Person-Centred Therapy

The person-centred approach is one of the most popular, enduring and respected approaches to psychotherapy and counselling. *Person-Centred Therapy* returns to its original formulations to define it as radically different from other self-oriented therapies.

Keith Tudor and Mike Worrall draw on a wealth of experience as practitioners, a deep knowledge of the approach and its history, and a broad and inclusive awareness of other approaches. This significant contribution to the advancement of person-centred therapy:

- Examines the roots of person-centred thinking in existential, phenomenological and organismic philosophy.
- Locates the approach in the context of other approaches to psychotherapy and counselling.
- Shows how recent research in areas such as neuroscience supports the philosophical premises of person-centred therapy.
- Challenges person-centred therapists to examine their practice in the light of the history and philosophical principles of the approach.

Person-Centred Therapy offers new and exciting perspectives on the process and practice of therapy, and will encourage person-centred practitioners to think about their work in deeper and more sophisticated ways.

Keith Tudor is a Director of Temenos and its Postgraduate Diploma/MSc in Person-Centred Psychotherapy & Counselling. He is also an Honorary Lecturer in the School of Health, Liverpool John Moores University.

Mike Worrall is a person-centred counsellor and supervisor in independent practice in Oxford.

LIVERPOOL
JOHN MOORES UNIVERSITY
AVRIL ROBARTS LRC
TEL. 0151 231 4022

WITHDRAWN

D1141891

Advancing Theory in Therapy
Series Editor: Keith Tudor

Most books covering individual therapeutic approaches are aimed at the trainee/student market. This series, however, is concerned with *advanced* and *advancing* theory, offering the reader comparative and comparable coverage of a number of therapeutic approaches.

Aimed at professionals and postgraduates, *Advancing Theory in Therapy* will cover an impressive range of individual theories. With full reference to case studies throughout, each title will

- Present cutting-edge research findings.
- Locate each theory and its application within its cultural context.
- Develop a critical view of theory and practice.

Titles in the series

Body Psychotherapy
Edited by Tree Staunton

Transactional Analysis: A Relational Perspective
Helena Hargaden and Charlotte Sills

Adlerian Psychotherapy: An Advanced Approach to Individual Psychology
Ursula E. Oberst and Alan E. Stewart

Rational Emotive Behaviour Therapy: Theoretical Developments
Edited by Windy Dryden

Co-Counselling: The Theory and Practice of Re-evaluation Counselling
Katie Kauffman and Caroline New

Analytical Psychology: Contemporary Perspectives in Jungian Analysis
Edited by Joe Cambray and Linda Carter

Person-Centred Therapy: A Clinical Philosophy
Keith Tudor and Mike Worrall

Person-Centred Therapy

A clinical philosophy

Keith Tudor and Mike Worrall

Routledge
Taylor & Francis Group

LONDON AND NEW YORK

First published 2006
by Routledge
27 Church Road, Hove, East Sussex BN3 2FA

Simultaneously published in the USA and Canada
by Routledge
270 Madison Avenue, New York, NY 10016

Routledge is an imprint of the Taylor & Francis Group

Copyright © 2006 Keith Tudor & Mike Worrall

Typeset in Times by Garfield Morgan, Rhayader, Powys
Printed and bound in Great Britain by TJ International Ltd, Padstow,
Cornwall
Paperback cover design by Sandra Heath

All rights reserved. No part of this book may be reprinted or reproduced or
utilised in any form or by any electronic, mechanical, or other means, now
known or hereafter invented, including photocopying and recording, or in
any information storage or retrieval system, without permission in writing
from the publishers.

This publication has been produced with paper manufactured to strict
environmental standards and with pulp derived from sustainable forests.

British Library Cataloguing in Publication Data
A catalogue record for this book is available from the British Library

Library of Congress Cataloging-in-Publication Data
Tudor, Keith, 1955–
    Person-centred therapy : a clinical philosophy / Keith Tudor and Mike
Worrall.
        p. cm. – (Advancing theory in therapy)
    Includes bibliographical references and index.
    ISBN 1-58391-123-5 (hbk) – ISBN 1-58391-124-3 (pbk)
    1. Client-centered psychotherapy. I. Worrall, Mike. II. Title.
III. Series.
    RC481.T83 2006
    616.89'14–dc22
                                                            2005025560
ISBN13: 978-1-58391-123-5 (hbk)
ISBN13: 978-1-58391-124-2 (pbk)

ISBN10: 1-58391-123-5 (hbk)
ISBN10: 1-58391-124-3 (pbk)

'This work is a unique contribution to person-centred inquiry and thought. It is a particularly timely and "deepening" addition to the burgeoning person-centred literature. It's a refreshing, original exploration that places the approach in context with major, related, historical and contemporary thought systems. Key aspects of person-centred theory are critically examined in ways that enlarge their meaning, challenge some features, and offer refinement and support to other elements. The book is often evocative in its ideas and is fresh in its information.'

Goff Barrett-Lennard, PhD, Honorary Fellow, Murdoch University, Perth, Australia

'This impressively mature book adds much analytical backbone to this centrally important therapeutic approach. With its appearance, no longer will person-centred praxis be open to the charge (albeit unwarranted) of theoretical flakiness. For what we find here is philosophy at its best: practically relevant to real-world concerns, passionate, committed – and with a quite breathtaking panorama of philosophical ideas weaved into the text. It is a particular delight to see Alfred North Whitehead's much-neglected philosophy given just prominence. With the acute analytic sensibility which they bring to their subject matter, and being unafraid to challenge sacred cows where they find it to be necessary, Tudor and Worrall have provided us with an excellent model of the richly fertile way in which therapy and philosophy can illuminate and inform each other. Person-centred praxis is substantially advanced with the appearance of this seminal *tour de force*.'

Richard House, PhD, Senior Lecturer in Psychotherapy and Counselling, Roehampton University

'As clinicians, Keith Tudor and Mike Worrall have spent years pursuing in-depth study of Carl Rogers' philosophy, methods and applications. Their intellectual curiosity and dedication to understanding the meaning of Carl's works and expanding the concepts is brought forth in this book. For theorists and clinicians alike, this book will be illuminating.'

Natalie Rogers, PhD, Professor (Adjunct), California Institute of Integral Studies, Institute of Transpersonal Psychology, and Distinguished Consulting Faculty at Saybrook Graduate School

Contents

Series preface

This series focuses on advanced and advancing theory in psychotherapy. Its aims are: to present theory and practice within a specific theoretical orientation or approach at an advanced, postgraduate level; to advance theory by presenting and evaluating new ideas and their relation to the approach; to locate the orientation and its applications within cultural contexts both historically in terms of the origins of the approach, and contemporaneously in terms of current debates about philosophy, theory, society and therapy; and, finally, to present and develop a critical view of theory and practice, especially in the context of debates about power, organisation and the increasing professionalisation of therapy.

As both the co-author of this book and the editor of the series in which it appears, it is perhaps a little invidious for me to introduce this particular volume. Dealing with the dual role involved in this task I am reminded of Gilbert and Sullivan's Lord Chancellor when, faced with being both judge and advocate, he sings: 'Said I to myself, said I'! Taking inspiration from this to differentiate myself in a similar way, as series editor I am delighted to introduce this volume on advancing person-centred therapy. It appears shortly after the anniversary of the birth of the approach sixty-five years ago, when Carl Rogers first presented his 'newer psychotherapy' which he described as a 'relationship therapy', a term which, currently, is increasingly being used across the theoretical spectrum of psychotherapy. In this book, the authors emphasise this relational perspective to the various subjects under discussion: the nature of the human organism and its tendency to actualise, the development of self and personhood, as well as the ways in which, as human beings, we become alienated from others, ourselves and our environment, and how, as therapists, we may work. This is particularly relevant and topical in a world in which governments and people appear to express their differences with others in increasingly conflictual ways, which further alienate relationships and co-create further alienation. Although widespread as a core model for many counselling courses, person-centred therapy has not always been taken seriously as a psychotherapy, in part perhaps because it does not distinguish between the two activities. In this volume the authors take on the broader task of advancing person-centred therapy as a well-founded and researched psychotherapy which embodies particular philosophical principles – in effect, a philosophy for and in therapeutic or clinical practice.

Keith Tudor

Acknowledgements

In this book we argue that the human organism cannot be understood outside of its environment, and that relationships are both inevitable and necessary for survival, enhancement and creativity. We want to acknowledge the personal and professional relationships which have sustained us especially over the past seven years of this book's gestation. We owe particular thanks to Louise Embleton Tudor, Natalie Rogers, Charlotte Sills, and Brian Thorne for their long-standing encouragement and support. Goff Barrett-Lennard, Yvonne Bates, Louise Embleton Tudor, Helena Hargaden, Dr Fiona MacKenzie, Briony Nicholls, Janet Radcliffe-Richards, Peter Schmid and Harry Van Belle read portions of and made specific comments on early drafts of the text. We are grateful to all of them for their close and exact reading. We remain, of course, entirely responsible for any deficits or inconsistencies. We thank the British Association for Counselling and Psychotherapy for permission to reproduce Figure 7.1 and some associated text from an article which first appeared in *Counselling* in February 2000. Keith acknowledges especially the first cohort of the Temenos MSc group for their willingness to wrestle with many of the ideas that find fruition in these pages. Mike thanks Anisha Mehta, Carole Shadbolt, and Geraldine Thomson for consistent love, kindness, and cheerfulness.

Kathi Murphy introduced us to one another in 1991. We dedicate this book to her with great appreciation, affection and respect.

Introduction

One couldn't carry on life comfortably without a little blindness to the fact that everything has been said better than we can put it ourselves.

George Eliot[1]

The English are incurious as to theory, take fundamentals for granted and are more interested in the state of the roads than in their place on the map.

R.H. Tawney

First there is experiencing, then there is a theory.

Carl Rogers and John K. Wood

Person-centred therapy is based on an organismic psychology which describes the innate and unforced tendency of human beings, given a conducive environment, to actualise their potential. Person-centred therapists work simply to support this tendency by co-creating as conducive an environment as possible.

Rogers dates the beginning of person-centred therapy from 11 December 1940 when he delivered a paper on 'A Newer Psychotherapy' at the University of Minnesota (see Rogers, 1959b, 1961/67b; Rogers & Russell, 2002). Over the years that Rogers wrote, he and others referred to this activity in different ways:

- 'Non-directive therapy' – in which terms, influenced by Jessie Taft, Frederick Allen and Virginia Axline, Rogers (1939) describes his therapeutic work with children.
- 'Relationship therapy' – a term with which Rogers (1942), influenced by Otto Rank and Taft, first describes his 'newer psychotherapy', one

1 References for all the epigrams in this book can be found in Appendix 1.

which began to emphasise the significance of the therapeutic relationship over and above particular therapeutic techniques.

- 'Client-centred therapy' – the first major exposition of which is in a book of the same name (Rogers, 1951) including, significantly, a view of the therapeutic relationship as experienced by the client.
- 'Person-centred therapy' – which offers a wider view of the client as person and implies the presence of the therapist also as person. Ivey, Ivey and Simek-Morgan (1993) date this last shift of terminology from 1961 and the publication of *On Becoming a Person*, and suggest that it reflects a therapy characterised by the increased personal involvement of the therapist, and a greater emphasis on relational issues.
- 'The person-centred approach' – which refers generally to the approach as it informs practice in fields other than therapy, such as education and training, groupwork, conflict resolution, and organisational consultancy. For a contemporary exposition of this see Embleton Tudor *et al.* (2004).

In our view these developments unfold one out of the other, and each enhances rather than replaces what went before. The different nomenclatures represent different emphases which still inform the theory and practice of person-centred therapy, and reflect particular strands of thinking and practice which we represent and develop throughout this book. As with other theoretical orientations, different personalities, interests and perspectives have made of the person-centred approach a broad church with a number of different wings or traditions. Sanders (2004) identifies five 'tribes' of the person-centred nation: classical, focusing, experiential, integrative and existential. To these, we would add two further tribes: the expressive therapy of Natalie Rogers (1993/2000) and pre-therapy as developed by Gary Prouty (1994) and others.

In the third decade since Rogers' death, we hope that this present work contributes to the continuing development of the approach to therapy he founded. Other sources of theoretical interest, development and support are to be found in the published papers from international person-centred and experiential conferences (Lietaer *et al.*, 1990; Hutterer *et al.*, 1996; Marques-Teixeira & Antones, 2000; Watson *et al.*, 2002) and in the international journal *Person-Centered & Experiential Psychotherapies*.

In our reading and research we have drawn on and cited publications written in or translated into the English language. There is also a significant and growing person-centred literature in Dutch, German, Japanese, Portuguese and Spanish, for details of which see the websites of Lietaer (www.pce-world.org) and Schmid (www.pca-online.net). A collection of person-centred literature may also be found in the International Archives of the Person-Centered Approach at the Universidad Iberoamericana in Mexico (www.aiep.bib.uia.mx/aiep). We are concerned to address an international audience and aim to write so as to address diversity of experience. Where we refer to something specifically to do with the United Kingdom (UK) we tend to signpost this as such, partly to acknowledge specific experience or local examples in areas such as legislation, and partly to invite you to draw or reflect on your own experience, situation, context, and equivalence.

From its beginnings, and largely because Rogers himself was a psychologist, person-centred therapy has been extensively researched: see, for example, Rogers (1942), Cartwright (1957), Rogers *et al.* (1967), Truax and Mitchell (1971) and Watson (1984). More recently, research compares the efficacy of person-centred therapy favorably with other approaches: see Friedli *et al.* (1997) and King *et al.* (2000). Despite such research and a resurgence of interest in the person-centred approach, represented by the number of counselling courses which espouse its principles, and the publication of more than fifty books on the subject in the past ten years, some critics still see the approach as overly positive or optimistic, naïve, lacking in theory and rigour, and overly reliant on certain attitudes of the therapist. Tudor and Merry (2002) and Thorne (2003) address some of these criticisms. Part of our motivation for writing this book in the context of this series is, precisely, to advance a more robust view of person-centred therapy, acknowledging, for example, that it offers theoretical and practical insights into working with people who are severely 'disturbed'. A second motivation, which also fulfils the brief of the series, is to advance the theory, to take it further. We do this in a number of ways, and specifically by reclaiming the centrality of the organism in the theory and its practice.

Person-centred therapy: Location, relation and integration

Most writers place person-centred therapy within the humanistic movement. Mearns and Thorne, however, (2000, p. 27) argue that 'it does not in fact have much in common with the other established humanistic therapies'. They continue: 'The governing feature of person-centred therapy (PCT) is not its "humanistic" orientation but its forsaking of mystique and other "powerful" behaviours of therapists. In this regard many humanistic therapies are as different from PCT as psychoanalysis.' Others, including Ellingham (1995, 1997), argue that the person-centred approach differs from other approaches in its most fundamental assumptions. It is precisely these fundamental assumptions which we examine and advance in this book. In doing so, we think that the traditional division into three or, now, four 'forces' or 'schools' of psychology – the analytic, the behavioural, the humanistic and the existential – is becoming redundant. Rather than locating person-centred therapy, or ourselves for that matter, within some

LIVERPOOL
JOHN MOORES UNIVERSITY
AVRIL ROBARTS LRC
TEL. 0151 231 4022

school, we are more interested in locating person-centred therapy with regard to other theoretical approaches on the basis of principles, values and meta-theoretical considerations. Warner's (2000) 'levels of interventiveness', for example, based on the degree to which practitioners intervene in their clients' processes, provides one framework for understanding, comparing and analysing different theories and practices.

In general the person-centred approach as a whole has tended to stand alone, and has not developed easy or significant relationships with other theories. The history of the approach shows Rogers developing its theory and practice, initially on his own, and then supported by like-minded colleagues and research students. Although he read widely, and although what he read informed his thinking and practice, he seems to have had little or no contact with contemporaries like Fritz Perls and Eric Berne, both of whom lived in California at the same time as Rogers, and with both of whom he shares significant philosophical ground (see O'Hara, 1984, and Tudor, 1999, respectively). We might even say that Rogers developed his thinking not only in isolation from sympathetic contemporaries, but in opposition to colleagues, like Skinner, whose thinking was largely inimical to his own. Of the public dialogues he had (see Kirschenbaum & Henderson, 1990a), he had none with psychologists or psychotherapists other than Skinner. We think that this isolation is due to a number of reasons which are:

- In part autobiographical – Rogers (1967) himself reports being 'socially shy'.
- In part theoretical – Rogers developed a view of the person as autonomous and free-standing, rather than relational and interdependent. We think that, to a certain extent, this also describes the theory itself.
- In part political – pioneers setting out to develop their own ideas or establish their own school of therapy often look inwards rather than outwards.

Against a background of a number of 'forces', schools and traditions, the *zeitgeist* now is one of integration. We think that person-centred therapy offers individual practitioners opportunity to integrate that which is personally and idiosyncratically important to them. Some may want to focus especially on the body, for instance; others may be interested in particularly cognitive or spiritual processes. These areas of interest are not exclusive to any one particular theoretical orientation. Person-centred philosophy emphasises holism and integrity, and demands of practitioners who want to integrate theories, concepts or methods from other psychological approaches that they make such integration personal. We take up this discussion in Chapter 9.

The nature, place and use of theory

Our aim, as we've said, is to advance the theory and practice of the person-centred approach. Perhaps we need to define what we mean by theory. Bohm (1980/83, p. 3) offers this:

> The word 'theory' derives from the Greek 'theoria', which has the same root as 'theatre', in a word meaning 'to view' or 'to make a spectacle'. Thus, it might be said that a theory is primarily a form of insight, i.e. a way of looking at the world, and not a form of knowledge of how the world is.

This catches the provisional nature of theory both as we understand it and as we want to advance it. Any particular theory is simply one way of looking at and making sense of what seem to be the facts of our experiences. 'The facts' says Rogers (1953/67b, p. 25) 'are friendly', and theory is an attempt (1951, p. 481) to 'contain and explain the observed facts'. The more adequately and comprehensively a theory does that, the more helpful it is. If we want to keep the theories we hold helpful and relevant, we must also be willing to amend them in the light of our changing experiences.

Although Rogers is known as a theorist, he says of himself that he saw experience, rather than theory, as primary. That is to say, he worked as a therapist, had the experiences that that entailed, and then looked for whatever sense and order seemed naturally to emerge from those experiences. The various elements of person-centred theory, then, are tentative descriptions of that emerging sense and order. If theory is 'to be profitable' he says (1951, p. 440), it 'must follow experience, not precede it'. Some years later (1959, p. 191) he describes theory as 'a fallible, changing attempt to construct a network of gossamer threads which will contain the solid facts'. More than fifty years on from this statement, and reading it with a postmodern scepticism, we may doubt the presence or viability of 'solid facts'. With that proviso, however, Rogers' description of theory as both fallible and changing locates theory in an appropriately humble relationship to experience. It seems to us both inevitable and desirable that we should evolve and amend whatever theories we hold so that they keep up with our evolving experiences and perspectives. Rogers (1959b, p. 190) endorses this view: 'Unless we regard the discovery of truth as a closed and finished book, then there will be new discoveries which will contradict the best theories which we can now construct.' This is similar to Karl Popper's point that science progresses through a process of conjectures and refutations. Rogers' theories and hypotheses are just that: theories and hypotheses to be tested against experience. Popper was a contemporary of Rogers, and Rogers cites his views of the 'open society' (Rogers, 1961/67c, p. 399). This book is our attempt, on the basis of our experiences as therapists, to contradict person-centred theory, and therefore to further its evolution.

Kurt Lewin is alleged to have said that there is nothing as practical as good theory. We've alluded to one of its uses above: that it allows us to see whatever orderliness there may be in our experience. This in turn affords us an opportunity to ask new questions of our experience, and in doing so to advance what we know. Angyal (1941, p. 7) puts it this way:

> The utility of a theory consists essentially in that it serves as a guide, as a point of reference, for empirical studies, which otherwise are likely to result in an utterly chaotic and incoherent mass of data. The utility of a good theory is twofold: it allows us to question nature intelligently and offers a background for the interpretation of empirical data.

Theory, however, is not specifically predictive. We've argued that it arises out of experience, and can therefore make sense only of what has already happened. It is, says Phillips (1994, p. 154), 'by definition, what we already know'. Mearns (1997, p. 146) recognises that it does not 'predict the behavior of an individual client'. In so far, though, as it provides a way of thinking about our experiences, it helps us examine what we know and develop curiosity about what we don't. Another way of saying this is that theory, at its best, helps us move from experience to discovery, from what we know to what we don't know yet.

This book is one of a series which focuses on advancing *theory*. We recognise that once ideas and suggestions are in print they can carry more authority than their authors intended. We don't want to be seen to be offering guidance about how to *do* person-centred therapy, and for this reason we are not necessarily going to spell out the implications of our thinking for your practice. We want rather to invite you, the reader and practitioner, to think about your own experiences, to recognise with Rogers (1953/67b, p. 25) that the facts of your experience are 'friendly', and to advance the theory in the light of those experiences.

We are also reluctant to give too many examples from our practice, partly because of our desire to honour confidentiality, and partly because we think that in a book of this sort their qualities of particularity and locality will fix thinking rather than free it. They are likely to distract rather than illustrate. We could, of course, invent examples, as Bryant-Jefferies does in a recent and continuing series of books (published by Radcliffe Medical Press). We have reservations about this approach. Reviewing one of Bryant-Jeffries' books, Schlebusch (2004. p. 71) says both that 'it gives us a deep insight into what actually happens between Dave (the client) and Alan (the therapist) in 12 completely transcribed therapy sessions' *and* 'that the book is not a transcription of a real therapy'! We agree with Spinelli

(1997, p. 3) that case-studies and case-examples, even if drawn from life, 'are highly selective "fictions" usually told from the perspective of one, highly biased participant in a shared experience whose "meaning" is open-ended and likely to change significantly over time'. Our objection to Bryant-Jeffries' methodology is that he tells the story as if from the perspective of three of the participants: client, counsellor and supervisor. This means that his books are more novels than case-studies, and although we value novels, and learn much from good ones, we question the moral and aesthetic integrity of novels written expressly to convey particular learnings. We do not see how transcriptions of a relationship that is itself fictional give us any insight at all into what 'actually' happens. So we compromise. We write mainly in the abstract, and will offer limited case-examples only where they seem to us to illustrate particular points that need particular illustration.

Back to the future

As we've written together, we notice that we've been looking backwards in order to advance. By this we mean that in order to take person-centred theory forward we've been looking back at the roots and root principles of the approach. This has seemed fruitful for a number of reasons. In the first place it has reminded us that person-centred ideas pre-date Rogers by millennia, even if no one at the time called them person-centred. Aristotle (384–322 BCE), for instance, prefigures Rogers' notion of an actualising tendency: 'The productions of nature have an innate tendency in the direction of the best condition of which they are capable' (1955, p. 44). Notions of this tendency and of the organism which it characterises appear in many psychological, philosophical and spiritual traditions, as well as in different health disciplines, such as acupuncture, homoeopathy and naturopathy. Polonius' advice to Laertes in Act 1 Scene 3 of Shakespeare's *Hamlet* is a lovely description of congruence, integrity and reliability:

> This above all: to thine own self be true,
> And it must follow, as the night the day,
> Thou canst not then be false to any man.

Marcus Aurelius (121–180 ACE) gave simple advice on what we might now call empathic listening: 'Accustom yourself to give careful attention to what others are saying, and try your best to enter into the mind of the speaker' (1964, p. 104).

These are simply a sample of some of the ideas we've come across. We don't intend them to be systematic or comprehensive, nor to suggest that Rogers was familiar with these particular authors. We mean only to point out that the ideas that Rogers brought together under one umbrella have a long pedigree in their own right, and are not exclusively person-centred. Whilst much ancient wisdom is still relevant, two tasks fall to each generation: to rediscover and review ancient wisdom; and to set it alongside more recent and current developments. Rogers did this in his own time, and we are offering to do something similar here.

Rogers himself acknowledges his debt to, and borrowing from, earlier writers and philosophers, such as Lao Tzu, the author of the *Tao Te Ching*, whom he quotes on leadership (Rogers, 1983), and Søren Kierkegaard, to whom he owes the title of chapter 8 of *On Becoming A Person* (1961/67b). In the same book he acknowledges his borrowing of the term 'personal construct' from George Kelly, the founder of personal construct psychology. He adopts the phrase 'I-Thou' from his near contemporary Martin Buber, with whom he dialogued in 1957 (see Kirschenbaum & Henderson, 1990; Anderson & Cissna, 1997), and reports (1963/78) his pleasure and surprise that almost identical ideas about holism are to be found in the work of Smuts. Kramer (1995) has traced Rogers' debt to Otto Rank and Jessie Taft, a debt which puts Rogers only two handshakes away from Sigmund Freud.

Rogers also imports significant terms from other disciplines. The word 'congruence', for instance, has a mathematical provenance; and both the word 'proposition', and the term 'necessary and sufficient', come from the language of philosophy, and in particular from the field of logic.

Rogers was not original as to the content of some of his ideas. He did, however, appropriate ideas from a wide range of sources, synthesise them into a (mostly) coherent and relevant philosophy, and use them as the basis for a new and radical form of psychotherapy. His research methodology was also radical. Listening to taped counselling sessions and drawing deductions about therapeutic conditions was, literally, client-centred. We use the word 'radical' deliberately here to connote a way of thinking that differs at its very roots from other contemporary ways of thinking.

Chesterton (1910/94) said that one of the troubles with Christianity was not that it had been tried and found wanting; but that it had been found too difficult, and therefore never fully tried. As with Christianity, so with the person-centred approach. In our view, the radical implications of Rogers' original formulations are still too little examined at the extremes. We intend to examine them, remembering that Rogers (1960/67a, p. 244) saw the theory of the approach not as dogma, doctrine or creed, but 'as a statement of hypotheses' to be tested and investigated.

The thesis of the book: Clinical philosophy

The person-centred approach is 'a way of being' (see Rogers, 1980a). That is to say it is a set of ideas which constitute a philosophy of life. Rogers

(1986/90, p. 138) describes the person-centred approach as 'a basic philosophy'. He goes on: 'When this philosophy is lived, it helps the person expand the development of his or her own capacities' and 'stimulates constructive change in others'. As Rogers articulated them, these ideas arose out of and apply most immediately to the relationship between therapist and client and, in this sense, person-centred therapy is a *clinical* philosophy: a way of being, underpinned by certain philosophical principles, embodied by the therapist, in a clinical setting. We use 'clinical' to refer to the field that is the clinic or the consulting room. It does not necessarily carry, for us, cold, medical or impersonal connotations.

This is a similar perspective to that of Frank Lake, the author of a volume on *Clinical Theology* (Lake, 1966, p. xxiv):

> The psychiatrist . . . must discourse on the meaning of pain and make sense of chronic suffering. He must communicate some of his own courage and share his personal philosophy for dealing with hard times . . . He is neither a professional philosopher nor a professional theologian. But he must attempt, as an amateur, to be both.

He continues (ibid., p. xxiv):

> If professional philosophers were so sure of the validity and effectiveness of their philosophies as to run clinics, this is the point at which the patient could suitably be referred to a professional philosopher, for a new style of wisdom appropriate to living in pain.

Person-centred practice is based on certain philosophical assumptions about human nature and the person, and emphasises the therapist's way of being and attitudes. Person-centred therapy, then, is an applied philosophy; and, in our view and at best, person-centred therapists are applied or clinical philosophers. Two implications follow from this. The first is that the practitioner needs to examine and be familiar with his or her own personal philosophy (see Tudor & Worrall, 2004b), not least to see to what degree it fits or is congruent with the philosophical assumptions that underlie the approach. The second is that the practitioner needs to understand both the assumptions of the approach, and the implications of those assumptions for practice. In this sense we want to advance person-centred theory by examining its philosophical assumptions from a clinical (rather than an abstract) perspective. Our thesis parallels Wittgenstein's notion of a 'therapeutic' philosophy, by which he refers to the practice of dissolving philosophical problems by showing what the terms of reference they depend on actually *mean* in their particular fields. Of course, this also parallels therapy in that therapists help clients to dissolve or resolve problems by understanding the various meanings they give to them.

Both implications, noted above, represent something of our own personal and professional journeys. If all theory is autobiographical, this is not surprising. The book itself is one of the fruits of our professional collaboration over fifteen years. Between us, we have been involved in a quartet of books which reflect our interest in defining person-centred psychology (Tudor & Merry, 2002), the approach as an *approach* (Embleton Tudor *et al.*, 2004), person-centred approaches to supervision (Tudor & Worrall, 2004a) and, in this present work, advancing theory.

As we review the person-centred and, for us, *present-centred* approach to therapy, we advance a number of propositions which we hope will assert, question and further the approach. We propose, amongst other things, that:

- The organism is central to the philosophy, theory and practice of the approach.
- Person-centred therapy is an environmental therapy.
- The human organism tends towards both autonomy and homonomy or belonging.
- The person and his behaviour are inseparable.
- Rogers' therapeutic conditions are neither necessary nor sufficient.
- The therapeutic condition of 'psychological contact' between therapist and client is best elaborated in terms of empathic understanding and unconditional positive regard.
- The client's experience and perception of 'being received' by the therapist is the one essential condition of therapy.
- Fluidity, creativity and the exercise of personal power are intrinsic qualities of the organism and observable outcomes of effective therapy.
- Person-centred literature and practice consistently undervalue the role of the client in the process of effective therapy.
- Effective psychotherapy depends upon active therapeutic relating and is therefore dialogic and co-created.

Structure of the book

The organisation of the book follows our concern to place philosophy at the centre of our understanding of person-centred therapy. In Chapter 1 we examine the inevitability and importance of philosophy and, from that, a number of philosophical traditions which influence person-centred theory and practice. For us, the organism lies at the heart of the person-centred approach to therapy. In Chapter 2, therefore, we reclaim the tradition of organismic psychology and consider its implications. The organism cannot be understood apart from its tendencies and these are the subject of Chapter 3. Chapter 4 on self and Chapter 5 on person represent developing and developed aspects of the organism in its environment, relating to others. In both chapters there is, again, a sense of reclaiming and relocating person-centred therapy, especially in the context of self psychology and debates about personhood. At this point, our focus on the clinical application of the person-centred approach becomes most apparent. A book on the *approach* would consider a number of applications and implications, as does Rogers (1959b) in his major formulation of the client-centred framework: relationships, groups, community, organisation and learning. For further discussions of these areas of application see Embleton Tudor *et al.* (2004). Here, following our reclamation of the reality of the organism at the heart of person-centred psychology and therapy, and having differentiated between the organism, self and person, we turn our attention to their respective organisation and disorganisation as a way of understanding psychopathology in terms of authenticity and alienation (Chapter 6). We then focus on the theory and practice of person-centred therapy, through discussions of the conditions of therapy (Chapter 7) and the process of therapy (Chapter 8). In Chapter 7 we review changing formulations and ideas about Rogers' therapeutic conditions. In Chapter 8, under the general title of process, we review the process and outcomes of therapy, the nature of the therapeutic relationship and the person of the therapist. In our own clinical practices we are concerned to hold the concept and actuality of the active exchange between organism and environment as central to an understanding of both. So in Chapter 9 we look at the environments person-centred therapy itself inhabits: intellectual, professional and ethical. We conclude with a discussion of person-centred therapy as an integrative or integrating therapy, and some final reflections on person-centred therapy.

We assume a high level of familiarity with the basic texts of the approach and a willingness to grapple with the ideas they offer. We see no difference between the activities of counselling and psychotherapy and thus use the terms interchangeably or, more commonly, use the generic term 'therapy'. To avoid the clumsy constructions 's/he', 'he or she', or 'they', we use personal pronouns alternately.

In a work of this nature and size, there are, inevitably, gaps. Some of these we have intended, and some not. Clearly we have chosen to advance our own particular view of person-centred therapy. We have not sought to represent the views of others more associated with particular 'tribes'. Sanders (2004) represents some of these traditions and, most recently, Purton (2004) introduces and advances the theory of 'focusing-oriented psychotherapy'. We have chosen also to focus mainly on the work of individual therapists with individual clients. We have not, therefore, addressed therapeutic groups, or the process of learning. The person-centred approach has contributed much to the theory of groups and their facilitation, beginning with Rogers' (1970/73) own work, developed by Barrett-Lennard (1979) and Wood (1984, 1999) and, more recently, by a collection of authors in a volume edited by Lago and MacMillan (1999). We have not discussed the implications of the theory of person-centred therapy for learning. Again, this is one of Rogers' major contributions to the wider field of education, learning and training (Rogers, 1969, 1983; Rogers & Freiberg, 1994). Others have discussed the implications of person-centred theory with regard to the training of person-centred therapists (Mearns, 1997) and we have discussed this elsewhere with regard to education (Embleton Tudor *et al.*, 2004), and the supervision of therapists (Tudor & Worrall, 2004b).

Chapter 1

Philosophy

Philosophy does not initiate interpretations. Its search for a rationalistic scheme is the search for more adequate criticism, and for more adequate justification, of the interpretations which we perforce employ.

Alfred North Whitehead

The attainment of biological knowledge we are seeking is essentially akin to this phenomenon – to the capacity of the organism to become adequate to its environmental conditions.

Kurt Goldstein

One cannot engage in psychotherapy without giving operational evidence of an underlying value orientation and view of human nature. It is definitely preferable, in my estimation, that such underlying views be open and explicit, rather than covert and implicit.

Carl Rogers

To do philosophy is to explore one's own temperament, and yet at the same time to attempt to discover the truth.

Iris Murdoch

'Philosophy' says Howard (2000, p. xiv) 'underpins therapy as a means to healing, identity, direction and meaning. It deserves more attention.' We want to begin this book by according philosophy some of that attention. Specifically, we want to look in this chapter at some of the ways in which philosophical principles underpin the practice of therapy, and especially the practice of person-centred therapy.

Before we do that we need to define what we mean by philosophy. 'Most definitions of philosophy' says Quinton (1995, p. 666) 'are fairly controversial, particularly if they aim to to be at all interesting or profound.' For our purposes we are taking philosophy to mean the underlying principles on which or out of which a person builds a life and chooses how to behave. This is a deliberately limited definition, in keeping with our conviction that the person-centred approach constitutes a functional, rather than an abstract, philosophy.

As we argue in the Introduction, we think that philosophy can help us understand ourselves, others and the world, and that we may ground many of the ideas and much of the practice of person-centred therapy in philosophical ideas. Wittgenstein (1921/2001, pp. 29–30) makes a number of points about philosophy:

- It is not a body of doctrine but an activity.
- It is a meta-activity, and not of the same order of things as the natural sciences.
- It results in the clarification rather than the creation of propositions.
- Its task is to make thoughts clear and to give them sharp boundaries.

We are citing Wittgenstein for a number of reasons. He is one of the most important philosophers of the twentieth century, and his work has influenced different schools of philosophy, including logical positivism and analytic philosophy. Some of his later work is compatible with radical hermeneutics and more postmodern perspectives. Although there is no immediate evidence that Rogers read his work, Wittgenstein was profoundly concerned with meaning in language and with symbolism, both of which underpin Rogers' work. Biographically they share a background in empirical sciences – Rogers in scientific agriculture, Wittgenstein in engineering and mathematics – which is reflected in their subsequent fields of psychology and philosophy. Wittgenstein's view of philosophy as a practice aimed not at solving problems but at resolving them through a better understanding of language supports our current interest in advancing person-centred theory and practice. In his last work (published in 1953, two years after his death) Wittgenstein compares philosophy with therapeutic practice, and a number of writers in the field of therapy have drawn on his work (see, for example, Lynch, 1997; Stige, 1998).

We suggest that the points Wittgenstein makes about philosophy are analogous to the practice of psychotherapy.

- Psychotherapy is not a body of doctrine but an activity.

From the beginning Rogers was interested in what worked. He took a pragmatic approach to his work, and grew the theory initially out of his observations and reflections. He saw, too, that descriptive theories could easily become prescriptive and doctrinal, leading to followers arguing about what therapists should or should not do in order to be effective. Writing appreciatively (1959, p. 191) about the way Freud showed 'more respect for the facts he observed than for the theories he had built', Rogers saw that 'insecure disciples' had taken Freud's 'gossamer threads' of theory and made of them 'iron chains of dogma'. He suggested 'that every formulation of a theory contains this same risk and that, at the time a theory is constructed, some precautions should be taken to prevent it from becoming dogma'. It's perhaps inevitable that any activity sustained purposefully over time will generate ideas that some practitioners will begin to hold as doctrine or dogma. 'Disciples are' after all, says Phillips (1994, p. 62), 'the people who haven't got the joke.' Wittgenstein and Rogers between them remind us of two things: that the activity comes first; and that, humourless disciples notwithstanding, theory need not, and probably should not, become doctrine.

- Psychotherapy is a meta-activity, and not of the same order of things as the natural sciences.

If the natural sciences describe and explore what *is*, philosophy and psychotherapy are meta-activities in that they offer opportunities to reflect upon the nature of what is. They sit, as Wittgenstein says of philosophy (1921/2001, p. 29), 'above or below the natural sciences, not beside them'. Clearly, psychotherapy as a process can often do little to change what is. The most effective bereavement therapist cannot bring a client's mother or lover back to life. Effective therapists can, however, offer their clients a space for them to reflect on what is, and, perhaps more significantly, to reflect on and amend their relationship with what is.

- Psychotherapy results in the clarification rather than the creation of propositions.

Wittgenstein (1921/2001, p. 23) describes a proposition as 'a picture of reality' and as 'a model of reality as we imagine it'. Philosophy, then, is primarily about articulating more clearly the propositions that currently are. Given this, we can read his statement as another way of describing congruence. Put into Rogers' terms, we can say that the process of therapy is not primarily about creating new propositions, or pictures of reality, although new propositions often do emerge. It is, rather, about symbolising and accepting the presence of the propositions we currently live by, and then, by implication, exploring and questioning their validity, accuracy, completeness and usefulness. This clarification, acceptance and examination of our own internal propositions or pictures of reality allows us to experience more clearly and therefore promotes a greater congruence between experience and awareness.

- The task of psychotherapy is to make thoughts clear and to give them sharp boundaries.

LIVERPOOL
JOHN MOORES UNIVERSITY
AVRIL ROBARTS LRC
TEL. 0151 231 4022

This point is implicit in the point above. Its two parts – *to make thoughts clear* and *to give them sharp boundaries* – signify two important elements in Rogers' thinking about psychotherapy. Saying that the task of therapy is to make thoughts clear is another way of saying that its task is to allow clients an opportunity to symbolise their experiences accurately. By this we mean it's a space within which they may find for themselves the words or other symbols that most accurately and completely describe their internal experiencing. Zimring (1995) suggests that this is exactly what is helpful about therapy. Saying that the task of therapy is to give those thoughts sharp boundaries is another way of describing one aspect of differentiation. Writing about the process of therapy, Rogers suggests that clients move gradually from thinking that is bound by rigid structures to thinking that is increasingly responsive to immediate experiencing, and that is therefore more discriminating of differences between past and present, self and other, fact and construct. One sentence from Rogers catches both of these elements. Writing about one of the seven stages of process (1958/67a, p. 138) he says that clients at this stage tend to show 'an increased differentiation of feelings, constructs, personal meanings, with some tendency toward seeking exactness of symbolization'.

A further reason for examining philosophical principles is that Rogers sees a significant relationship between private beliefs, or philosophy, and public behaviours, a notion which has immediate roots in Angyal (1941, p. 165):

> Any sample of behavior may be regarded as the manifestation of an attitude. Attitudes may be traced back successively to more and more general ones. In so doing one arrives at a limited number of very general attitudes which are unquestionable, axiomatic for a given person. These have been called *axioms of behavior*. When such axioms are intellectually elaborated we may speak of *maxims of behavior*. The axioms of behavior form a *system of personal axioms*. The system of maxims may be called a *philosophy of life*.

In Angyal's terms, then, a philosophy of life is a set of intellectually elaborated or articulated attitudes towards oneself and others, attitudes which show in the way we live. Rogers picks up both Angyal's idea that a person's behaviour is an outward showing of his philosophy of life, and his process of working back inferentially from observed behaviour to personal philosophy. Doing so he enshrines (1951, p. 19) a therapist's personal philosophy as an important variable in the process of therapy:

> In any psychotherapy, the therapist himself is a highly important part of the human equation. What he does, the attitude he holds, his basic concept of his role, all influence therapy to a marked degree.

Further to this, Rogers suggests (1951, p. 20) that an individual's personal philosophy of life helps determine the ease and speed with which he becomes a therapist:

> Our experience in training counselors would indicate that the basic operational philosophy of the individual (which may or may not resemble his verbalized philosophy) determines, to a considerable extent, the time it will take him to become a skillful counselor.

In other words, a student whose personal philosophy sits easily with the philosophical values of the person-centred approach will become a person-centred therapist more easily and more quickly than one whose philosophy does not.

Rogers' allusion to a possible discrepancy between 'operational' and 'verbalized' philosophy suggests that what we say we believe, or think we believe, or would like to think we believe, may differ from what our behaviour shows about what we believe. This gives us a way of expanding our thinking about congruence. As Rogers formulates it in the context of a theory of therapy (see Chapters 7 and 8), congruence describes a relationship of consistency between a person's experience, awareness and communication. We expand that definition so that it also describes a relationship between a therapist's verbalised philosophy and his behaviour; and further between both of those and the philosophical values of the approach to which he subscribes (see Figure 1.1). Swildens articulates (2004, p. 17) 'one

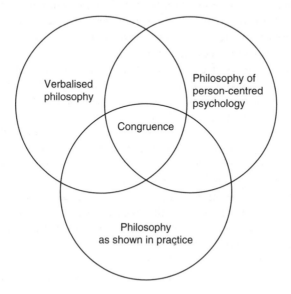

Figure 1.1 Philosophical congruence.

of the fundamentals of psychotherapy as a trade: that there should be a basic connection between a working hypothesis and therapeutic practice'. We suggest that this area of congruence precedes the congruence Rogers believed was necessary for therapeutic work. It is, as it were, a background congruence, out of which or against which emerges the more acute and immediate congruence of a therapist's experiencing in the moment as she works with her client.

Rogers also asserts that philosophical values, however accurately articulated or intrinsically therapeutic, are not enough in and of themselves. Values are helpful only in so far as they manifest in the lived reality of the relationship between therapist and client. It is, for instance, little use a therapist believing, even genuinely, in the importance of empathic understanding if he has no way of implementing that belief in the moment as he sits with his client. This suggests that effective therapists develop fluid and creative ways of living or implementing their philosophy of life, so that what they believe at the philosophical level becomes a genuine, specific and perceptible way of being in particular lived relationships.

Rogers' use of philosophical terms

At critical points in his writings Rogers appropriates from the language of philosophy terms which have precise meanings within their original sphere. The phrase 'necessary and sufficient' is perhaps the most striking example of this, and suggests that Rogers was at least familiar with philosophical discourse. We think it's appropriate therefore to examine his work as if it were a philosophy, albeit functional rather than abstract, pure or academic.

Rogers' theory of therapy (1957, 1959b) depends on what he called the *necessary* and *sufficient* conditions of personality change. From his own experience with clients, from the experiences of his colleagues, and from relevant research, he draws out (1957, p. 95) the conditions which seem to him 'to be *necessary* to initiate constructive personality change, and which, taken together, appear to be *sufficient* to inaugurate that process'. His formulation is of an 'if-then' variety: 'if these six conditions exist, and continue over a period of time, this is sufficient. The process of constructive personality change will follow' (ibid., p. 96). In another paper he asserts that 'for therapy to occur it is necessary that these conditions exist' (1959, p. 213). The sense he makes, then, is that the six conditions are both *necessary* for personal growth, in that they need to occur; and that they are *sufficient* for personal growth to begin, in that no other conditions need to occur. He uses the words, we think, in their ordinary, everyday senses to describe a causal relation rather than a logical one.

In philosophical discourse, the meaning of the words 'necessary' and 'sufficient', and of the phrase 'necessary and sufficient', differs from the meaning those words carry in everyday use, and therefore also from the meaning they have come to have in person-centred thinking, writing and practice. Wittingly or unwittingly Rogers has used terms with a precise meaning in one area to mean something subtly different in his own. This may or may not be a problem. At the very least, however, it offers us another way of looking at Rogers' formulation.

In philosophical logic necessity and sufficiency are used in two ways. The most common way is to describe logical relationships between propositional variables, as in 'if p then q', where p is a necessary condition of the truth of q. The second use, which is the one that we draw on, is to describe two aspects of the relationship between conditions and events. As Hospers has it (1967, p. 293) necessary conditions are 'conditions in the absence of which the event never occurs'; and sufficient conditions are 'conditions in the presence of which the event always occurs'. One event (x) is said to be a necessary condition of another (y) if x always has to occur in order for y to occur. Oxygen is a necessary condition of fire in that a fire cannot happen without it. This is not a causal relationship: oxygen does not cause fire. It's just that oxygen has to be present in order for there to be fire. Oxygen can, of course, also occur without there being a fire. One event (x) is said to be a sufficient condition of another (y) if x always occurs in the presence of y. In this formulation, x will never happen without the occurrence of y, although y can occur without x happening. Wind, for instance, is a sufficient condition of a tree's movement, in that whenever the wind blows, the branches of the tree move. The tree, of course, can move for other reasons, and so wind is not a *necessary* condition for its movement. To sum up: oxygen is a necessary condition of fire because fire never occurs in its absence; wind is a sufficient condition of a tree's movement because a tree always moves in its presence. In this formulation, says Hospers (ibid., p. 292), 'necessary condition and sufficient condition are the reverse of each other'.

Taken individually, the terms 'necessary' and 'sufficient', then, have both ordinary and specialised meanings. The phrase 'necessary and sufficient' has a more exclusively precise meaning within the field of logic, where to describe conditions as 'necessary and sufficient' is to say that something happens *if and only if* those conditions are present: both *if* those conditions, and *only if* those conditions are present. This has profound implications for person-centred practice. If Rogers is arguing that the six conditions are, strictly, 'necessary and sufficient' then he is saying that therapeutic growth can occur if and only if those conditions are present: that therapeutic change never occurs in their absence, and always occurs in their presence. A statement from the 1959 paper suggests that this is indeed what he meant. He writes (1959b, p. 213) that the process of therapy 'often commences with only these minimal conditions, and it is hypothesized that it never commences *without* these conditions being met'. This is a staggering hypothesis. It rules out the possibility of anyone growing or developing or changing through reading a book, or watching a sunset, or hearing a piece of music, or learning to juggle, or watching a film. It rules out the possibility of anyone feeling better on anti-depressants, or after a brush with death that helps her see her current troubles in a different perspective. It also asserts that therapeutic change will, always and inevitably, follow the six conditions. Given that Rogers developed an approach to therapy that values fluidity, responsiveness and a tentative attitude to experience, we think it's ironic that he should have couched his thinking at this point in such absolute, all or nothing terms.

We'll suggest later when we look at the history of each of the six conditions in more detail that Rogers may have been moving away from this position towards the end of his life. Subsequent theorists too have questioned the necessity and sufficiency of the conditions, particularly in the light of the part clients themselves play in effective therapy. Rodgers, for instance (2003), reviews some of the qualitative studies of clients' experiences, and suggests (p. 20) that 'it is the client's involvement in therapy that is found to be of key importance'. Bohart (2004) agrees that most descriptions of the process of therapy are (p. 103) 'therapist-centric' in that they privilege the therapist's intentions and behaviour, and discount or minimise the role the client himself plays in his own therapy. There is also, Bohart says (p. 106), 'evidence that many individuals with problems recover or solve them without our help as all-seeing benevolent therapists'. Schmid (2004, p. 49) echoes this. 'Therapy' he says 'is more than a matter of therapist variables; it is a matter of the client's self-healing capacities.' Moreover, in perhaps the most extensive piece of research conducted into person-centred therapy, in this case with schizophrenics (Rogers *et al.*, 1967), the report concludes (Kiesler, Mathieu & Klein, 1967, p. 310): 'that the results of this study have not been interpreted as supporting our theoretical specifications of a *causal* relationship between therapist conditions and patient process movement' (our emphasis). Instead, they conclude that patient factors and therapist attitudes create a mutually interactive process and thus (p. 309) 'it seems most appropriate to conceive of therapy outcome as a complex function of their dynamic interaction'.

What do we get if we look at the six conditions through this framework? We argue that the six conditions prove to be neither necessary nor sufficient, in this strict, philosophical sense of the words.

Look at necessity first. We agree that the conditions are intrinsically helpful and often implicated in therapeutic growth. The question, though, is whether they must *necessarily* be present in order for growth to occur. Put another way, can therapeutic growth ever occur independently of the six conditions? Our experience is that it can and does. People do make therapeutic changes on their own, in the gym, walking on a mountain, reading a book or listening to music. The changes may have roots in moments of relationship. A person's perceived or subceived experience of being understood and accepted may precipitate therapeutic change. But often the moments of change themselves take place in solitude, out of any psychological contact with another human being, and therefore out of any immediate experiencing of empathic understanding or unconditional positive regard.

If the conditions are sufficient for therapeutic change, then therapeutic change happens inevitably in their presence. Barrett-Lennard (2002, p. 146) questions this: 'If there is one feature within the theory that is basically unconvincing, it resides in the notion of '"sufficiency" of the conditions.' Our experience supports this, and suggests that change depends upon many more conditions than the six Rogers describes. Outcome research too seems to bear this out. Reviewing the literature, Bozarth (1998, p. 19) sums up:

> The most clear research evidence is that effective psychotherapy results from the resources of the client (extra-therapeutic variables) and from the person-to-person relationship of the therapist and client. The specificity and systematizing of these variables remain somewhat murky, although they do include Rogers' hypothesized variables of the attitudinal qualities.

At best, then, Rogers' hypothesis covers the most that therapist and client can bring to bear for the time that they are together. The hypothesis is limited to the immediacy of the therapeutic relationship and says nothing about the inner resources of the client, or the outer realities of the client's life, both of which may have profound implications for whatever changes individual clients are able to make at particular points in their lives. We cannot say that the six conditions are sufficient for therapeutic change if, even when they occur, a client's lack of inner resources or the intractable realities of her life in society can prevent that change.

Cain (1990, p. 359) argues that there may be 'no definitive answer' in the debate about whether the conditions are really necessary and sufficient. He suggests that the particular skills and styles of particular therapists, and the individual needs of individual clients 'must be factored into the equation of what contributes to the effectiveness' of the therapeutic relationship. We would add an individual client's inner resources and outer situation to that equation. And, writing about the conditions as attitudes, Bozarth (1993, p. 100) suggests that it is 'theoretically consistent and functionally true that people do improve therapeutically without being in relationship with therapists who consistently hold these attitudes'. We think, then, that the conditions are, broadly, 'necessary', using the word in its everyday sense. At the very least, they're often implicated in the process of therapeutic change. Given the significance of extra-therapeutic variables, we cannot agree that the conditions are 'sufficient', even in that word's everyday meaning. We see, too, that therapeutic growth happens in all sorts of ways, in and out of psychological contact, in and out of relationship, and that therefore the conditions are not, in the strict philosophical sense, either 'necessary' or 'sufficient', and certainly not 'necessary and sufficient'.

We noted at the start of this section that Rogers states his hypothesis as an if-then proposition: *if* certain conditions pertain, *then* therapeutic change will follow. Although Rogers stated his case dogmatically, we suspect that he offered his formulation more as a description of what he'd observed in his work, and as a hypothesis to be tested, than as a statement of fact. However, the tone in which he offers it, and the nature of if-then propositions themselves, both make it easy for description to become prescription. By this, we mean that the descriptive statement 'if *x* occurs, *y* will then follow' can easily become 'if you want *y* to happen, then you have to do *x*'. We believe that this is behind recent insistence on the significance of the conditions, and particularly the so-called 'core' conditions, in current training and literature. In effect, therapists are coming to believe that if they want clients to change they have to 'offer' the 'core' conditions. This reverses the emphasis of Rogers' original formulation, which abstracted from experience, described a process, and invited continuous testing and re-assessment. It also allows for a skills approach to the training of therapists and the practice of therapy, on the assumption that if a therapist can but learn the skills to communicate empathic understanding and unconditional positive regard, then this will suffice to initiate a process of change. Along with others, we contest this notion.

These ideas carry implications for theory and practice. In theoretical terms, our relegation of the conditions to a less central position allows us to see instead a trust in the organism's tendency to actualise as central to the therapeutic process. In relation to practice this allows us to work in whatever ways honour and manifest that trust given our own individual way of being in the world and the demands of our individual client. This both echoes Bozarth's notion (1984) of idiosyncratic empathic responses, and expands it beyond empathic responses and into the whole range of therapist responses. Bozarth suggests (1984, p. 59) that if we're to avoid making empathic responses which are merely technical, we need to let them emerge as 'idiosyncratic to the therapist, to the client, and to their experiencing of each other'. In other words, genuinely empathic responses emerge as a function of the person of the therapist, the person of the client, and the quality of the relationship between them in the immediate moment. We suggest that this notion of the idiosyncratic response can hold true for any of a therapist's responses, as long as she is working from and acting out of a profound and unconditional trust in her client's tendency to actualise.

Philosophical influences on Rogers

Wood (1996, p. 168) declares that the person-centred approach is not a philosophy, even though 'many have noted "existential" positions in its attitudes and others have referred to "phenemenologic" perspectives in its intentions'. From time to time, however, even though he says (1961/1967a, p. 199) that he 'was not a student of existential philosophy', Rogers aligns himself and his ideas with both existentialism and phenomenology. He contributed, for instance, to a volume on existential psychology (May, 1961a) and to another on behaviourism and phenomenology (Wann, 1964), and held public dialogues with existential theologians Martin Buber (1957) and Paul Tillich (1965). Showing an interest in broader philosophical matters, he also spoke in public with philosophers of science Michael Polanyi (1966) and Gregory Bateson (1975). Kirschenbaum and Henderson (1990) collect these dialogues and others in one volume, while Anderson and Cissna (1997) offer a new transcript of and commentary on Rogers' dialogue with Buber. Van Belle (in press, 2005) views the origins of the person-centred approach as a therapy movement in continental (European) rationalism (encompassing thinkers such as Descartes, Leibnitz and Kant), one of the central beliefs of which was that human beings could perfect themselves through self-reflection.

For these reasons, we think it's important to look at the relationships between person-centred thinking as it evolved and other philosophical systems to which Rogers was exposed and by which he was informed. We begin with Christianity, which we see as a philosophy in the sense that it offers a framework of beliefs by which to live and act. We then look at empiricism, humanism, phenomenology and existentialism.

Christianity

Rogers grew up in a devout, hard-working and evangelical Protestant family. He described his mother (1967, p. 344) as 'a person with strong religious convictions, whose views became increasingly fundamentalist as she matured'. He considered a career in the Christian ministry and travelled to China as a delegate in an evangelical mission in 1922. It's ironic that this trip to China opened his eyes and stretched his thinking to the point where he questioned the most basic tenets of the faith he'd grown up in. Describing his journey home after six months away, he reports (1967, p. 351):

> It struck me one night in my cabin that perhaps Jesus was a man like other men – not divine! As the idea formed and took root, it became obvious to me that I could never in any emotional sense return home. This proved to be true.

By the time he returned from China, then, Rogers had broken, 'with a minimum of pain', what he called (ibid., p. 351) 'the intellectual and religious ties' with his parents.

The remaining traces of Rogers' early Christianity in his later thinking and practice as a psychologist and psychotherapist are less explored. Interviewed by Russell shortly before he died (Rogers & Russell, 2002, pp. 51–2), Rogers says that he is embarrassed by his early commitment to Christianity and that his embarrassment may be 'due to the fact that possibly I hold similar convictions now, but they're not religious'. One way of understanding this is to say that Rogers divorced himself from the formal trappings of the Christian church as an organised religion while staying committed to the essence of some of the principles it enshrined. 'His deconversion from theological orthodoxy did not' as Fuller puts it (1984, p. 364) 'diminish his spiritual sensibilities'. In this deconversion Rogers is prefiguring a more widespread societal drift away from what he described (1975/81, p. 158) as 'highly structured, inflexible, bureaucratic institutions' like the church, the universities, marriage and the armed forces. He saw this movement (ibid., p. 158) as typical of the emerging person of the latter half of the twentieth century, who would 'leave an institution rather than give in to what to him are meaningless dictates'. This is consistent with Rogers' insistence on the validity and authority of his own personal experience, even or especially against the weight of the established authority vested in institutions like the church.

We see in Rogers' thinking at least two strands which have roots in Christianity and which carry some of its essences stripped of its organised trappings: salvation and teleology.

Salvation

Reviewing the work of the earlier theologians Oden and Browning, Fuller (1984, p. 358) suggests that 'client-centered therapy could be argued to be the anthropological correlate or expression of the Christian scheme of salvation'. By this he means that a therapist's unconditional acceptance of a client is both healing in itself and also a human expression or analogue of God's unconditional love and acceptance.

Teleology

Christianity is teleological in that it carries within it a vision of ends, both individual and universal. Individual Christians who live this life according to God's will expect to live in God eternally when this life ends. Christian scriptures describe a planned end to humanity, an end to which life on earth is tending. We suggest that these two ends – individual and universal – have possible correlates in person-centred thinking: the actualising tendency and the formative tendency. A teleological reading suggests – or at least leaves room for – an intelligent creator who has chosen the *telos*, or end. Given what we know of Rogers' upbringing, this might be an attraction for him in that it allows him to maintain a belief in the meaning, purpose and orderliness of life without using overtly religious terms.

Brodley (1999, p. 109) suggests that the actualising tendency is indeed teleological, and that the particular *telos* or end towards which it works is the survival of the organism. The idea is not new. 'Nature' says Aurelius (1964, p. 125), writing in the second century after Christ, 'always has an end in view.' Although this is credible, we may also see the actualising tendency as a tendency to express, to manifest, to realise potential – as a movement, then, from within to without. That doesn't necessarily make it teleological. The actualisation of potential is a push from within. A teleological process requires a goal for that push, or a pull from without.

Rogers (1979, p. 106) describes the formative tendency as 'an evolutionary tendency toward greater order, greater complexity, greater interrelatedness'. Van Belle (1990, p. 49) describes it as a 'total evolutionary process of becoming' which 'has its own ends in view and its own organizational principle within itself'. We think that this notion of a formative tendency is problematical for a number of reasons. The first is that it presupposes a *telos* to which the universe tends. This raises questions of what and who: What *telos* and who chose it or sets it? The second is that it enshrines the idea of progress, which Gray (2002/03, p. xiii) calls 'a secular version of the Christian belief in providence'. We explore the implications of these ideas further in Chapter 3.

Thorne (1991a) has explored the legacy of Christianity in Rogers' thinking through the notion of original sin. Christianity holds, or has come to hold, the view that men and women are born in sin and redeemed only through the suffering and death of Jesus Christ. Person-centred thinking holds that men and women are born whole and pristine, are shaped and mis-shaped in and through their relationships with others, and can be redeemed to their original pristine congruence through the loving and authentic acceptance of another man or woman, who may or may not be a therapist. The two bodies of thought start from radically different views of humanity. Thorne describes introducing Rogers to the pre-Augustinian doctrine of original righteousness. Although Rogers seems not to have heard of this, Thorne describes him (ibid., p. 131) as 'one of the chief secular exponents of precisely this doctrine in the twentieth century'. Thorne is adamant (ibid., p. 132) that he is not trying 'to claim Carl Rogers for the Christian fold posthumously'. He is, however, one of a number of writers who find in Rogers elements of thinking that, even if not explicitly Christian, stand in friendly relation to some elements of Christian thought.

Perhaps the most obvious way to read this aspect of Rogers' biography is as a move from theology to psychology, from Christianity to humanism, and as part of a wider cultural trend towards what Fuller (1984, p. 365) has called the 'secularization of theology'. However, Fuller suggests (ibid.,

p. 365) that what Rogers offered was, rather, a 'spiritualization of psychology'. This is consistent with what we know of Rogers' increasing interest, towards the end of his life, in mystical, spiritual and paranormal phenomena.

Empiricism

'I like myself best' says Rogers (O'Hara, 1995, p. 143) 'as a pure scientist and realize that each departure from that has been a bit disappointing.' Rogers grew up on a farm and learned early in his life what he called 'the essential elements of science' (Kirschenbaum, 1979, p. 14). Kirschenbaum (ibid., p. 14) notes 'the beginning of a scientific inclination toward careful observation, collection and organization of objective data'. And Rogers says (ibid., p. 14):

> The design of a suitable experiment, the rationale of control groups, the control of all variables but one, the statistical analysis of results – all of these concepts were unknowingly absorbed through my reading at the age of 13 to 16.

This empirical and scientific frame of mind shows in a number of ways in Rogers' subsequent thinking and practice. It shows first in his pragmatic approach to therapy. He describes (1967, p. 358) working with children in Rochester: 'There was only one criterion in regard to any method of dealing with these children and their parents, and that was "Does it work? Is it effective?"' As he began to evolve his own way of working and thinking about his work, he wanted to articulate his thinking as precisely and objectively as possible, and to validate what he did empirically. His desire to articulate his ideas led ultimately to his chapter in Koch (1959), which stands as a vigorous and rigorous attempt to couch his ideas in the orthodox scientific language of his day. His desire to validate what he was doing empirically led to dozens of funded research projects, some of which are reported in Rogers and Dymond (1954) and Rogers *et al.* (1967). It also led to Rogers and his colleagues recording and transcribing therapy sessions so that they could look collaboratively at what seemed to be happening between individual therapists and clients.

Humanism

If Rogers grew up believing in the centrality of God, he spent most of his adult life believing in the central importance of individual men and women. It's in this loose sense that we can call him a humanist: he sought meaning, purpose and satisfaction in his relationships with individual men and women, rather than in his relationship with God. Fuller, though, (1984, p.

365) says that 'the humanistic psychology for which he has been the preeminent spokesman has never been humanistic in the strictest sense'. He goes on to make the point (ibid., p. 365) that the idea of 'a preconscious, biologically-based actualising tendency' allows Rogers to see the personal as an expression or manifestation of the universal, and that this renders his approach (ibid., p. 366) 'a metaphysical doctrine', and therefore not strictly humanist.

Gray (2002/03, p. 31) goes further, and describes humanism itself as 'a secular religion thrown together from decaying scraps of Christian myth'. These critiques allow us to ask whether, even in his apparent humanism, Rogers held on to some aspects of Christian philosophy, albeit without overtly religious language and trappings. We touched on this idea above in the section on Christianity.

Phenomenology and existentialism

Although Rogers identified himself at times with both phenomenology and existentialism, we think he was, strictly speaking, neither a phenomenologist nor an existentialist. Van Belle (1980, p. 190) notes that Rogers confirmed to him in a letter 'that there were no direct contacts with any existential or phenomenological thinking until he was teaching at the University of Chicago', a post he took up towards the end of 1945. The person-centred approach, however, shares some of the assumptions and values of both philosophies, and draws freely on the ideas they provide. For this reason we think it's worthwhile looking briefly at each.

'Phenomenology' says May (1961b, p. 26) 'is the endeavor to take the phenomena as given.' Writing specifically about its use in therapy, he goes on:

> It is the disciplined effort to clear one's mind of the presuppositions that so often cause us to see in the patient only our own theories or the dogmas of our own systems, the effort to experience instead the phenomena in their full reality as they present themselves. It is the attitude of openness and readiness to hear – aspects of the art of listening in psychotherapy that are generally taken for granted and sound so easy but are exceedingly difficult.

Although phenomenology, as a philosophy and as a practice, is more complex than May's definition suggests, it's an accurate and adequate definition for our purposes. Phenomenology takes as one of its assumptions that we bring our own individual biases to our experience of the world, and experience the world through the filter of those biases. It recognises, therefore, the inviolable subjectivity of individual experience: two people will bring different filters to the same phenomena and therefore experience them differently. It offers, also, a method by which we can, if we're interested, begin to recognise some of our own filters and approach the phenomena of our lives more immediately. Briefly, this method involves three steps or rules (Spinelli, 1989):

1   That we *bracket* anything and everything we think we know about whatever it is we're experiencing.
2   That in our own thinking and articulating we *describe* what we experience as simply as possible.
3   That we approach the different aspects of whatever phenomena we're experiencing *equally*, and allow for the possibility that any one aspect of what we're experiencing may be as important as any one other. We resist, therefore, any temptation to give those aspects a differential or hierarchical significance.

Spinelli (1989, p. 148) says that 'most textbook accounts of Rogers' client-centred therapy fail to reveal his obvious indebtedness to the phenomenological method'. Although we think that Rogers drew from phenomenological *principles* rather than from the phenomenological *method*, we agree with Spinelli's point. Since he wrote, some writers, including Brazier (1993, p. 87), have acknowledged Rogers' debt. The first three of the nineteen propositions, for instance, (Rogers, 1951, pp. 481–533) articulate a thoroughly phenomenological perspective, sceptical of the notion of an objective reality, enshrining the importance of the subjective and describing the relationship between what we perceive and how we behave. And, writing in 1974, Rogers asked (1978/80, p. 104) whether we still needed, or could indeed afford, one agreed reality:

> Can we today afford the luxury of having 'a' reality? Can we still preserve the belief that there is a 'real world' upon whose definition we all agree? I am convinced that this is a luxury we *cannot* afford, a myth we dare not maintain.

The phenomenological aspect of Rogers' work is significant at least in part because it justifies the centrality of empathic understanding in the theory and practice of the approach. If the first of the nineteen propositions is true, and if we each of us live at the centre of our own 'continually changing world of experience' (Rogers, 1951, p. 483), then the only understanding that can possibly be meaningful is an empathic one. Anything else at best assumes a shared reality, or asserts a reality and insists that it be shared.

Existentialism is a development of phenomenology. The phenomenological insistence on the primacy of the subjective grows into a recognition that we are all isolated one from another, that one subjective being never has access to another's subjective world, that we each have to make our own sense of the world around us, that we must each choose for ourselves what to believe and what to do, and that we will all, eventually, die alone. In terms which Rogers himself could have used, Tillich (1952, p. 125) describes existentialism as 'the expression of the most radical form of the courage to be oneself'.

In this original European formulation existentialism is a stark and bracing philosophy, not immediately attractive to American humanistic psychologists. Allport, for instance (1961, p. 94), suggested that most Americans found European writing and theorising on the existential approach 'turgid, verbalistic, and reckless', and the Europeans themselves (ibid., p. 97) 'too preoccupied with dread, anguish, despair, and "nausea"'. Interviewing Rogers, Evans (1975/81, p. 70) suggests that 'much of the French existentialism has been beset by a kind of cynicism', and that American existentialism 'seems to be a good deal more optimistic'. Rogers agrees with both points. Recognising that it emphasises 'the more discomforting aspects of life', Cooper (2004, p. 106) suggests also that it does so only as 'part of an attempt to help people live life more fully and intensely'.

Kirschenbaum (1979, p. 29) says that as early as the 1920s Rogers was 'developing an "existential" slant in religion and morality', even if he wouldn't have used that term himself to describe it. Specifying what he means by this, Kirschenbaum offers the following (ibid., p. 29):

A person is a Christian not on the basis of her words or beliefs, but in her actions. He came to believe that good works were more important than ritual or doctrine in Christianity. One must take responsibility for one's actions.

To this, we would add another comment from Rogers himself. Writing a paper on Martin Luther shortly after his return from China he formed the idea (1967, p. 351) 'that man's ultimate reliance is upon his own experience'. He adds that this 'has been a theme which has stayed with me'. Whether or not Rogers had come across existentialist thinking this early in his life, his recognition of the importance of action, responsibility and individual experience clearly prefigures existential concerns. If Rogers was indeed thinking in this way he would have found ready affinity with some aspects of existential philosophy as soon as he met it.

Rogers says (Kirschenbaum, 1979, p. 231) that he was encouraged to read the existential writers Kierkegaard and Buber in the early 1950s by some of his theological students at Chicago. He described them both (Evans, 1971/85, p. 70) as 'friends of mine that I never knew I had', and took especially to Kierkegaard. Writing a later introduction to one of the papers he wrote at about this time, he says (1967b, p. 273): 'I am sure that his honest willingness to call a spade a spade influenced me more than I realized.'

It's easy to see why some strands of existential thinking should have appealed to Rogers. Its recognition of individual freedom, its emphasis on action and its insistence on authenticity are all elements that echo throughout Rogers and his contemporaries. It seems to us that those Americans, including Rogers, who identified with existential thinking took selectively from the European tradition, and rendered it both more optimistic and more pragmatic than it had been in Europe. They adopted the existential recognition of individual freedom, and its emphasis on action and authenticity, and used those concepts to support their own optimistic notions of individuality and actualisation. They overlooked or chose to ignore the European recognition that if we are free we are also responsible, and that, in an isolated and meaning-free life that ends necessarily in death, responsibility is, potentially, as distressing as the idea of freedom is exhilarating.

Reading Rogers from contemporary viewpoints

In this part we consider the relevance of a number of contemporary influences on person-centred theory and therapy. We think that this is important for a number of reasons:

- Ideas do not exist outside a social context. It is nearly fifty years since Rogers (1957, 1959b) originally formulated his theory of therapy. As the social context changes, so too does the lens through which we view his ideas.
- Rogers (1959b) himself views theory as fallible, temporary, fluid and, at best, stimulating.
- Intellectual and scientific developments in a numbers of fields both during Rogers' lifetime and since his death confirm, support, challenge, question and contradict his original ideas. In our view it behoves anyone who identifies with person-centred therapy as practitioner, trainer or supervisor to take both person-centred psychology and these developments seriously by addressing rather than avoiding them.

We look first at structural perspectives, postmodernism, and constructivism.

Structural perspectives

This title encompasses a variety of structural critiques of individual and individualising psychotherapy. These critiques have often been forged in the crucible of struggles against inequalities and for access, on picket lines and demonstrations, in consciousness-raising groups, marches and direct action more than in the study, library, seminar or training group. Essentially such critiques, from feminist, cultural, class, disability and gay perspectives, argue that the world is organised through the influences of, respectively, gender, race, class, disability, and sexuality; that environmental pressures affect or even determine our identity in terms of these divisions; and that, therefore, they shape our behaviour. Historically, economically and socially, men, white people, the ruling class and so on have held power and maintained this by oppressing others.

To take an example from psychology: feminists argue that men and women are not the same and that they develop differently because of history, environment, socialisation and expectations. Men tend to view the world in terms of power, competition and hierarchy; women through relationship with and connection to others. Applying this in the fields of psychology and psychotherapy, we have many hierarchical, structural theories of personality which not only do not account for women's experience, but also further marginalise and pathologise women. This, in effect, has led pioneers such as Karen Horney (1939) and, in more recent times, Juliet Mitchell (1975), to criticise a patriarchal psychoanalysis and to develop a feminist theory and practice. Being oppressed leads to alienation. Marx's concept of alienation has resonances in Kierkegaard's notion of 'losing one's own self', which Rogers (1973) takes up in his discussion of a disintegrating marriage. These perspectives share a critique of the individual focus and individualising effect of psychotherapy. In the words of Hillman and Ventura (1992) and the title of their book: *We've had a Hundred Years of Psychotherapy and the World's Getting Worse*. In her feminist critique Waterhouse (1993, p. 68) argues that 'in failing to politicize personal life, the Rogerian approach can be naïve and even, at times, harmful'. We think this criticism is inaccurate, as Rogers and others who followed do precisely politicise personal life and promote social change.

These different structural critiques have something in common, especially when they are experienced by an individual person, a situation which is well discussed and illustrated by Moodley (2003) in a chapter entitled 'Double, triple, multiple jeopardy'. Of course, there are also differences of emphasis between these structural critiques. We summarise these with regard to psychotherapy:

- Feminism – has contributed to a focus on the relational both theoretically and in therapeutic practice. In their discussion of the person-centred and feminist approaches, Proctor and Napier (2004a, p. 5) suggest that '. . . the biggest point of conflict between the two approaches is the focus of study'. They view these as, respectively, the individual and gender dynamics.
- Culture – critiques from cultural perspectives often focus on the monocultural roots of white, western/northern psychology. This has been levelled against humanistic psychology by Spinelli (1989), and

against person-centred psychology by, amongst others, Holdstock (1990, 1993) and Laungani (1999).

- Class and disability – analysis from these viewpoints tends to focus on issues of access and segregation. In the therapeutic field, this manifests as a critique of the inaccessibility and exclusivity of psychotherapy in terms of cost and language, as well as physical barriers such as steps and stairs. This covers a range of concerns with regard to affording a psychotherapist in the private sector or getting to see one in any reasonable length of time in the public sector, let alone affording to train as one (see Kearney, 1997). The issue of language centres on the inaccessibility of therapeutic jargon and theory. Disabled activists, therapists and clients are still having to educate professionals about disability and especially about those disabilities which are invisible or not apparent (see Corker, 2003).
- Gay – 'queer analysis' offers a critique of psychotherapy's monosexual roots, and the pathologising and mistreatment of gay, lesbian, bisexual and transgender (glbt) clients. Psychoanalysis, in particular, has a history of discrimination against glbt clients (see O'Connor & Ryan, 1993). Glbt therapists have also developed 'gay affirmative therapy' (see Maylon, 1982; Davies & Neal, 1996, 2000).

How does Rogers stand up to critiques from these perspectives? In his later years Rogers wrote a number of books about people in wider contexts in which he acknowledges both some of his own limitations and the changing context of relationships and society.

- In *Becoming Partners: Marriage and Its Alternatives* Rogers (1973) tries to get inside the experience of partnership. In doing so he acknowledges some of the limitations of the sample studied, and identifies a number of themes, which Embleton Tudor *et al.* (2004) elaborate and bring up to date. Specifically he acknowledges (1973, p. 18) that a relationship will have *permanence* 'only to the degree to which it satisfies the emotional, psychological, intellectual and physical needs of the partners'. He also predicts that (in the year 2000) 'partners will be demanding more of the relationship than they do today'. Elsewhere in the book he reflects candidly on his own shortcomings as a husband.
- In *On Personal Power* Rogers (1978) talks about oppression, citing approvingly the work of the Brazilian educator and revolutionary, Paulo Freire (1921–1997). He acknowledges the impact of changing culture and discusses the revolution in marriage and relationships, and how people deal with jealousy. He refers (1978, p. 45) to the Women's Liberation Movement as '. . . one of the most rapid and effective "quiet revolutions" of our time'. In other papers he talks about 'cultural conditioning' and discusses working with intercultural tensions and

their resolution, and refers to the emergence of a 'new political figure' or 'emerging person'.

- In *A Way of Being* Rogers and others write about the political impact of the person-centred approach, especially in and through large community groups. He acknowledges (Rogers 1980b, p. xvii) the influence of his daughter and other friends with feminist leanings on his greater sensitivity to 'the linguistic inequality between the sexes'.

Notwithstanding his general openness to criticism and his own willingness to change, Rogers did not account theoretically for the kinds of critiques from the structural perspectives under discussion. It has been left to others to consider the relationship between person-centred therapy and specific concerns from these social movements. Three edited books, recently published and written largely from person-centred perspectives, have contributed to the development of a more sophisticated understanding of these relationships: Fairhurst (1999); Moodley, Lago and Talahite (2004); and Proctor and Napier (2004). We consider some theoretical implications.

Person and context, person-in-context

A number of writers comment on the view amongst person-centred therapists that focusing on the uniqueness of the individual client means that we cannot comment on any analysis of social factors unless the client mentions it (see, for instance, Proctor & Napier, 2004). We disagree. From an organismic perspective, we cannot understand an individual outside of her environmental context. Even referring to someone as 'her' is a social construct. In a similar vein, Wilkins (2003, p. 16) cautions against the separation of person-centred therapy from the broader person-centred approach: 'To entirely separate person-centred therapy from the context of the person-centred approach means that any consideration of it is incomplete.' The implication is that a person-centred *approach* to therapy is a wider, contextual and more permissive activity than 'person-centred therapy'. Whilst we appreciate the subtlety of the word-play we think that reclaiming the centrality of the organism, as we do in this present work, offers us a way of working therapeutically with the person-in-context.

The development of theory

Wilkins (2003) addresses and, in our view, largely repudiates the argument that person-centred therapy is monocultural. It is an easy and strangely personal, individualistic jibe. As we observe, particularly in this chapter and throughout the book, the roots of much of Rogers' thinking derive from Ancient Greek philosophy, via European and North American existentialists. Many people all over the world find Rogers' ideas compatible with their own. There is a large interest in the person-centred approach in Japan, and Wilkins (2003) reports on a gathering in South Africa at which Zulu participants were pointing out similarities between person-centred concepts and the practice of their 'folk medicine'. A number of people have written about the person-centred approach and its relationship to Buddhism, Taoism, Sufi, Soto Zen, and Christianity, for references to which see Tudor and Merry (2002) and Wilkins (2003). As we acknowledge in the Intro-duction, a part of our interest in writing this book is to reclaim the diversity of sources for an organismic, person-centred psychology.

The theory of human development

The criticism stands that person-centred theory does not sufficiently account for gender or cultural differences. Addressing the first point, Wolter-Gustafson (1999, p. 208) argues that Rogers' theory offers 'a sophisticated and substantial approach to understanding human development primarily because of his insistence on starting with the schema as it is apprehended by the person'. This, of course, includes apprehending discrimination and oppression. Wolter-Gustafson is critical of how human development theory continues to split people along gendered lines, and holds that Rogers' organismic psychology, with its emphasis on the internal valuing process, and its redistribution of epistemological authority from the (external) expert to the person, is a radical and empowering psychology (see Wolter-Gustafson, 2004). Further, given that the organism differentiates (for dis-cussion of which see Chapters 2 and 4), the precise nature, phenomeno-logical and social reality of such differentiation (woman/man, black/white, gay/straight/transgender) is personal, contextual and constructed.

The challenge to person-centred psychology of critiques from different cultural perspectives centres on the issue of whether it is an individualistic psychology, reflecting dominant 'me cultures', rather than a collectivist psychology more associated with 'we cultures'. Taking Stark's (2000) taxonomy of one person (traditional psychoanalytic), one and a half person (object relations), and two person (relational) psychologies, person-centred therapy definitely falls into the last model. Furthermore, if our therapeutic practice is based on engagement in relationship, as distinct from the enhancement of knowledge or the provision of experience, then therapist and client must both appreciate the inevitability and impact of relationships and context outside of the consulting room. Adding to Stark's taxonomy, this may allow us to describe person-centred psychology as a 'two person in context' psychology.

Person-centred therapy emphasises present-centred human development, as distinct from past-centred child development. We do not have to ask clients questions about their past, as they experience and express the impact of their past in the present. The view that psychotherapy is a present-centred process of learning and healing reduces the danger of infantilising adult clients and trainees, which happens when 'growth' or development is defined within the framework of an expert therapist and an inexpert client.

The social/political world in the consulting room

Those who are familiar with the philosophy and principles of the person-centred *approach* to life may be used to taking concepts and theories drawn originally from therapy and applying them more widely, as Rogers did. It is less common to draw ideas and practice from the external, social world and apply them to the therapeutic encounter and process. A rare example of this is Keys (1999) who discusses how key concepts of the *Universal Declaration of Human Rights* (United Nations, 1948) underpin the work she does with clients in a counselling service operating within a drop-in project in London. To us this is an example of viewing both person (persons) and therapeutic practice in a wider, social, environmental context, and one which accounts for the organisational context of therapy. That therapists are willing to engage actively with their clients is not a departure from person-centred principles, but an embodiment of them. This is perhaps most challenging with regard to the person-centred principle of being 'non-directive', a discussion we take up in Chapter 3. Analysing Rogers' coun-selling interview with a black client in 1984, Lago and Clark (2004, p. 149) suggest that it 'clearly demonstrates Rogers' increasing capacity to recog-nise, acknowledge and address explicitly the societal conditions of dis-crimination and racism that affect minority group members'.

Language

Language can be both liberating and oppressive. Consistent with Rogers' (1959b) provisional and fluid conception of theory is an open, critical approach to the changing use of language and the need for language to change. Rogers' (1980b) own observation about sexist language is one example of this. Writing about anti-disabling practice, Corker (2003) points out the importance of the root metaphors in therapy and cites an example from Freud who refers to the ego as wearing 'an auditory lobe'. We discuss the impact of language and metaphor further below (pp. 40–4). More generally, Warner (1999) criticises the use of compacted language in which psychological phenomena such as 'boundaries', 'confidentiality' and 'safety' are objectified. She argues for a descriptive and action-oriented language which is clearer and, psychologically, more personal and accurate. Thus:

- 'Fred enters or allows others to enter areas of body space that are private, without consent', rather than 'Fred's boundaries are inappro-priate.'

LIVERPOOL
JOHN MOORES UNIVERSITY
AVRIL ROBARTS LRC
TEL. 0151 231 4

- 'I'll trust you to maintain my confidence', rather than 'Confidentiality is an important rule in this group.'
- 'I don't feel safe here right now', rather than 'Safety is important. Why aren't you (the therapist) providing it?'

Education and learning as therapists

The implications of many of these structuralist critiques for the education and 'training' of therapists are framed in terms of an increased curriculum (to include input on discrimination, oppression, anti-oppressive practice, and so on), or a particular focus, say on gender studies. Such additions can detract from the experiential and phenomenological integrity of the person-centred approach to student-led and process-led learning. Discussing the 'desirable preparation' for a person in training as a therapist, Rogers (1951, p. 437) says:

> It seems desirable that the student should have a broad experiential knowledge of the human being in his cultural setting . . . Such knowledge needs to be supplemented by experiences of living with or dealing with individuals who have been the product of cultural influences very different from those which have molded the student.

Rogers wrote a lot about learning (Rogers, 1969, 1974/80), and Mearns (1997) has written specifically about *Person-Centred Counselling Training*. Cornelius-White and Godfrey (2004) take up the challenge of integrating feminist critical pedagogies and the person-centred approach to education, concluding (p. 174) that, whilst there is a need for an explicit openness to different ideas of theory, self, subjectivity, helping or therapeutic relationships and so on, it is only 'through empathy and compassion [that] students can more likely liberate and accept themselves and others'. We adopt a similar approach in this present work, drawing on a variety of sources, in order to discuss and develop the theory and practice of person-centred therapy.

Postmodernism

Brazier (1993, p. 11) says that Rogers 'was brought up in the "modern" world but was able to open the door for us to a "post-modern" universe'. O'Hara (1999, p. 63) suggests that Rogers 'started out as a logical positivist and ended up as a post-modern romantic'. Schmid (2004, p. 37) says that he 'came to view every individual as a unique being' and stood therefore, 'in the tradition of phenomenology, existentialism, hermeneutics and con-structivism'. We wouldn't go so far as to say that Rogers opened a door for us to a postmodern universe. At best, we think, he saw that there was a door and looked through it himself. We agree, though, the general point that Rogers straddled the divide between modern and postmodern. In some ways this is a product of chronology. He was born at the beginning of the twentieth century, and grew up a modernist. He was confident that empirical and scientific methods were, or could lead to, adequate tools with which to examine and measure the subtleties of therapeutic processes. He saw progress as desirable and inevitable, and he cherished the notion of truths and principles that were universally true. Yet by the time he died postmodernism was on the rise, sceptical of science, interested in local, subjective, individual and therefore relative truths, and dismissive of the plausibility or possibility of universal ones.

This leaves a dissonance in much of what Rogers wrote. He wrote about processes which he saw as organic, holistic, phenomenological, and even mystical; and yet he sought increasingly objective ways of measuring and articulating them, and wrote about them often in linear, rationalist, scientific language. He admits as much himself (1967b, p. 200): 'I have felt an increasing discomfort at the distance between the rigorous objectivity of myself as scientist and the almost mystical subjectivity of myself as therapist.' He's so at the cusp of the change from modern to postmodern that he has only, or largely, modern language with which to describe increasingly postmodern experiences. This is ironic. Rogers argued that congruence, integration and fullness of function come as a result of having or developing the capacity to symbolise experience accurately in awareness. The irony is that Rogers probably never had the language, the conceptual vocabulary, with which to symbolise to himself, accurately and adequately, the depth and breadth of his professional experience. As a therapist and as a theorist, then, Rogers was incongruent. Born when he was, he simply did not have the words for his experience. We can see his writings perhaps as a striving for increasingly full symbolising of his experiences. This may explain why he wrote so much about so little. He wrote all that he wrote around a small cluster of ideas, as if he had the experience early and spent the rest of his life seeking to articulate it. This would explain too the attraction Rogers came to feel for mystical and spiritual philosophers such as Lao Tzu, Kierkegaard and Buber, as though he knew that their language was more likely than his own to be adequate for what he wanted to say.

Writers since Rogers have examined his thinking in the light of postmodernism. Others have used person-centred principles to critique postmodern assumptions. Postmodernists dismiss the possibility of universal truths or theories, and hold that truths are local, individual, subjective and relative. Jones (1996, p. 20) argues, therefore, that postmodern thinking 'stands in direct opposition to the kind of universal claims that Rogers makes for his theories'. Postmodern thinkers don't question the claims themselves, so much as the *nature* of the claims, the fact that Rogers asserts them to be *universally* true. From their perspective, his assertion (1979, p. 106) of a formative tendency, for instance, that 'can be traced and observed in stellar space, in crystals, in micro-organisms, in organic life, in human beings' is clearly out of date and untenable. Ellingham, though (1997, 1998, 1999), critiques postmodern thinking as bleak and nihilistic, and argues, with Rogers, that the formative tendency is an idea fertile enough to generate a paradigm which will unify the practice of counselling and psychotherapy. The search for a paradigm is, in itself, inimical to postmodern thought. The idea that there is or can be one grand explanation of a whole field of endeavour is simply inconsistent with its insistence that there are only local and individual truths.

Ellingham's description of postmodern thinking as bleak and nihilistic recognises that its extremes render theory irrelevant, and allow therapists to champion any behaviour as legitimate. If all truths are local, who can say what's true and what's not, or what's therapeutic and what's not? Jones, too, who is more willing than Ellingham to embrace postmodern thinking, considers, and ultimately decides against, the possibility of abandoning theory, and (1996, p. 23) of working 'without the support of any explanatory theoretical discourses'. He argues that postmodern thinking need not mean an end to person-centred theory, but held lightly may be a practical way (ibid. p. 25) for us 'to remain uncertain to its "truth"'. It may, in other words, help us see it as one possible truth among others, a truth that came from and may be more relevant to a particular race, culture and class. We find Jones' argument attractive. It allows us to hold person-centred theory as relatively true, or true in the particular fields to which it is relevant, and also therefore to acknowledge the possibility of fields where more local truths have more to offer. Ironically, one recent book on the subject of psychotherapy and postmodernism (Frie, 2003) summarises Rogers' emphasis in its title: *Understanding Experience*.

Social constructivism

Anderson (1990) tells (or retells) an old joke about baseball umpires which explains some of the complexity of constructivism, social constructivism and radical constructivism.

> One says, 'There's balls and there's strikes, and I call them the way they are.' Another says, 'There's balls and there's strikes, and I call 'em the way I see 'em.' The third says, 'There's balls and there's strikes, and they ain't *nothin'* until I call 'em.'

Commenting on this joke, Allen and Allen (1997, p. 89) says that it shows 'an objectivist and two kinds of constructionists, the last umpire the more radical'.

In his dialogue with Rogers, Skinner tells a story about a time Rogers went out duck hunting. After a long cold morning in the blind sighting no ducks, a lone duck came by and Rogers shot at it. At the same time a few hundred yards away another man shot at the same duck. In the dialogue, Rogers clarifies both the story and the punch line, which was that when Rogers and the other man met over the body of the duck, they flipped a coin, the result of which, reports Rogers, 'proved that I had shot the duck' (Kirschenbaum & Henderson, 1990a, p. 92). Calling it in a similar vein to the baseball umpire, this clearly shows Rogers as a radical constructivist!

'Constructivism holds that the structure of our nervous systems dictates that we can never know what is "really" out there' (Hoffman, 1993, p. 34). All we can ever know about anything is our construction or construing of people, events, phenomena and 'reality'. In this sense the truth is not 'out there' but 'in here'. We construct or co-construct the meaning of these truths in our encounters with each other. This view of the world may be traced back, philosophically, to the tradition of European rationalism which held that the mind is active, not passive, and that it constructs 'reality', rather than being informed by it. This perspective will be familiar to personal construct psychologists, whose work derives from George Kelly, and whose core theory is based on the notion of construing reality. Rogers (1958/67a) acknowledges Kelly in his borrowing and use of the term 'personal constructs'.

Social constructivism, which is closely aligned with the postmodern tradition, understands that everybody has equally valid perspectives and that there are no 'transcendent criteria of the correct' (Gergen, 1991, p. 111). That truth is local and subjective supports the importance of Rogers' sixth condition: that the client perceives (or subceives) the therapist's positive regard and empathy. No matter how empathic or accepting a therapist is or construes himself to be, his client's experience of him is more important. We discuss this further in Chapters 7 and 8.

A number of points follow from these perspectives:

- Knowledge within a culture is embedded in language. Thus, he (sic) who has the language has the knowledge has the power (see p. 35). Language and images are provided by experts, sanctioned by what Becker (1967, p. 241) refers to as 'superordinate groups in the society'. The media provide daily examples of this. One recent example was of a report of a murdered teacher 'and his wife' which, in later editions, was changed to 'two schoolteachers'. The first edition defined the woman in terms of her relationship to her husband. The second identified her as a professional in her own right.
- Science, in the modernist tradition, seeks to reduce rather than enhance thinking and seeks 'monocrop' rather than diversity. This critique informs John Taylor Gatto's thinking on education and schooling which, he argues, seeks to 'dumb down' children (for more on which see Embleton Tudor et al., 2004).

- Language is not so much a device for reporting one's experience, but a defining framework for it. If we agree that perception *is* reality (Rogers, 1951, 1959b), then the language we use to describe that perception is also reality (see Whitehead, 1929/78, 1933). This also means that a change in language connotes a change in experience. If I say of myself that I'm untidy, lazy and just made that way, I'm expressing a history of internalised external evaluations. If I say that I know where to find my things, I'm making a self-referential statement which reframes, deconstructs and reconstructs both my perception and my experience.

- Language socialises people into a way of thinking about themselves. White and Epstein (1990, p. 74) suggest that all human science disciplines in the modernist tradition 'characterize, classify, specialize; they distribute along a scale, around a norm, hierarchize individuals in relation to one another, and if necessary disqualify and invalidate'. It is not surprising that social constructivists are critical, for instance, of diagnostic categories such as those promoted by the American Psychiatric Association in its *Diagnostic and Statistical Manual* (*DSM*) (now in its fourth revised edition). This critique was prefigured both by Rogers (1951) in his objections to the external nature of diagnosis, and by Steiner (1971, p. 5) who said that 'everything diagnosed psychiatrically, unless *clearly* organic in origin, is a form of alienation'.

- The principal way to think about our lives (from a constructionist perspective) is through stories or narratives which are a set of explanatory concepts that explain our relationship with others and the world. Change the language, change the story; change the story, change the experience.

Summers and Tudor (2000, p. 24) summarise the principles of constructivism which are particularly relevant to and inform therapy:

- That meaning constantly evolves through dialogue.
- That discourse creates systems (such as particular understandings of personality), and not the other way around.
- That therapy is the co-creation, in dialogue, of new narratives which provide new possibilities.
- That the therapist is a participant-observer in this dialogue.

These are all compatible with and embodied by person-centred therapy.

Language and metaphor

As we observe, one of the defining characteristics of recent philosophy is a particular interest in language. Postmodernism (Norris, 1995, p. 708) is specifically interested in language 'as the object of its own scrutiny', an interest which can lead to a 'dizzying rhetorical regress' in which nothing seems to make any sense. At the same time postmodernism and constructivism have challenged and sharpened our appreciation of the impact of language in therapy. In concluding this chapter we consider the significance of the language we use to describe therapeutic processes.

We're interested especially in metaphor, which is a condensed, economical and therefore powerful way of describing one thing in terms of another. In strict rhetorical terms, a metaphor (Rogers was a pioneer) is a more concentrated or elliptical form of a simile (Rogers was like a pioneer). For our purposes, and consistent with one of the original meanings of the word, we're using metaphor in a wider sense to mean any figure of speech that works by associating or comparing one thing with another.

Psychological accounts of brain functioning, consciousness, motivation, personality, the therapeutic relationship and so on are shaped by the metaphors used, a subject explored in Leary's (1990) major work on *Metaphors in the History of Psychology*. Also, it's not just that some us are more interested in language than others; our capacity for metaphor may have a neurophysiological basis. Synaesthesia is a phenomenon whereby looking at numbers or listening to tones for some people evokes the experience of a particular colour. Based on his research in this field, Ramachandran (2003) suggests that this reflects the functioning of the angular gyrus, the part of the brain where the occipital, parietal and temporal lobes meet and which is responsible for cross-modal synthesis. He goes further to suggest that the angular gyrus may have evolved precisely so that the ability to engage in cross-modal abstraction could allow the emergence of other, more abstract functions such as the construction and use of metaphors. This provides a neurological basis and location for cross-modal symbolisation which, from a person-centred perspective, is a necessary process in the understanding of experience and experiencing (see Chapter 2).

'Language' says Keen (1983, p. 233) 'governs perception.' He goes on: 'The metaphors we use limit what we can see and experience. The category into which we place a thing determines how we will deal with it. An entire logic and philosophy is smuggled into seemingly innocent words.'

We would add that 'seemingly innocent words' then smuggle that 'logic and philosophy' into any discourse or conversation of which they are a part. Given this, we think it's important to attend to the words we use to describe the work we do. We've already pointed out that Rogers uses mainly linear, scientific and modern language to describe experiences and processes that are, rather, dynamic, organismic and postmodern. Making the same point on a larger scale, Ellingham notes (2001, p. 96) that the person-centred approach is 'a mix of concepts deriving from two disparate "paradigms," two fundamentally different guiding visions of the world'. He identifies one as deriving from Descartes and Newton, and as underpinning 'our contemporary common-sense understanding of reality'; and one as still emerging, and characterised by such terms as holistic, organismic and process. Our current interest in this is that Ellingham identifies the root metaphor of the first paradigm as a machine, and the root metaphor of the second as a living organism. Both metaphors make statements about the way we see the work we do, and carry implications for the way we think about our work. They also, therefore, inform how we work. We contend that metaphors are freighted with meaning and implications, and that it's important to use metaphors that are consistent with the root metaphor and therefore with the nature of the work we do. If sensitive dependence on initial conditions applies, the metaphors we choose to describe aspects of therapy carry powerful messages and unforeseeable implications.

In our view, person-centred practice is, in its nature, organic rather than mechanical, seminal rather than technical. If they're to be helpful, the metaphors we use to describe the work, and to further the development of practice and theory, need to reflect this nature. The approach begins with natural images. Rogers (1979, p. 100) uses organic images to describe different aspects of the approach: potatoes in a cellar (1979, p. 100) describe an organism's tendency to actualise; seaweed on a rocky outcrop (1963, pp. 1–2) illustrates an organism's resilience in the face of an inhospitable environment; white blood corpuscles dealing with an infection describe (1970/73, p. 50) a group's capacity to deal with 'unhealthy elements in its process'. Given what Van Belle (1990, p. 47) calls Rogers' 'almost religious reverence for growth', the metaphors he uses to carry his thinking can only be natural ones. Compare Rogers' images with this from Freud (1926/62, p. 142):

> we picture the unknown apparatus which serves the activities of the mind as being really like an instrument constructed of several parts (which we speak of as 'agencies'), each of which performs a particular function and which have a fixed spatial relation to one another.

Freud's image is mechanical rather than seminal, lifeless rather than vital, man-made rather than natural. His metaphor comes from and is symbolic of a different paradigm, and is neither meant to carry nor capable of carrying the idea of inherent growth or actualisation.

More recent writers have used particular images to describe aspects of their work and thinking. From a person-centred perspective, Mearns (1994) writes about the 'dance' of psychotherapy. Whilst this has some merit, as a metaphor it is too general. Is the dance a slow waltz, an enticing tango, a disco dance, or what?

Brazier (1995, p. 27) describes therapy as surgery, and the therapist as surgeon. He makes the point that the therapist, like the surgeon, must be scrupulously clean so as not to introduce any infective or contaminating material into an open wound. Although we might disagree with this, it's a legitimate point of view and the metaphor carries the idea vividly and persuasively. Push the metaphor a little further, though, and its limitations become clear. The patient, or client, is not in a position to effect his own change, and puts himself passive, prostrate and anaesthetised, into the hands and under the knife of an expert technician who acts upon him. The surgeon, or therapist, must not introduce anything of her own into the surgical field for fear of infecting the wound and compromising the health and recovery of her patient. Even if we recognise that Brazier is using this metaphor for limited ends, to make a particular point, we suggest that its implications are at odds with the spirit of the approach and therefore problematical. Rogers, for instance, (1959b, p. 221) says that 'psychotherapy is the releasing of an already existing capacity in a potentially competent individual, not the expert manipulation of a more or less passive personality'.

Wyatt (2001) describes congruence as a diamond. Like Brazier, she's making a local and legitimate point: that the practice of congruence has many facets. Outside of its locality, though, the metaphor becomes unhelpful. Although diamonds are originally organic, by the time they become diamonds they are fixed, hard, impermeable and not living at all. We suggest that this metaphor risks encouraging a belief in congruence as a fixed attitude, desirable and expensive, as diamonds are, and difficult to attain.

Other metaphors in the generic field of therapy define and dominate discourse. A major example of this is the term 'depth psychology', from the German *Tiefenpsychologie*, originally coined by Eugen Bleuler. This term generally refers to those psychotherapies which are based on notions of the unconscious. The topographical metaphor indicates a geological and archeological structure to the personality (see Chapter 5). It is also exclusive in that it implies that those psychotherapies which don't place the unconscious at their centre or bottom are shallow and irrelevant. Within person-centred therapy Mearns (1996) talks about working at 'relational depth' with clients. This metaphor carries the same risks, we think, as the term depth psychology.

We deconstruct these metaphors simply to endorse the truth of Keen's point above, that 'seemingly innocent words' can carry unforeseen and unhelpful implications. Ellingham (2002) suggests that the person-centred approach may be sufficiently supple and comprehensive to provide the conceptual vocabulary for a new paradigm which will unify the current variety of psychotherapies. If that is to happen, we think it's important to pay close attention not only to the images and metaphors we use, but also to the ways in which those metaphors and their secondary implications cohere with the root characteristics of the approach, which are organic, holistic and vital. 'Of course,' says Sontag (1989, p. 5) 'one cannot think without metaphors. But that does not mean there aren't some metaphors we might well abstain from or try to retire.' In terms of their use in therapy, both Gordon (1978) and Barker (1996) discuss the practical manifestations and applications of metaphors, including the use of anecdotes and short stories, analogies and similes, and relationship metaphors.

The person-centred approach draws philosophically from several streams: Christianity, empiricism, humanism, phenomenology and existentialism. The assumptions contained in each of those streams carry implications for the language we use. Learning the discipline of the language may be a way into more congruent and therefore more effective practice. Having laid out the philosophical ground of our enquiry, we now turn to the heart of organismic psychology: the organism.

Chapter 2

Organism

Biological knowledge is continued creative activity, by which the idea of the organism comes increasingly within reach of our experience.

Kurt Goldstein

No organism is self-sufficient. It requires the world for the gratification of its needs . . . there is always an inter-dependency of the organism and its environment.

Fritz Perls

We must recognize that the human organism is not an isolated entity, sufficient unto itself. Every individual is born, lives, and dies inseparably from the larger contexts of physical, social, political, and spiritual influences. The laws governing the physical universe are not separate from those governing the functions of living organisms . . . we must begin by comprehending clearly the setting in which the human being is found, how it influences him, and in turn how he affects it.

George Vithoulkas

The person comes to be what he is, as clients so frequently say in therapy. What this seems to mean is that the individual comes to be – in awareness – what he is – in experience. He is, in other words, a complete and fully-functioning human organism.

Carl Rogers

At the heart of the person-centred approach and the theory and practice of person-centred therapy lies the organism, a pulsing biological entity and a significant and enduring image. Spielhofer (2003, p. 80) clarifies Rogers' use of the term: 'Rogers does not see "organism" either as a metaphor used to present and explain our experiencing and acting, or as a theoretical construct like the self, but rather as a real, given entity.'

Rogers' use of the concept signifies both a unified concept of human motivation and a focus on all organisms, and in this sense it may be more accurate to talk about a *people*-centred or even *species*-centred approach to life and to therapy. The use of the concept 'organism' means that our approach to working therapeutically with people emphasises the nature of the human organism, and the integration of the person and personality, more than it does notions of the self. As Rogers (1953/67a, p. 80) himself put it:

> ... one of the fundamental directions taken by the process of therapy is the free experiencing of the actual sensory and visceral reactions of the organism without too much of an attempt to relate these experiences to the self. This is usually accompanied by the conviction that this material does not belong to, and cannot be organized into, the self. The end point of this process is that the client discovers that he can be his experience, with all of its variety and surface contradiction; that he can formulate himself out of his experience, instead of trying to impose a formulation of self upon his experiences, denying to awareness those elements which do not fit.

This also addresses the traditional and mainly Western separation of mind from body. We think that Rogers' point is a particularly important one as, in our view, both person-centred psychology and practice, and generic theoretical and meta-perspectives on the fields of psychoanalysis, psycho-therapy and psychology, have tended to sideline the organism in favour of the more popular concept of the self. For instance, in his work on psy-chology and psychoanalysis, Pine (1988, 1990) identifies four conceptual domains: drive, ego, object and self. He omits organism and organismic psychology. Even within the person-centred approach and person-centred therapy few books list 'organism' in their index, let alone as a central consideration. To date (in addition to our own work), we have found only five: Rogers (1939, 1969), Barrett-Lennard (1998), Thorne and Lambers (1998) and Wilkins (2003). In four of these 'organism' is only a one-line entry. In their major work on *Theories of Personality*, Hall and Lindzey (1970) acknowledge Rogers as adopting an 'organismic orientation', although they do not categorise him as an organismic theorist as such. In the third edition of their work they revise this significantly. 'It is clear from his recent writings' they say (Hall & Lindzey, 1978, p. 279) 'that the emphasis should fall on the organism, not the self.'

Hall and Lindzey acknowledge, alongside Rogers, a number of other psychologists who have also expounded organismic theory: Kantor (1924), Wheeler (1940), Murphy (1947) and Werner (1948), to which we would add Brunswik in his early work (Tolman & Brunswik, 1935). More recently, Brown (1990) writes about organismic psychotherapy from the perspective of neo-Reichian body psychotherapy and, on the basis of the centrality given to organismic experience, Fernald (2000) claims Rogers as a body-centred counsellor.

We too view person-centred therapy as based on an organismic psychology, as distinct from a self psychology, an assertion we discuss both here and in Chapter 4. Whilst Rogers' contribution to the development of self theory may be better known, we view his contribution to organismic theory and psychology as more significant in that it marks person-centred psychology as one which consistently views the organism *as a whole*, and as the source of subjective experience. In this it differs, for instance, from early gestalt psychology, as developed by Wertheimer, Koffka and Köhler, which tended to restrict its attention to the phenomena of conscious awareness, a discussion developed in Chapter 3.

Organismic psychology also emphasises the indissolubility of organism and environment and, therefore, the inevitability of interpersonal relationships. The organism cannot be understood outside of its environment. Angyal (1941) makes this point strongly throughout his work. 'Any attempt' he says (p. 89) 'to make a morphological separation of organism and environment fails and necessarily leads to endless hair-splitting dialectic.'

History, knowledge and philosophy

The notion of the organism is central to person-centred psychology, to the person-centred approach, and to the nature of the knowledge it represents and promotes. As the neurologist Goldstein (1934/95, pp. 307–8) puts it: 'the attainment of biological knowledge we are seeking is essentially akin to this phenomenon – to the capacity of the organism to become adequate to its environmental conditions'. Asserting his view of the tendency and striving of the human species, Rogers (1951) acknowledges his debt to Goldstein who, in 1934, had published his major work entitled *The Organism*, and to Angyal's *Foundations for a Science of Personality* (1941). We have gone back to these original influences in order to familiarise ourselves with them, and have found not only a wealth of research and detail about the nature and properties of the organism, but also significant links between the ideas contained in these early works and more recent studies in neuroscience on the brain and emotions. An early definition of the term comes from Angyal (1941, p. 99): 'The term itself, "organism" (organ = tool) means a system in which the parts are the instruments, the tools, of the whole.' Feldenkreis (1981, pp. 21–2), the founder of a form and method of bodywork, defined it, almost casually, as consisting of 'the skeleton, the muscles, the nervous system, and all that goes to nourish, warm, activate, and rest the whole of it'. In his foreword to the re-publication of Goldstein's work, Sacks (1995) traces a brief history of neurology, seeing Goldstein and others, including gestalt psychologists, as important in rebutting more modular views of neural organisation and the human organism. These people, Sacks says (p. 8):

> . . . were intensely conscious of the plasticity of the nervous system, the organism's powers of coming to terms and adapting, and the general powers of symbolization, of conceptual thought, of perspective and consciousness, so developed in humans, which seemed to be irreducible to mere elementary or modular capacities.

Damasio (1994/96, p. 87) also defines living organisms as 'changing continuously, assuming a succession of "states," each defined by varied patterns of ongoing activity in all its components'.

Together these ideas, based on developments in research and clinical practice in a number of fields over nearly a century and in different continents, can provide us with a more robust person-centred theory and clinical practice centred on a psychology of the organism. A number of these early works, such as Goldstein (1934/95) and Angyal (1941), refer to gestalt psychology. This is in part because Goldstein himself was closely identified with gestalt psychology through his work with Gelb on figure–ground relationships in visual perception (Gelb & Goldstein, 1920), and in part because, historically, gestalt psychology as such is older than what was originally 'client-centred', now person-centred, psychology and therapy. We see a number of similarities and links between these two psychological traditions, which we refer to and explore throughout this book. Part of our intention in this chapter is to reclaim this history for the theory and practice of person-centred therapy. Moreover, this enterprise is itself organismic, as there is a direct link between the nature of knowledge and the nature of the organism. As Goldstein (1934/95, p. 22) puts it: 'Biological knowledge is possible because of the similarity between human nature and human knowledge. It is an expression of human nature.' Our desire for knowledge of the organism is, in itself, organismic, and crucial therefore for our understanding of what it is to be human and to be knowledgeable.

In keeping with the theme of the book, we discuss first the philosophy of the organism. We recognise the impossibility of separating the organism from its inherent tendencies (which we consider in the next chapter) and, at the same time, the need to make such artificial separations in a linear, literary format. That said, we focus in the second part of this chapter on the nature and qualities of the experiencing organism, and elaborate ensuing implications for clinical practice. In the shorter third and final part, we reflect on the broader implications of organismic psychology for person-centred theory and practice. We agree throughout with Angyal that any morphological separation of organism and environment is unhelpful. He goes on (1941, p. 89) to make the point that:

It will, however, be useful to go into this dialectic to some extent, not because one might expect positive results, but because it will demonstrate that the consideration of organism and environment as structures in space is not a workable point of view.

We consider the psychopathology or, more properly, the disorganisation of the organism, along with the psychopathology of the self and the person together in Chapter 6.

Process philosophy and the philosophy of the organism

Alfred North Whitehead (1861–1947), mathematician and philosopher, founded a movement called 'process philosophy', although he himself did not use the term. The antecedents of this movement can be traced back to Heraclitus (540–480 BCE) and David Hume (1711–1776). Other influences include William James (1842–1910) and John Dewey (1859–1952). We find no evidence that Rogers ever read Whitehead's major work on the philosophy of the organism (Whitehead, 1929/78), although he does make one secondary reference (1963/80) to Prigogine citing Whitehead. Nonetheless, we see *Process and Reality* as the *philosophical* ground for organismic psychology and for the theory and practice of person-centred therapy. Although complex and dense, it gives philosophical weight to the importance in person-centred therapy of experience, process and perception.

Process philosophy holds that the central task of philosophy is to develop a metaphysical cosmology that is adequate to all experienced facts. To be adequate, these facts or 'actual entities' must give equal weight to all intuitions grounded in human experience, such as the aesthetic, ethical and religious or spiritual, as well as to those of the natural sciences. In this Whitehead anticipates modern and postmodern concerns about holistic thinking, interconnectedness, and interdisciplinarity, and provides the philosophical base for enquiry into the nature of the organism in a number of disciplines (see, for instance, Lewontin, 2000). In order to integrate experience and science, process philosophy is equally critical of what it views as the exaggerations of science, such as 'scientific materialism' and the 'sensationalist' doctrine of perception; and of religion, principally the notion of divine omnipotence.

Some of these terms warrant brief explication. Scientific materialism describes the view that everything, including human experience, can be explained in terms of the movement of matter, which has no spontaneity, internal process or intrinsic value. The alternative is to conceive the basic units of the world as processes. The 'sensationalist' doctrine of perception posits that we perceive of things only by means of our physical sensory organs, a doctrine Whitehead rejects in favour of a view that experience can be confirmed by subjective evaluation. In a rare reference to the (then) modern psychology, Whitehead (1929/78, p. 141) bemoans its limitations: 'one difficulty in appealing to modern psychology, for the purpose of a preliminary survey of the nature of experience, is that so much of that science is based upon the presupposition of the sensationalist mythology.'

In promoting the value of common-sense beliefs, such as the intuitive knowledge that humans can think and feel at the same time, and that thoughts and actions are not wholly determined by antecedent causes, Whitehead and other process philosophers are adopting the pragmatic maxim of James that, if an idea cannot be lived in practice, it should not be affirmed in theory.

The key points of process philosophy are:

- A concern with what Whitehead (1929/78, p. xiii) calls 'the becoming, the being, and the relatedness of "actual entities"'. This prefigures both Allport (1955/83) and Rogers (1961/67b), for more on which see pp. 63–7 and Chapter 5.
- That experience or feeling is the hallmark of human existence, rather than abstract thinking or metaphysics. In this Whitehead's work offers a critique of most modern(ist) philosophy, in particular positivism, and has inspired more recent work examining organic life as subjective activity (see Diefenbeck, 1995), and the making of consciousness (Damasio, 1999, who cites Whitehead).
- That the task of philosophy is to make our immediate experience intelligible so that we can discover how we can experience the actual world. In this Whitehead is reaching back to Plato and Aristotle. In the preface to *Process and Reality* Whitehead (1929/78, p. xi) said that 'the writer who most fully anticipated the main positions of the philosophy of organism is John Locke', and like Locke, Whitehead is certainly an empiricist. Although working independently, Whitehead's concerns parallel those of Martin Heidegger, and there is a sense in which we may see Whitehead as a phenomenological empiricist.
- That 'the reality is the process' (Whitehead, 1925/67, p. 72). In a subsequent book *Adventures of Ideas* (1933, p. 355), one which Whitehead said he most wanted to write, he summarises the process of what happens between the time an external experience impinges on body, spinal column and brain, and the time it is uttered forth: '*The process is itself the actuality.*' This echoes Goethe's view of nature as a dynamic, process-based phenomenon, a view which has, in turn, inspired a movement called 'process theology' (see, for example, Griffin, 1976), and which prefigures quantum physics and its dynamic understanding of particles and waves.
- That 'prehension' is more fundamental than sensory perception (Whitehead, 1925/67). This refers to a more primitive mode of perceptual experience, which may or may not be conscious, and represents the

concrete fact of relatedness. In a previous work, *The Concept of Nature*, Whitehead (1920) had constructed a powerful phenomenology of perception based on the rejection of the 'bifurcation of nature', arguing that disjunction between subject and object, *res cogitans* and *res extensa*, renders the world of life and the world of science incompatible. We see a similarity between Whitehead's concept of prehension and Rogers' (1959b) reference to 'subception', a term he adopted from McCleary and Lazarus (1949) to mean discrimination without awareness.

- That mind and body are one. This is based on the 'nondualistic inter-actionism' of process philosophy which avoids the problems of both dualism and materialism. 'The philosophy of organism' writes Whitehead (1929/78, p. 219) 'is a cell-theory of actuality. Each ultimate unit of fact is a cell-complex, not analysable into components with equivalent completeness of actuality.' In a passage which prefigures current research in neuroscience, Hartshorne (1962, p. 229) says that 'cells can influence our human experiences because they have feelings that we can feel. To deal with the influences of human experience on cells, one turns this around. We have feelings that cells can feel.'

Having given something of the philosophical background to the organism, we turn to an elaboration of its nature and qualities.

The nature and qualities of the organism

As formulated in his theory of personality and behaviour, Rogers (1951, p. 487) asserts that the human species, as with other species, has one basic tendency and striving: 'to actualize, maintain, and enhance the experiencing organism'. Angyal (1941) sees the organism as having two related tendencies: one towards increased *autonomy*, and one towards *homonomy*. He defines the organism (p. 23) as autonomous in the sense that it is 'to a large extent, a *self-governing* entity', and homonomous (p. 172) in the sense that it longs 'to be in harmony with superindividual units, the social group, nature, God, ethical world order, or whatever the person's formulation of it may be'. Angyal also acknowledges (p. 33) the notion of *heteronomy*: 'The organism lives in a world in which things happen according to laws which are heteronomous from the point of view of the organism.' Human beings live autonomously and homonomously in a world that is heteronomous or other (see Figure 2.1).

Angyal uses the term biosphere (from the German *Lebenskreis*), meaning the realm or sphere of life, to convey the concept of a holistic entity which includes both individual and environment (p. 100): 'not as interacting parts, not as constituents which have independent existence, but as aspects of a

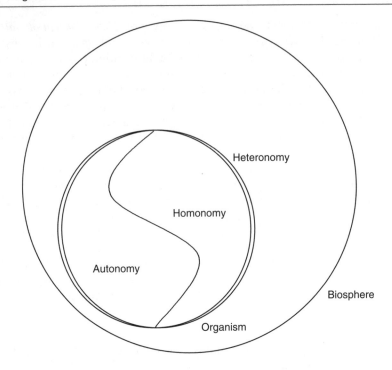

Figure 2.1 The organism's tendencies to autonomy and homonomy.

single reality which can be separated only by abstraction'. Thus (p. 101): '*The subject-matter of our considerations are not organic processes and environmental influences, but biospheric occurrences in their integral reality.*'

In addition to this basic tendency, or tendencies, Barrett-Lennard (1998, pp. 75–6) identifies five properties of the organism. We think that the term 'property' has mechanistic, empirical and prescriptive connotations. We prefer instead to use the term 'quality' which we think describes the fluidity of the organism more accurately.

1 The organism functions as an organised whole, responding to its own, moving perceptual field.
2 The human organism interacts with perceived 'outer' and 'inner' reality in the service of the actualising tendency.
3 Human beings engage in an organismic valuing process.
4 Differentiation is an important effect of the actualising tendency.
5 The organism is always in motion.

Drawing on the literature regarding the philosophy and psychology of the organism, and process philosophy, we take these qualities as a starting point for our own elaboration. Out of this we describe a number of other qualities in the hope that such an elaboration will deepen our under-standing of person-centred psychology, theory and practice. We don't intend this list to be exhaustive.

'The organism' says Rogers (1951, p. 484) 'reacts to the field as it is experienced and perceived. This perceptual field is, for the individual, "reality".' Barrett-Lennard (1998, p. 75) describes the organism as 'a pur-poseful, open system, in particularly active interchange with its environ-ment'. From these two brief quotes, we see that the organism:

- is holistic,
- is experiential,
- is concrescent, and
- construes reality according to its perception.

Holism

We have discussed holism as a philosophical stance in Chapter 1. Goldstein (1934/95, p. 99) describes the organismic wholeness of our experience:

> The pattern of the excitation that occurs in the system as the result of a stimulus cannot be sufficiently characterized by noting merely the state of excitation in the 'near part.' The rest of the system, the 'distant part,' as we shall call it, is also in a very definite state of excitation. Each movement of one part of the body is accompanied by a definite change in the posture of the rest of the body.

We can most easily see this in babies and infants when they are excited, sad, angry or scared. Whatever state they are in, they are in it wholeheartedly, unless they have taken in or learned to interrupt such whole field experi-encing. Even in the infant's 'turning to' reaction, which is in the foreground at a particular phase of development due to the fact that other reactions are not yet possible, we can observe her trying to move her *whole* body towards the stimulus. In adults we may see more of the ways in which we interrupt this excited process or compartmentalise our movement. For example, the middle-aged woman, sitting upright and 'properly', and who talks quietly about her love of opera, is showing only some 'part' of her excitement.

Goldstein was concerned about the 'whole' and wholeness of the organism, devoting an entire chapter of *The Organism* to this concept: 'Certain essential characteristics of the organism in the light of the holistic approach' (pp. 229–83). At the same time, as he stood firmly in the empirical scientific tradition, he argues (p. 67) that the only way of ascer-taining knowledge of and about the whole was 'the scientific or *analytic*, "*anatomizing*" method'. However, from his studies of investigations into reflex reactions, and his observations of the behaviour of patients with brain lesions, he concludes (p. 173) that these 'have repeatedly taught us one thing: the relationship of each individual performance to the whole organism'. He goes on to explain (p. 182) that 'every reaction is a "Gestalt reaction" of the whole in the form of a figure–ground configuration.' Everything relates, and thus, from an organismic perspective, reactions cannot be compartmentalised or made into parts (p. 182): 'the process in the rest of the organism is, by nature, part of the individual, apparently isolated performance'. A therapist may respond to the person described above with empathy: at the same time he is reacting or responding to 'middle-aged', 'woman', 'sitting upright', 'properly', her way of talking, her love of opera, his own love of certain operas and composers, his dislike of others, and her suppressed excitement. Goldstein refers to this as the 'holistic relation of performances' (ibid., p. 183). Although holism is more associated with gestalt psychology and, in particular with the work of Smuts (1926/87), it is, as we shall see, also central to an understanding of the organism. Sanders (2000), for instance, views it as one of the secondary principles of the person-centred approach. Recent research in neurology, neuroscience and developmental psychology supports the holistic nature of the organism. Damasio (1994/96, pp. xviii-xiv) anchors this in a series of statements:

> The human brain and the rest of the body constitute an indissociable organism, integrated by means of mutually interactive biochemical and neural regulatory circuits . . . (2) The organism interacts with the environment as an ensemble: the interaction is neither of the body alone nor of the brain alone; (3) The physiological operations we call mind are derived from the structural and functional ensemble.

Experientiality

Based on the view of the experiencing organism, person-centred psychology views experience as present, constructed and reciprocal.

In some ways the emphasis on the experiential is in contrast to Goldstein's ontological view that there is an 'essence' of the organism. Sacks (1995) sees in Goldstein's work and his focus on the actual *experiences* and 'life-worlds' of his patients, a move towards an existential neurology. However, Sacks (p. 12) also suggests that Goldstein, influenced by Kantian idealism, shrank away from a completely existential viewpoint or, at least, that 'he felt it necessary to propose a more general ontological viewpoint as a necessary *antecedent* to any personal one'. Kant (1781/2005) argues that we have a subjective representation of things that we are able to conceive like God, friendship or love, without the real *intuition* that we have of physical objects, and refers to this as 'transcendental idealism'. We are not convinced of the need for a general ontology, of an 'essence' of what it is to be human, before we explore or understand a particular person's sense of herself.

The priority and authority of experience, which Rogers emphasises throughout his work, also challenges philosophical views of *a priori* knowledge which, by definition, is prior to and does not depend on experience. The value of experience is confirmed by the work of neurobiologists such as Schore (1994, p. 33): 'the core of the self lies in the patterns of affect regulation that integrate a sense of self . . . thereby allowing for a continuity of inner experience'. As Knox (2004) puts it, reviewing this field: 'There is no suggestion of a pre-experiential self that guides this development.' We think that Aristotle's view of ontology helps us here. He distinguishes between two categories of 'things':

- 'Universals' – things in a number of particular substances which we grasp through symbolising 'thisness', e.g. whiteness, cat, anxiety.
- 'Particulars' – those things of which we have *direct* experience and which give us a sense and understanding of the quality of the particular 'thisness', i.e. *this* white paper, *this* cat, *this* (my) anxiety. For Stern (1985) we make sense of such particulars through representations of interactions which are generalised, for further discussion of which see Chapter 4.

The therapeutic emphasis on experience and experiencing has led to some within person-centred psychology, notably Eugene Gendlin (1961, 1981), to focus on this as a therapeutic method.

It is through our experienc*ing* that we make sense of the world. As Bronson (2000, p. 2) puts it, in the context of a discussion about self-regulation in early childhood: '"Experience" includes support and guidance from other people and from the mental and material tool kit provided by culture.' In his autobiography, the actor Sidney Poitier (2000, p. 6) puts this well:

. . . our minds are actually *constructed* by these thousands of tiny interactions during the first few years of life. We aren't just what's directed by our genes, and we certainly aren't just what we're taught. It's what we experience during those early years – a smile here, a jarring sound there – that creates the pathways and connections of the brain.

In their description of the development of the brain and, specifically, the prefrontal lobes, Solms and Turnbull (2002, p. 282) describe this more technically:

LIVERPOOL
JOHN MOORES UNIVERSITY
AVRIL ROBARTS LRC
TEL. 0151 231 4022

The experiences that shape the activity of these executive mechanisms in the earliest years of life will determine their individual structure. The application of their inherent (neurochemical) inhibitory capacities is, accordingly, literally *sculpted* by the parental (and other authority) figures who guide this aspect of the child's development during the critical early years. This 'sculpting' process appears to be governed by at least two things: first, by what parents *do*; second, by what they *say*.

In the field of psychology this view derives largely from the work of Kelly (1955) who founded and developed personal construct psychology, which posits that we are constantly trying to make sense of our worlds through interpretation, anticipation and experimentation. Rogers was critical of Kelly's work, and in 1956 had written a review of Kelly's *Personal Construct Psychology* under the title 'Intellectualized Psychotherapy'. He nevertheless borrowed '*Kelly's helpful term*' (1958/67a, p. 132), 'personal constructs', to describe a person's 'cognitive maps of experience' (p. 157). This borrowing links Rogers directly to constructivism (see Chapter 1).

Concrescent

We describe the nature of the organism as concrescent rather than integrative. Deriving from the Latin *concrescere*, to grow together, Whitehead (1929/78) used this concept to carry the sense of many diversities growing together into a new unity. He describes becoming (p. 45) as a dipolar process, 'constituted by the influx of external objects into a novel determinateness of feeling which absorbs the actual world into a novel actuality'. This concrescence is based on prehension (see pp. 50–1) and symbolisation (p. 108): 'The integration of the physical and mental side into a unity of experience is a self-formation which is a process of concrescence.' Integration implies, and in our view requires, an organising principle to such growth. The basis of a perceptual theory of integration can be traced back to Aristotelian philosophy. In his *Metaphysics* Aristotle emphasises perceptual integration, a process which itself is not sensory. In other words, in order to process and make sense of what we experience and perceive, we need to abstract it. When we work with a client, we are aware through our senses of many things, but our *experience* is not of separate attributes. There is, literally, a common sense (*koine aisthesis*) which 'is not to be taken as itself a sense but as some process common to all the senses, by which experiences are forged out of the separate contributions from the different sense organs' (Robinson, 1995, pp. 48–9). This is important as it asserts that the process of assimilation or integration is situated in all our senses and cells. If this process is seen as separate, as a 'sixth' sense, as it were, then we have to conceptualise a 'higher', 'integrating self' (for more on which, see Chapter 4). For Whitehead (1929/78) life is in the millions of individual cells of the organism. As Emmet (1932/66, p. 186) puts it: 'there is no "life of the whole" as an entelechy over and above this. But there is co-ordinated and organised activity, so that a plan of the body as a whole is served by this particular type of organisation of its millions of centres of life.' She goes on (p. 186) to make an important point about the nature of theory and difficulties of language:

> So if we are to try to formulate a thoroughgoing organic theory of nature something like this view of the integrated subjective aims of the individual actual occasions will be necessary; and the apparent pathetic fallacy or anthropomorphisms it at present involves may be due to the difficulties of expressing these things in a language which is not misleading.

Thus, the language of 'self' is itself (no pun intended) a distracting and literal anthropomorphism of the metaphors of organic life and organism – which is why we think the rediscovery, reclaiming and use of language is so important. Campos (1980) acknowledges this in the title of an article: '"Cure" as finding the right metaphor'. This echoes Rogers' (1951) view that diagnosis is a process whereby a client finds the words or the metaphors for his own distress.

In the field of psychotherapy and counselling in general, and in humanistic psychology in particular, the theme of integration is an important one. Our tendency to integrate or seek integration has, perhaps unsurprisingly, found root and form in the training and organisation of psychotherapy, in which 'integration' is of the *zeitgeist*, a trend we critique in Chapter 8.

Construction of reality

In the second proposition of his theory of personality and behaviour Rogers (1951, p. 484) states that '*The organism reacts to the field as it is experienced and perceived. This perceptual field is, for the individual, "reality."*' Rogers goes on to argue that it seems unnecessary (to him) to posit or try to explain any concept of 'true' reality. Indeed, in another paper (Rogers, 1978/80), he wonders whether we need 'a' reality. Continuing with his theory of personality, Rogers then makes a point (ibid., p. 485) which is both interesting and crucial for practice: 'We live by a perceptual "map" which is never reality itself. This is a useful concept to keep in mind, for it may help to convey the nature of the world in which the individual lives.' A therapist listens to a client. He wants to understand his client empathically, by which Rogers (1959b, p. 210) means 'to perceive the internal frame of reference of another with accuracy, and with the emotional components and meanings which pertain thereto, as if one were the other person, but without ever losing the "as if" condition'. This both distinguishes empathic understanding from the technique of reflective listening, with which it is sometimes confused and equated, and emphasises the attempt on the part of the therapist to understand the client's *perceptual 'map'* or frame of reference, rather than his 'essence'. A person-centred therapist is interested in how her client sees, experiences and makes sense of his world rather than in who he is any fundamental or apparently objective way.

Gestalt psychology has contributed to our understanding of perception a view of how perception is organised, that is, by a certain form, *Gestalt* (plural: *Gestalten*), or quality of the whole, *Gestaltqualität*. The Gestalt laws of organisation include:

- Continuation – whereby, for example, a diamond is seen as such and not as two incomplete triangles.
- Closure – whereby the observer attempts to complete an unfinished image.
- Proximity or grouping – the perceptual putting together of lines or figures.
- Similarity – whereby figures that are similar to each other are seen as belonging together.

These laws or principles of organisation have been famously represented by pictures which may be perceived as representing either a young or an old woman, a face or a vase. The incompleteness of a particular form, figure or quality, including a breakdown in communication or relationship may, in this sense, be referred to as an 'incomplete gestalt'. Aristotle is alleged to have said that Nature abhors a vacuum, and the organism proves this in seeking wholeness and completeness. As Robinson (1995, p. 356) puts it: 'It is by virtue of this filtering and transforming of stimulus elements that the organism is able to deal with the demands of the environment in an economical and orderly way.' This also gives us a certain constancy of experience, even when perceiving things from a different angle: we see this book when closed as oblong irrespective of the angle of regard.

Differentiation

Rogers (1959b, p. 223) states that 'a portion of the individual's *experience* becomes differentiated and *symbolized* in an *awareness* of being, *awareness* of functioning'. 'Such awareness' he says 'may be described as *self-experience*.' Some psychologists have criticised what they perceive to be a cultural and a male bias towards emphasising differentiation as a primary process in development (see, for example, Nobles, 1973, and Gilligan, 1982, respectively). A close reading of Rogers, however, reveals symbolisation as an equally important and integrating process. Kegan (1982, pp. 5–6) asks an important question about this: 'Is it possible to evolve a model of personality development which takes account not only of both sides of this tension but of the tension itself?' In this section whilst we are examining differentiation, we do so in the context of the inevitable tension between differentiation and integration, which resembles that between autonomy and homonomy. Barrett-Lennard (1998, p. 76) puts the importance of differentiation more directly: '*Differentiation is an important effect of the actualising tendency.*' 'At both extremes of existence, the microscopic and the human,' says Zohar (1991, p. 94), 'individuals are the focal points of events and differentiations.' Again we pick up the implications of this process in the following chapters on tendencies and self. Whilst Rogers emphasised differentiation in awareness, we also consider the organism's ability to differentiate out of awareness or at a level of 'subception', a term Rogers (1957) himself adopted from McCleary and Lazarus (1949) precisely to signify discrimination without awareness. Rogers' use of the term prefigures more contemporary references to pre-symbolic, pre-verbal, intuitive 'knowing'.

The concept of differentiation is not unique to person-centred theory or to Rogers. Indeed, two other contributors to the volume (Koch, 1959) to which Rogers contributed his seminal paper also describe differentiation as an important principle of psychoanalytic theory (Rapaport, 1959) and of a theory of action (Parsons, 1959). It is also a central concept in Piaget's (1937/54) theory of physical-cognitive development and neo-Piagetian theories of development (see Kohlberg, 1976; Kegan, 1982). Macmurray (1957/91, p. 33) argues that 'the full form of the organic is represented as a dynamic equilibrium of functions maintained through a progressive differentiation of elements within the whole'. Notwithstanding its application in different theories, the choice of the word is significant. Lewin (1951/64, p. 72) comments: 'A shift from the theory of association or conditioned reflex to a theory of differentiation . . . means a change from a physical analogy (namely that of links in a chain) to a more biological approach.' Recent research in the fields of neuroscience, infant development and human communication points to the fact that infants are capable of differentiating themselves, their bodies, faces and hands from those of their mothers and, therefore, knowing themselves.

Angyal makes a further point about differentiation. He acknowledges that the process of differentiation always involves a risk of disintegration, and that it is also inherently destabilising. 'A whole' he says (1941, p. 322) 'may differentiate into so many specialized parts that their unification and their control may present a serious problem for the organism.' This makes sense to us. Differentiation is another word for change or growth, and to change or grow is, inevitably, to go beyond where we are, where we know and where we feel comfortable. To go too far beyond where we know, or to go too quickly, or in too many directions, is to risk the kind of instability we see in some artists, writers, philosophers and scientists, whose process of differentiation leaves them simultaneously creative and unstable.

Here we discuss the significance of the organism's capacity to differentiate through three discussions on:

- figure and ground,
- the dialogic nature of the organism, and
- becoming.

Figure and ground

The concept of figure and ground is key to understanding the structure of the organism. As Hall and Lindzey (1978) put it: 'the primary organization of organismic functioning is that of figure and ground . . . In terms of action, the figure is the principal, ongoing activity of the organism . . . The background is continuous; it not only surrounds the figure but extends behind it' (pp. 246–7). Goldstein (op. cit., pp. 123–4) elaborates:

> . . . a certain ground process accompanies each figure process. In performances of the normal organism, the total organism forms the background against which the figure process, taking place in a certain circumscribed area, stands out. But the entire organism does not form the background in a homogeneous way. In the execution of a movement the 'ground process,' in the rest of the motorium, is probably more closely related to the figure process than the rest of the processes at large. But the whole system always participates to some extent.

Pally (2000, p. 25) echoes this: 'Perception is very sensitive to the sensory context in which a stimulus is encountered. This means that a stimulus can be perceived differently depending on what other environmental stimuli are close by.'

As we have seen, differentiation is an important effect of the actualising tendency, such differentiation of the organism's experience being symbolised in an awareness of being, or 'self-experience'. Hall and Lindzey (1978, p. 246) observe that 'the organism consists of differentiated members which are articulated together'. The emergence of a figure from the total background of the organism 'is determined by the task which the nature of the organism at the time requires' (ibid., p. 247), a 'task' which is often expressed in terms of needs (see pp. 72–6). Goldstein (op. cit., p. 100) regards the foreground–background relation, the configuration of excitement, as 'the basic form of the functioning of the nervous system'. This echoes Aristotle's doctrine of form, which describes the organisation of a certain structure to serve a certain end: the structure of the organism is the way in which the organism organises in order to become itself. The centrality of the figure–ground concept also gives a present and future orientation to our understanding of organismic needs and development – what Whitehead (1929/78) refers to as 'appetition' (see pp. 83–4), and to our therapeutic responses to them, as distinct from focusing on the past in order to understand need, motive and drive (see Chapter 3). Arriving at this idea by another route, Bohart *et al.* (1993, p. 13) view 'persons as ongoing purposive future-oriented organisms'. They suggest (p. 20) that Rogers' own responses to clients were often 'future-oriented' and that as therapists we may usefully choose to respond empathically to whatever is future-oriented in our clients' experience.

The concept of figure and ground derives from field theory (Lewin, 1951/64), which Rogers (1951, p. 491) draws on implicitly when he refers to the organism seeking to satisfy its needs as experienced '*in the field as perceived*'. In considering and working with the organism and notions of the self and, for that matter, ego, we find the idea of figure and field or ground useful. As Goldstein (op. cit., p. 123) puts it: 'in performances of the normal organism, the total organism forms the background against which the figure process, taking place in a circumscribed area, stands out'. Thus, we view 'self' and 'ego' as more or less useful concepts in elaborating a portion of the perceptual field in which the total organism stands for the total human being.

Dialogic

The human organism behaves as an organised whole. This is most clearly seen in infants. The organism, however, is not isolated. Unlike the young of some other mammals, human babies are born before they are independently viable, largely because otherwise their heads would be too big to pass through the birth canal. As Goldstein (op. cit., p. 19) puts it: 'The infant is able to live because the people around him, particularly the mother, organize his world in such a way that he is exposed as little as possible to demands that he cannot fulfill.' In mammals the mother regulates the body physiology of the infant until the infant brain matures enough to provide 'self'-regulation, and the brain grows after birth (see Pally, 2000). Goldstein (op. cit.) continues:

> Thus the behavior of the infant is not at all an expression of his concrete capacity alone *but also of the abstract attitude of someone else*. Thus normal behavior in infancy becomes comprehensible as the result of the activity of two persons. [Our emphasis.]

We have emphasised this as it highlights the dialogic nature of what can be seen as individual behaviour. Behaviour cannot be understood without being symbolised and, at least initially, a baby cannot symbolise on its own.

She needs the 'abstract', empathic and symbolising attitude of an other. Warner (1997, p. 135) describes exactly such a moment with her 3-year-old nephew:

> His mother had left the room to pay attention to his younger brother, and he had begun throwing his toys. I said, 'You feel angry.' He looked at me with a sense of surprise and discovery and tried on the words 'I feel angry.' He threw his toys a few more times, saying the words with greater conviction each time. Then he went into the kitchen to tell his mother about his new discovery, that he felt 'angry'.

Person-centred therapy values mutuality (see Chapter 8). In this sense we can say that all affect regulation is co-regulation: the mother or primary carer regulates the baby, *and* the baby regulates the mother (see Putnam, Spritz & Stifter, 2002).

Also, in order to be valuable, symbols must have some 'intersection', as Emmet (1932/66) puts it, with the symbolised: 'the process of abstraction ... is not a purely arbitrary one'. In the clinical context, this refers to and supports the importance therapists give to checking that they have understood what meanings their clients' words, phrases and metaphors carry.

Behaviour cannot be understood outside of the context in which it is expressed, and that context, whether in the home, on the street or in a clinical setting, is the result of two or more people's activity. In a recent article about a course promoting emotional literacy in schools, Naysmith (2003, p. 4) reports that teachers are encouraged 'to ask themselves whether their own inability to form relationships with pupils could be partly responsible for misbehaviour in the classroom'. It does indeed take two to tango – and two to teach!

The other on whom we are initially dependent, not least for help with symbolising, and others with whom we later symbolise and dialogue, are crucially important. In psychology, the school of object relations has emphasised the importance of the emotional bonds between oneself and another, and, like the person-centred approach, has placed relationship at the heart of what it is to be human. As Gomez (1997, p. 1) points out 'the term "object" does not refer to an inanimate thing, but is a carry-over from the Freudian idea of the target, or object, of the instinct ... it is used in the philosophical sense of a distinction between subject and object'. Gomez (ibid., p. 34) summarises Klein's contribution:

> She envisages the person as subjective agent within a subjective world of relationship, conflict and change. The outer world is experienced through the medium of this subjective world; the outer world also reaches into the inner world, influencing its nature and structure.

Compare this with Emmet (1932/66, pp. 93–4):

> Since an actual entity arises by objectifying aspects of other actual entities in its own nature, it has an immediate feeling of every part of its own subjective experience as involving other actual entities . . . Every actual entity emerges from the background of the world which it feels, and its own nature might be described as the way in which it organises its perspectives of the rest of the world.

Whilst the use of 'object' in object relations makes some sense, especially when applied to abstract others such as a blanket, a house, art or Rome, it also literally objectifies the other. Furthermore, it discourages viewing the human other as another subject and, thereby, as another with whom to dialogue. For these reasons we prefer the notion of 'subject relations'. As Fernald (2000, p. 175) puts it: '. . . one does not *have* an experience. Rather, trusting one's organism, one *is* the experience. And accordingly, self is subject, not object.' Interestingly, in discussing the work of Melanie Klein, Gomez (ibid., p. 34) uses this term: 'Klein's work is a theory of "subject relations" which marks the beginning of the Object Relations school.'

Becoming

Along with being, the notion of becoming is present in Rogers' writings and in person-centred literature. It refers to the process as distinct from the outcome of human potentiality (see also Chapter 5). Rogers (1967b/54) refers to the process of becoming as one in which we get behind the mask or roles with which we face life, and in which we experience feeling and discover unknown elements of ourselves. He goes on to describe the characteristics of the person who emerges from, and in, this process of becoming a person as: having an openness to experience; having trust in one's organism; having an internal locus of evaluation; and willingness to 'be a process'. In a sense, as human *beings* we are in a continuous process of *becoming*.

We become who we are through differentiation. It is a fact of life that as soon as we are conceived an embryonic, single-cell, human zygote with 46 chromosomes immediately produces specifically human proteins and enzymes and genetically directs his or her growth and development. This cell splits into two cells, four cells, eight cells and so on, and multiple rounds of cell division result in a microscopic ball of cells referred to, briefly at around 4 days, as a morula, until as an adult our bodies comprise around one hundred trillion cells. The development of the organism may be described essentially as becoming through differentiation, at least from a person-centred perspective. This view is supported by more recent studies in developmental psychology. Stern, for instance, (1985, 2000) argues that differentiation between self and other is in place and in process from almost the very beginning of life, and that the infant's major developmental task is to create ties with or attachment to others. Macmurray (1961/91, p. 91) argues that 'personal individuality', his term for 'personality', 'is achieved through the progressive differentiation of the original unity of the "You and I"'. We develop these ideas further in discussions about homonomy in Chapter 3, the development of the self in Chapter 4 and belonging in Chapter 5. Psychological approaches to human development from Freud onwards have started with consideration of the neonate at birth. However, recent advances in both intellectual and technological spheres have meant that the development of the foetus *in utero* has become a focus of study, enquiry and conceptualisation (see, notably, Piontelli, 1992). This is important from an experiential perspective as, according to Northrup (1998, p. 359) 'Babies remember their lives – *all parts* of their lives – and their experiences have a potentially large effect on them. All of us retain the imprint of our entire lives within our cells.' In his work, which complements traditional developmental psychology with a transpersonal view of human development, Wilber (1980) describes stages of 'self sense'. However, by his own account (p. 7) 'neither the fetus in the womb nor the infant at birth possesses a developed self sense'. We think that some of Wilber's descriptions and detail are useful in describing the early development of the organism; we find it more consistent with our present concern, however, to refer to this sense of 'self' as organismic. Although he states that he wishes to avoid 'intricate debate' about certain lines of development, Wilber does speculate about cognitive, affective, motivational and temporal lines or elements of the developing human. Here we summarise the first three stages:

- The pleromatic self/organism – 'which essentially means that the self and the material cosmos are undifferentiated . . . The self is embedded in the *materia prima*, which is both the primal chaos of physical matter and the maternal matrix' (ibid., p. 7).

Cognitive style	Absolute adualism, objectless, spaceless, protoplasmic
Affective atmosphere	Total oceanic, unconditional omnipotence, pleromatic paradise
Motivational factors	Almost entirely absent
Temporal mode	Timeless (pre-temporal)

This accords with Fordham's (1957) view of development *in utero*, although he too refers to an undifferentiated 'self'; and with the Taoist metaphor of chaos, which Hayashi and Kara (2002, p. 75) describe as denoting 'the initial state of the universe where nothing is differentiated'.

- The alimentary uroboric self/organism – 'At this point, then, the infant's self no longer *is* the material chaos, for he is beginning to recognise something *outside* of himself . . . this global, undifferentiated, prepersonal environ we call the *uroboric other*' (Wilber, 1980, p. 9). The word uroboros refers to the mythical serpent which, eating its own tail or, at least, turning in on itself, forms a self-contained, pre-differentiated mass, rather like pictures of foetal scans. It is also referred to as alimentary as the organism is dominated by what Wilber refers to as 'visceral psychology', as a part of which he sees the beginning of reflex reactions.

Cognitive style	First subject–object differentiation, acausality, hallucinatory wish-fulfilment
Affective atmosphere	Oceanic euphoria, primordial fear
Motivational factors	Early urges to survival, psychological needs (hunger)
Temporal mode	Pre-temporal

- The typhonic self/organism – in which 'the infant's sense of self begins to shift from the pre-personal uroboros to the individual organism' (ibid., p. 12). Again drawing on archetypal images, Wilber views this as the realm of the typhon: half serpent, half human. Although he subdivides this sense of self, we summarise it as one.

Cognitive style	Feeling, sensorimotor, multivalent images
Affective elements	Elementary emotions, later sustained emotions, wishes, rudimentary desires
Motivational factors	Immediate survival, the pleasure–unpleasure principle, wish-fulfilment, anxiety reduction, prolonged survival and safety
Temporal mode	Concrete, momentary, later extended present

We have given some details of Wilber's ideas here as, in our view, they elaborate our early differentiation. Given that we retain the imprint of our initial organismic development, this appears important for our continuing development and, theoretically, supports us as therapists to understand and support our clients' differentiation and direction: 'the free experiencing of the actual sensory and visceral reactions of the organism' (Rogers, 1953/67a, p. 80). We also find the concept of differentiation more useful in understanding the development of a variety of human behaviours (see Lewin, 1951/64) than stage theories which attempt to link a child's behaviour with often pre-theorised views of what is 'age appropriate', views which underpin much current obsession with 'standards' and achievement in education. At the same time, the infant's development through differentiation is not homogeneous. Schore (1994, p. 13), for instance, suggests that:

> . . . a critical period of synaptic growth and differentiation of an affect regulating limbic structure in the prefrontal cortex of the right hemisphere commences at the end of the first year, and that this developmental process is significantly influenced by the stimulation embedded in the infant's socioaffective transactions with the primary caregiver.

In other words: the less stimulation from the environment, the more reduced the infant's limbic structure. It used to be thought that specific tissues (structures) are susceptible to particular environmental influences at specific 'critical periods', at that time and no other. The lack of stimulation and experience can lead to the death of cells, and the 'use it or lose it' principle of brain development. Schore (ibid., p. 76) says that 'the mother's emotionally expressive facial displays provide a rich source of visual stimulation' and that 'this acts as an imprinting stimulus for the continuing development and differentiation of the infant's right hemisphere'. Other studies suggest that neural pathways in the adult brain can be activated and developed if the adult experiences an equivalent 'gaze'. As the brain's development is an 'experience-dependent' process, this offers a neurobiological argument for the impact and efficacy of unconditional positive regard and empathy. The continuing plasticity of the brain, or how open it is to further development throughout the lifespan, remains an open question.

Sander (1982, p. 317) describes the organism gaining coherence 'as ever new coordinations between organism and environment are created in new combinations of action and function that serve to bridge the disparities generated within and between systems'. Becoming inevitably requires constant, and often subceived, adjustments in and adaptations to the organism–environment system. These experiences are laid down as neural pathways in the brain through right-hemisphere cognitive processing 'of facial, prosodic, and bodily information embedded in emotional communications, for attention, for empathy, and for human stress response' (Schore, 2003, p. xv). He continues: 'These essential processes – central to both regulation of homeostasis and the capacity to flexibly alter the internal environment to optimally cope with external perturbations – take place extremely rapidly, at levels beneath conscious awareness' (ibid., p. xv). The significance of this as regards person-centred therapeutic practice is that it provides further research-based support for the client's capacity to respond to what he may experience as the challenge of the therapist's positive regard and empathic understanding. Schore and others suggest that the therapist acts as an 'interactive affect regulator'. Whilst we are uneasy with the language and metaphor of the therapist as a regulator, we concur with the theory and research that supports the practice of right brain/left brain interactions, and the efficacy of empathy. Neuroscientific findings and developments also support the importance of the therapist's contact reflections in pre-therapy work with clients, often operating at a subceived level.

The becoming, directional human organism has parallels with Jung's theory of the psyche which in some sense is teleological, in that it is concerned with design and purpose and, specifically, that it relates to ends or final causes. This gives a sense of directionality to the unconscious mind as it operates developmentally towards maturity or what Jung refers to as individuation. Also from an analytical psychological perspective, Cambray and Carter (2004, p. 132) reaffirm the importance of the relationship in response to incongruence and anxiety:

> Every living system must cope with uncertainty that places it in a state somewhere between continuity and change . . . In the therapeutic setting fluctuations in relational certitude and doubt provide an emergent edge through which the co-constructed third of the relationship becomes the locus of the transcendent function.

Barrett-Lennard (1998) describes the human organism as interacting with perceived 'outer' and 'inner' reality in the service of the actualising tendency. Bearing in mind that the organism's tendency to actualise is the focus of Chapter 3, and our general caveat about the artificial separation of these subjects, we consider four further aspects of the organism in response to these 'realities':

- that it is 'self'-regulating,
- that it behaves according to need,
- that it has a sphere of immediacy, and
- that it is interdependent with its environment.

Regulation

This is more commonly referred to as 'self'-regulation. We think that this term, like the unhelpful term 'organismic self', confuses two concepts which person-centred psychologists and therapists need to separate in order to clarify the distinctions between the two. This confusion also prevails in the generic psychological literature. One excellent book on *Self-Regulation in Early Childhood* (Bronson, 2000), which is, in our view, predominantly about organismic regulation, contains no discussion of the 'self', and no references to organism! (For ease of reference and style, and to maintain

LIVERPOOL JOHN MOORES UNIVERSITY
LEARNING SERVICES

historical accuracy, however, in this section we maintain the original term used by the various authors cited.) In addition to differentiation, which we discuss above, we identify two characteristics of organismic regulation:

- excitation and balance, and
- antagonistic effects.

Excitation and balance

Goldstein (op. cit., p. 101) describes organismic regulation in the context of a discussion about the distribution of excitation in the organism:

> the organism can deal with the respective environmental demands and actualize itself. The possibility of asserting itself in the world, while preserving its character, hinges on a special kind of 'coming to terms' of the organism with the environment. This has to take place in such a fashion that each change of the organism, caused by environmental stimuli, is equalized after a definite time, so that the organism regains that 'average' state that corresponds with its nature, which is 'adequate' to it. Only under this condition can the organism maintain its consistency and identity.

Here, Goldstein is emphasising the homeostatic, balancing aspect of organismic regulation, sometimes referred to as 'equalisation', a process which is predominantly unconscious or, to use Stern's (2004) more helpful term 'non-conscious' (for more on which see Chapter 2). Rogers (1968) refers to organic processes, such as the regulation of body heat, as aspects of the organism's actualising tendency. Goldstein also refers to research which discloses 'an extraordinary number of facts that demonstrate a far-reaching interaction between vegetative and mental processes'. Examples of this range from anxiety to trauma, held in the body. Other writers, especially in the Reichian and neo-Reichian tradition of body psychotherapy refer to 'vegetative processes', based in and on the vegetative or autonomic nervous system (see Reich, 1947/83; Boyeson & Boyeson, 1981, 1982; Carroll, 2002), and to vegetotherapy, which Eiden (2002, p. 42) describes as 'a free association through the body' which 'aims to release physical tension to free the mind, the mental belief structure'. Therapists working in this way may work directly on a client's muscular holding 'in order to free blocked energy, expressed emotionally or physically through involuntary movements . . . to free physical mobility and breathing . . . [to] lead to a capacity for more intense emotional experience of self and other' (ibid., p. 35). Despite its organismic, holistic and integrative approach to the person, person-centred therapy has not engaged much with body therapies. Exceptions to this are: Tophoff (1984); Gendlin (1986) from an experiential/

focusing perspective; a recent, special themed issue of *Person-Centred Practice* (*PCP*) on 'Psyche and soma' (Embleton Tudor & Tudor, 2002); and Natalie Rogers' expressive therapy in which she uses movement and dance. Fernald (2000) writes of similarities between Rogers' approach, based on organismic experiencing and Reich's body-oriented psychotherapy. One of the papers in the special issue of *PCP* by Geggus (2002, pp. 88–9) describes Zero Balancing, which the author describes as person-centred bodywork or body-centred personwork:

> The basic premise of Zero Balancing is that holding a client's energy body and physical body simultaneously and consciously in relationship, using a specific kind of touch, can result in a more harmonious state of balance between them. This balance is a dynamic state, reflecting and responding to life in a way that can release old patterns of stress within the body and inhibit the development of disease.

Along with many others, we assert that mind and body are inseparable. Our emotional processing is also integral and inseparable. From an evolutionary perspective our emotions evolved to enhance survival. As Pally (2000, p. 73) puts it: 'emotions organise an animal's sustained responses to rewarding and aversive stimuli'. This echoes Rogers' (1959b, p. 222) view that the human infant 'behaves with adience toward positively valued *experiences* and with avoidance toward those negatively valued'. Pally (ibid., p. 73) continues: 'The function of emotion is to co-ordinate the mind and body. Emotion organises perception, thought, memory, physiology, behaviour and social interaction so as to provide an optimal means for coping with the particular situation that is generating the emotion.' We believe, with Pally, that understanding this is helpful in working with people with regard to anxiety, psychosomatic conditions, attachment and non-verbal communication (see also Chapters 6 and 7). A major contribution in this field is Schore's (1994) work on the neurobiology of emotional development: *Affect Regulation and the Origin of the Self* from which we have quoted. In her work Pally (2000) presents many of the ideas in the field of neurobiology and neuroscience in an accessible way. For example, she notes the changes in the sympathetic and parasympathetic nervous systems: the 'fight or flight' and 'rest and digest' responses to emotional processing of stimuli. We discuss the relevance of this for psychotherapists specifically with regard to perception and subception in Chapter 7.

The organism's tendency to what we refer to as 'homeostatic balance' is not the act of a couch potato, seeking a 'giving up' or passive rest. It is literally a dynamic balancing act. Macmurray (1957/91, p. 33) conceives of the organism 'as a harmonious balancing of differences, and in its pure form, a tension of opposites'. As we discuss in Chapter 1, the significance of balance, of harmony, of being 'at one' with ourselves, others and the world, has its philosophical origins in the Ancient Greek Stoic school, and theological echoes in the Christian concept of atonement.

The two characteristics, organismic regulation and differentiation, together form what Goldstein (op. cit., p. 224) refers to as 'the natural situation':

> as long as no pathology exists, one finds, in the natural situation, only unitary, total performances that are not caused through isolated excitation of single apparatuses, but are formed through differential configuration of the excitation course, in the various sectors of the whole.

In other words, the 'normal' or usual development of the organism is based on excitation in response to stimulus, balance, and differentiation. Bronson (2000) identifies four major issues in relation to what she refers to as 'self-regulation' in young children: definition, development, integration and support. These relate to our discussion in this part of the chapter as follows:

- Definition: the definition of organismic regulation, especially with regard to balance (see above pp. 67–8).
- Development: the development of organismic regulation through differentiation (see below pp. 58ff.), and in response to antagonistic effects (see below).
- Integration: the tendency to integrate.
- Support: and the necessity of environmental support for the regulating organism (p. 73).

Antagonistic effects

The third characteristic of organismic regulation is in response to antagonistic effects or stimuli. In some experiments which applied contradictory or antagonistic stimuli to the right and left cerebellum, Goldstein observed that the response of the patient's left arm (1) did not deviate; or (2) stopped; or (3) staggered 'in the form of an alternating horizontal wobbling to the right and left' (ibid., p. 225). He goes on to reflect: 'Which one of the three reactions sets in depends on the relationship of intensity of the left and right stimulus.' This can equally be applied to psychological and/or social stimuli. Someone who enjoys cheese and red wine may know that they are not good for him: they are mucus forming and he wakes up the next morning feeling 'bunged up'. He both wants to eat and drink and doesn't want to. *A client reports feeling undermined by her mother's comments about her own mothering. One example is that her mother refers to the client's son as 'a little monster'. Her instinct is to confront her mother. The comments are hurtful both to her and her son. However, whilst the client wants to confront her mother, she's sure that her mother will make a lot of it, that she'll probably try and drag other family members into it, and that she'll generally make her, the client, feel worse. She doesn't want to ignore the problem or the hurt, and also doesn't want to suffer the consequences of confronting her mother. One response to this might be for the therapist to help the client make a decision about which course of action to follow. Another is to accept her accepting that she has a conflict.*

The latter is, in our view, the more subtle therapeutic response. It is also one which acknowledges that we have a split perceptual system (LeDoux, 1995, 1998), based on two survival mechanisms: one of which gives us speedy responses (to detect food, foes and mates), the other of which provides us with accuracy (to distinguish between edible and inedible food, and between friends and foes). In the example above the client's instinctive, non-conscious response is to respond and confront her mother. It is non-conscious as the sensory stimuli involved in our capacity for quick response bypasses the cortex and passes from the sensory end organ, in this case the ear, through the thalamus and directly to the amygdala. The slower response is more considered and based on more detailed input from the environment, sensory stimuli from which travel the longer route from the thalamus, to the sensory cortex, the hippocampus, the amygdala and orbitofrontal cortex. It is, therefore, a fuller or more comprehensive response. Goldstein (p. 225) poses the more general problem of this antagonistic innervation: 'How does the organism behave when it is exposed simultaneously to stimuli, one of which would lead to the opposite reaction as compared with the other?' This question is, in part, addressed by this split perceptual system, which Pally (2000) refers to as 'the conflicted brain', and which, in part, leads us to consider the behaviour and needs of the organism.

Behaviour according to need

Discussing the structure of the organism, Goldstein discusses figure–ground differentiation and behaviour. He identifies three different kinds of behaviour:

- performances – voluntary, consciously experienced activities,
- attitudes – feelings, moods and other inner experiences, and
- processes – bodily functions, experienced only indirectly.

More broadly he distinguishes between concrete and abstract behaviour. When an organism reacts to the stimulus automatically or directly, this is viewed as concrete behaviour; when an organism reacts to the stimulus after thinking about it, or acts upon the stimulus, this is conceptualised as abstract behaviour.

Rogers (1951, p. 491) considers behaviour as '*basically the goal-directed attempt of the organism to satisfy its needs as experienced, in the field, as perceived*'. It is, in other words, goal directed and needs driven. A number of implications follow from this Proposition (V):

1   Behaviour is inextricably linked to needs.
2   Behaviour is a reaction to the field, *as perceived.*
3   All behaviour is to meet a present need (although past experience modifies present meaning).
4   All needs have what Rogers refers to as 'a basic relatedness' (ibid., p. 491), and spring from and refer to the organism's tendency to actualise.
5   Needs are experienced, whether or not they are symbolised in awareness.
6   The satisfaction of needs is designed to reduce tension and to maintain and enhance the organism.
7   In pursuing this satisfaction, the organism *is* its behaviour at any one moment.

Rogers (1951) suggests that this proposition is somewhat modified by the development of the self, a modification we discuss in Chapter 4. Scheerer (1954, p. 123), a contemporary of Rogers, was saying something similar about behaviour from the perspective of cognitive theory: '. . . behavior may be conceptualized as being embedded in a cognitive-emotional-motivational matrix in which no true separation is possible. No matter how we slice behavior, the ingredients of motivation-emotion-cognition are present in one order or another.' Writing about evolutionary psychology, Evans and Zarate (1999, p. 160) state that:

> Every kind of behaviour results from the way our minds interact with our environment, and the mind results from the interaction of the environment with our genes. Different environments will lead the mind to develop differently and change the way in which the mind causes behaviour.

This provides further support for the importance of the interchange between organism and environment and the inseparability of the holistic mind/body organism/environment from its behaviour.

In a brief passage in his book on *The Clinical Treatment of the Problem Child*, Rogers (1939) identifies two great classes of needs of the human organism:

1   *Affectional response* – which includes recognition, affection and, in the mature (adult) human organism, sexual response. This is echoed by

neurobiologists such as Schore (1994) who observe and discuss the importance of smiling and of positive, open expression between mother and baby.

2   *Achievement* – which consists, for Rogers, of accomplishment and self-esteem.

Later (Rogers, 1951), he viewed these needs as physiological and, therefore, having a biological base. To this binary division, we would add:

3   *Affiliative needs* – which Allport (1955/83, p. 32) sees as 'the ground of becoming', on which more below. Affiliation also involves a sense of belonging, and therefore echoes Angyal's notion of homonomy.

In our view, however, the needs Rogers describes appear strangely unidirectional, and not relational or interactive, let alone demanding of the environment. Rogers (1939, pp. 487–8) continues: 'it seems entirely possible that all organic and psychological needs may be described as partial aspects of this one fundamental need . . . the words used are an attempt to describe the observed directional force in organic life'. Murray (1938), writing about needs at the same time as Rogers, took account of the impact of the environment. He defines a need (p. 123) as:

a construct (a convenient fiction or hypothetical concept) which stands for a force . . . in the brain region, a force which organizes perception, apperception, intellection, conation and action in such a way as to transform in a certain direction an existing, unsatisfying situation. A need is sometimes provoked directly by internal processes of a certain kind . . . but more frequently (when in state of readiness) by the occurrence of one of a few commonly effective press [forces] . . . Thus, it manifests itself by leading the organism to search for or to avoid encountering.

We discuss environmental 'press' further in Chapter 6.

This perspective on needs describes an outward-looking organism, seeking security; homonomy (see Angyal, 1941); development (see Rogers, 1959b); contact (see Fairbairn, 1952, and the first of Rogers' 1957, 1959b therapeutic conditions); and, crucially, opportunities to express love and affection (see Brazier, 1993, and Erskine, 1998, who identifies eight *relational* needs).

Most people accept the view that children need love. It is less understood that they also need to express love, and a nurturing relational environment in which to do so. In this sense these relational needs describe and expand Rogers' view of needs as expressing a basic relatedness. One practical and clinical implication of this is the consideration that as therapists it may be important to accept gifts from clients (see, for instance, Stamatiadis, 1990). Of course, as with any transaction, we need to understand the meaning and significance of such a gesture in the context of the person, the situation and the therapy, rather than refuse or reject it as a matter of course or policy. Barrett-Lennard (1998, p. 75) makes the point that 'Motivational constructs in the form of a scheme of specific needs . . . [are] unnecessary and even heuristically unsound.' This is an important caution against any prescriptive and fixed taxonomy of needs.

The points of implication (above, 5 and 6, p. 72) about needs being *experienced* and *satisfied* elaborate the view of organismic regulation as outlined earlier (pp. 67ff.). It is, however, the final implication (point 7) noted above that is the most radical and controversial. If behaviour is an organismic attempt to satisfy current need, then I am that behaviour, whether that is loving/lovable, hating/hateful, generous, jealous, aggressive or even violent. This has huge implications, especially for those humanistic psychologists, therapists and trainers who seek to separate the person from his behaviour, so as to criticise the behaviour and not the person. From a holistic and organismic perspective, this artificial separation is both a nonsense and unrealistic. It is unhelpful and misses the point. Faced with cruelty, oppression, nastiness, or evil in the world, the issue is how to respond to, deal with and work with people who are, *at that moment when they do something cruel,* themselves cruel. It is unrealistic to suggest that, in some way, 'underneath', everyone is 'in essence' simply 'good'. Human organisms are more complex and life more complicated than that. Such liberalism about ontology is unhelpful in that it sets up a false idealism about human nature and life itself. Finally, the attempt to claim a comforting 'niceness' about an essence of human nature does not allow for entropy, or disorder, alongside syntropy, or unity. Take the example of smoking. Most people agree that smoking is unhealthy. Taking the view that a person is not his behaviour, we can love someone who smokes but not like the fact that he smokes. We can give him a hard time about his 'filthy habit', how bad it is for him and for us, whilst at the same time reassuring him that we love him *as a person.* This is a pertinent example not only in the personal and social sphere but also in the clinical setting. A number of therapists take this 'separation' view and justify their interventions with clients who smoke on the basis that they are confronting a death wish, suicidal tendency or harmartic script. This approach misses a number of things:

1   That the vast majority of people who smoke know more about the effects of smoking than non-smokers, and that therefore any comments or advice along these lines are, at best, redundant and, at worst, patronising. Also, evaluative comments or exhortations work against what Rogers (1958/67b) says about wanting to free people from the threat of external evaluation.

2   That the person who smokes will have his own complex feelings and thoughts about the fact that he smokes, as well as physical responses to nicotine, and possibly, pathological addiction. This is supported by the importance Rogers (1942) gives to the free expression of feelings, and also by his view (Rogers, 1951, p. 223) that therapy is complete when 'the client is able to make, to experience, and to accept the diagnosis of the psychogenic aspects of his maladjustment'.

3   That friends, colleagues or therapists often reassure for their own sake. Such reassurance that a smoker is loveable anyway risks detracting and distracting him from reflecting on and exploring what he feels and believes about his smoking.

4   That, when one person says that he loves another as a person despite the fact that the other smokes, he implies a love or acceptance of the whole person. In fact, and ironically, what he is saying, and often what the smoker hears and experiences, is that he loves him (only) as a part person – the part that doesn't smoke! This is an atomistic rather than an holistic or organismic perspective.

5   That there is a point and purpose to smoking which ranges from enjoyment to different forms of retroflection. Simply rehearsing the humanistic mantra that the behaviour is not the person separates the person from their smoking, encourages dissociation and passivity, misses the point about the 'positive intention' that a person has in smoking, and flies in the face of the importance of empathising with a person's internal frame of reference in its completeness and complexity.

We know several people who feel ashamed or embarrassed that they smoke and have experienced negative and punitive responses from their therapists. Several said that they hadn't even told their therapist that they smoked. One person described smoking as 'a route to belonging', an attitude which, in our experience, is common in both psychiatric and penal systems where smoking is a ritual, and tobacco a form of exchange value. Another saw it as 'an attempt to soothe painful feelings'.

This leads us to a final point on organismic behaviour which is expressed by Goldstein's question about being exposed simultaneously to two stimuli that invite mutually contradictory responses:

- Knowing that smoking is bad for my health, why do I smoke?
- Feeling loved by my partner, why am I reluctant to confide in him?
- Wanting to enjoy close relationships, why do I feel cold, detached and flat?
- Having studied biology, why do I think that my internal organs are dislocated?
- Knowing that I'm upsetting the neighbours, why do I play music so loud?

- Knowing that my therapist is reliable, why do I get so upset and feel abandoned when she takes a break?
- Knowing that I'm loved by my friends, why do I feel compelled to show off in social situations with them?
- Knowing that I'm respected by my colleagues, why am I always seeking to be more admired?
- Even though I know I could enjoy going out with a friend, why do I always make excuses and end up staying in on my own?
- Even though I often know what to do, why do I always have to seek advice and reassurance from others?
- Even when I'm taking a break, why do I always have to make lists and even lists of lists?

We can answer these questions in terms of reflex reactions in the organism, and of the difference between two tendencies: our organismic tendency to actualise, and the tendency to self-actualisation, both of which we consider in the next chapter. As far as organismic reactions to simultaneous stimuli are concerned, Goldstein (p. 225) concludes with a 'general law', that: 'the reaction that corresponds to the stronger stimulus is more extensive and slower than the other; whereas the latter reaction, which corresponds to the weaker stimulus, is less extensive and faster'. Thus, in the above examples, which hint at each of the ten personality disorders identified in *DSM-IV* (APA, 1994), the second clauses of each question reflect the respective reactions to stronger stimuli. From this and Goldstein's earlier observations, we discern a number of factors that influence the organism's reaction and behaviour:

- the strength of the stimulus,
- the relationship of intensity between two stimuli, and
- the extensiveness, speed, and chronicity or acuteness of the reaction.

Thus, a child brought up with values based in the two different cultures of home and school may well experience a strong stimulus from the school environment to do something which contradicts the values she and her family hold at home.

Sphere of immediacy

Goldstein takes up the point about the relationship between organism, other and the world and suggests that, in addition to our subjective experience and the heteronomous world, there is another sphere by and in which we know ourselves and the world more deeply and fully. He refers to this as the 'sphere of immediacy', and compares this to the 'subject–object' world in which both the subject and the world are considered from an isolated and isolating point of view: 'The experience of immediacy cannot be reached by the discursive procedure or by any kind of synthesis. It may achieved only by surrendering ourselves to the world with which we come into contact without fearing to lose our relation to the ordered world' (ibid., p. 21). What this means, and our own experience supports this, is that we inhabit both the subjective sphere and the sphere of immediacy, and that both are part of our human nature. This sphere is, for us, akin and parallel to how Barrett-Lennard (2005) sees community, as a 'zone' lying somewhere beyond the family but 'as a closer, more personal context of activity and configured meaning than the pluralist nation state or other big systems in the modern world'. That we are able to live in both or a number of spheres is due to our capacity for the abstract attitude which, in turn, is based on our ability to differentiate. Indeed, we would argue that this sense of immediacy, between 'ourselves' and the world is necessary, for instance, for the development of regard for and empathy with another, and for the development of our capacity to receive acceptance and understanding. For Goldstein (op. cit., p. 21) this sphere of immediacy 'creates a deeper existence that affords not only the possibility of living in the static condition of the abstract–concrete sphere but also of tolerating uncertainty without losing our existence'. Allport (1955, p. 32) puts it this way:

> Having known acceptance in an affectionate environment [the child] learns more readily to accept himself, to tolerate the ways of the world, and to handle the conflicts of later life in a mature manner . . . early affiliative needs (dependence, succorance, and attachment) are the ground of becoming.

This concept helps us to understand and support the fluid movement between an individual and an other, an individual and his world: 'the organism is part of the world, but it can also experience the world as something apart from itself – as something as real as itself' (Perls, 1969, p. 38).

Interdependence

The interplay between organism and environment is characteristic of Goldstein's work, of Angyal's, and of our own, present work. Angyal (1941, p. 48) goes so far as to describe life as 'an autonomous dynamic event which takes place between the organism and the environment'. Although Rogers was alive to this interdependence he does not emphasise it in his work. This lack of emphasis has, in turn, led to some criticism of Rogers' lack of focus on the positive impact of social and environmental conditions on the human organism. Holland (1977, p. 74), for instance,

LIVERPOOL
JOHN MOORES UNIVERSITY
AVRIL ROBARTS LRC
TEL. 0151 231 4022

criticises Rogers for making a false split between the organismic and the social, 'projecting exclusively good qualities onto the organismic level'. We agree with Holland that there is at times a naïve quality to some of Rogers' ideas, and an individualistic conception of human action in his and others' approach to one-to-one therapy. In this chapter (and book) we are concerned to advance person-centred therapy as one which is as mindful of the impact of the social/environmental context as it is focused on the nature of the organism. As we discuss later (in Chapter 5) it was psychologists such as Henry Murray who combined and articulated an appreciation of the individual complexity of the human organism with a 'field' orientation. We also examine such criticisms in Chapter 9 when we discuss the implications of organismic psychology for person-centred theory and practice.

'Coming to terms' with the environment is one of the main dynamic concepts presented by Goldstein (op. cit.). The environment provides both the source of disturbance to which the organism has to respond, and the source of supplies on which the organism can draw in order to actualise. Perls (1947/69) examines what he refers to as the cycle of the interdependency of organism and environment and offers a phased formulation of it (Box 2.1).

Perls comments that this cycle or circle leads to the fact of 'organismic self-regulation', which, for Reich, Perls, others and us, is very different from moral regulation (see Chapter 8). Again, it is important to note that, in both examples, the organism does not return to where it was before. In the first example, in response to the 'disturbance' of an internal need, the subject sets the book aside, and is open to the next sensation. In terms of the gestalt cycle of awareness, this represents a movement from satisfaction to withdrawal. In the second example, the return of organismic balance is characterised by engagement with others.

Recent research on brain development also emphasises the importance of the environment and the dynamic relationship between the mental phenomena of the organism and environment (Damasio, 1994/96, p. xix):

> mental phenomena can be fully understood only in the context of an organism's interacting in an environment. That the environment is, in part, a product of the organism's activity itself, merely underscores the complexity of interactions we must take into account.

There seem to be, for example, a number of emotional systems which are genetically determined or 'hard-wired' in the brain's subcortical structures, regulating care, rough and tumble play, seeking, lust, fear, rage, separation and distress. The activity in the subcortex which produces fear, rage or distress is also influenced by 'higher structures' in the cortex, particularly the frontal lobe, which can inhibit subcortical activity and, therefore, the expression of emotions. However, at birth, the subcortex of the human

Box 2.1 The cycle of the interdependency of organism and environment (Perls, 1947/69) with examples.

The cycle of the interdependency of organism and environment (Perls, 1947/69)	Example of internal disturbance cycle (from Perls, 1947/69)	Example of external disturbance cycle
(1) The organism at rest.	I am dozing on the settee.	I am lying on the settee, drifting in and out of consciounsess.
(2) The disturbing factor, which may be		
(a) An external disturber – a demand put upon a person, or any interference that puts her on the defensive.		The children come in, throw their things down, run up and then down the stairs, and demand their tea.
(b) Internal – a need.	The wish to read something interesting penetrates my consciousness.	
Either of which requires:		
(3) The creation of an image or reality.	I remember a certain bookshop.	I become aware of this disturbance.
(4) The answer to the situation, aiming at:	I go there, browse and buy a book.	I get annoyed.
(5) A decrease of tension – achievement of gratification or compliance with the demands, resulting in:	I am reading.	One of them comes over and gives me a hug. I feel less annoyed. I wake up fully and prepare their tea.
(6) The return of the organismic balance.	I have had enough. I put the book aside.	I sit with them and we talk about our respective days.

infant is not fully connected to the cortex, so at this stage we are not wired up for self-regulation – and hence the importance of the regulating other. This interdependence of organism and environment is the basis, in organismic terms, of the significance of interpersonal relationships or, as Trevarthen (1980/93) puts it, 'the foundations of intersubjectivity', a subject we examine in Chapter 4. Thus (Pally, 2000, p. 1):

old notions of dichotomy between mind versus brain, nature versus nurture, have been supplanted by a rich web of synergistic relations between mind and brain, nature and nurture. Specifically, according to modern neuroscience, this means that all mental phenomena are assumed to be the result of biological activity of neuronal circuits in the brain. The development of these circuits relies in part on genetic programmes, but is also heavily dependent on the individual's experiences within the environment.

One example of this is Sander's (2002) research in which he set up two groups of babies. In one group, babies were fed on demand, and in the other fed every four hours regardless of their state. Within a few days babies in the demand-fed cohort began to show the emergence of one or two longer sleep periods in each 24 hours and, after a few more days, these longer sleep periods began to occur more frequently at night. This was in contrast to the group of babies fed every four hours, who showed no such changes. Sander concludes: 'The emergence of a new and continuing 24-hour circadian rhythm in the demand-fed infant–caregiver system can be seen as an emergent property of a system in a state of stable regulation . . . the infant becomes a system within a larger system' (p. 24).

Internal valuing process

Through healthy development, human beings engage in an *organismic valuing process*, which Rogers (1959b, p. 210) defines as 'an ongoing process in which values are never fixed or rigid, but experiences are being accurately symbolized and continually and freshly valued'. Whilst our tendency to actualise is the criterion for such evaluation, we do not, of course, exist or operate outside of an environmental context: 'whether or not a reflex occurs, seems . . . to depend partly on the "value" of the stimulus – on its functional significance for the whole organism' (Goldstein, op. cit., pp. 72–3). 'This awareness of worth in human beings' says Whitehead (1954, p. 295) 'develops very early. Most attempts to formulate it in words fail.' Experiences which maintain or enhance the organism are valued positively, and we move with *adience* towards such experiences; we move away from, that is, we avoid, negatively valued experiences. Stinckens, Lietaer and Leijssen (2002) also emphasise the interrelationship between organism and environment arguing (p. 48) that: 'Inborn, intuitive experiencing should enter into a continuous dialectical relationship with the laws of social reality for the valuing process to correspond with the social embeddedness of the individual.' Whilst we agree with an emphasis on the dialectical, we think that these authors make too much of their criticism of Rogers' theory as too individualistic.

Recent research in neuroscience confirms these views about the development of values. It confirms, for instance, that the whole brain is involved in the process of evaluating the meaning of experience (e.g. Cortina, 2003). The brain consists of groups or units of neural networks which consist of between 50 and 10,000 neurons, and there are estimated to be perhaps a hundred million such groups. 'Experience that proves to be of value for the organism' says Cortina (2003), 'is "mapped" into these neuronal networks.' Edelman (1992) talks about 'values' as the way in which the developing organism selects a limited amount of stimuli from an enormous and potentially bewildering array of possibilities. A person being out of contact, withdrawing, 'cutting off', or even disassociating, may thus be understood as discriminating their environmental stimuli. We think that personality 'disorder' is more usefully understood as personality *process*, a discussion we develop in Chapter 5. In terms of therapeutic practice this research supports the importance of understanding both the value the client *himself* gives to a particular stimulus, and his own response from within his frame of reference. We see no contradiction in holding this attitude alongside an understanding of the correspondence between the individual's internal frame of reference and external, societal values, or the lack of correspondence between the two. To take an example: the human infant is polymorphous, having a sexual temperament that moves simply towards its own satisfaction. The phrase 'polymorphous *perverse*' represents an external evaluation of that polymorphism. As human beings we are polyvalent, having many values. An example of this is when somebody says that she is feeling ambivalent, a common response to which is to help her decide between the two values or positions. It seems to us to be more consistent with the theory of person-centred psychology to help the person to 'own' both or multiple values rather than simply to 'sort it out'. For us, this reflects the acceptance of difference and diversity, and is the theoretical and organismic basis for working with diversity therapeutically within the individual, between individuals and in and between groups.

Siegel (1999, p. 124) suggests that, in a matter of microseconds, following an 'initial orienting response', the brain processes the representations of the body and the external world. As this occurs, 'elaborative appraisal and arousal processes' begin which 'assess whether a stimulus is "good" or "bad", and determine whether the organism should move toward or away from the stimulus'. Furthermore, '*Emotional processing prepares the brain and the rest of the body for action.*' Thus, the infant needs a stimulating and responsive environment in which need is valued and values are needed.

Holland (1977, p. 74) criticises what he sees as a split in Rogers' conceptualisation between the organism and the social environment. He argues that Rogers projects exclusively good qualities onto the organismic level. 'On the social side of the split' he continues 'are all those unfriendly, limiting and distorting influences, the expectations of others and the social pressures to conform, against which Rogers prefers to trust his organismic feelings.' Although Holland acknowledges Rogers' (1951) view of the socialised nature of the organism, he views this as a weak attempt to integrate the organism/social split. We have some sympathy with aspects of Holland's criticism of the emphasis on the individual, apparent especially in Rogers' early work, and we appreciate his unusually close reading of Rogers. We think, though, that his view of an organism/social split is a distortion of the theory. Rogers (1951, p. 524) is clear about the necessary adjustments an individual makes in the context of need and socialisation, and the implications for a social system of values:

> It is in the outcome of this valuing of values that we strike the possi-
> bility of very basic similarities in all human experience. For as the
> individual tests such values, and arrives at his own personal values, he
> appears to come to conclusions which can be formulated in a
> generalized way: that the greatest values for the enhancement of the
> organism accrue when all experiences and all attitudes are permitted
> conscious symbolization, and when behavior becomes the meaningful
> and balanced satisfaction of *all* needs, these needs being available to
> consciousness. The behavior which thus ensues will satisfy the need for
> social approval, the need to express positive affectional feelings, the
> need for sexual expression, the need to avoid guilt and regret as well as
> the need to express aggression. Thus, while the establishment of values
> by each individual may seem to suggest a complete anarchy of values
> by each individual, experience indicates that quite the opposite is true.
> Since all individuals have basically the same needs . . . [there results]
> a high degree of commonality and a genuinely socialized system of
> values.

We think this addresses the criticisms levelled at Rogers by Stinckens *et al.* (2002) and others.

Barrett-Lennard (1998) suggests that the organism is always in motion. As Feldenkreis (1981, p. 23) puts it: 'Most of the organism . . . is pre-occupied with movement in our environment.' We explore two aspects of organismic motion:

- direction, and
- appetition.

Direction

For Goldstein (op. cit., p. 84) 'direction is what we actually find as the outstanding characteristic in the performance of an organism'. He suggests that this directionality is effected both through a specific environment in which the organism lives and 'a certain determination and force issuing from the organism itself', otherwise the organism would be a static organic system of regulation and balance, in homeostasis but not in action. The environment, too, is in motion. Our own planet spins on its axis at 67,000 mph, and in circles at over 1,000 mph. The organism does not live in its immediate environment alone but, in Goldstein's words, 'in a world in which all possible sorts of stimuli are present and act on it' (ibid., p. 85). He goes on to say that we make some sort of continuous selection from all the events in the world 'from the point of view wherein events are, or are not, pertinent to that organism' (ibid., p. 85). The point about multiple stimuli appears to draw on force field analysis (Köhler, 1940) and is also reminiscent of a (later) field theory perspective (Lewin, 1951/64); we know that in his work Goldstein refers to Köhler, and that Lewin refers to both Goldstein and Köhler.

It is precisely because of this innate directionality of the organism and its tendency to actualise that the person-centred therapist has no need to be directive and can, with specific regard to a client's experience, embody a non-directive attitude.

Appetition

'Appetition' according to Whitehead (1929/78, p. 32) 'is immediate matter of fact including in itself a principle of unrest, involving what is not and what may be.' The statement 'I'm hungry' implies unrest and describes both what is (hunger) and what may be (satisfaction). Furthermore, he argues (ibid., p. 32): 'All physical experience is accompanied by an appetite for, or against, its continuance.' Sharing the same etymological root as the word 'appetite', appetition carries the meaning of seeking after something, only with a stronger sense of desire and direction towards an object or purpose. It is a concept found in Leibniz's philosophical work, and has echoes of the broader meaning which the gestalt psychologists, Perls, Hefferline and Goodman (1951/73, pp. 100–1), give to the word aggression, which they say 'includes everything that an organism does to initiate contact with its environment'. However, importantly for Whitehead (1958/71) and for us, appetition also carries a sense of the future: it describes 'an urge towards the future based on an appetite in the present'. This is particularly significant as it gives an organismic basis for future focus and direction, based on a sense both of what is *and of what may be*. Whitehead uses the example of thirst to argue this point. Thirst is and represents an appetite towards difference, towards something relevant in the sense that its future satisfaction *will* meet a present need or desire. Part of our 'unity of satisfaction' is our ability to evaluate both our own needs and those external objects which, in this case, will satisfy our thirst. For Whitehead (1929/78, p. 32) appetition has an immediate and a broader relevance: 'This is the ultimate, basic adjustment of the togetherness of external objects on which creative order depends. It is the conceptual adjustment of all appetites in the form of aversions and adversions. It constitutes the meaning of relevance.'

Appetition has a neurobiological basis in the seeking system, the source cells of which are located in the ventral tegmental area (see Solms & Turnbull, 2002). Solms and Turnbull talk about appetitive states such as hunger, thirst and craving and also curiosity, interest and expectancy. Their location is relevant as the command neurotransmitter of this system is dopamine. When this seeking system is damaged people lose interest in objects in the world, and stop dreaming; together with these symptoms there is a decrease in psychotic symptoms such as hallucinations and delusions. Conversely, when the system is stimulated, for instance, through medication, energy levels and dreaming increase – as does the likelihood of psychosis.

As we have indicated throughout this chapter, one major implication of organismic psychology is the differentiation of the 'self', a differentiation which we elaborate in Chapter 4. As a preface to that discussion, we turn our attention to the organism's tendency to actualise and to the formative tendency.

Chapter 3

Tendencies

Always think of the universe as one living organism, with a single substance and a single soul; and observe how all things are submitted to the single perceptivity of this one whole, all are moved by its single impulse, and all play their part in the causation of every event that happens. Remark the intricacy of the skein, the complexity of the web.

Marcus Aurelius

It's never too late to support nature in its tendency to cure.

Alfred Vogel

The human organism is active, actualizing, and directional. This is the basis for all of my thinking.

Carl Rogers

Taken together, says Rogers (1979, p. 98), the actualising and formative tendencies constitute 'the foundation blocks of the person-centered approach'. That is to say they are, at the level of philosophical belief, assumptions without which the approach does not make sense, and the basis for everything a therapist says or does while she is working.

Rogers describes the formative tendency as universal and evolutionary, and says that it tends towards greater order, complexity and interrelatedness in the universe. The actualising tendency is a localised manifestation of the formative tendency, and tends towards maintaining and enhancing the health and well-being of the experiencing organism. Articulating the relationship between the tendencies, Van Kalmthout (1998, p. 8) says that the formative tendency is 'the cosmic source of the actualizing tendency, which is at work within the individual'.

In our view we can speak of the formative tendency and the actualising tendency only as matters of faith that are not yet empirically verifiable. Writing specifically about the actualising tendency, Brodley (1999, p. 109) allows that it is a hypothesis that 'cannot be conclusively proved or disproved'. We choose, therefore, to believe in the tendencies or not in the light of our own convictions, experiences and temperament.

In our discussion of the tendencies we follow the chronology of Rogers' thinking and begin with the tendency to actualise. In the second part of the chapter we discuss an important manifestation of this tendency: that of self-actualisation. In the third part of the chapter we discuss from a person-centred perspective questions raised by other viewpoints regarding motivation and drive, and consciousness. In the fourth and final part of the chapter we discuss the formative tendency.

The organism's tendency to actualise

Rogers (1959b, p. 196) describes the actualising tendency as 'the inherent tendency of the organism to develop all its capacities in ways which serve to maintain or enhance the organism'. He later (1979, p .98) describes it as 'a characteristic of organic life'. He holds that the organism's tendency to actualise is dependable; that it can be the basis of therapeutic endeavour; that a therapist can rely on an individual client's organismic tendency to actualise; and that her only role is to facilitate that tendency by attending to the relational conditions that are most conducive to it. Brodley (1999, p. 109) says that it 'functions as an assumption that influences the way the therapist proceeds as a helper'. The non-directive attitude, for instance (see Chapter 8), follows from this belief in the organism's tendency to actualise.

The idea of an actualising tendency is neither new nor unique to Rogers. Writers from antiquity onwards have noticed a natural tendency in living organisms to preserve, renew and enhance themselves:

- 'The productions of nature' says Aristotle (1955, p. 44) 'have an innate tendency in the direction of the best condition of which they are capable.'
- 'At length' says Lucretius (1951, p. 93) 'everything is brought to its utmost limit of growth by nature, the creatress and perfectress.'
- 'No one' writes Spinoza (1677/1993, p. 154) 'unless he is overcome by external causes and those contrary to his nature, neglects to seek what is useful to himself, *i.e.*, to preserve his being.'
- Ferenczi (1932/95) writes about *orpha* or an organising drive. Stanton (1990, p. 198) states that this term derives from spiritualist terminology where it denotes 'creative destiny': 'it indicates the unconscious, vital, organizing instincts that nourish people and prevent them from falling apart during moments of severe crisis'.
- Taft (1933, p. 13) notes that living beings, including human beings, 'are geared to movement and growth, to achieving something new, leaving the outworn behind and going on to a next stage'.

- Berne (1947/71, p. 98) writes about *physis* as 'the force of Nature, which eternally strives to make things grow and to make growing things more perfect', and cites Zeno the Semite as having thought much about physis in connection with the growth and development of living things. Ferenczi (1932/95) refers to *physis* as '*determined* by the past, to which it is bound' (p. 40); Edwards (1967) sees physis in the works of the Stoics and the Epicureans; and Clarkson (1992) quotes Heraclitus and Aristotle on the subject.
- Merry (2003, p. 83) describes it as 'the non-conscious and inherent property of living organisms to become whatever they are capable of becoming'.

Rogers grew up on a farm, surrounded by examples of natural growth, and at the University of Wisconsin initially studied agriculture. It's understandable that he should base his work as a therapist on a principle of natural growth. As a metaphor, the actualising tendency is organic and natural, and stands against the earlier inorganic or mechanical metaphors of Freud and Skinner.

It's important to recognise that the actualising tendency isn't a thing or an entity, that how we talk about it is significant, and that there's a difference between 'is' and 'has'. An organism doesn't *have* a tendency to actualise, or even have *an* actualising tendency, in the same way that we might say it has an arm or an ulcer or a raging headache. We think it's more accurate and more useful to say that the organism *is* a tendency to actualise. The actualising tendency is then functionally synonymous with life: an organism that is alive is necessarily tending to actualise; an organism that is not tending to actualise is dead. Rogers (1978, p. 239) puts it this way:

> This tendency is operative at all times, in all organisms. Indeed it is only the presence or absence of this total directional process that enables us to tell whether a given organism is alive or dead.

In this sense, a therapist's role is simply to facilitate the life of the individual organism, where to facilitate means to make the unfolding of life easy or easier.

An organism tends to actualise, to grow, to develop, to realise its potential. Its tendency to actualise is simply one of its properties. As such it's of the same order as weight in relation to gravity. If we step off a ladder we fall. We don't need to think about it. Given the environment we live in, once we've made the choice to step, the fall is inevitable. If we were on the moon or at the bottom of the ocean, we'd be in a different environment, gravity would operate differently and the fall would be different. Similarly with the actualising tendency. If the environment is conducive, actualisation is inevitable. In different environments, different degrees of actualisation are possible. We could go further and say that the organism is always actualising to the extent that its environment is conducive.

Fowles (1964/81, p. 160) says of sex that it is 'like all great forces: simply a force. We may judge this or that manifestation or situation of the force as moral or immoral; but not the force itself.' We think the same is true of the actualising tendency: it is simply a force, an expression of nature, and in itself neither moral nor immoral. We may judge individual manifestations of it, but the force itself is amoral. Brodley agrees. She reminds us (1999, p. 116) that the actualising tendency is 'a biological concept rather than an ethical one'.

It is also unselfconscious. That is to say, the process of actualisation doesn't depend on an organism's conscious decision to make it happen. Although consciousness allows human organisms to reflect upon their environment and to make choices about what they do, the tendency to actualise goes on independently of this consciousness. It may even be the case that consciousness gets in the way of optimal actualisation, at least in the short term. As a result of introjected ideas about what's right and wrong, we may find ourselves torn between conscious desires or prohibitions on the one hand, and organismic promptings towards actualisation on the other. 'I have' says Rogers (1978, p. 247) 'gradually come to see this dissociation, rift, estrangement, as something learned, a perverse channeling of some of the actualizing tendency into behaviors that do not actualize.'

The actualising tendency is the ground of unconditional positive regard. That is to say that a therapist's unconditional positive regard is the minute-to-minute manifestation of his willingness to be non-directive, and that that willingness is possible only if he believes in and relies on the integrity and dependability of his client's organismic tendency to actualise. It's this that we hold in unconditional positive regard: not what a person does; nor even who he is; but his tendency to actualise as fully as possible in any given environment. This way of thinking supports from another angle our contention that it is simplistic and naïve to offer unconditional positive regard for the person but not for her behaviour. In our view that constitutes an untenable dichotomy, in that a person's behaviour is an intimate and accurate expression of who she is as a person in the moment of her behaving (see Chapter 2). It makes more sense to us to say that we hold unconditional positive regard for her tendency to actualise, and to see that she is tending to actualise whatever she or we or others may think of the behavioural manifestations of that tendency.

This train of thought supports and sheds light on Proposition V of Rogers' (1951) personality theory (p. 491): '*Behavior is basically the goal-directed attempt of the organism to satisfy its needs as experienced, in the field as perceived.*' In other words, a person's behaviour, however bizarre, destructive or self-defeating it may seem to us from the outside, is always both an expression of his tendency to actualise, and as full an expression of it as is possible in the environment as he experiences it. We may understand behaviour, then, always, as the best a client can do in any given moment, given his perception of his inner and outer environment.

Some have criticised the notion of the actualising tendency on a number of counts: that it's naïve; that it's overly optimistic; and that it accounts for neither the complexity of life nor the prevalence of evil. Rogers (1979, p. 101) notes himself that there are those who 'regard it as too optimistic, not dealing adequately with the negative element, the evil in persons'. Land too (1996, p. 69) says that 'reports of humanity's essential goodness are premature. Any openminded observation of human behavior must validate innate destructiveness as at least an equal possibility.' A more substantial critique, again based on the assertion that it's overly optimistic, is that the actualising tendency both supposes and enshrines the notion of progress, a more or less continuous process of improvement and betterment. This belief in progress may be a particularly American notion, or an expression perhaps of the spirit of the time in which Rogers was writing (see Barrett-Lennard, 1998). Rogers and some of the other writers we have cited talk about the tendency to actualise and the formative tendency as explicitly positive tendencies towards the maintenance and enhancement of the organism. They don't talk much about the organism's inevitable death, destruction and recycling. Paglia, though, recognises that everything that's created must eventually die. 'Organicism' she says (1994, p. 20) 'is the true deconstruction.' As she puts it in a subsequent online discussion forum (1995): 'from the perspective of the cosmos, society is very artificial and frail. Society is nothing compared to the vastness of outer space. The cosmic perspective is the real instrument of deconstruction.'

While valid, these critiques overlook three things:

1   that the actualising tendency is, as Brodley puts it (1999, p. 113), a *'tendency'* towards growth rather than *'a guarantee* of full health',
2   that it depends, at least in part, on external circumstances, and
3   that it is in itself neither moral nor immoral.

Self-actualisation

We noted earlier Rogers' comment (1978, p. 247) that an organism's tendency to actualise might occasionally result in 'behaviors that do not actualize'. To examine and make sense of this we need to look at Rogers' ideas about the development of the self, which he sees as a differentiated aspect of the organism.

Rogers' view is that we are born an unselfconscious organism, and that we develop a self-picture in response to the sense we make of the way those

around us behave towards us. There is, inevitably, some degree of difference or incongruence between our original organismic integrity and the self-
picture we develop. The greater this incongruence, the greater the likelihood
of emotional and psychological distress.

Given a conceptual map that includes organism and self, or self-picture,
we can say that the organism tends to actualise, and that a part of that
process of actualisation involves us actualising in ways that are more
immediately and obviously consistent with our self-picture than with our
organism. Rogers calls this second process a process of self-actualisation. It
follows that the greater the incongruence between organism and self, the
greater the likelihood that actualisation and self-actualisation will manifest
in different and incompatible behaviours.

We notice two misunderstandings of this. The first is that some practitioners and writers use actualisation and self-actualisation as if they refer
to the same process. This confusion is especially understandable when
Rogers himself, at least until the mid-1950s, uses the terms as synonyms.
Rogers (1951) uses 'self-actualisation' to describe the move towards optimal
psychological functioning. By 1959 he prefers the term 'actualisation' and
uses 'self-actualisation' to describe more specifically the actualisation of the
self. The confusion is compounded when some person-centred writers and
therapists, and many from other traditions, use the term 'self-actualisation'
consistently to refer to the kind of growth and development for which
Rogers reserves the term 'actualisation'. We think that this misunderstanding is simply that – a misunderstanding of the theory that we can clarify by
a more disciplined use of terms.

The second misunderstanding is that some practitioners see actualisation
as, broadly, good and healthy, and self-actualisation as bad and unhealthy.
Tolan (2002, p. 144) describes practitioners who act 'as though they had
received the "message" from their reading and training that their clients'
organismic experiencing was the only valuable and trustworthy aspect of
the client's personality'. We think that this is a more serious misunderstanding, and that the relationship between the two processes is too complex to reduce to that kind of dialectic. We have reservations about Tolan's
use of the term 'self-structure' to mean a person's construing of his world,
but agree with her recognition (ibid., p. 144) that 'it would run counter to
the whole philosophical base of client-centred theory to believe that *any*
part of the personality had no purpose'. She describes a number of ways in
which what she calls the self-structure serves the organismic tendency to
actualise:

- it helps us organise and evaluate our experience,
- it helps us stay acceptable within our family or society,
- it 'enables us' (ibid., p. 147) 'to predict the world and, in particular, to
  anticipate how people will respond to us', and

- ultimately (ibid., p. 147), it 'helps us to balance our own organismic needs with the needs of others' so that we can 'live in a world peopled with others rather than in an isolated world of our own'.

Addressing the same misunderstanding Merry (2003, p. 87) asks a number of questions:

> How can a 'tendency' be in conflict with a 'part' or 'subsystem' of itself? If the actualising tendency is the only source of motivation, how can it give rise to a part of itself that provides a second (and conflicting) motivation? Finally, if the actualising tendency is constructively directional, trustworthy and moving always in the direction of maturation, how does it create a secondary system that can sabotage it?

Merry answers those questions by suggesting that the organism's primary need is to survive, and that in order to do so it will adapt and 'close down some potentials if the alternative threatens survival'.

Both Tolan and Merry offer us a way to see all of a person's behaviour as a manifestation of her tendency to actualise. In this way, they help the theory itself become both more parsimonious and more holistic.

Questions raised by other viewpoints

In this part we discuss the implications of the theory of the organism's tendency to actualise for the concepts of motivation, drive and consciousness. In doing so we are echoing the title of a chapter by Rogers (1951) in which he addresses the questions of transference, diagnosis and the applicability of client-centred therapy. We want to do something similar here. It's not that person-centred psychology ignores these phenomena, or that its practitioners don't believe in them. It's simply that we view and work with them differently. Although these concepts derive from other approaches, we think it's useful to understand them and elaborate them from a person-centred perspective.

Motivation

The question of motivation arises in practice when therapists talk about 'unmotivated' clients or, indeed, when clients themselves feel unmotivated. This seems to imply that there is a lack of movement, inducement, desire, or response to influence. Much psychological literature reflects this and refers to motivation in a number of forms: primary drives, need systems, incentives, as an energiser of behaviour, and so on. Nearly fifty years ago Littman (1958) identifed fifty-two motivation terms. However, to ascribe particular motivations to people, and then to value those motivations as good, poor, high or low, both asserts a hierarchy and posits a person of separated parts. In their review of (then) contemporary schools of psychology, Woodworth with Sheehan (1931/65, p. 334) reflect that the 'problem of motivation takes on special significance when emphasis is laid upon the wholeness of the organism'. Distinct from most other schools, organismic psychology offers a unitary view of motivation: the actualising tendency. This concept, originally influenced by Goldstein's (1939) work is, as we discuss in the first part of this chapter, a first principle of person-centred psychology and, as Brodley (1999, p. 109) puts it, is 'a meta-motivation that subsumes all specific motivations'. Thus the question or debate is between those who view human beings as having a number of motivations (Freud, Jung, Klein, Maslow); those who think in terms of a sole motivating tendency (Adler, Goldstein, Angyal, Lecky, Combs and Snygg, Rogers); and, perhaps most radically, those who find it unhelpful, like Kelly (1962, pp. 83–4), who calls it 'an invented construct' for which he has 'no use'. Patterson (1964/2000a, p. 16) puts it pithily: 'There's no such thing as a lack of or absence of motivation. To be alive is to be motivated, to be unmotivated is to be dead. Thus we cannot say that a client is unmotivated.'

One problem with suggesting a number of motivations, such as Maslow's (1954) hierarchy of needs, is that they need organising. The most serious objection to the unitary theory of motivation appears to be whether maintenance and enhancement imply a dualism in the organism's tendency to actualise. Angyal (1941, p. 218) sees no problem with this: 'Human behavior, as a rule, is multiply motivated: a given activity may express more than one tendency at the same time.' Patterson too (1964/2000a, p. 16) addresses this point, arguing that 'preservation or maintenance, and enhancement or actualization may be seen as two aspects of the same motive, operating in different situations' and links this to pathology (see Chapter 6).

Traditional theories of motivation from Freud onwards tend towards tension reduction. This, in turn, is based on a negative or problematic view of tension, such as a tension between autonomy and homonomy, or between actualisation and self-actualisation (see pp. 89–91). Organisms tend rather to maintain than reduce tensions. Allport (1955) attempts to bridge these two perspectives by borrowing Maslow's (1954) distinction between *deficit* and *growth* motives. Allport suggests that, whilst growth motives maintain tensions, motives based on deficit attempt to reduce tension. This makes sense to us if we link these distinctions to the distinction between actualisation and self-actualisation. In other words, tension is a normal part of the organism's maintenance and growth. This view is backed up by neuro-scientific research which, for instance, explains the observation that it is the affective state that underlies and motivates attachment behaviour. Through the affective relationship with her child, a mother can, in effect, 'kick start' the psychic energy that activates the child's attachment and, in Schore's terms (1994, p. 104), her 'exploratory motivational systems'. At the same time, when we are more concerned with self-actualisation, we will attempt to meet the deficit caused by our differentiation along those lines. So, developing Schore's example, a child who is concerned to please her mother will anticipate her mother's need, say, for attachment, or will attempt to fill the deficit of a lack of stimulation.

Drive

A drive is generally viewed as a motivational state produced either by deprivation of a needed substance (to be desired), or the presence of something noxious or undesirable (to be avoided). This is echoed in Rogers' view of the organism's movement towards adience or avoidance. In the same years as Rogers published his paper on motivation, Butler and Rice (1963), also exploring this issue from a person-centred perspective, presented their findings on drive reduction theory and came up with the concept of 'adient motivation', which they refer to as stimulus hunger, a term also used by Berne (1964/68). Commenting on this, Browning (1966) suggests that the concept of stimulus hunger gives the actualisation concept clearer empirical specificity, while sacrificing none of its original meaning. As with motivation there is a similar debate as to whether human beings have a number of drives, such as sex and aggression, or whether there is only one, as Goldstein (1934/95) suggests. We can summarise as follows:

1   Drives are conceptualised as releasing tension.
2   The healthy organism is in a state of tension.
3   Therefore, drives are a pathological phenomenon.
4   The tendency of the sick or pathological organism to discharge tension is the only means of actualising itself (self-actualisation). This represents a drive for self-preservation.
5   The concept of different, separate drives is based on research conducted under experimental conditions on young children and animals, and represents an atomistic or decentred view of the organism.
6   Therefore there is only one *drive*, that of *self*-actualisation.

Rogers (1951, pp. 487–8), who refers to Goldstein, puts it organically: 'it seems entirely possible that all organic and psychological needs may be described as partial aspects of this one fundamental need . . . the words used are an attempt to describe the observed directional force in organic life'. Fromm (1971, p. 67) puts this in more relational terms:

Man's 'drives' . . . are an expression of a fundamental and specifically human need, the need to be related to man and nature, and of confirming himself in this relatedness . . . The need for self-realization in man is the root of the specifically human dynamism.

We see connections here between the person-centred approach's emphasis on organismic experiencing and the vegetative processes of Reichian and neo-Reichian theory and body therapies (see Chapter 2). Reich moves beyond Freud's libidinous drive theory, and reclaims sexual expression as essential to health. His concept of 'orgastic potency' (1922/83, p. 102) is clearly organismic: 'Orgastic potency is the capacity to surrender to the flow of biological energy, free of any inhibition; the capacity to discharge completely the dammed-up sexual excitation through involuntary, pleasurable convulsions of the body.' Notwithstanding the common slip of the tongue between the two words, there is a real sense in which orgasm is itself a manifestation of organismic vitality.

Consciousness

Rogers sees consciousness as a potential impediment to the full and free-flowing functioning of the organism. He concludes his view of 'the good life' and 'the fully functioning person' (1957/67, pp. 194–5) with the following lines, which describe a tension between organismic functioning and consciousness:

> Man's behavior is exquisitely rational, moving with subtle and ordered complexity toward the goals his organism is endeavoring to achieve. The tragedy for most of us is that our defenses keep us from being aware of this rationality, so that consciously we are moving in one direction, while organismically we are moving in another.

Consciousness is, basically, a state of awareness. Beyond that it is notoriously difficult to define. Psychoanalysis emerged out of Freud's neuropsychological studies of consciousness and cognition and thus consciousness holds a central place in the history of psychotherapy. However, whilst we may define consciousness as an electrochemical function of the nervous system, no amount of 'scientific' description can convey a subjective grasp of conscious experience, or what it means and feels like to have consciousness. When asked about consciousness (Evans, 1975/81), Rogers talked in terms of a range of phenomena: from those in sharp focus in awareness, which he refers to as 'the height of consciousness'; through a range of material which could be called into consciousness, but which is not figural; to phenomena which are more dimly connected with awareness, which some person-centred practitioners refer to as sitting on the 'edge of awareness'.

From a perspective based on organism, tendency and *process*, it's problematic to conceive of consciousness as a *domain* of the mind or as a *structure* of the psyche. Nonetheless, such topographical or structural views of consciousness are implicit in some person-centred thinking on the subject. For example, the 'edge of awareness' sounds similar to the notion of the preconscious, and suggests a reified view of consciousness that emphasises structure and topography rather than process. The same applies when we talk about *the* conscious, *the* preconscious, *the* subconscious, *the* unconscious, what is 'in awareness', and what is outside awareness. Another problem with traditional perspectives regarding the unconscious (or dynamic unconscious) is that it is viewed as a domain of the psyche which encompasses repressed functions and desires, primitive impulses, and memories, images and wishes which are too anxiety-provoking to be admitted into consciousness, or which have been, as it were, exiled to the unconscious.

By contrast, Rogers (1951, p. 483) says that 'consciousness consists of the symbolization of some of our experiences' and acknowledges Angyal's (1941) influence in his thinking about this. This, in turn, has its roots in James' view of consciousness not as a thing but as a process. Rogers continues:

> only a portion of that experience, and probably a very small portion of that experience, is *consciously* experienced. Many of our sensory and visceral sensations are not symbolized. It is also true, however, that a large portion of this world of experience is *available* to consciousness, and may become conscious if the need of the individual causes certain sensations to come into focus because they are associated with the satisfaction of a need.

As Whitehead (1929/78, p. 53) puts it: 'consciousness presupposes experience, and not experience consciousness'.

It is clear from this that we focus on or attend to particular elements of our perceptual field according to what we need. Panksepp (1998, p. 310) views this 'primary-process consciousness' as *'that ineffable feeling of experiencing oneself as an active agent in the perceived events of the world'*, and argues that this consciousness is rooted in low-level brain circuits 'that first represented the body as an intrinsic and coherent whole'. From a person-centred perspective, Brodley (1999) sees the capacity for such self-awareness or reflective consciousness as a salient human channel of the actualising tendency. Solms and Turnbull (2002) view consciousness as intrinsically introspective and intrinsically evaluative, which again gives a biological basis for the organism's internal valuing process. In our view this active focus or attention offers a theoretical basis for the practice of focusing (Gendlin, 1961, 1981, 1986), which demands an attention that is more active, directed and effortful than simple awareness.

Rogers distinguishes what is consciously or *explicitly* known from what is unknown or *implicitly* known, and potentially available to consciousness.

LIVERPOOL
JOHN MOORES UNIVERSITY
AVRIL ROBARTS LRC
TEL. 0151 231 4022

This distinction has been elaborated in more recent work by neuroscientists and neuropsychologists. When we remember, say, a connection between what we do now and our past, our conscious memory system is mediated by the hippocampus and related cortical areas. These areas help us to retain facts, concepts and ideas and, importantly, are involved in assessing the emotional significance of a stimulus and the meaning we attach to it, and in formulating our response. Another type of implicit, emotional memory system involves the amygdala and related structures which respond more quickly, albeit by less than a quarter of a second, through what LeDoux (1998) refers to as 'the quick and dirty route'. *A therapist informs his client that he is taking a break. Almost before he has finished his sentence, his client says angrily: 'I knew I was too much for you.' Both client and therapist know that she has been and has felt abandoned by men but hitherto they have talked about this mainly in cognitive terms, even about her fear. The client's immediate reaction to the prospect of a break in contact bypassed her usual, considered response.*

In order to understand this, we don't have to conceptualise an area called the unconscious which is full of repressed material about abandonment, or develop therapeutic techniques for 'getting to' or 'breaking through' this. We simply have to work with what becomes explicit and present, however it emerges (see Rogers, 1961/80; Gendlin, 1986; Jennings, 1986; Finke, 1990; Vossen, 1990). This is the sense of the presenting past (see Jacobs, 1998; Edelman & Tononi, 2000; Stern, 2004). In the field of psychology there has been considerable debate as to whether experience is a present phenomenon or whether it is an amalgam of past experiences. James (1890) argues that each moment of consciousness appropriates each previous moment and, furthermore, that the knower is embedded in what is known. Drawing on quantum physics, Zohar (1991, p. 104) argues that both past and present form our memory and sense of self:

> This weaving of the self moment by moment as the wave functions of past selves overlap with the wave functions of the present self is what I mean by quantum memory. It is a necessary, definitive link between our past, present and future selves, and gives us the mechanism by which we have a personal identity that abides across time. I am, in part, the person that I was yesterday because that person is woven into the fabric of my being. In quantum mechanical terms, the past has entered a 'phase relationship' with the present – because both past and present produce wave functions on the ground state of consciousness.

Although we say 'simply' (above), the provision of a therapeutic environment in which the client may react quickly rather than respond in a more considered way is no easy task (see Chapter 7). It requires the therapist to know herself and, by implication, to have space (such as supervision and/or personal therapy) in which she can process her own implicit memories, drawn from the field of her experience.

Rogers (1954/67b, p. 119) comments on the practical implications of this approach to experience and consciousness:

> In general then, it appears to be true that when a client is open to his experience, he comes to find his organism more trustworthy. He feels less fear of the emotional reactions which he has. There is a gradual growth of trust in, and even affection for the complex, rich, varied assortment of feelings and tendencies which exist in him at the organic level. Consciousness, instead of being the watchman over a dangerous and unpredictable lot of impulses, of which few can be permitted to see the light of day, becomes the comfortable inhabitant of a society of impulses and feelings and thoughts, which are discovered to be very satisfactorily self-governing when not fearfully guarded.

In their recent work on consciousness Edelman and Tononi (2000, p. 147) discuss the general properties of conscious experience, including consciousness as a differentiated process, arguing that 'the number of conscious states that we can discriminate within a fraction of a second is exceedingly large'. They go on to relate 'the extraordinary differentiation of conscious experience' to other properties such as informativeness, global access and flexibility. Again, we see in these ideas an elaboration entirely consistent with organismic psychology.

Equally, what is unconscious or not known, then, is not necessarily problematic or pathological. As Rogers acknowledges, organic processes, such as the regulation of body heat, are unconscious. Indeed, as Solms and Turnbull (2002) remind us, an entire hemisphere, or about half of the forebrain, can function unconsciously. In the same spirit, Stern (2004) distinguishes between aspects of implicit relationship that are neither conscious nor defensive nor pathological. He terms these aspects 'nonconscious', and reserves the term 'unconscious' for dynamically repressed material and, therefore, defended aspects of self.

The formative tendency

According to O'Hara (1999, p. 64):

> Rogers held the metaphysical belief that the inborn capacities for self-healing and creative agency are reflections of a formative tendency in the universe impelling all of nature – from molecules to galaxies – to evolve towards greater complexity and expanded levels of consciousness.

On these grounds, she calls Rogers a Romantic (1995, p. 134; 1999, p. 63). Finke (2002) makes the same point. Rogers' optimism about human nature, and his love of the natural world support this assertion. We can also see both the actualising tendency and, especially, the formative tendency as manifestations of nature or spirit, a typically Romantic notion. This, for instance, is Wordsworth, from Book 1 of the 1850 edition of *The Prelude* (ll. 401–4):

> Wisdom and Spirit of the universe!
> Thou Soul that art the eternity of thought,
> That givest to forms and images a breath
> And everlasting motion . . .

There are other precedents and parallels. In a sense, any cosmogony that posits a purpose or destiny to which the world is tending prefigures the formative tendency. So too does any mythical, theological or political system that assumes or asserts an order in the universe. 'All things' says Aurelius (1964, p. 106) 'are interwoven with one another; a sacred bond unites them; there is scarcely one thing that is isolated from another. Everything is coordinated; everything works together in giving form to the one universe.' Bohm (1980/83, p. xii) echoes this when he describes reality as 'a set of forms in an underlying universal movement or process'.

Whereas the actualising tendency is a universal tendency located in individual organisms, the formative tendency is assumed to animate the whole universe, organic and inorganic, sentient and non-sentient, alive and inert. Whereas the actualising tendency tends towards complexity and differentiation in the service of an individual organism's continuing health and well-being, the formative tendency tends towards form and order throughout the whole universe. Rogers (1979, p. 103) defines it as 'the ever-operating trend toward increased order and inter-related complexity evident at both the inorganic and the organic level'.

As with the organism's tendency to actualise, the language we use is significant. The universe does not *have* a formative tendency. It *is* a tendency to form, or it tends to form. Here 'form' can be verb or noun. Where form is a verb, we may say that the universe tends to form itself in an orderly or coherent way. This supposes an intelligent universe, capable of choosing order over disorder, and coherence over incoherence. Where form is a noun, we may say that the universe tends towards form, or that it tends to be orderly or coherent. This supposes a set of universal laws which result in order rather than disorder, and coherence rather than incoherence. Rogers believed in an orderly universe from early in his life, and spent much of his life seeking the order that he believed was there beneath, behind or beyond the apparently unruly.

Rogers defines in detail neither the quality of the order he believes the universe to manifest, nor the end or purpose to which he believes the world is tending. He does, however, assert (1979, p. 107) that there is both order and purpose, and suggests that 'perhaps we are touching the cutting edge of our ability to transcend ourselves, to create new and more spiritual directions in human evolution'.

We know that Rogers was influenced by Angyal. Rogers' 1959 paper in particular shows many traces of Angyal's thinking. We suspect that Rogers' notion of the formative tendency may be informed by Angyal's notion of homonomy, which is an idea that Rogers doesn't really make much of in any other way. Briefly, Angyal sees that human beings tend towards homonomy, which he describes (1941, p. 172) as 'a trend to be in harmony with superindividual units, the social group, nature, God, ethical world order, or whatever the person's formulation of it may be'. He also suggests (1941, p. 170) that in their 'religious attitude' men and women experience themselves as members 'of a meaningful cosmic order'. We've argued in an earlier chapter that even at his most apparently humanistic or existential, Rogers maintained a 'religious attitude' towards life. Angyal's formulation of an organismic tendency towards homonomy allows Rogers a place for that religious attitude. We can see the formative tendency as a development of the trend towards homonomy. If Angyal is right, and human beings tend to want to belong to something larger than themselves, then a formative tendency of which they are a part both expresses and satisfies that tendency.

Whatever view we each take of the formative tendency, it poses questions even within Rogers' own system of thinking. We've seen, for instance, that he professed some affinity with existential beliefs. It's hard to square these beliefs – in contingency, isolation and a meaningless universe – with the notion of a formative tendency, with all that that implies of order, meaning, purpose and interconnectedness. We're not saying that Rogers has to be consistent. He wrote a great deal over many years, and we'd be foolish to expect a complete consistency. We're acknowledging, though, that there are inconsistencies internal to the approach, and that those inconsistencies give each of us the opportunity, and perhaps the responsibility, to think about where we stand in relation to the approach, and in relation to the formative tendency in particular. Van Kalmthout, for instance, questions the validity of the concept. In the context of the Holocaust, and of a more recent history characterised by wars, genocides, violence and abuse, he sees (2002, p. 129) that any 'philosophy of life based on the assumption that the cosmos and the history of man have some purpose and that human nature is basically good quickly gives rise to an impression of naiveté'. Ellingham (2002, pp. 16–7) takes a different view. He suggests that the formative tendency, like Newton's idea of gravity or Darwin's idea of evolution, might serve as the central and unifying idea around which the field of psychology can unify and become a bona fide science.

These questions matter not only for us as individual practitioners, but for the approach as a whole, and perhaps for the practice of therapy more widely.

Having discussed the organism in the previous chapter and its tendency to actualise in this chapter, we now turn to the major differentiation of the organism: the self.

Chapter 4

Self

Perhaps one explanation of therapy is that the inconsistencies in self are recognized, faced, re-examined, and the self is altered in ways which bring about consistency.

Carl Rogers

[T]he self is self only because it has a world, a structured universe, to which it belongs and from which it is separated at the same time.

Paul Tillich

The paradigm instance of the self is, of course, indisputably, the organism – from primitive amoeba to highest mammal.

Freya Mathews

Not many people think about themselves in terms of organism or tendencies. Some of us, however, think about and are fascinated by ourselves – literally, our *selves*. Arguably, no subject is more personal or interesting to us than our 'self' or selves. From ancient times, philosophers have studied and debated what it means to be human and attempted to define the concept of the self, which seems to describe the core of what it means to be 'I' or 'we'. Our use of the plural pronoun in this context refers to a collective self-concept, as distinct from the individualised self-concept prevalent in narcissistic 'me' cultures (for a critique of which see Lasch, 1979), and acknowledges an awareness of an historical and cultural reference group (see Nobles, 1973). In modern times, psychologists since William James (1842–1910) have also been studying this most personal of subjects, although, as Robinson (1976/95) points out, 'self-awareness', 'self-actualisation' and related expressions of self-concern, are directly attributable to the German philosopher Georg Hegel (1770–1831) and neo-Hegelian idealists. As a background to some of the debates about self in the field of psychology, we summarise a number of contributions to understanding this subject (Appendix 2). These derive predominantly from philosophy but also include ideas from spiritual traditions, anthropology and physics.

The way in which we experience ourselves as multi-dimensional is matched, appropriately enough, by a multiplicity of theories and models of 'self' and 'the Self' in the fields of psychology and psychotherapy and within person-centred theory.

However, the capitalisation of the 'Self' implies a core, more important or higher 'Self' or, in keeping with some theories, a kind of divine presence within human beings. It tends to reify the idea and, as Van Kalmthout (1998, pp. 58–9) puts it, 'can very easily lead to abstract theoretical speculation about the characteristics of the Self, and take us far from the actual experiencing of ourselves'. From a philosophical view, Macmurray (1961/91, p. 17) argues that any conceptualisation of the 'Self' as 'the Thinker', 'the Knower', 'the Subject' or a reflective spectator is itself a 'mere idea': 'It is more illuminating to recognize it frankly as a solipsism; and to accept this solipsism for what it is – a *reduction ad absurdum* of the theoretical standpoint.' This solipsism has, nevertheless, taken hold of the imagination of psychologists, psychotherapists and lay people alike, and is somewhat less easy to dislodge than philosophers such as Macmurray and Murdoch would like. We write from a sceptical perspective, and consider in this chapter the usefulness of various definitions, concepts and constructs of self.

There is no one agreed definition or meaning of the word 'self'. In his theory of personality and behaviour, Rogers (1951, p. 497) acknowledges that 'there are many puzzling and unanswered questions in regard to the dawning concept of the self'. Winnicott (1960/65) describes the 'true self' in organismic terms: 'The true self comes from the aliveness of the body tissues and the working of body functions, including the heart's action and breathing.' Even Heinz Kohut (1913–1983), whose work led to and inspired the tradition of self psychology (see pp. 116ff.), said of his work (1977, pp. 310–11) that 'it never assigns an inflexible meaning to the term self, it never explains how the essence of the self should be defined . . . The self . . . is not knowable in its essence . . . only its introspectively or empathically perceived manifestations are open to us.'

Despite its origins in organismic psychology, within person-centred psychology in general much more has been written about the self than the organism. The *Dictionary of Person-Centred Psychology* (Tudor & Merry, 2002) reflects this in its thirty entries on 'self'-related words. Rogers wrote about the self (1951, 1959b, 1963); and one recent development in person-centred theory advances it as a therapy addressing configurations of self (Mearns, 1999). A number of writers view Rogers' theory as a 'self theory', including: Combs (1948); Hall and Lindzey (1957), although, as we noted in Chapter 2, in the third edition of their work, published in 1978, they acknowledge that the emphasis should fall on the organism; Beck (1963);

and Patterson (1965). From an organismic perspective, it is interesting that Fujio Tomoda, who was one of the main proponents of client-centred therapy in Japan, and who translated much of Rogers' work, translated 'self' as 'a living organism commonly equated with "I"' (quoted in Hayashi *et al.*, 1994, p. 4).[1]

One of the problems with the concept of self is the fact that the same word is used to describe different aspects of the human being and her experience. In his theory of personality and behaviour, Rogers (1951, p. 497) suggests that: '*A portion of the total perceptual field gradually becomes differentiated as the self.*' In this chapter, based on and grounded in the ideas about the organism and its tendency to actualise that we explored in the previous two chapters, we differentiate the concept of self. We do this first by reviewing Rogers' concept of self (including his own self-concept). We then set these in context by means of a brief history of self, which includes a comparison between self psychology and person-centred psychology. We then review more recent developments in person-centred literature, which encompass social, personal and reflective selves, self in social context, and pluralist conceptions of self. We conclude this chapter by returning to our theme of organism and environment.

Focusing on the self, personally, clinically and theoretically, carries a certain danger of being accused of being too selfish, too self-obsessed. This selfish self has been critiqued by, amongst others, Schwartz (1986). The self is seen as synonymous with the individual and individualism. Etymologically, the origins of the English word 'self' lie in the Anglo Saxon *selbha* which, Ryce-Menuhin (1988, p. 4) suggests, contains within its root 'the symbolic union of separation and belonging' or, from an organismic perspective, the tendency to autonomy *and* to homonomy. This is echoed in Jung's (1944/67, para 104) view that: 'Natural man is not a self – he is the mass and a particle in the mass, collective to such a degree that he is not even sure of his own ego.' From his study of the etymological roots of the word 'self' in a number of languages, Ryce-Menuhin (ibid., p. 5) concludes that:

> Two striking motifs emerge in the etymology of the self concept [i.e. the concept of self]: one, that of belonging to a clan but, associated with this, the notion of freedom and individuality; the other that of omnipotence of the individual self.

These motifs are reflected in the philosophy and psychology of the self and, indeed, the modern history of the study of this subject. The American

---

1 Tomoda's work has not been translated into English and hence the secondary source; see also Moore (1997).

philosopher and social psychologist George Herbert Mead (1863–1931), a younger contemporary of James who preceded Rogers at the University of Chicago, emphasised the emergence of self-consciousness in a human being through interaction with others. Since this interaction depends on the existence of language or symbol systems, his work is referred to as 'symbolic interactionism'. Although we have no evidence that Rogers ever read Mead, the influence of symbolic interactionism may be seen in Rogers' writing such as his (1959b) theory of personality. Given our emphasis on the active interchange between organism and environment (see Chapter 2), we place an equal emphasis in this chapter on understanding self in the context of its cultural and social environment.

Rogers' concept of self

The word self is used in person-centred writing in at least two ways, and it is important to distinguish between them if we are to avoid confusion. The first usage is reflexive, and carries the meaning: I did it myself. When Rogers asserts that the organism maintains itself, he means that the organism both initiates and benefits from the process of maintenance. It works, as it were, for its own good. The second usage derives from the use of the word self as a noun. Thus, when Rogers writes about self-actualisation he means the actualisation of the self. One implication of this is that the term self-actualisation can mean one of two things in any one context. It can mean:

1 that the organism self-actualises, or actualises itself; or
2 that the organism actualises its 'self', which is a conceptual element within the organism.

On the subject of the self, Rogers drew on the work of Angyal (1941), Raimy (1943, 1948), Lecky (1945) and Standal (1954), influences he acknowledges in his own work (Rogers, 1951, 1959b, 1963) and later in an interview published after his death (Rogers & Russell, 2002).[2] Rogers (1959b, p. 200) disclaims any early interest in the notion of the self, viewing it as 'a vague, ambiguous scientifically meaningless term which had gone out of the psychologist's vocabulary with the departure of the introspectionists'. However Barrett-Lennard (1998) points out that Rogers' (1931)

---

2 This acknowledgement is important as, in his presidential address to the American Psychological Association in September 1947 (later published, Rogers, 1947), Rogers drew heavily on Raimy's (1943) doctoral thesis, as he later put it (Rogers & Russell, 2002, p. 130) 'without even being aware of that'. At the time another student took him to task for this lack of acknowledgement and Rogers reports feeling 'great humiliation' about this (ibid., p. 130).

early work includes the development of a test for children approximating the concepts of actual and ideal self. In a dialogue with Rogers, Evans (1975/81, p. 16) acknowledges that Rogers was among the earliest group of individuals in psychology to emphasise the self. Rogers responds with a definition of the self. He says that it 'includes all of the individual's perceptions of his organism, of his experience, and of the way in which those perceptions are related to other perceptions and objects in his environment and to the whole exterior world'.

Significantly, this quote emphasises the unified picture of self which Rogers favoured. Whilst he acknowledges that some person-centred theorists have developed the notion of different selves, a development which has, wittingly or unwittingly, influenced some person-centred practitioners since, the notion of different selves did not have much meaning for Rogers himself. Despite Evans' acknowledgement, some texts on the self in American psychology omit Rogers even from discussions about the development of self psychology and the centrality of empathy. We discuss self psychology, including Rogers' own comments on the differences and similarities between his work and that of Kohut, below (pp. 116–23). In reviewing and advancing the concept of self in person-centred theory we aim to bring some clarity to theory and practice.

Rogers develops his theory of self in three key papers:

1   In the context of a number of propositions about personality and behaviour (Rogers, 1951), in which he views the self in the context of the *organism*.
2   In his major formulation (Rogers, 1959b), in which he defines *self* and related constructs and offers a fuller account and illustration of the history of these constructs.
3   In a paper on the *actualising tendency* (Rogers, 1963), in which he reiterates its unitary nature.

In 1951 Rogers (p. 497) describes the self as emerging from a portion of the *'total perceptual field'* and says that it is, specifically (p. 498), 'the awareness of being, of functioning':

> As a result of interaction with the environment, and particularly as a result of evaluational interaction with others, the structure of self is formed – an organized, fluid but consistent conceptual pattern of perceptions of characteristics and relationships of the 'I' or the 'me', together with the values attached to these concepts.

This definition and conceptualisation of self is based in the organism, and is highly interactive. Rogers' description of infant development in the pages following this proposition (IX) prefigures the intersubjective view of self and developmental psychologists, notably Stern (1985), by over thirty years.

Angyal (1941, p. 113) says that the self 'is symbolically elaborated by the organism and then appears as self-awareness or consciousness of self'. Our self-awareness, he suggests, extends to objects outside our bodies such as clothes and property. Furthermore, the greater my governance of an object, the greater my sense of that object belonging to me. Thus, I have more self-awareness of 'my hands' than 'my shirt', and more awareness of 'my shirt' after I have bought it than before when it was on a rack in a clothes shop. This is also true in the learning of skills or the rediscovery of lost skills: 'we ascribe a given factor to ourselves or the external world, respectively, on the basis of whether it is prevalently under autonomous or heteronymous government' (ibid., p. 114). In this we can see the psychological significance of political autonomy, self-government and independence. In his first formulation of a theory of the self, Rogers (1951, p. 497) echoes Angyal on this point: 'Whether or not an object or experience is regarded as part of the self depends to a considerable extent on whether or not it is perceived as within the control of the self.'

In the seminal paper in which he outlines his theory of therapy, personality and interpersonal relationships, Rogers (1959b) acknowledges that Raimy (1943) produced a careful and searching definition of the self-concept based on the categorising of self-attitudes. Generally, the self-concept is seen as the *mental* notion a person has about her *physical*, *psychological* and *social* attributes as well as her *attitudes*, *beliefs* and *ideas*. It comprises the image we have of ourselves, and how we value ourselves (self-esteem). Raimy (op. cit., p. 154) defines the self-concept as: '. . . the more or less organized perceptual object resulting from present and past self-observation'. Raimy's was the first objective study of change in the self-concept, and he is widely acknowledged as an innovative researcher and thinker in this field. He went on to introduce measures of self-concept in counselling interviews (Raimy, 1948), arguing that psychotherapy is basically a process of altering the ways that individuals see themselves and, some years later, he published a book on *Misconceptions of the Self* (Raimy, 1975). From Raimy's work Rogers (1959b, p. 201) took the following:

1   That self-referent attitudes alter significantly in therapy, from a predominantly negative evaluation of the self to a predominantly positive one.
2   That 'violent fluctuation' in the client's concept of self is not uncommon, even within one session.
3   That this picture of self (or 'product') was a gestalt, or configuration.

Lecky's (1945) work informed Rogers and may also be a source of confusion between concepts of organism and self. As Lecky himself (p. 75) puts it: 'There is a coherence in the behaviour of any single organism which argues against explanation in terms of chance combinations of determiners and points to an *organized dynamic subsystem* which tends toward self-determination' [our emphasis].

Rogers (1959b, p. 200) defines the self, which he equates with concept of self and self-structure, as:

> the organized, consistent conceptual gestalt composed of perceptions of the characteristics of the 'I' or 'me' and the perceptions of the characteristics of the 'I' or 'me' to others and to various aspects of life, together with the values attached to these perceptions. It is a gestalt which is available to awareness though not necessarily in awareness.

This both echoes and elaborates his 1951 proposition. A number of points follow from this:

1   The self is a concept.
2   The self is a gestalt. It is thus inherently moving between figures or what Mearns (1999) refers to as configurations (see p. 130). It is fluid, not fixed, and is constantly changing in the light of new experiences.
3   The self is also consistent. No matter how much change occurs, there remains within individuals a constant internal sense that they are still the same person at any given moment. Lecky (1945) contributed the notion that self-consistency is a primary motivating force in human behaviour; and, in his review, Barrett-Lennard (1998, p. 77) suggests that it is the organism that 'applies a criterion of consistency in organizing experience as part of the self'. Discussing the impact of time on identity, Davies (1995, p. 16) argues that 'the very concept of selfhood hinges on the preservation of personal identity through time'. The self, then, is, at any given moment, a specific entity which is definable in operational terms by means of research methods such as a 'Q sort' (see Dymond, 1954; Vargas, 1954; Rogers, 1955/67; Cartwright & Graham, 1984).
4   The self is itself perceptual. 'The self' says Murdoch (1970/85, p. 93) 'the place where we live, is a place of illusion.' This perspective echoes Macmurray's (1961/91) sceptical view of the 'Self' (see p. 127). The notion of 'I' or 'me' also carries an implicit reference to Mead's famous distinction between these two aspects of self (see p. 113).

Like a number of theoreticians in this field, Rogers was not the most rigorous or consistent in his use of language. This has given rise to confusions, interpretations and debates, and to a certain amount of textual analysis. For instance, in a paper on creativity (written in 1954), he refers to the 'real self' emerging, in response to empathic understanding and acceptance. A few years later, he wrote a paper on a therapist's view of personal goals (Rogers, 1960/67b) in which he takes his title from the existential philosopher Kierkegaard: 'To be that self which one truly is'. Although this implies that there is a true or real self, this was not the particular focus of Rogers' paper. Rogers describes his view of personal goals and purpose in terms of directions:

- away from façades (from behind which people face life); from 'oughts'; from meeting expectations; from pleasing others, and
- towards self-direction; being process; being complexity; openness to experience; acceptance of others; and trust of self.

Two aspects of this are both interesting and problematic. The first is that Rogers frames such directionality in terms of personal 'goals', implying an achieved end rather than a continuous process. Second, he mixes references to self, such as 'self-direction' and trust of 'self', as distinct from organismic direction and a trust in the organism, with references to more fluid concepts, such as 'being process' and 'being complexity'. Others have taken this as permission to think in terms of a 'real' self as distinct from a 'false' self, conditioned in response to external conditions of worth; or a 'core' self, as distinct from more peripheral selves. One term applied to this is that of the 'organismic self', a term coined by Seeman (1983), which he equates with a core sense of self, and taken up by others, including Mearns and Thorne (1998). We find this particularly unhelpful as it confuses and conflates two distinct concepts which Rogers, amongst others, strove to distinguish from each other. One implication of this conflation is, as Tolan (2002) points out, that it makes Rogers' (1951) concept of the self-structure redundant.

The other, related term which Raimy, Rogers and other researchers used at that time was the 'ideal self' or 'ideal self-concept'. Again, this is not to be confused with Maslow's concept of self-actualisation, that is, the achievement of an ideal state. According to Butler and Haigh (1954, p. 56), who conducted research into the relationship between self-concepts and ideal concepts consequent upon client-centred counselling, the ideal self-concept is:

> the organized conceptual pattern of characteristics and emotional states which the individual consciously holds as desirable (and non desirable) for himself. The assumption is that the individual is able to order his self-perceptions along a continuum of value from 'what I would most like to be' to 'what I would least like to be' or, more briefly, from 'like my ideal' to 'unlike my ideal'.

In other words the ideal self = self-concept + added value.

Rogers' third major paper on the self, 'The actualizing tendency in relation to "motives" and to consciousness', was written in 1963. Mearns (2002, p. 15) views this paper as 'extremely important for students of the approach in that it documents the qualitative change of emphasis in Rogers' thinking that heralded his forsaking of the university sector and the move to California'. In it Rogers (1963, pp. 19–20) characterises the actualising tendency as purely positive and acknowledges that his thinking has changed:

> Ten years ago I was endeavoring to explain the rift between self and experience, between conscious goals and organismic directions, as something natural and necessary, albeit unfortunate. Now I believe that individuals are culturally conditioned, rewarded, reinforced, for behaviors which are in fact perversions of the natural directions of the unitary actualizing tendency.

In other words estrangement and dissociation are learned, and are the basis for all psychological and social pathology. Bifurcated systems and theoretical concepts (conscious, unconscious; self, experiencing process) are also the result of particular social learning and, as it were, constitute theoretical pathology. Although he does not say this directly, as far as the theory of self is concerned, this paper constitutes a reassertion of his organismic view whereby self is the awareness of being organism and of the functioning organism.

Rogers' theory of development

One purpose of any theory of self is in what it has to say about our development: literally, our self-development. For Rogers (1951, p. 498), the self is 'the awareness of being, of functioning' and is thus synonymous with self-awareness and self-experience (see also Chapter 3 regarding consciousness). As self is a differentiated portion of the perceptual field (Rogers, 1951, 1959b), our sense of self is born out of differentiation: 'This is my arm . . . when I lift my arm to my face I feel my skin . . . I am my arm . . . my arm is part of me.' Stern (1991) describes this well in his *Diary of a Baby*, his inventive version of his earlier theoretical work (Stern, 1985) (see pp. 123ff.).

Rogers (1959b, p. 223) continues: 'This representation in *awareness* of being and functioning, becomes elaborated, through interaction with the environment, particularly the environment composed of significant others, into a *concept of self*, a perceptual object in [the individual's] *experiential field*.' With regard to human development, Rogers did not greatly elaborate this. In his 1959 paper he devoted just over a page to 'Postulated

Characteristics of the Human Infant'. Nevertheless, his idea of representations prefigures the work of neuroscientists and self psychologists.
Compare, for example, Siegel (1999, p. 167):

> These complex conceptual representations are an important part of the
> information processing of the mind. They . . . are created by the
> computations of the mind in its interactions with the world and other
> people within it. In this sense, sensory-perceptual representations
> attempt to symbolize the mind's creation of ideas and of the mind itself.

For an infant, non-verbal experiencing initially comprises a relatively
undifferentiated totality of sensations and perceptions that constitute
reality for that infant. At 6 weeks a sighted baby can see well and is aware
of different colours, shapes and intensities. Later, interaction with significant others results in part of the infant's experiencing becoming differentiated into a 'self' or 'self-concept'. Later still, perceptions become
discriminated as being related to 'me' or 'I', perceptions which Rogers
termed 'self-experiences'. The development of self is based on differentiation and the elaboration of the individual's being and functioning, through
interaction with their environment and especially their significant others.
We consider that Stern's (1985) work, based as it is on the infant's interpersonal interactions with her environment, with its reference to 'representations of interactions which are generalised' (RIGs), is an elaboration of
the development of self, consistent with Rogers' theory. Interestingly, from
our present perspective, in the second, revised edition of his work, Stern
(2000) echoes Rogers when he refers to RIGs as 'ways-of-being-with'.

   Following his postulated characteristics of the human infant and comments on the development of the self, Rogers (1959b) describes the conditions required for the development of personality. This theory may be viewed
as an unfolding cycle of self-development, which we elaborate with some
commentary:

The awareness of self emerges.

⟶ The individual develops a need for positive regard . . .

Rogers views the need for positive regard as universal in humans, and
pervasive and persistent in individuals. Standal (1954), who developed the
concept, argues that this need is learned. For Rogers whether it is inherent
or learned is irrelevant to theory of its satisfaction.

⟶ . . . which is reciprocal (⟷) . . . and potent.

Its potency is based on Rogers' (ibid., p. 224) view that 'the *positive regard*
of any social other is communicated to the total *regard complex* which the

individual associates with that social other'. He goes on to suggest that this can become more compelling than the organism's internal valuing process, with the result that the individual can become more adient to the positive regard of others. This is why, as therapists, it is more important to focus on the value the client gives to the emotion, than on the emotion itself (see also Keil, 1996).

⟶ The individual comes to experience positive regard independently as self-regard . . .

⟶ . . . which develops out of the association of self-experiences with the need for positive regard.

⟶ Thus the individual experiences positive regard and its loss independently of transactions with social others.

Rogers (ibid., p. 224) states that, in this regard, 'The individual becomes in a sense his own significant social other. This is similar to the notion in object relations theory of the internalised self-object.'

⟶ Rogers (ibid., p. 224) continues: 'When *self-experiences* are discriminated by significant others as being more or less worthy of *positive regard*, then *self-regard* becomes similarly selective' . . .

⟶ . . . and when an experience is avoided or sought solely on this basis, then the individual acquires a 'condition of worth'.

We consider the effect of such conditions on the development of self disorders in Chapter 6. Rogers (ibid., p. 224) concludes this section of his theoretical outline of self-development with a comment that if no conditions of worth developed then '*self-regard* would never be at variance with *organismic evaluation*'.

Rogers' self-concept

Before leaving Rogers' view of self and self-concept, we want to comment briefly on his own self-concept. The notion that 'all theory is autobiographical' is not new. Indeed in the field of psychology, there was a series of volumes published between 1930 and 1967 under the title *A History of Psychology in Autobiography*, to volume five of which (Boring & Lindzey, 1967), Rogers (1967) contributed a chapter. He describes himself (p. 343) as:

> fundamentally positive in my approach to life; somewhat of a lone wolf in my professional activities; socially rather shy but enjoying close

LIVERPOOL
JOHN MOORES UNIVERSITY
AVRIL ROBARTS LRC
TEL. 0151 231 4022

relationships; capable of a deep sensitivity in human interaction though not always achieving this; often a poor judge of people, tending to overestimate them; possessed of a capacity for setting other people free, in a psychological sense; capable of a dogged determinism in getting work done or in winning a fight; eager to have an influence on others but with very little desire to exercise power or authority over them.

In a critical reflection on Rogers' life and major work, Holland (1977, p. 70) suggests that 'client-centred therapy is modelled precisely on the man himself: its goal a continuous process of movement away from the expectations and values of others toward self-determining, self-respecting (actualising) choice'. Examining Rogers' own self-concept, Holland (ibid., 1977, p. 71) observes that throughout his life: 'There is a clear direction here of retreat from external and religious principles into the self. "The theme of retreat" he is saying, "is a constant one."' Elsewhere, Rogers (1980a) describes certain qualities of the 'person of tomorrow', including: having a scepticism regarding science and technology; having a closeness to and a caring for nature; having authority within; being anti-institutional; and being fundamentally indifferent to material things. These qualities reflect something of Rogers' own personality, and have informed and influenced the development of person-centred thinking. We take issue with some of the consequences of this. We don't, for instance, believe that person-centred therapy is necessarily sceptical of science and technology. As therapists, we need to deal with science, new science, technology and the industrial, even post-industrial world; with external authority; and with materialism. Just as in art it is necessary to kill your father, so in psychology it is necessary to 'kill' the euhemerus or dead primal leader in order to revitalise and enhance his theory.

Before turning our attention to other developments on self within the person-centred approach, we offer a brief history of the self in order to place these developments in their intellectual and environmental context.

A brief history of self

Me, myself, I[3]

James discriminates two aspects of the self: the self as known (the empirical self or ego, or 'me') and the self as knower (the pure ego, or 'I'), a distinction which Zimring (1988) echoes and explores within person-centred

3 This heading not only echoes the title of a song by Joan Armatrading but also represents what Harré (1998) refers to as an ontology of selfhood: self 3, self 2 and self 1, respectively.

psychology (see pp. 125–6). Mead (1934) also distinguishes between these words, but on the basis of different arguments. James suggests that the known self comprises:

- The material me – body, clothes, our immediate family, home, and property.
- The social me – based on the recognition we get from others: 'Properly speaking, *a man has as many social selves as there are individuals who recognize him*, and carry an image of him in their mind' (James, 1892/ 1999, p. 70). The centrality of recognition has echoes in the work of Eric Berne (1910–1970), the founder of transactional analysis, who suggests that recognition is, alongside our need for stimulus (contact and sex), structure and incident, one of a number of inherent 'human hungers'.
- The spiritual me – the entire collection of my states of consciousness, which, in James' description, is close to our present understanding of the organism.

For Mead (1934, p. 175), 'The "I" is the response of the organism to the attitudes of the others; the "me" is the organized set of attitudes of others which one himself assumes.' Thus, the 'me' part of the self comprises all those incoming messages and attitudes that are carried and presented by significant others in the context of our interactions with them. We necessarily introject these messages and attitudes, and thus the 'me' cannot be anything but conformist. It is the way in which social institutions and cultural mores 'get inside' us.

James (ibid., p. 74) describes the self as knower as 'that which at any given moment *is* conscious . . . In other words, it is the *Thinker*.' Martel (1996, p. 2) catches this well:

I became aware of a voice inside my head. What is this, I wondered. Who are you, voice? When will you shut up? I remember a feeling of fright. It was only later that I realized that this voice was my own thinking, that this moment of anguish was my first inkling that I was a ceaseless monologue trapped within myself.

This sense of self-consciousness derives from the consciousness we have about what we often refer to as our 'self'. Despite his differentiation of a 'self as knower' James (1890) concludes that there is not a substantive self which is distinct from the sum total of experiences. 'Each moment of consciousness' he says, 'appropriates each previous moment, and the knower is thus somehow embedded in what is known: the thoughts themselves are the thinker.'

Along with other critics of James, we consider his argument inconsistent. Passing thoughts cannot regard themselves. The logic of James' analysis of self and, indeed, of other philosophers who predate James, such as Kant, who introduces the term 'transcendental Ego', is that the self as knower is a synthesising or integrating part of the self: a self of selves. Famously, the term 'ego' is used by Freud to describe one of three systems of the personality (the others being the id and the superego), which fulfils an executive function, based on the 'reality principle'; and which identifies the appropriate satisfaction of needs, by means of the 'secondary process' of realistic thinking. In his critique of the concept of self, Allport (1955, p. 55), who frames his discussion in the language of personality (see Chapter 5), concludes that 'what is unnecessary and inadmissable is a self (or soul) that is said to perform acts, to solve problems, to steer conduct, in a trans-psychological manner, inaccessible to psychological analysis'.

Theories of knowledge

This debate about the self has its origins in debates about what is known, what can be known and how we know things, in other words: epistemology or the theory of knowledge. The epistemological debate between rationalism and empiricism (see Table 4.1) concerns the extent to which senses contribute to knowledge. Rationalism, which dates back to the work of Plato, does not trust senses because they can be deceptive; argues that reason alone provides real knowledge, and that mathematics is the paradigm of real knowledge; and asserts that there are innate ideas. Empiricism, the origins of which may be traced back to the work of Aristotle, argues, on the other hand, that senses are the primary or only source of knowledge, and that mathematics deals only with the relation of ideas; and that there are no innate ideas. In his work, which brought together ideas from both traditions, Kant (1781/2005) argues:

- That both rationalism and empiricism are wrong when they claim that we can know things *per se*, that is, in themselves. Kant demonstrates that the mind constructs our experience, and thus may be viewed as the forerunner of modern and postmodern constructivism (see Chapter 1).
- That rationalists are wrong not to trust senses. In the phenomenal world senses are all we have.
- That rationalists are right about innate ideas. Kant distinguishes between the *phenomenal* world (the world for the agent), and the *noumenal* world (the world in itself, outside consciousness).
- That both traditions overlook the fact that the human mind is limited by *a priori* constraints of location in space, time, causality and identity.

James' idea of 'self as knower' appears consistent with Kant's reworking of the rationalist view of innate ideas. When people refer to the 'real self', they are wittingly or unwittingly, drawing on the rationalist tradition of philosophy. Furthermore, this 'real' self, as part of the noumenal world, is itself outside consciousness. On this basis, when we realise or 'discover' something about ourselves, we bring it into consciousness, and thus it becomes part of our phenomenal world. Whenever someone says 'I never thought of it like that' they are bringing something new into their pheno-menal field. We place the word 'discover' in inverted commas to highlight the view that, in this context, what is discovered is, in some way, created. Columbus did not 'discover' the New World. He set foot on land that was known to those who lived there, and unknown to others. Furthermore, 'the New World' is a construction. Freud did not 'discover' the unconscious. It is a theory and does not exist as land does. Also, in the sentence 'I never thought of it like that', 'I' is the subject, the knower and claimant of the new thought or perception. However, this promotes a somewhat hierarchical model whereby 'I' is, to use von Broembsen's (1999) phrase, 'the sovereign self', and one which leaves the 'I' 'self as knower/organiser' itself as unknown and, therefore, an innate idea. Later, existential philosophy counters this abstract universal Self with the notion of authenticity, which, precisely because of existential objections to objective and objectifying language, resists positive definition (see Golomb, 1995).

Different concepts of self

What these ideas and theories describe is the sense we attempt to make of our daily experience of ourselves in a number of ways.

- 'I feel great: alive and whole' – This describes a view of a 'whole self' akin to Masterson's (1985, p. 15) concept of the self: 'The sum total of self representations in intimate connection with the sum total of object relations.'
- 'You know, I feel more myself when I'm with you' – This describes a sense of self which is inextricably and interdependent on an other and, from a developmental point of view, necessarily so: 'I am because we are.' On an individual level, this is the self of object relations: a self which is only developed interpersonally, initially with undifferentiated part-objects such as the mother's nipple (or 'nibble' as one child put it!). On a wider level, we relate this to cultural perspectives on social psychology which emphasise a 'we'-concept (see, for instance, Nobles, 1973).
- 'I like myself in this: it's the new me' – This implies a changing, moving sense of self or selves. Implied in this notion is the view, and the phenomenological experience, that we can 'cathect' or put energy into

different aspects of our personality (see Federn, 1952; Berne, 1961/75). Rogers' (1951) model of the total personality is one of way of describing such shifts of energy; Berne's ego state model is another.

These examples reflect three of Clarkson and Lapworth's (1992) interrelated concepts of self: whole, interpersonally developed, and moving. We refer to the others in Chapter 6. In their conceptualisation, they also view the self as the organising principle of physis, which we view as the organismic tendency to actualise, as distinct from self-actualisation (see Chapter 3).

Self psychology

In general terms, 'self psychology' describes any approach to psychology which places the self as the central concept of its theory. More specifically, it refers to a development in psychology which has its roots in psychoanalysis, but which places empathy rather than interpretation at the centre of its method and practice. In this way, self psychology has helped reclaim and relocate the curative role of empathy in the wider fields of psychoanalysis and psychotherapy. From a person-centred perspective this is a welcome development and, indeed, much of the writing in this field echoes Rogers' own writings and even phrases. This is not without its irony, however, as the contribution of Rogers and other person-centred psychologists to the understanding and development of empathy goes entirely unacknowledged by Kohut himself, and is rarely acknowledged or referenced by other self psychologists. Tobin (1991) reminds us that Rogers and Kohut were both at the University of Chicago between 1945 and 1957 and whilst there is no record of or reference to the fact that the two men themselves ever met, Elizabeth Kohut, a psychologist and Kohut's wife, did have some contact with Rogers. Tobin also observes that in his work Kohut refers to few other writers who influenced him, so his lack of acknowledgement of Rogers may not have been a specific lapse or slight. Less understandable is the continued lack of cross-referencing amongst more recent self psychologists. In one volume edited by Jackson (1991), only one contributor (Donner, 1991) quotes Rogers (once) on empathy. We are not claiming that Rogers 'discovered' empathy since, as a concept, it is to be found in the work of Freud (1912/58), Jacobson (1964), Winnicott (1965) and others. From a personal perspective, Rogers (1986) comments on some similarities he sees between himself and Kohut; and a number of other writers have commented on similarities and differences between the two psychologies (Stolorow, 1976; Graf, 1984; Kahn, 1985, 1989a, 1989b, 1996; Bohart, 1991; Tobin, 1991; Warner, 1997, 2000; Kahn & Rachman, 2000; Stumm, 2002). Generally, Kohut's work is seen as offering a bridge between psychoanalysis and humanistic psychology. Here we summarise the key concepts of self psychology, acknowledging that, as a field, this too is changing, and compare them with a person-centred theory of therapy.

Originally developed by Kohut, self psychology breaks from Freudian theory in arguing that archaic narcissism is not transformed into object-love but rather is a developmental driving force. Kohut postulates that if parents and/or significant others are empathically responsive or attuned to the infant, then the child transforms necessarily narcissistic needs, and narcissistic experiences, into a cohesive and dynamic self-structure including healthy self-love. This is akin to Rogers' (1959b) description of the development of positive self-regard (see pp. 110–11). In this sense self psychology puts the self, rather than instinctual drives, ego or object relations, at the centre of psychological concerns, theory and method, and is thus viewed by Pine (1988, 1990) as a fourth psychology of psychoanalysis.

Rogers acknowledges that he shares with Kohut a view of human nature as a constructive, assertive whole. Kohut's healthy re-reading and reclaiming of rage as a response to narcissistic injury, rather than as an untamed aggressive drive, also finds resonance in Rogers' positive motivational psychology.

In self psychology the self is viewed as a psychic 'self-structure' at the core of the personality which is 'experience-near' (Kohut, 1984), or close to a person's experiencing. This compares with Rogers' (1951) theory of personality with its self-structure based on the symbolisation of experience. Masterson's (1988, p. 23, original emphasis) definition of the real self, from a perspective which integrates object relations and self psychology, is striking in its echo of a person-centred understanding of self: 'the real self . . . is made up of *the sum of the intrapsychic images of the self and of significant others, as well as the feelings associated with those images, along with the capacities for action in the environment guided by those images*'.

In terms of human development and personality, Kohut proposes three 'sectors' or constituents of the self-structure, together with their corresponding sets of needs: the grandiose-exhibitionist; the twinship or alterego; and the idealising. Table 4.1 summarises these sets of needs, the child's needs in these sectors, and the maturational process.

Kohut refers to 'others' as 'selfobjects' because they function in an internalised/symbolised way as part of the self. Thus a child needs (1) to be able to internalise the qualities of a 'good enough' parent, and (2) to be able to idealise material selfobjects in her world. This is why an empathic parent or carer, and toys, are both important. The parent or carer needs to respond to the needs of the child and to do so empathically. What Kohut refers to as 'transmuting internalisation' on the part of the child is based on the parent maintaining a relationship of consistent 'empathic intuneness'. An empathic response is more important than necessarily meeting the child's needs. It is neither possible nor desirable to meet all a child's needs;

Table 4.1 Self-structure, needs and maturational processes in self psychology

'Sectors' of self (Kohut)	Need	Maturational processes
Grandiose-exhibitionist	For mirroring, echoing and admiration	Dependent upon receiving confirming or mirroring responses from significant others[a]
Twinship or alterego	To identify and affiliate with the parent[b,c]	Dependent upon being in the presence of a benign human presence
Idealising	To be allowed to idealise the parent, and to merge with the parent's perceived omnipotence	Dependent upon receiving responses that soothe and calm the child's fear and anxieties

Notes

a It is interesting to note that, following his dialogue with Martin Buber in 1957, Rogers (1958/67b) adopted the term 'confirmation' to refer to the acceptance of the person as a process of becoming. Also, despite Rogers' (1951) critique of transference, he was, as Stolorow (1976) points out, skillful at fostering what self psychology refers to as 'mirror transferences'.

b This has echoes both of Rank's (1914, 1941) work on the twin or double, and of Bion's (1961) concept of twinning in a group.

c Tobin (1991) observes that the following quote from Rogers (1951, p. 42) could have been made by a self psychologist as a summary of a mirroring selfobject transference: 'the therapist endeavors to keep himself out, as a separate person . . . to understand the other so completely that he becomes almost an alter ego of the client'.

sometimes we will gratify them, sometimes we will frustrate them. This is a process described by Kohut as one of 'optimal frustration', a phrase which has echoes of Perls' notion of the 'safe emergency' of therapy. As Lynch (1991, p. 19) puts it: 'This process of empathic attunement informs the selfobject as to what kinds of responses may be in the child's interest; it is empathy that guides which response is made.' Indeed, it is dealing with the alternating combination of gratification and frustration of needs that leads to mature self-development or becoming fully functioning. On the other hand, someone experiencing persistent and pervasive empathic failure as a child is likely to develop a disorder of the self-structure, a subject which, together with the concept of selfobject transferences, we discuss in Chapter 6. Kohut believes that people never stop needing selfobjects and suggests (Kohut, 1984) that analysis cures people in so far as it helps us find and use selfobjects that are appropriate. It follows from this that empathy is the key therapeutic tool. Donner (1991, pp. 53–4) states that:

In any therapy in which relationship serves as the crucible for change, empathy is imperative, as it is the connection which sparks the relationship. Without empathy there is no meaningful relationship and no access to experiences and data by which the self becomes known. Only empathy can offer a convincingly safe invitation to a meeting attended by patient and therapist in which the subjective world of the patient creatively unfolds. As such, empathy is a prerequisite for all other therapeutic interventions.

For her part, the child also needs to be able to idealise material selfobjects in her world. This is facilitated initially through her projection of qualities (good, bad and ugly!) onto her toys.

In Chapter 7 we take up the issue of whether it is empathy or contact that sparks the relationship. Ornstein (1986) sees empathetic (*sic*) interpretations as comprising three components: acceptance, understanding and explanation. Again, this is similar to Rogers' notion of empathic *understanding* (as distinct from empathy) and his distinction between empathy and emotional identification. This has been developed further by Greenberg and Elliot (1997) who identify four forms of empathic responding in addition to understanding: evocation, exploration, conjecture and interpretation. Similarly, Stern (1985, p. 145) identifies four distinct and probably sequential cognitive processes to empathy: '(1) the resonance of feeling state; (2) the abstraction of empathic knowledge from the experience of emotional resonance; (3) the integration of abstracted empathic knowledge into an empathic response; and (4) a transient role identification'. He argues that, whilst affect attunement shares with empathy the initial process of emotional resonance, they are different processes in that attunements occur largely out of awareness. Kohut's own views on empathy changed from the date of his first essay on the subject (1959) to his last address (published in 1981), for more on which see MacIsaac (1997) and Chapter 7.

It also follows from this theory that empathic failures are important opportunities for what Donner (1991, p. 66) refers to as 'optimal responsiveness':

> The intensity of the response to something . . . quite minor serves as a clue that the selfobject tie has been disrupted and that the event has evoked something psychically meaningful. This is an opportunity to discover with readily available affect something very significant about the self . . . [and] a patient's selfobject needs, which have suddenly been pushed into awareness.

Haule (1996) argues that therapy breaks down when empathy breaks down, and that it's the second breakdown that is more important. A therapist's misunderstanding of a client, although significant, and painful, may not be crucial. A therapist who misunderstands that a client has previously felt misunderstood risks compromising the relationship to the point of breakdown. To acknowledge such ruptures in the relationship is, often, the therapy. Whilst it may be important for a therapist to apologise for an apparent mistake, it may also be important not to apologise too quickly, so as to allow a client time or space to feel whatever he feels about the empathic failure or misattunement, and to reflect upon what it might mean for him.

Beech and Brazier (1996, p. 338) argue something similar. On the basis that the therapist's role is to help the client to see her world more fully, they suggest that therapists do this most effectively by being alongside but separate from the client, in effect offering 'a second viewpoint on the client's world, giving a fuller experience than the client has hitherto been able to achieve.' They continue: 'The slight inaccuracies in the therapist's understanding of the client's world view provide the second viewpoint which serves to increase the clarity of its perception.'

Whilst Rogers himself acknowledged that he shared with Kohut many common ideas about the self and the restructuring of the self through therapy, he criticises Kohut for, as he views it, his lack of interest in the testability of his theories. Specifically, Rogers cites Kohut's theory of the 'grandiose self' and the 'idealised parent image' as examples of this. Rogers argues that as we can never enter the infant's conceptual world to verify this, such theory exists only in a speculative realm. However, Graf (1984) suggests that Kohut's self psychology goes beyond Rogers', especially in his notions of creativity and healthy creative tension, and idealising conceptual processes which guide ideals and values. Graf (p. 7) concludes that a synthesis of Rogers and Kohut would 'create a more comprehensive humanistic theory of healthy self functioning'. Also comparing the two, Kahn (1985) argues that Kohut provides more depth and complexity to our understanding of the self. In two separate contributions Warner (1997, 2000) offers articulations between person-centred therapy and self psychology with specific reference to working with clients with 'fragile process', a theory which has parallels in gestalt psychology and the work of Beaumont (1993) on 'fragile self process'. We discuss her elaborations of empathy in Chapter 7. The similarities and differences between the person-centred psychology of Rogers and the self psychology of Kohut and others are summarised, respectively, in Tables 4.2 and 4.3.

Most of the commentators cited conclude that person-centred therapy has something to gain from studying self psychology. We agree with this, specifically regarding:

1   A more detailed and robust understanding of self and self processes. In this sense many of Kohut's (1971, 1977, 1981) views may be taken as an elaboration which is consistent with Rogers' (1951, 1959b) outline of self and personality.
2   The value of understanding the client's idealisation of the therapist in terms of a deep-seated need. This is consistent with Rogers' (1951) perspective on behaviour and needs (see also Chapter 2).
3   The usefulness of the concept of narcissistic rage, which, as Stumm (2002) reminds us, does not diminish in its intensity when the present

Table 4.2 Similarities between the person-centred psychology of Rogers and the self psychology of Kohut and others

Person-centred psychology (Rogers)	Self psychology (Kohut)
Human nature	
– is essentially constructive,	
although Kahn (1985) and Stumm (2000) argue that Kohut	
is more pessimistic in his view of the human condition	
Re phenomenology and phenomenological method	
– primacy given to this	
(see Rogers, 1941; Kohut, 1959)	
Self	
is holistic (see Rogers, 1986)	
The total personality comprises experience and self-structure (Rogers, 1951)	'Experience-near' concept of the self (Kohut, 1984)
Self-development	
– both have a field theoretical view (see Tobin, 1991)	
Positive self-regard (see Rogers, 1959b)	Healthy narcissism (see Kohut, 1971)
Defence	
Two defences (denial and distortion) which are protective and self-preserving in the interests of the survival of the self	Defence is an adjustment
Psychological climate	
– both emphasise its importance	
Empathy and emotional identification	
– there is distinction between these	
(see Rogers, 1951) (see Stolorow, Brandschaft & Atwood, 1987)	
Empathic understanding	Empathetic interpretation (Ornstein, 1986)
Application of theories to societal issues	
(see Tobin, 1991)	

perceived threat is removed. As with other concepts, such as sexual undertones in the therapeutic relationship, or the extent of the therapist's own injured feelings, the usefulness of the concept or any theory is gauged against whether it enhances the therapist's empathy (see Mearns, 1997).

4   Its understanding and support for the disruption and restoration of the therapeutic relationship. Whilst this is outlined by Rogers (1959b), it is

Table 4.3 Differences between the person-centred psychology of Rogers and the self psychology of Kohut and others

Person-centred psychology (Rogers)	Self psychology (Kohut)
Philosophical/intellectual background	
Existential, humanistic frame of reference	Background in psychoanalytic ego psychology
The potential of human beings	
Belief in the organism's tendency to actualise	Kohut's concept of the 'tragic person' is less optimistic
Growth and outcome of therapy	
In the direction of greater independence and separation (autonomy)	Interdependence – from Kohut's ideas about necessary dependency of the self on external sources
See Tobin (1991) and Stumm (2000) on the impact of the respective personalities of the founders on this theory	
Theory of change/cure	
Expansion of consciousness	Strengthening of the self
Self	
Changing, perceptual view (Rogers, 1951)	As bi-polar configuration (Kohut, 1977)
Self-development	
Focus is in the present therapeutic situation	Shows that certain categories of parental behaviours are also necessary attitudes for therapists
Theory of disturbance – Aetiology	
Deficit model	Dissociation model
Empathy	
The therapist's attempt to perceive the internal frame of reference of the other is itself curative (see Rogers, 1959b)	Viewed as an 'information-gathering activity' (Kohut, 1982) . . . and in order to make good interpretations
(see also Warner, 1997, and Chapter 7)	
Transference	
The therapist endeavours to understand and accept transference attitudes but does not foster dependence	Transference is a manifestation of the patient's manner of organising her experience
Theory and research methodology	
Importance given (especially by Rogers) to theories being testable by empirical means and operationalised (see Rogers, 1986)	Subjective experience is only accessible through introspection and empathy
Re therapeutic method	
Against interpretation	Against unempathic interpretations but in favour of genetic interpretations linking present events with past experiences

more elaborated in self psychology and by intersubjective theorists such as Stolorow (1976), Sapriel (1998) and Orange, Atwood and Stolorow (2001).

5   The challenge of Kohut's emphasis on introspection and subjectivity for person-centred approaches to research.

Intersubjective senses of self

Based on infant observation, and on theories from psychoanalytic self psychology and developmental psychology, Stern (1985, 2000) suggests how an individual's sense of self develops. He describes four ways in which the self is experienced. The major contributions of Stern's work are:

1   A layered, as distinct from a stage, model of development. For Stern (2000, p. xi), this 'assumes a progressive accumulation of senses of the self, socioaffective competencies, and ways-of-being-with-others . . . [which] remain with us throughout the life span'. One implication of this, which supports much person-centred practice, is that we live and can access 'developmental issues' in the present and, therefore, do not need to do past-centred therapeutic work by means of techniques which encourage retrogression (a return to a type of behaviour characteristic of an earlier time in a person's development) or regression (a change to an earlier, younger behaviour, irrespective of whether the person has actually behaved like that, and opposite to development). The distinction between the two comes from Barker, Dembo and Lewin (1941) and suggests that what many psychotherapists refer to as 'regression' is, in their terms, 'retrogression'.

2   The view that self/other differentiation begins at birth. As we discussed in Chapter 2 this refocuses personal and professional interest on increasing relatedness which, again, is in line with our reading of Rogers and, before him, Angyal (1941). As for such process beginning at birth, we take this logic further and say that this differentiation begins at conception (see Tudor, 2003), and that organism/other differentiation, and attachment and relatedness take place *in utero*, both literally and psychologically. Stern (2000, p. xiii) argues that this layered, process theory 'places more emphasis on strategies and problems in attachment when viewing pathology, and it minimizes, even does away with, the need to conceptualize phases of "normal autism," "primary narcissism," and "symbiosis."' Again, this supports the person-centred critique of the traditional medical/psychiatric and psychoanalytic models of diagnosis.

3   The importance of the non-verbal. Stern (ibid., p. xiv) describes a natural tension, 'a sort of zone of turbulence', where the verbal and

non-verbal meet. On the one hand, we know the impact of non-verbal communication: some studies put the non-verbal communication of the meaning of a message as high as 90% (see Fromkin & Rodman, 1983). On the other hand, most forms of psychotherapy, including person-centred therapy, are primarily 'talking therapies'. On the one hand, units of human behaviour are miniscule: observers of babies have been working with smaller and smaller behavioural units, currently looking at fractions of seconds. Larger units of time often appear to be repetitions of these smaller units. On the other hand, psychotherapists tend to deal with the larger picture of patterns of behaviour over time and our reflection on and understanding of these. Talking is only one mode of communication and other forms of expression in therapy would appear an essential complement to talking if we are to facilitate pre-verbal and non-verbal experience and experiencing. 'What we cannot speak about' says Wittgenstein (1922/74, p. 89) 'we must pass over in silence.' Zuckerkandl (1973, p. 66), a musicologist, disagrees: 'Not at all: what we cannot speak of we can sing about.' Stern (2000) himself acknowledges the usefulness of non-verbal psychotherapies involving dance, music, body and movement. Natalie Rogers (1993/2000) brings the expressive arts to person-centred therapy, in what she refers to as *The Creative Connection*. We see this as an important development in encouraging the holistic expression of whole organisms.

4   The emphasis on intersubjectivity. Based on observation and clinical practice, Stern (1985) presented evidence for the idea that internal objects are constructed from patterns which are interactive and inter-subjective. In 1985 he introduced the concept of 'representations of interactions which are generalised' (RIGs) which (in 2000, p. xv) he subsequently refers to 'ways-of-being-with', thereby 'deemphasizing the process of formation in favor of describing the lived phenomenon in a more experience-near and clinically useful way'. The emphasis on 'experience-near' phenomena echoes Kohut directly and, as we have discussed above, Rogers indirectly. The emphasis on intersubjectivity represents a move from a focus on internalisations to interactive and co-created experiences (see Summers & Tudor, 2000).

From Stern's observation and experience, the child enjoying healthy development has, by the age of two, a full, multi-faceted sense of herself. Throughout life, relationships and experiences can either enhance or impede the repair or further development of different aspects of the sense of self. Stern proposes an account, based on an organising principle which concerns the subjective sense of self in relation to self-and-other, comprising four senses of self and domains of relatedness which build one upon the other. Whilst he suggests (1985, p. 32) that there are formative phases in the development of self up to and around fifteen months, 'once formed, the domains remain forever as distinct forms of experiencing social life and the self. None are [*sic*] lost to adult experience'.

The self in person-centred literature

Against this psychological history of self, in this part of the chapter we consider, in chronological order, a number of different theoretical views of self found in person-centred literature.

Self-concept as a cognitive structure

Cartwright and Graham (1984) consider the self-concept as a structure of cognitions about the self in which there is a hierarchy of categories based on decreasing levels of generality. Thus, they argue, 'I am different from others' is the highest category of generality. Other beliefs such as 'I can't decide' or 'I don't face things' represent less general categories. Each of these will be based on the evidence of experience. A childhood experience of not being able to choose, for example, might lead to the first of these beliefs, and an experience of being allowed to stay off school when things were difficult might lead to the second.

Social, personal – and reflexive – selves

As we have seen, the notion that the self is essentially and developmentally *social* has its origins in the work of James and Mead. James first distinguished between 'I' (self as knower) and 'me' (self as known). For Mead (1934) there are two aspects of the self: 'the "I" is the response of the organism to the attitudes of others; the "me" is the organized set of attitudes of others which one himself assumes' (p. 175). Broadly then, we may take 'me' as the *social self*, or *myself* as others see me and as 'me' perceives, accommodates, assimilates and integrates the perceptions of me of these 'significant others'.

In an article arguing that we attain mastery by shifting from 'me' to 'I', Zimring (1988) compares 'me' and 'I' modes of functioning (see Table 4.4). Interestingly, mastery over one's environment was one of Marie Jahoda's (1958) concepts and determinants of positive mental health.

To complete the picture, we suggest that 'myself' is the *reflexive self*, that is, the self as perceived and reflected upon by the individual subject. In terms of linguistic and psychological development these develop first as 'me', then 'myself' and, later, 'I'. As different symbolisations of three aspects of self, it seems important that the therapist supports the client's experiential and constantly developing self-awareness: 'me' awareness, 'myself' awareness, and 'I' awareness. When a client says anything beginning 'I . . .', the therapist has at least two choices: of reflecting that back as

Table 4.4 Comparison of the 'me' and 'I' modes of functioning (Zimring, 1988)

Me	I
Socially defined self	*Personally defined self*
Behaviour guided by incorporated social standards	Goals set by own plans and values
Morality defined by society's values	Personal values and morality
Agenda for what has to be done set by others	Agenda set by self
Enables problem solution according to social standards	New, creative solutions
Repository of social knowledge and expectations	Contains self-knowledge
Provides social viewpoint in line with assimilated social values	Reacts creatively to 'me' attitudes and interactions
Passive recipient or reactive self	Proactive
Concerned with past and future	Experiencing the present
Focus on others	Focus on self
Lives in roles	Acts from present personal values

'You . . .' or echoing 'I . . .' as if he (the therapist) is that client. Thus, when a client says 'I'm feeling bad about not being kinder to my child', the response 'You're feeling bad . . .' represents the client's social self ('me') as reflected by the therapist saying 'You . . .'. Echoing 'I'm feeling bad . . .' represents the client's personal self. The difference between the two is significant as is reflected in the exercise in Box 4.1.

Our own experience of doing and facilitating this exercise is that individuals experience various and often powerful reactions to the two responses of reflection or echoing. In discussion, people often talk about the

---

Box 4.1 Exercise regarding the social self and the personal self

Exercise, in pairs, for two or three minutes each way. One person (A) completes sentences beginning 'I am . . .', the other (B) reflects back accurately 'You are . . .'. Then, for another two or three minutes, A again completes sentences beginning 'I am . . .'. This time B echoes accurately 'I am . . .'. The sentences may be the same as the previous ones or may be varied. At the end of the time the two debrief, both reflecting on how they experienced the two parts to the exercise. The whole exercise may then be repeated with B taking the lead 'I am . . .', etc. and A reflecting back.

relative comfort or discomfort they feel in owning their various statements ('I'm feeling self-conscious', 'I'm feeling good about myself', 'I'm scared', 'I'm a good mother/father', etc.). For some, saying and hearing reflected '*I'm* a good father' (personal self) is more difficult than hearing 'You're a good father' (social self) which may be heard as an external affirmation. For others, to have an element of their social self reflected back to them, e.g. 'You're a confident woman', is harder to hear and to allow in than when they say it themselves. Zimring (1988, p. 174) concludes: '"I" and the "me" are important self-configurations with different degrees of mastery. The attainment of mastery is the change from the self-configuration with less mastery to the configuration with more.'

Self in social context

This strand of thinking within person-centred psychology offers a critique of narcissistic individualism, acknowledges that self is constituted by social context, and informs a dialogic view of self-in-relationship. This is supported by Macmurray's (1961/91, p. 17) critique of the inherently abstract concept of 'Self':

> We may say . . . that the Self only exists in dynamic relation with the Other . . . the Self is constituted by its relation to the Other . . . it has its being in relationship; and . . . this relationship is necessarily personal. Our main effort, therefore, must be directed towards determining the formal characters of personal relationship.

On the first point Rogers (1979, p. 12) expresses himself strongly: 'We seem as a culture to have made a fetish out of complete individual self-sufficiency, of not needing help, of being completely private except in a very few selected relationships.' In the same year Lasch (1979, p. 13) was making his criticism of *The Culture of Narcissism*, including what he views as the narcissistic nature of therapy:

> Even when therapists speak of the need for 'meaning' and 'love,' they define love and meaning simply as the fulfillment of the patient's emotional requirements. It hardly occurs to them – nor is there any reason why it should, given the nature of the therapeutic enterprise – to encourage the subject to subordinate his needs and interests to those of others, to someone or some cause or tradition outside himself.

Writing about the culture of narcissism from a gestalt perspective, Philippson (2004a) argues that, in order for a child to support the project of self-actualisation in the face or blank screen of an unavailable parent, 'the infant must learn to deflect any sense data which might contradict this image: this would include most real emotional contact! So the infant develops a sense of self based on retroflection rather than contact.' We discuss narcissistic processes in Chapter 6 and the implications of this perspective for a person-centred theory of contact in Chapter 7. Here, it is sufficient to acknowledge the necessity of an empathic other in order for the infant to process experiences (see Stern, 1985, and Chapter 2). In this sense it may be more useful to consider the notion of a 'relational self', developing and known only through dialogue. This fits with some criticisms of Rogers for promoting an individualistic concept of self. We think this criticism of Rogerian and person-centred theory is largely unjustified, especially when we incorporate Angyal's (1941) concept of homonomy, although we accept this critique of some individual and individualising therapeutic practice. Writing about identity development in women, Josselson (1987, p. 170) observes that: 'Boundaries of the self are never as rigid in girls as in boys, and the basic female sense of self is connected, with a good deal of fluidity, to the world.' From a developmental point of view, however, this fluidity relies on the parent or carer being able to hold and reflect back the child's sense of self, including her gender, in order that she can 'take in' this sense of her self (see Stern, 1985; Wolter-Gustafson, 1999). In self psychology this is the self-regulating function of the self, and is akin to organismic regulation (see Chapter 2). Lapworth (2003) makes a similar point about the need many lesbian, gay and bisexual clients have to receive empathic attunement in a therapeutic relationship precisely because, in many instances, this was specifically missing in their childhood regarding their sexuality. He gives examples of working with unmet developmental needs through mirroring, idealised and twinship introjective transferences (see Box 4.1 above).

If being relational is a way out of narcissism, psychological isolation and impasse, then participation is the way out of social isolation and passivity. Tillich (1952, pp. 90–1) puts it well:

> Self and world are correlated and so are individualization and participation. For this is just what participation means: being a part of something from which one is, at the same time, separated . . . The identity of participation is an identity in the power of being. In this sense the power of being of the individual self is partly identical with the power of being his world, and conversely.

Within person-centred psychology, Holdstock (1990, 1993, 1996) has represented the view that self cannot be understood outside its context and, indeed, is constituted by its social context. He has argued consistently for a revision of the concept of self in client-centred theory and practice. In one article (Holdstock, 1993) he cites references to sixteen different cultures in which self is seen in terms of social context and not, as Miller (1988, p. 273) puts it, as 'an individuated psychological core'. A number of person-centred theorists and practitioners, in common with those from other theoretical orientations, have questioned the monocultural roots of therapy and the impact of this on concepts such as that of the self. See, for example, Nobles (1973) on the 'we'-concept, and Moore's (1997) discussion of Japanese responses to Rogers' self-theory.

One of the reasons for this internalised separation of self from context is, according to Holdstock (1993), historical: whilst the 'self as experienced' ('me') became theorised and understood as multi-faceted, the 'self as experiencer' ('I') remained nuclear and somewhat one-dimensional. Rogers (1959b) himself presents experiencing, a key component of the self-concept, as a passive rather than an engaged and relational process. Neither does he formulate his concept of self in cognitive terms, although Wexler (1974) argues that experiencing is created by actively processing available information. Although Rogers (1958/67a) himself acknowledges his debt to George Kelly, the founder of personal construct theory, Holdstock (1993) goes on to argue that cognitive and constructionist perspectives have developed and contributed to our understanding of these two selves, with more recent constructivist thinking emphasising the dialogical nature of the self. In this sense 'me' and 'I' – and, for that matter, 'myself' – become multifaceted narrations of an evolving and fluid identity and life story. Whilst Rogers' original hypothesis of conditions was interactional, he did not emphasise either the intersubjective or the dialogic, a perspective we develop in Chapter 7. In an article reclaiming three 'lost' conditions of therapy, Tudor (2000, p. 37, our emphasis) argues that 'viewing the conditions in the context of person-centred personality theory also illustrates more clearly the *dynamic* between the therapist . . . and the client'.

Pluralist conceptions of self

As in the field of psychology and psychotherapy in general, there are a number of pluralist conceptions of self in person-centred psychology: self conceptualised as a systemic process of interactions of 'inner persons' (Keil, 1996); configurations of self (Mearns, 1999; Mearns & Thorne, 2000); and the concept of multiple contextual selves (Hayashi & Kara, 2002).

On the basis that the self is constantly evolving, and that one's relationship with oneself is analogous to relationships with others, Keil (1996) draws on communication theory and her experience of working with families to describe a therapy of 'inner persons'. She argues convincingly that the laws of communication (Watzlawick, Beavin & Jackson, 1967) may apply equally to internal communication. Keil (1996, p. 60) draws on Rogers' (1959b) view of self as a gestalt-like configuration and suggests that, in response to inevitable failures in parental attention, what we may refer to as failures in empathic attunement and ruptures in relationship, the child responds by slipping into a particular role:

> Since the environment is a very complex structure, one role is not sufficient for all situations, so one develops many . . . the network of inner relations is built up between persons created in response to one's environment and persons developed in reaction to persons already developed.

We find a number of problems with Keil's arguments:

1   She makes an unsubstantiated and unnecessary conceptual leap from defence/s to role theory.
2   She equates roles with persons. This, again, is unnecessary and, given person-centred theory of the person (see Chapter 5), somewhat confusing.
3   By using the term 'inner relations' in this way, there is a danger of reifying a personal and subjective internal process. Generally we don't find this helpful unless the client himself talks in terms of inner relations, persons or characters, as some people do who are working with their own 'dissociative processes'.

As we have seen, the term configuration is found in Rogers (1959b) referring to the changing gestalt-like nature of the self-concept. Both Zimring (1998), in his use of the term 'self-configurations', and Keil (1996) echo this. However, it is Mearns (1999, p. 126) who is most associated with the term, which he uses to describe 'a number of elements which form a coherent pattern generally reflective of a dimension of existence within the Self'. In his writings, however, Mearns consistently capitalises the 'Self' which seems to elevate and reify the notion of self as organiser. We think that the concept of configurations invites us to see a self of many parts, allows for polarisations and hierarchies, and risks distracting us from viewing the organism as a whole.

More recently, Mearns and Thorne (2000, p. 102) have expanded their definition of a configuration: 'a hypothetical construct denoting a coherent pattern of feelings, thoughts and preferred behavioural responses symbolised or pre-symbolised by the person as reflective of a dimension of existence within the "Self"'. As Mearns (2002) acknowledges, pluralist conceptions of self are not new and the concept of 'configurations' has conceptual similarities with Jung's 'complexes'; the 'objects' and 'part objects' of object relations theory; ego states in transactional analysis; 'subpersonalities' (Rowan, 1990); and other psychological literature which refers to 'voices' and even 'parts'. Nevertheless Mearns and Thorne's definition of configurations of self has a particular resonance with Berne's

(1961/75, p. 17) definition of ego states: 'phenomenologically as a coherent system of feelings related to a given subject, and operationally as a set of coherent behavior patterns, or pragmatically, as a system of feelings which motivates a related set of behavior patterns'. For a number of years Mearns has been concerned to develop a person-centred perspective on self-pluralism and 'to lay down a distinctly person-centred and purely phenomenological orientation to the work i.e. staying close to the clients' symbolisation' (personal communication, 16 August 2004), thereby avoiding an 'expert' orientation on the part of the therapist.

Mearns (1999, p. 126) has developed person-centred practice in working with configurations of what he refers to as the client's 'existential self' in ways which stay close to the client's own symbolisation – 'It's something to do with sadness', 'There's a part of me that is dreadfully vulnerable' – without trying to move the client on:

> Not changing the client's symbolisation of parts of his Self is respectful but it is also functional. The symbolisation, however poorly formed, expresses the closest which the client can get to its meaning in his existential world at that time. The skill of the person-centred therapist is to work *without* imposing external constructions.

In one paper, which in our view is an overlooked and undervalued contribution, Rogers (1958/67b) asks himself – and us – a number of questions about creating a helping relationship, one of which is this: 'Can I free [the client] from the threat of external evaluation?' This question seems highly pertinent with regard to the therapist's ability to help the client with *internal* constructions about her*self* or him*self* rather than imposing, however subtly, further external constructions or configurations of the self. From a phenomenological perspective, working this way with configurations of self demands that the therapist observes the 'rule of horizontalisation', that is, treating each configuration with equal empathic understanding.

Finally, Hayashi and Kara (2002), drawing on Taoist philosophy, refer to multiple contextual selves as a way which is equally horizontal, and abstinent or empty, but which goes further in challenging values. They advocate (p. 73) 'an attitude of regarding *all things as equal* and free from all values'. For us, this articulates the therapeutic necessity of maintaining a radical neutrality about the organism's internal valuing process.

Acknowledging the pluralities within, Keen (1983, p. 164) puts this well:

> To love the self is not to come upon an unchangeable image or essence, but to welcome all the diversity of experience into consciousness. To love myself is to proclaim that I will live in a democratic rather than a dictatorial relationship to the plurality within. I will allow all my

subpersonalities, contradictory impulses, alien wills, strange desires, forbidden needs, to live together within the commonwealth of my consciousness. Once my self-image has been shattered, I will always be more than I can know. I will never wholly understand myself. The complexities that have been interwoven to form me are equal to the complexity of being itself. I can no more comprehend the width, height, depth of myself than I can embrace the totality of the world. Thus, knowing I will never be the all-knower, I learn to accept what I cannot comprehend. Loving myself, I respect the mystery that I am. I open myself to be more than I can ever know. It is in coming to respect the unfathomable depths of myself that I discover that love ranks higher than knowledge or action. Self-love is to the explorer of consciousness what curiosity is to the pure scientist. I must agree to respect what is the case before my quest for knowledge may begin.

As we view the self in the context of the organism, we conclude this chapter by drawing together our reflections on the relationship between organism and self.

Organism and self

One issue raised by the emphasis on organism found in the work of Whitehead (1929/78), Goldstein (1934/95), Angyal (1941), Raimy (1943), Perls (1947/69) and Rogers (1951, 1959b) is the relation between organism and self. It is relatively straightforward to argue that the organism is and describes a 'natural' state or process, while the self is and represents a self-conscious interruption to this blissful, desired and desirable way of being. Such polarisation, however, does not account for the dynamic relationship between organism and self. The self is a function of the organism and, for instance, sometimes to actualise the self is to enhance the organism.

Angyal (1941, pp. 116–17) talks about the relationship between organism and environment, between which, there is at times 'a peculiar split': 'With the conscious elaboration of the biological subject–object relationship, a peculiar split arises in the subject organization. It is a remarkable fact that we exclude from our self-awareness certain factors which are very important components of the subject.' He cites two examples: one when we act under the influence of strong affects or feelings, the other the state of inspiration. In both these examples, he argues, we feel or believe that we are, in some way, out of control, and passive. For Angyal, 'the expression "passion" has definite reference to passivity' (ibid., p. 117). When someone looks back on a time when he was passionate he might say 'I wasn't myself'. People use the expression 'I was beside myself with anger'. People who are violent may claim that a 'red mist' came over them. Being inspired is another example. When someone says 'I was inspired by such and such', although she is, literally, the one doing the inspiring or breathing, and taking in whatever it is she needs from the environment, she might say it in such a way as represents her as a passive recipient of external inspiration. In everyday life, the first example is used, often by men who are violent, to minimise and deny responsibility for their violence. The second example is, in our experience, often noted in the context of learning, where the focus, traditionally, is on the inspiring teacher, rather than the inspiring, breathing student. In his theories and perspectives about learning, Rogers (1969, 1983; Rogers & Freiberg, 1994) reverses this tendency.

Given that affect and similar experiences are activities of the organism, why do we not always experience them as such? We think there are two answers, one which concerns the organism, the other, the environment. The first is provided by Angyal (1941, pp. 117–18), who states that:

> The important fact is that such processes – although they are deter-mined by the autonomy of the organism – are not governed by our *will*. In order to clarify the meaning and origin of the concept of 'will' we should recall that the biological total process is differentiated into an autonomous component or subject and a heteronymous component or environment. In the psychological realm the subject is elaborated symbolically as the consciousness of self . . . it is a highly significant fact that the conscious self, which is only a part, namely the symbolic part of the biological subject, *tends to establish its own autonomous government. What we will call 'will' represents the autonomous deter-mination, the self-government of this narrower conscious or symbolic self.* The symbolic self becomes a state within a state. Thus a split is created within the subject organisation.

In other words, two crucial aspects of the differentiation of the organism are:

1   first, between a conscious self and ongoing, autonomic, unconscious processes (see Rogers, 1968), and,
2   subsequently, between what we have some control over (ourselves) and what we have less control over (the environment).

The first differentiation leads us as human beings to develop a sense of self and self-concept which is well symbolised but at the cost, at times, of organismic experiencing, which is perhaps less well symbolised and expressed. Over-differentiating can lead to over-valuing isolated problems and losing contact with the human personality as a whole, which is the basis of a person-centred perspective on personality disorders (see Chapter 6). Perls (1947/69), for instance, is critical of those analysts, such as Rank, who, in his view over-emphasise the historical point of the birth trauma *ad absurdum*. (Perls is equally critical of Jung's inflation of the concepts of the *libido* and the unconscious such that they cover everything and explain nothing.) The second differentiation leads to an artificial distinction between organism and environment and a view that we only have dominion over ourselves in the face of an alienating, hostile environment.

Thus, to pursue our examples above, a man who is violent to his partner is, in some sense, expressing a need, to adopt Rogers' (1951, p. 491) phrase, '*in the field as perceived*'. However, both the man and his behaviour are more complex than the polarised and equally simplistic reactions 'He's a nasty bastard' and 'Ah, but he's a lovely man when he's not drinking'. In attempting to understand this complexity, we draw on Rogers' (1951, p. 503) theory of personality and behaviour in which he identifies one congruent or integrated response and three defensive responses to experiences (Proposition XI):

> As experiences occur in the life of the individual, they are either (a) symbolized, perceived, and organized into some relationship to the self, (b) ignored because there is no perceived relationship to the self-structure, (c) denied symbolization or given a distorted symbolization because the experience is inconsistent with the structure of the self.

At the moment at which a man is violent, his is a limited field in which he denies his awareness of different options with regard to communicating in the relationship; furthermore, he distorts his perceptions both of himself and, say, his partner as whole persons. In this sense his violence is a *passive* behaviour (see Schiff *et al.*, 1975), and not the active behaviour of an organism interacting with his environment in the service of his tendency to actualise. Rather, violence is the behaviour of, in this instance, a self-seeking man, actualising, if at all, in the service of a self-concept which is supported by certain and fixed views of himself and of society about being a man and being violent as an aspect of being a 'real' man, in control, and laying down domestic law. Similarly, the passive student is differentiating from an organismic valuing process by which she can accurately assess her learning needs, perhaps in favour of an external locus of evaluation.

We think there is a second answer to Angyal's question which is to do with the environment, both psychological and social, which by and large encourages the artificial splitting of 'the person' from his 'behaviour'. Elsewhere (Embleton Tudor *et al.*, 2004), we refer to the injunction to criticise the person, not the behaviour as a humanistic mantra which obfuscates rather than clarifies a person's behaviour in an environmental context. As we suggest (in Chapter 2), from an organismic perspective, a person *is* his behaviour. Let us take the example of the violent man. To suggest that we simply separate the person from his behaviour is naïve in that it ignores all the environmental influences on him, man and boy, to be violent. It ignores the fact that many men see being violent as a part of what it means to be a man. To attempt to separate a particular act of violence from an individual man is to violate the integrity of the organism in the context of its environment.

Having elaborated the concepts of organism (in Chapter 2) and self in this chapter, we now turn to the third related conceptual elaboration of the human organism: that of the person.

Chapter 5

Person

After this cold considerance, sentence me;
And as you are a king, speak in your state
What have I done that misbecame my place,
My person, or my liege's sovereignty.
William Shakespeare

We are not organisms, but persons. The nexus of relations which unites
us in a human society is not organic but personal.
John Macmurray

Despite its centrality in the person-centred approach, Rogers does not
define the term or concept 'person' in his writing. Schmid (1998, p. 47)
reports asking Rogers about his definitions of the terms 'organism', 'self'
and 'person', a question to which Rogers replied:

> I use the term organism for the biological entity. The actualising
> tendency exists in the biological human organism. I use the term self
> when I am referring to the concept a person has of himself, the way he
> views himself, his perceptions of his qualities and so on . . . I use the
> term person in a more general sense to indicate each individual.

From this response, Schmid comments that, of these terms, 'person' is a
superordinate concept, superior in rank to the concepts of self and
organism. We disagree. It seems to us that Rogers is, simply, and somewhat
surprisingly, using the word person synonymously with the word individual,
although elsewhere (1958/67b, 1960/67b) he does distinguish between
individuals and persons. To argue that the person or individual is superordinate is, in our view, to move away from an interconnected, organismic
perspective on the person as a whole individual and as an individual-in-
relation, in a whole, holistic context. We do, however, agree with Schmid

that the term 'person' is omnipresent in Rogers' work. With its meaning largely assumed and undefined, it is also strangely absent.

In this chapter we hope to make person and persons more known first by exploring aspects of the person in a broader philosophical and psychological context with specific reference to personalism and personology. Woodworth with Sheehan (1965) places Rogers in the context of his consideration of 'personalistic psychology'. In the second part of the chapter we review Rogers' different conceptions of the person: that is, the 'fully functioning person', and his various formulations of the 'emerging person' or the person in process. For Schmid (1998), these represent, respectively, the individualistic and the relationist conceptions of the person. We elaborate these conceptions through discussions of experience and relationship; and the existential concepts of being, becoming and belonging. For some authors such as Strawson (1959), Macmurray (1961/91) and Harré (1998), it is precisely the sense of belonging that distinguishes persons from organisms. In the third part of the chapter we consider the concept of personality itself with reference to a structuralist, Marxist conception of personality. As with the parallel chapters on organism (Chapter 2) and self (Chapter 4), we discuss the pathology of the personality, that is, personality disorders, in Chapter 6.

The philosophy and psychology of persons

In the epigram above, from Shakespeare's *Henry IV Part 2*, the word 'person' carries a number of senses which reflect its usage in philosophy, psychology and literature, as:

- agent,
- personage,
- actor, and
- physical body.

Person as agent may be traced back to the work of Aristotle on *orexis*, the fundamental drive or appetite that defines life itself, and *entelechy*, the end within, and of St Thomas Aquinas and the doctrine of intention, according to which individuals learn about the world by acting into it and change themselves in accordance with the consequences of their own actions. Liebnitz views the person as the source of acts, a perspective echoed in Macmurray's (1961/91) work, although he does not cite Liebnitz. Allport (1955, p. 12), who does discuss the Liebnitzian tradition, argues that this source is not to do with agitation or stimulation, but rather that it is a result of a purposive person who is oriented to the future: 'To understand what a person is, it is necessary always to refer to what he may be in the future, for every state of the person is pointed in the direction of future possibilities.' This is particularly significant and perhaps challenging for person-centred psychologists and therapists who are, by and large, present-centred in their focus and therapeutic work. Bohart (Bohart *et al.*, 1993) is one exception to this trend. He discusses the therapeutic possibilities of attending to a person's orientation towards the future.

The person as personage carries a sense of standing and status, whether standing out from the crowd or *hoi polloi* as distinctive in some way, or in terms of social standing ('as you are a king'). Given the egalitarianism of the person-centred approach, this sense of person has only a negative connotation, for instance, in terms of a criticism of the cult of the individual.

By contrast, the sense of the person as actor is present in Rogers' (1960/67b) work. The *persona* was the mask that actors in the ancient world wore on stage, and Rogers talks about people moving away from hiding behind such a mask, or façade.

Rogers does not greatly emphasise the person as physical body in the body of his own work. He sees the organism as visceral, and in his description of the process of therapy (1958/67a) he noted bodily relaxation as one of the indicators of change. The body is more present in the expressive therapy work of Natalie Rogers (1993/2000). When we say 'This is me', 'This is my body', 'This is my person' we are, in effect, referring to our sense of embodied uniqueness which is encapsulated in the particular physical shape and boundaries of our own bodies. If the image of the organism is amoeba-like, the image of the person is the personal body.

As Whitehead is the philosopher of the organism, so Macmurray is the philosopher of persons. Indeed, the second volume of his Gifford Lectures, delivered at the University of Glasgow during the spring term of 1954, is entitled *Persons in Relation* (Macmurray, 1961/91). In the previous year's Gifford Lectures, later published as *Self as Agent* (Macmurray, 1957/91), he challenges (p. 12) the assumptions of a theoretical and egocentric view of the Self: 'Against the assumption that the self is an isolated individual, I have set the view that the Self is a *person*, and that personal existence is *constituted* by the relation of persons.' His logic is as follows:

> The idea of an isolated agent is self-contradictory. Any agent is necessarily in relation to the Other. Apart from this essential relation he does not exist. But, further, the Other in this constitutive relation must itself be personal. Persons, therefore, are constituted by their mutual relation to one another. 'I' exist only as one element in the complex 'You and I'.

In seeking the union of many into one, both Whitehead and Macmurray articulate a feeling for community. There are some differences: Macmurray uses the term 'action' instead of 'process', and the phrase 'persons in mutual relation' instead of organs, within an organismic metaphor. 'Macmurray would argue' suggests Kirkpatrick (1991, p. xiv) 'that process thought has

chosen the wrong initial controlling model (organism) for understanding the
unity of reality through agency.'

Personalism

Another strand of thinking about the person derives from personalism,
which refers to the quality of being characterised by purely personal modes
of expression or behaviour, or idiosyncrasy. In philosophy it refers to any
of various theories of subjective idealism regarding personality as the key to
the interpretation of reality. According to Gallagher (1998, p. 1): 'Personalism can be defined as the attempt to place persons and personal
relationships as the center of theory and practice, and to explore the significance of personal categories across a variety of disciplines and traditions.' He goes on to suggest that personalism is a philosophical and
theological approach with roots in nineteenth-century thought, and cites
Allport as a proponent in the field of psychology. There are a number of
implications of this approach:

1   Personality is seen as the supreme value (see, for example, Murray,
    1938; Allport, 1955).
2   As a philosophy it asserts the primacy and irreducibility of personal
    categories of meaning. Kohak (1997) speaks about the significance of
    'categories of meaning rather than cause, of respect rather than force,
    of moral value rather than efficacy, of understanding rather than
    explanation'. This is consistent with the interest and focus in person-
    centred therapy on meaning, respect, values and understanding.
3   Disciplines need to be studied as if people mattered, and need to
    address issues which confront actual persons and not abstract categ-
    ories. Personalism has impacted on and been developed in a number of
    fields such as philosophy and theology (Martin Buber, Teilhard de
    Chardin, John Macmurray, Emmanuel Lévinas), psychology (William
    James, Mary Whiton Calkins, William Stern, Henry Murray, Gordon
    Allport), and economics (see Zúñiga, 2001 and www.acton.org). In its
    Christian humanist form it has inspired religious and political leaders
    such as the late Pope John Paul II and the current British Prime
    Minister Tony Blair. In this sense, Rogers' book, written with Barry
    Stevens (1967), *Person to Person: The Problem of Being Human*, may be
    viewed as a personalistic text.[1]

1 The book interleaves papers written by Rogers and his associates with Stevens' personal
'warm, human reaction' to the papers. Rogers' own writings on values, freedom and
interpersonal relationships are followed by three contributions on work undertaken with
people diagnosed as having schizophrenia.

4   Ultimate reality is personal, not impersonal, in terms of drives or
     gratification, or suprapersonal in terms of history or system; reality is a
     society of persons. These personalistic perspectives find echoes in
     Rogers' (1953/67b) emphasis on the authority of experience and in his
     argument (p. 26) that *What is most personal is most general'*.
5   The definition of 'personhood' remains open. Again this is consistent
     with person-centred process and theory.

We shall return to Murray's ideas later when we consider the concept and
nature of personality. For now it sets the scene for discussion of the person
in her perceived environmental context.

Schmid (1998, p. 43) sees personalism as the philosophy of dialogue and
the philosophical rationale, as it were, for encounter: 'This is why ethics is
the foundation of every philosophy and why responsibility – Lévinas calls it
"*diakonia* [service]" which precedes every dia-logue – is the fundamental
category of being a person; from the encounter arises the obligation to
respond.' This argues for a therapy that is more active, engaged and relational than person-centred therapy is often thought to be or allowed to be,
even by its proponents. We have referred at several points to the criticisms
of the individualistic, even egocentric concepts of organism (Chapter 2) and
of self (Chapter 4). O'Hara (1989) advances a similar criticism of Rogers'
concept of personhood and Caspary (1991) makes a distinction between
Rogers' sense of personhood and Boyte's (1984) sense of 'peoplehood'.
O'Hara (1989, p. 17) contrasts Rogers' views with those of the Brazilian
educator, Paolo Freire: 'For Rogers a person is seen as distinct from
society, separate, individual . . . Freire's view, in contrast is more socio-
centric. He considers a "person" both as an individual center of consciousness and as a social reality.' Whilst we share the critique of individualism
offered by O'Hara and others, such as Holdstock (1996a, 1996b), we think
that there is, in our reading of the philosophy and psychology of the
organism, more of a relational perspective inherent, if not explicit, in the
theory of the person and the practice, therapeutic or otherwise, between
persons.

Personology

Personology was first used in 1938 by the American psychologist Henry A.
Murray (1893–1988) to describe his own work and that of others in the
field of personalistic psychology, which emphasised a primary concern with
a full understanding of the 'complex whole' that is the individual. Essentially, personology is the study, from different perspectives, of single,
complex, *lived* lives over time. This has led, for instance, to a broad interest
in psychobiography (see www.psychobiography.com). In this Murray was
sympathetic with and close to organismic theory. He also emphasised the

environmental context of individual behaviour and in this respect, at least in the person-centred community, he is the unacknowledged inspiration for a more field-relational perspective on the person and persons. As a counterweight to his theory of motivational need, Murray (1938, p. 121) developed the notion of 'press', that is, the impact of the environment on the subject, for further elaboration of which see Chapter 6. His emphasis on the past or history of the individual, and the importance attached to unconscious motivation, however, places him closer to psychoanalysis than to the practice of person-centred therapy. Hall and Lindzey (1978, pp. 236–7) summarise Murray's contribution:

> his theory possesses the unique feature of a simultaneous emphasis upon the importance of the past of the organism and the present context within which behavior takes place . . . His interest in the field or environment within which behavior takes place led to the distinctive system of press concepts that permits the investigator to represent the perceived environment as well as the objective environment.

Rogers' concepts of the person

In his writing Rogers describes two apparently different conceptions of the person: on the one hand, the fully functioning person (Rogers, 1960/67b, 1969) and, on the other, the emerging person (Rogers, 1978), the political person (Rogers, 1978) and the person of tomorrow (Rogers, 1980a). Schmid (1998) views these as reflecting different philosophical conceptions of the person: the individualistic and the relationalist.

The fully functioning person is synonymous with optimal psychological adjustment, complete congruence and extensionality, and is characterised by: an openness to experience, the ability to live in the present and to be attentive to each moment, and a trust in organismic experiencing. One of the problems with the phrase 'fully functioning', however, is that it sounds more complete and fixed than the theory or Rogers intends, more akin to Maslow's (1954) notion of the self-actualised person than a person in process. For Rogers the fully functioning person is the outcome of therapy, a discussion we take up in Chapter 8.

In his later writings Rogers uses a number of terms to describe a person in process:

- The political person – 'a new political figure' gaining influence and fostering an emerging culture (Rogers, 1978).
- The emerging person – the characteristics of which are: openness to experience, a trust in one's organism, an internal locus of evaluation, and a willingness to be a process (rather than a product or a goal) (Rogers, 1980a).

- The person of tomorrow – Rogers (1980a) describes twelve qualities of such a person: openness; caring; having a desire for authenticity, a scepticism regarding science and technology, a desire for wholeness, the wish for intimacy, a closeness to and caring for nature, an authority within, and a yearning for the spiritual; being process persons, anti-institutional, and fundamentally indifferent to material things.

Although these persons and their qualities appear more open and fluid, the descriptions of them are framed in individualistic language. All the qualities or ascribed attributes somehow reside in the individual, separately from others. Compare them with eight relational needs identified by Erskine (1998): for security; to feel validated, affirmed and significant; for acceptance by a stable, dependable and protective other person; for confirmation of personal experience; for self-definition; to have an impact on others; to have another initiate; and to express love – all of which imply and require relationship and may be viewed as inter-human needs.

Experience and relationship

Schmid (1998, p. 45) views experience and relationship as the two most important principles of the person-centred image of the human being: 'we live through *experience*, and we live in *relationships*'. We agree with Schmid that there is an interdependence between these two principles: we experience relationship, and relate experientially. One cannot exist without the other. Indeed, we cannot exist without the other. We emphasise this point as it seems to us somewhat lost in the culture of narcissism and the reification of individuality which, for Rank (1941), is linked to beliefs in personal immortality.

One client, who herself was a counsellor, would regularly get cross with her own therapist for, as she put it 'not trusting my experience'. The client often missed appointments, came late to sessions, sometimes forgot to pay, although she would always settle up at the next appointment. The client genuinely felt that she was 'doing my best' in difficult circumstances, and the therapist acknowledged this. The client argued that the therapist should support her more by trusting her and supporting her experience. The therapist disagreed, saying: 'I do acknowledge your struggle. I also acknowledge your experience. However, it's not for me to support your experience or to disagree with it.' The client didn't accept this but continued to attend therapy. Some time later she missed two consecutive sessions. When she arrived the following week the therapist asked: 'What happened?' The client got angry and critical of the therapist for asking her a question. Later in the session the therapist said: 'You know, it seems like you expect me to support your experience, but not my experience of our relationship.' The client looked puzzled, paused for a while, and asked what she meant. The therapist responded: 'You want me to support you unconditionally and somehow separately, as if we're not relating to each other, and as if my experience of you and our relationship doesn't matter.' The client went very quiet. After some reflection she acknowledged that she was looking for unconditional support from her therapist and perhaps seeing it almost as a test of her therapist's trust in her. She hadn't seen therapy as a place to relate.

Here, the therapist is inviting the client to consider relationship, or relating, alongside her experience. This way of working therapeutically moves away from a somewhat linear and mechanistic model of person-centred therapy whereby the client is vulnerable, the therapist is loving and understanding, the client experiences this and feels better. It also challenges individualistic and absolutist views of experience, and invites, even challenges the client to reflect on and engage with her experienc*ing* in relationship. It is the logic of the view that, as human persons, we can't not be in relationship; and that we are and become persons only by being in relationship. Drawing on philosophical and theological traditions, Schmid (ibid., p. 46) argues that 'Man's primordial situation is a dialogical one. Therefore the person can be considered a response in an act of communication into which man was born.' In our experience as therapists and supervisors, the struggle described above is not uncommon. It is exacerbated by, in our view, an overemphasis on experience, often characterised by 'the right to have my experience', and an underemphasis on relationship and working with and within the therapeutic relationship (see Chapter 8).

Exploring the range of human experience, Schmid (ibid., pp. 45–6) acknowledges the experience of becoming or developing: 'we are and become persons through the experience of and in the relationship – through the experience we are having at the very moment (awareness in the present) and biographical experience (the developmental aspect of becoming a person)'. This connection between the developmental aspect of becoming and being a person is an important one. Rogers' (1951) original criticisms of the transference relationship, and Shlien's (1984) countertheory of transference, have fostered in person-centred therapy and therapists a healthy scepticism of the traditional psychoanalytic emphasis on the childhood origin of all distress. However, some person-centred therapists have, as it were, thrown the significance of the baby and childhood development out with the bathwater of theoretical invention and interpretation. That we are at least influenced by our past is uncontentious; the significance of the past, and how we work with the past in the present, is. Angyal (1941, p. 344) puts it this way: 'Nobody questions the fact that the present state of the personality is significantly determined by its past. The nature of

LIVERPOOL
JOHN MOORES UNIVERSITY
AVRIL ROBARTS LRC
TEL. 0151 231 4022

interconnection and the mode of influence upon the present, however, can be conceived in various ways.' Rank (1941, p. 49) discusses his break with Freud and his shift of emphasis from the individual's past to his present self, 'respecting emotional expression as a positive will manifestation without condemning it as "resistance"'. Existential therapy too has contributed to our understanding of working with and in the present, and, as we discuss in Chapter 4, process theories, especially those of developmental psychology, notably Stern (1985), have advanced the notion that development continues in the present. As a result, there is more therapeutic interest in the 'presenting past', as Jacobs (1998) puts it; the implications for how we might view the structure of a present-centred personality or *neopsyche* (see Tudor, 2003); and on the psychotherapy of the present moment (Stern, 2004). One client described his therapy as 'working in the present whilst acknowledging the past':

One example related to just one word: 'matter'. It became apparent that I thought other people did 'matter' quite a lot, but that I didn't. The phrase 'I matter' seems now to have at least two interpretations: that I matter to other people, and that I (am) matter in the physical sense. That insight is still echoing round my head two years later. The effect was that of an unescapable truth. I am composed of matter; therefore I can't deny that in some way 'I matter'. This insight, I believe, has profoundly changed my view of myself, at what I might describe as identity level.

Interestingly, 'I matter, You matter, They matter' was coined by Virginia Satir, a phrase which Berne (1972/75) later reformulated as 'I'm OK, You're OK – and They're OK'.

In a sense, the word 'person' is *per se* somewhat fixed. Unlike the metaphor and image of the organism, which is both amorphous (having no determinate shape) and fluid, our image of the person is shaped by the form and shape of our own body, by that of others and by the images of bodies that surround us in the media. In order to develop a more fluid image of the person, a fuller picture of a person in process, and a more intersubjective picture of persons in relation, we now consider the concepts of being, becoming and belonging.

Being, becoming and belonging

The concepts of being, becoming and belonging derive from existential philosophy, although the distinction between *being*, the quality of enduring existence, and *becoming*, the quality of change in systems such as an organism, may be traced back to Ancient Greek philosophy. As a concept, being refers to the active existence and existing of humankind, which leads to a focus on and acceptance of 'being' in the present. Aristotle argues that the important distinction in metaphysics is between the *potential* and the *actual*: all substances consist of potentiality and actuality. According to Woodfin and Groves (2001, p. 73), the former represents 'a chaotic and characterless pool of potentiality', the latter, the actual, or fully actualised, is the Supreme Being or Supreme Cause to which humans aspire and which was, for Aristotle, the determining force in human nature. This is the tradition and sense in which Maslow (1954) developed his ideas about self-actualisation and self-actualised persons. Organismic philosophy and psychology take a different view, focusing more on process (Whitehead, 1929/78; Rogers, 1958/67a) than on outcome, and more on the 'actualising tendency' or the organism's tendency to actualise (Rogers, 1959b, 1963) than on self-actualisation. The philosophy and psychology of the organism reverses Aristotle's teleology, anthropology and theology: where Aristotle argues that being or actuality emerges from becoming or potentiality, organismic psychology sees that becoming emerges from being. Whitehead (1929/78, p. 22) summarises this: 'it belongs to the nature of a "being" that it is a potential for every "becoming." This is the "principle of relativity."'

Early existential philosophers such as Kierkegaard and Nietzsche emphasise the aloneness and isolation of the individual. Later philosophers, including Heidegger, emphasise *dasein* or 'being-in-the-world', which conveys, especially in its hyphenated form, a sense of what Cooper (2003, p. 18) calls 'the indissoluble unity of person and world'. This describes existence as *between* the person and their world, and *daseinanalysis* (Ludwig Binswanger, Medard Boss) provides the foundations for an existential therapy (see Cooper, 2003).

Becoming describes the *process*, as distinct from the outcome, of human potentiality – and, as such, stands in the same relation to 'be' as the actualising tendency does to self-actualisation (see Chapter 3). Rogers (1961/67d) refers to this process as one in which people get behind the mask or roles with which they face life, in which they experience feeling and discover unknown elements of self in experience. The person who emerges from or, more accurately, is *in* this process, is characterised as having: openness to experience; a trust in his organism; an internal locus of evaluation; and a willingness to be a process. These characteristics are undoubtedly more concerned with process than outcome and Rogers' language and references here are different from the somewhat ambiguous language and mixed references to both organism and self in his chapter on personal goals (Rogers, 1960/67b). Keen (1983, pp. 129–30) describes the existential process of becoming more poetically:

The decision to become an individual, to allow oneself to be moved by the deepest impulses of the self rather than the social consensus, can only be made with fear and trembling. It is, by definition, a lonely decision. It necessarily involves anxiety and self-doubt. At first it will seem awkward, embarrassing, unnatural, and will require a high degree of painful self-consciousness. One will stumble and fall often. Frequently the path will disappear into the brambles. The outlaw will often wonder whether asserting the right to know, to taste, to experience, to judge is not an act of arrogance. The individual's way always is an unbeaten path.

Whitehead's (1929/78, p. 45) description of the process of becoming supports Rogers' description of the symbolisation of experience and creativity: 'The process is constituted by the influx of external objects into a novel determinateness of feeling which absorbs the actual world into a novel actuality.' Compare this with Rogers' (1954/67a) notion of the product of creativity being 'novel constructions' (see Chapter 3).

In his essay 'What it means to become a person' Rogers (1954/67b) asks two questions: 'Who am I?' which is about personhood, and 'How may I become myself?' Schmid (1998, p. 51) suggests that:

> In these words he expresses the specifically person-centred contribution to man's personhood: the question about the person is the question about being a person *and* the question about becoming a person – linked to the question as to what sort of encounter must take place in order to bring this 'becoming' about.

We comment at various points in this book on a certain lack of emphasis on relatedness in Rogers' work. This is, in some part, autobiographical. Rogers (1967, p. 343) describes himself as 'somewhat of a lone wolf in my professional activities; socially rather shy but enjoying close relationships' (see Introduction and Chapter 4). Significantly, Whitehead (1929/78, p. viii) describes the philosophy of the organism as concerned exclusively with 'the becoming, the being, *and the relatedness* of actual entities' (our emphasis). This sense of relatedness is encapsulated in the concept of belonging. If 'being' emphasises a person's subjectivity, then belonging emphasises inter-subjectivity between people, the relationship and encounter between persons, or, as Atwood and Stolorow (1996) describe it, 'reciprocal mutual influence'. We link this to what Goldstein (1934/95, p. 20) describes as the 'sphere of immediacy': 'the feeling of unity comprising ourselves and the world in all respects and particularly our relation to other human beings', and to what Barrett-Lennard (2005) says about community (see Chapter 2). Holdstock (1996b) argues that, whilst Rogers' theory of the self focuses on individual autonomy, his theory of therapy stresses unconditional positive regard and empathy, thereby reflecting the importance of relatedness. We develop this further when discussing the process of the therapeutic relationship in Chapter 8.

We discuss the implications of this for the person of the therapist in Chapter 7.

Personality

Having discussed some of the philosophical and psychological influences on a theory of the person, we now turn to the concept of personality. Referring to the person in everyday life raises questions of and distinctions between:

- Personality – often referred to in terms of personality clash or personality disorder, implying that nothing can be done about it.
- Disposition – which Allport (1955, p. 24) sees as 'the raw material for the development of personality'. He, in turn, identifies three factors which make up inborn dispositions:

  - Survival tendencies, common to the species.
  - Inheritance, which is linked to our genes.
  - Latent or potential capacities which, for Allport, play a crucial role in becoming.

  Cartwright and Graham (1984, p. 110) suggest that a disposition refers to 'a tendency to behave in a certain way'.
- Habit (*habitus*) – an acquired disposition, according to William of Ockham (1300–1349).
- Temperament – seen in medieval physiology, at least, in terms of the cardinal humours of the human condition: sanguine, choleric, phlegmatic or melancholic.
- Character – viewed as being inherently good or bad, strong or weak.
- Characteristics – which, according to Cartwright and Graham (1984, p. 110), plurally are 'relatively stable and distinctive features of a person that are likely to be manifested in particular instances'.
- Trait – as in a character trait like her mother's way of talking; a local, behavioural manifestation of character.

Often such distinctions or attributions imply 'natural' inherent qualities, which are viewed as an inevitable aspect of our human nature, about which it is often, though erroneously, argued that we can do nothing. As we have discussed, views from organismic, developmental and evolutionary psychology, and neuroscience, all suggest that our human nature is based on the interrelation of organism and environment, and that the environment directly and indirectly affects our development, genes, brain and behaviour. In this part we explore what personality is by discussing personality and theory, and by comparing a structuralist (Marxist) conception of personality with aspects of person-centred psychology. We conclude with a brief discussion of whether we need a theory of personality.

Personality and theory

Just as a person's personality *appears* to be given and fixed, so too the concept of personality appears to describe a generalised aspect of the person, common to all persons. We think that Rogers, amongst others, contributes to a more fluid and individual understanding of personality in relation to other understandings, and, not surprisingly, a more organismic one. He says (1953/67a, p. 92) that 'the inner core of man's personality is the organism itself, which is essentially both self-preserving and social'. Rogers expounds his own view of personality theory in *Client-Centered Therapy* (Rogers, 1951), and further elaborates it in his main formulation of theory (Rogers, 1959b). Despite his organismic inclination, however, Rogers uses the language of structure to talk about personality, and his (1951) diagram of the 'total personality' implies a more fixed and topographical view of personality, comprising certain areas, for further discussion of which see Chapter 6. Elsewhere, we and others (Embleton Tudor *et al.*, 2004) have reviewed Rogers' personality diagram, representing its experiential basis. We agree with A. Rogers (2001, p. 41) who considers Rogers' personality theory to be '*one of many* potentially interesting ways of considering what it means to be a person'. This is important, as a fixed or reified theory of personality lends weight to the use of instrumental therapeutic techniques or even attitudes designed on the part of the therapist to effect change. The other problem with Rogers' original conception of personality is that it appears more individualistic than other, more relational aspects of his theory (see Chapter 6).

Other theoreticians we have already cited have also made important contributions to a more fluid understanding of personality theory:

- Henry Murray – Although initially heavily influenced by Freudian thinking, Murray was, according to Hall and Lindzey (1978, p. 212) 'strongly oriented toward a view that gives adequate weight to the history of the organism'. Unlike Rogers he is wary of the word 'structure' with regard to personality. He acknowledges that an individual's personality is an abstraction and conceptualisation formulated by the theorist, and proposes that an individual's personality refers to and reflects the enduring and recurring elements of a person's behaviour over time, as well as to the new, distinct and unique behaviour. It follows that, with regard to research, Murray was interested in detailed study of individual subjects (see Murray, 1959).
- John Macmurray – Macmurray (1961/91, p. 25) critiques the way in which 'personality' is used to refer to the quality or set of characteristics which distinguish one person from another, arguing, rather, that this should be referred to as 'personal individuality'.

- Gordon Allport – In many ways Allport (1955) puts the personal back into personality. He argues that personality, defined as including habits and skills, frames of reference, matters of fact and cultural values, never seems warm or important. He suggests another term, the *proprium* to include (1955, p. 40): 'what is warm and important also – all the regions of our life that we regard as peculiarly ours . . . The proprium includes all aspects of personality that make for inward unity.' He goes on to offer eight aspects or properties of the proprium:

  – Bodily sense or *coenesthesis* – the bodily *me* which (p. 42) 'remains a lifelong anchor for our self-awareness'.
  – Self-identity – which provides a sense of continuity over time.
  – Ego-enhancement – i.e. self-seeking.
  – Ego-extension – the extension of me to 'mine' with reference to objects and others of importance.
  – Rational agent – that functioning of the proprium that is capable also (p. 46) 'of yielding true solutions, appropriate adjustments, accurate planning, and a relatively faultless solving of the equations of life'.
  – Self-image or phenomenal self – which includes our self-regard and evaluation of our abilities, status and roles, as well as our aspirations.
  – Propriate striving – which refers to a higher level of motivation characterised by its resistance to equilibrium and the maintenance of tension (see Chapter 3).
  – The knower – 'a blended unit of a sort that guarantees the continuance of all becoming' (p. 54).

Allport acknowledges that person and personality are broader conceptions than the proprium, and that personality includes 'adjustive activities' (a point we pick up when we discuss adjustment and maladjustment in Chapter 6). Nevertheless, he finds these terms more useful than many 'doctrines' of the self which (p. 61) 'are so inclusive as to blur these distinctions'.

A structuralist, Marxist conception of personality

We are interested to explore a structural and, specifically, a Marxist conception of personality for a number of reasons:

1   It is influential – the Marxist and feminist re-readings of Freud (see, for example, Mitchell, 1975) have been highly influential in the development of psychoanalysis and, more generally, psychotherapy. Such

critiques have not been so prominent with regard to person-centred psychology, with the exception of a recent volume (Proctor & Napier, 2004) edited by two feminists.

2   It emphasises human relations in their social context, under the pre-dominant economic system, i.e. capitalism. It thus offers a contextual (economic/social/cultural) view of the person, which in many ways is compatible with person-centred psychology.

3   Its starting point is the 'ensemble of social relations' rather than the individual or individuality. It thus emphasises relationship, relation-ship-in-context, and context-in-relationship, which is also compatible with a person-centred psychology that emphasises relationships.

4   It provides a theory of alienation which, as a concept, is largely missing from person-centred accounts of human experience, and which we develop in Chapter 6.

A Marxist perspective views personality as the organisation of forces within the individual in response to need. Since needs are relative and developed in relation to others and the world, personality too is constantly developing. This describes a process conception of personality.

The methodological basis of Marxism has been described as historical or dialectical materialism. Politzer (1976) identifies four laws of dialectics which we compare with person-centred principles and values (Table 5.1).

Historical materialism sees experience, life and consciousness as determined by social existence. Traditional psychoanalysis views these as

Table 5.1 Laws of dialectics and person-centred principles

Laws of dialectics (Politzer, 1976)	Comparison with principles of and concepts in person-centred psychology
i. That things must be studied in motion and change.	The organism is always in motion.
ii. That, as everything has a transitory and not a universal or absolute character, the object of study must be seen in a spiral rather than linear process.	People are viewed in personal subjective terms not as having universal or absolute qualities or characteristics. Person-centred psychology has a process rather than a linear view of human development (see Chapters 2 and 4).
iii. That it is internal contradiction that stimulates change.	This is in keeping with the view of the organism's inherent tension and differentiation.
iv. That historical progress comprises a series of gradual changes which accumulate and result in sudden and substantial change.	Personal progress and change is often experienced in a similar way. Rogers' (1958/67a) process conception of psychotherapy offers a description of his personal process.

determined by instinctual drives. Both Marx and Freud view consciousness as helping to grasp the nature of reality so that individuals can organise their existence. Person-centred psychology sees consciousness as the symbolisation of experience (see Chapter 3) and symbolisation as the organisation of experience or existence. For Freud and Freudians there are universal conflicts, such as the Oedipus complex, irrespective of the type of society or mode of production. For Rogers and most person-centred therapists conflicts are particular, personal, and phenomenological. For Marx and Marxists any conflict which exists in the personality is an expression of conflict in the structure of society. For example, a conflict between, say, a man and a woman about housework, cannot be understood without some reference, at some level of consciousness, to:

- Capitalist modes of production and reproduction, that is, the view that capital needs labour power to be reproduced on a daily and generational basis – which reproduction is generally considered to be 'women's work'.
- Waged and unwaged labour – and hence the debate amongst feminists in the 1970s about wages for housework (see Dalla Costa, 1972; James, 1975; Smith, 1978).
- Changes in women's expectations in and about domestic life and the world of work, which may be traced back one or two generations, often personally, to the impact of changing roles as a result of the Second World War.

We think that such consideration is useful in that it helps the therapist hold a contextual and historical view of what she may otherwise view as a personal conflict between partners. From a person-centred perspective, the ultimate or fundamental test of the usefulness of such analysis or understanding, however, remains its contribution to the therapist's regard and empathy.

In terms of the emphasis on human relations, the Marxist science of biography is based on the historical materialism of the individual and, therefore, involves a dialectical approach to the individual in their social relations. On this basis, it is impossible, for instance, to understand the personality of a working-class woman without at least studying the effects of class and gender (as above). That said, scientific Marxism demands a *specific* historical and social analysis of the individual, in some ways akin to the approach of Murray (p. 148). The work of both Marx and Rogers shares an empirical basis, even if Marx was more concerned with the empirical analysis of social relations, and Rogers with an understanding of intrapersonal and interpersonal relations. From a Marxist perspective, the structure of personality at least reflects the structure of society and, some would say, is in the mathematical sense absolutely congruent with it. Thus, in a static society in which no significant change occurred for hundreds of years, such as 'the Asiatic mode of production' identified by Marx (1858/1964), we could hypothesise that people's personalities did not change much either. As the mode of production changes, so does the personality. With regard to the development of Rogers' ideas, Barrett-Lennard (1998) considers the impact of Rogers' milieu: the Great Depression, reform and Franklin Roosevelt's 'New Deal'. The following quote from Dewey (1928/60, pp. 286–7) (which Barrett-Lennard uses as an epigram to a chapter in his book) makes the link between this context and the potential of personality:

> The possibility of freedom is deeply grounded in our very beings. It is one with our individuality . . . But like all other possibilities, this possibility has to be actualized: and, like all others, it can only be actualized through interaction with objective conditions . . . the conditions that form political and economic liberty are required in order to realize the potentiality of freedom each of us carries within him in his very structure.

To focus on social relations and context, however, is generally viewed within person-centred psychology as introducing something from the therapist's frame of reference and, therefore, ultimately, directive. Discussing the intersections of feminism and the person-centred approach, Proctor and Napier (2004b, p. 5) see the fact that feminism has a different focus of study as a point of conflict with the approach: 'A person-centred approach does not include gender analysis or analysis of any other societal factors unless an individual specifically mentions them as being personally relevant.' We agree that a person-centred therapist does not normally or gratuitously introduce such factors. We think, however, that such analyses are both relevant and legitimate areas of study which help us understand the organism in its environment. In our view, a greater appreciation of the client's social relations addresses the criticism that person-centred therapy is too individualistic (see Buber in Kirschenbaum & Henderson, 1990a; Vitz, 1997).

From a Marxist perspective it is clear that the human essence *is* the ensemble of social relations, and that people are irreducibly social and not independent of social relations. We only have to consider some of the issues involved in the exchange of money for psychotherapy in private practice (see Tudor & Worrall, 2002) to have a practical sense of this. Molina (1977, p. 241) describes this well: 'social relations (society) are not a mere "social framework" with respect to individuals, but they stand as the very structural "ensemble" which *constitutes* individuality itself'. As Einstein put it (cited in Newnes, 2004): 'Individuality is an illusion created by skin.' For example, from this perspective, the family, as the predominant psychological agency of society, stamps its specific structure on the child. The repetition of childhood experiences (play and discipline, as well as abuse) are not so much repetitions of *content* (a particular game, being tidy in a certain way, a particular form of abuse) as *structure*. In their ethnographic study of the authoritarian and prejudiced (anti-semitic) personality, Adorno *et al.* (1969, p. 971) describe it thus:

> A basically hierarchical, authoritarian, exploitative parent–child relationship is apt to carry over into power-oriented, exploitatively dependent attitudes towards one's sex partner and one's God and may well culminate in a political philosophy and social outlook which has no room for anything but a desperate clinging to what appears to be a strong and disdainful rejection of whatever is relegated to the bottom. The inherent dramatization likewise extends from the parent–child dichotomy to the dichotomous conception of sex roles and of moral values, as well as to a dichotomous handling of social relations as manifested in stereotypes.

Elsewhere, Horkheimer and Adorno (1972, p. 211) describe a personality determined by the economic context: 'Here in America there is no difference between a man and his economic fate. A man is made by his assets, income, position, and prospects. The economic mask coincides completely with a man's inner character.' This Marxist perspective on social relations gives a sharper edge to our understanding of people in relationship. In this sense relations and relationships are both personal and political or social: they *are* social, and are *experienced* personally. Where Marxist and Rogerian perspectives part company is the degree to which people are viewed as determined by social forces and having little or no individuality. However, if we substitute 'conditioned' for 'determined', then the two perspectives appear closer. Bozarth (1998, p. 83) argues that 'conditionality is the bedrock of a person-centered theory of pathology', and Van Kalmthout (2002, p. 140) says that 'Living in the grip of the conditioned self only leads to feelings of meaninglessness, depression and other signs of alienation' (see Chapter 6).

In practical terms a psychotherapy which integrates ideas from a structuralist approach to personality such as Marxism holds, amongst other things:

1   A focus on the pathological features of society before those of the individual. Indeed our understanding of the pathological features of an individual can only be understood in this context (see Chapter 6).
2   A critique of the dominant constructions of pathology in terms of illness and madness (see Sanders & Tudor, 2001).

Having explored and elaborated organism (Chapter 2) and its tendency to actualise (Chapter 3), self (Chapter 4) and person in this present chapter, we now turn our attention to the disorganisation of these entities.

Chapter 6

Alienation

Every self-estrangement of man from himself and nature is manifested in the relationship he sets up between other men and himself and nature.

Karl Marx

Mental health is an ongoing process of dedication to reality at all costs.

M. Scott Peck

Conditionality is the bedrock of Rogers' theory of pathology.

Jerold Bozarth

A person becomes inauthentic if they are alienated from self and Others, i.e. from the experiencing organism and the necessary genuine relationships.

Peter Schmid

In previous chapters we explored the nature of organism (Chapter 2), self (Chapter 4) and person (Chapter 5). These, in effect, describe and elaborate the authenticity of the human organism. We agree with Schmid (2004, p. 39) that the notion of inauthenticity

> differs qualitatively from the common meaning of illness or disorder. What is experienced from an internal frame of reference as 'psycho-logical suffering' is seen from an external point of view as alienation or maladjustment. If it is called 'disorder', one must *permanently* keep in mind that the 'order' always is also a cultural norm.

In the first part of this chapter we elaborate this point by discussing alienation in the context of authenticity, a discussion which reframes and relocates discussions about health and illness or 'disorder'. In order to discuss particular disorders, we first address the concept and subject of process differentiation, which stands as a necessary introduction to the subsequent parts. Following this, we take up Schmid's challenge to develop a genuinely person-centred systematic description of inauthentic processes, and discuss the pathology of organism, self and person. Whilst maintaining our perspective on alienation, we consider such pathologies in their different forms and with regard to terms which are more generally used in both person-centred literature and in the field of mental illness: for the organism, disorganisation; for the self and the person, disorder. The examples we use to illustrate our discussion reflect broader changes in psychopathology and reflect the 'disorders' of our times; that is, those which have become more identified in the last thirty years in affluent societies: compulsive overeating, dependency-related disorder and narcissistic personality process. These also represent a range of 'disorders' across the three groupings or 'clusters' identified by the American Psychiatric Association's (2000) *Diagnostic and Statistical Manual of Mental Disorders* (*DSM*) (now in its fourth edition). We recognise that some disorders, including anxiety and obesity, may be symptoms of organic rather than psychological pathology. Any sophisticated differential diagnosis will take this into account. Given our backgrounds we focus on the psychological and the social aspects of pathology or alienation. We recognise also our limitations and believe that it's both beneficial and necessary to work with professionals from other disciplines who may have particular diagnostic skills. In the final part of the chapter, we draw on Murray's (1938) concept of environmental 'press' and consider briefly the ways in which our tendency to actualise is thwarted.

Authenticity and alienation, health and illness, order and disorder

For Rogers authenticity is synonymous with congruence. In his 1959b paper he defines a number of terms, viewing them all as forming a cluster which grows out of the concept of congruence (p. 207):

> Congruence is the term which defines the state. Openness to experience is the way an internally congruent individual meets new experience. Psychological adjustment is congruence as viewed from a social point of view. Extensional is the term which describes the specific types of behavior of a congruent individual. Maturity is a broader term describing the personality characteristics and behavior of a person who is, in general, congruent.

Rogers' point about openness to experience is interesting in the light of personality research (Cloninger, Svrakic & Pryzbeck, 1993; Benjamin *et al.*, 1996) which suggests that some characteristics, including novelty-seeking and adaptability, are inherited; and that some of us are temperamentally open to new experience and seek it out, while others are cautious and prefer things to stay the same. People who are autistic, for instance, can find apparently minor differences in their environment difficult to accept and manage. The way they process information means generally that they prefer sameness.

The authentic person is, in effect, fully functioning, for further discussion of which see Chapters 5 and 8.

In a later paper, Rogers (1975/81) sees a deep concern for authenticity as a quality of the multifaceted, emerging person. He goes on to describe this person in polemical and political terms, citing examples of people who are prepared to reject a culture they see as hypocritical, to confront those in authority, to refuse orders, to work for civil rights, and to take full personal responsibility in situations (p. 158): 'Such painful honesty, such willingness to confront, and the willingness to pay the price of such utterances are indications of the value this emerging person places on being authentic.' Schmid (2004, p. 38) says simply that: 'To be a person can truly be called living the process of authenticity.'

This authenticity describes mankind in relationship and unity with itself and nature – and, if not united, being prepared and willing to do something about it, to be, in Barrett-Lennard's (1998, p. 75) words describing the purposeful, open system that is the organism, 'in particularly active inter-change with its environment' (see Chapter 2). Alienation is the opposite. Alienation, for Marx, the philosopher of alienation, is the distortion of such unities. Marx talks in terms of 'distorted relations', Rogers (1951) of 'distorted perceptions'. The difference is that a Marxist point of view argues that the distortion lies in oppressive forms of society, such as feudalism and capitalism, and not only in the individual's perception of distorted relations, as Rogers suggests in his theory of personality. Marx conceptualises alienation as four basic but closely related social relations within capitalism: man's (*sic*) relation to his product, his productive capacity, to other people, and to his species, a framework which Tudor (1997) draws on to describe examples of class-conscious therapeutic practice. Roy (1988) adds to this taxonomy a further set: that of man's alienated social relations with the earth, a perspective which informs contemporary concerns about the environment, and a developing interest in ecopsychology. Again, we find in the work of Angyal and, specifically, in his holistic theory of *Neurosis and Treatment* (1965/73), more of a relational perspective on alienation. He uses the term 'alienness' to describe (p. 92) 'the central figure of the neurotic mythology . . . [which] results from the persisting state of isolation of the child whose attempts at relating himself to the world have largely failed, so that no communication and no real community has been established'.

A number of therapists from different traditions have taken up the concept of alienation. Here we refer to two, from gestalt psychology and from transactional analysis:

- Discussing alienation in the context of the malfunctioning process of projection, Perls, Hefferline and Goodman (1951/73, p. 259) describe this as a psychological process:

> Alienated from his own impulses, yet unable to obliterate the feelings and acts to which they give rise, man makes 'things' out of his own behaviour. Since he then does not experience it as himself-in-action, he can disclaim responsibility for it, try to forget it or hide it, or project it and suffer it as coming from the outside.

A person who is passive, who disowns her feelings and behaviour, who blames 'them' or 'the world' is, in these terms, inauthentic or alienated in some way. On the other hand, therapy which invites a client to 'own' her impulses and behaviours, and to experience herself as herself-in-action in a social world, describes a process of dis-alienation, a process which, Bulhan (1980) argues, is impossible without a total restructuring of society.

- Based on a theory of alienation, and an analysis of oppression and power, derived from Marx and influenced by Reich, Marcuse, Fanon and Laing, the tradition of radical psychiatry within transactional analysis offers particular co-operative ways of working with individuals and groups to reclaim autonomy (see Steiner *et al.*, 1975). Steiner and his colleagues came up with a formula which defines Alienation as equal to (=) Oppression + Mystification + Isolation. Echoing Marx's analysis, Steiner (2000) talks in terms of people being alienated from their hearts, or from love; being alienated from their minds, or from the capacity to think; being alienated from their bodies, or from their feelings; and being alienated from their hands, or from their work. Echoing the tradition of civil disobedience, Steiner (1981, p. 50) asserts: 'The first step in becoming powerful without using power to control others is to learn to be disobedient . . . Refusing to be controlled against your will and judgement frees your own powers for whatever you may decide is good for you.' This analysis of power and responses to 'power plays' is echoed in the person-centred approach to personal power (Rogers, 1978) and collaborative power (Natiello, 1987, 1990).

We suggest (in Chapter 5) that Rogers frames his theory of personality in individualistic terms and that a structuralist conception of personality focuses more on the impact of the environment and social relations *in* the subject or client.

After some months of therapy a client said to her therapist: 'You know, I don't like people.' She was, in effect, describing her alienation from her species which in part she knew, and in part discovered, had its roots in her childhood and the ways in which her parents had stamped their structures on her (see Chapter 5). This affected all aspects of her life: from how she viewed herself and her capacity for enjoying life, through to how she organised her daily routine and even how she drove her car without much care for herself or others. She and the therapist spent the first few months of her therapy exploring the ways in which she felt isolated and alienated from the world, and how she protected herself against feeling the implications of this. She acknowledged the ways in which she distorted certain perceptions of herself ('That's how I am'), others ('. . . are out to get me'), and the world ('. . . is against me'). She was also quite certain of the impossibility of change for herself, although she recognised this and even facilitated this in others. One day some birds flew past the window of the consulting room. The client interrupted what the therapist was saying to point this out and, with great knowledge and animation, described the difference between the birds in some detail, and, in doing so, revealed her passion for nature. She then apologised for the interruption. The therapist acknowledged the affective vitality of the client (Stern, 1985) and the significance of the 'interruption'. As he saw it the temporary 'rupture' in relationship had actually had the effect of helping him to refocus on her vitality and authenticity. Drawing on his understanding of the different forms of social relations and alienation, the therapist followed the client and discovered, as it were, a whole world of the client's authentic social relations with nature and the earth, in terms of her love of flora and fauna, and of walking. This, and its origins in her childhood, became a significant theme in therapy. Acknowledging this, client and therapist were able to return to other areas and reassess her relationship with both the 'product' she produced and her productive capacity. By acknowledging and working with all of this, the client was able to talk more about her difficulty in relating to others and the social world. Reflecting on this process sometime later, the client acknowledged that it was the therapist's non-judgemental, acceptant response which had been most helpful and reparative as, in her childhood, she had been consistently told off for interrupting.

This vignette highlights the value of thinking in terms of authenticity and alienation rather than health and illness. 'In psychotherapy' says Phillips (1994, p. 49) 'one always has to remember that anyone who is failing at one thing is always succeeding at another.' Schmid (2004) critiques terms such as 'health', 'normal', 'in order', 'in-firmity' and 'dis-ease' (p. 38): 'authenticity has nothing to do with being firm or at ease. These common terms are not only misguiding, but completely wrong, because a severely ill person can very well live most authentically.' Whilst we agree with this in principle, we have two modifications, one strategic and the other a reframe.

Our strategic concern is that we think there is a missing stage in Schmid's argument. He refers to health and illness as if the two terms are used separately. In our experience this is not the case. There is such widespread conflation of these terms, especially in the field of 'mental health', i.e. mental *illness*, that we think there is a strategic need first to argue that health is something different from illness (see Antonovsky, 1979) and then that mental health or well-being is something different from mental illness and 'disorder' (see Tudor, 1996, 2004) – two terms, incidentally, which themselves are also conflated and used synonymously, e.g. in current mental 'health' legislation and policy in the UK and elsewhere.

The reframe we want to offer concerns the concepts of order and organisation. The correlative of 'order' is 'dis-order' and, in any context in which there is a tendency to polarise, these can be equated, respectively and somewhat simplistically, with health and illness. However, going back to Whitehead (1929/78) we discover a more inclusive and dynamic sense of order. He argues:

1   That both order and disorder are 'given', that is, that the basis of the organism's experience is given. This represents a more even-handed view of both order and disorder, and a less pathologising approach to disorder.

2   That order is differentiated from 'givenness' by virtue of the notion of adaptation, i.e. that an organism adapts in order to attain a particular end or goal (see the discussion of needs in Chapter 2).

3   That (p. 84): 'There is not just one ideal "order" which all actual entities should attain and fail to attain.' This challenges the reification of health over illness, and the kind of health fascism which promotes the notion of the perfect body and which leads to obsessive concerns about physical ability, fitness and strength, body image and weight.

4   That, as Emmet (1932/66, p. 217) summarises: 'order is always a balance on the verge of chaos . . . the depth or intensity of order depends on the capacity to hold together diverse elements in experience as contrasts'. This acknowledges the inherent tension in organisms, and provides a link with chaos and complexity theory.

Thus, in its congruent, integrated state the human organism, as any other organism, is more or less organised and unified from moment to moment (see Chapter 2). Lewin (1951/64, p. 101) makes a similar point with regard to his preference for the term 'organisation':

Mathematically integration is the reverse of differentiation. However, it has been rightly emphasized that psychological 'integration' does not mean dedifferentiation. It may be better to replace this term by the term 'organization.' This use of the term 'organization' seems to be well in line with its use in embryology and also in sociology.

Before turning our attention to the specifics of process with regard to organism, self and person, we want to remind ourselves and the reader of the sheer complexity involved in order and organisation, organismic or otherwise. Whitehead (1929/78, p. 108) reflects that:

> All the life in the body is the life of the individual cells. There are thus millions upon millions of centres of life in each animal body. So what needs to be explained is not dissociation of personality but unifying control, by reason of which we not only have unified behaviour, which can be observed by others, but also consciousness of a unified experience.

At times, and especially regarding the beginning of a human life, we may focus on the risk that a foetus may not be 'perfect' and worry about the statistical chances of there being something 'wrong' with it – and, at this stage, it is often referred to as 'it'! We may equally be amazed at the chances and actuality of relative genetic and chromosomal order and organisation. As Emmet (1932/66, p. 214) puts it: 'the miracle of a living organism, is not dissociation, but *unified control*'. Peake (1950) puts it more poetically: 'To live at all is miracle enough.' In this sense the focus of the philosophy of the organism (Whitehead, 1929/78), the neurobiology of the organism (Goldstein, 1934/95), and the psychology of the organism (Angyal, 1941; Raimy, 1943; Perls, 1947/69; and Rogers, 1951, 1959b) promotes an appreciation of authenticity, order and organisation from which we may develop an understanding of pathology of the organism, self and person, grounded in an understanding of alienation.

Inauthenticity

In response to external threat, the human organism may become anxious. In his 1959 paper, Rogers, to a certain extent, paralleled his description of the cluster of terms around the concept of congruence (see p. 156), with some terms describing incongruence or, more broadly, inauthenticity. Browning (1966) views incongruence as estrangement and, from a Christian theological perspective, describes it as a bondage (to the self and its conditions of worth), and idolatrous (in absolutising relative values). Here, we summarise the relevant terms and complete this part of Rogers' framework.

• Incongruence – defines or describes the state. It describes the discrepancy between the self as perceived and the actual experience of the organism.

- Closed to experience – describes the way in which an internally incongruent individual meets new experience.

These represent two elements or continua in Rogers' (1958/67a) process conception of psychotherapy (see Appendix 3).

- Psychological maladjustment – is incongruence as viewed from a social point of view. This exists (and here we combine Rogers' 1951 and 1959b definitions) when the organism denies to awareness or distorts in awareness significant sensory and visceral experiences which, consequently, are not accurately symbolised and organised into the gestalt of the self-structure. Schmid (2004, p. 39) takes this concept further, defining it as 'a deficit of relational authenticity'. He sees two types of deficit: autonomy deficit, the incongruence between self and experience; and relationship deficit, the incongruence between others as perceived and as they are. Drawing on Angyal's (1941) work, we recast this as:

  – Autonomy deficit – which describes the incongruence between self and experience.
  – Homonomy deficit – which describes the incongruence between self and self-in-relationship.
  – Heteronomy deficit – which describes the incongruence between self and differentiated 'Other', representing actual others or, more generally, difference.

- Intensionality – is the term which describes the specific types of behaviour of an incongruent individual and, as Rogers (1959b, p. 205) describes it, is characterised by a person who tends 'to see experience in absolute and unconditional terms, to overgeneralize, to be dominated by concept or belief, to fail to anchor his reactions in space or time, to confuse fact and evaluation, to rely upon abstractions rather than reality-testing'.

- Immaturity – describes the personality characteristics and behaviour of a person who is, in general, incongruent.

These terms describe rather than judge the inauthentic organism. Being intensional or closed to experience is not bad or wrong. We want to acknowledge the possibility and wisdom of being knowingly closed to some kinds of experience. In this sense the ideal is not to be continuously and gratuitously 'open', but to be discriminating about those experiences to which we can be open. This view of authenticity and alienation is akin to a psychodynamic perspective which values balanced and mature defences.

Later in this chapter we elaborate this broad view of alienation and inauthenticity in terms of organism, and self and person. This is preceded by a discussion concerning process differentiation.

Process differentiation

This is defined by Swildens (2004, p. 16) as 'the diversification of the client-centred attitude and its implementation on behalf of clients with actual or supposed difficulties in receiving therapeutic interventions in one or more phases of therapy'. There is currently a lively debate within the person-centred and experiential therapeutic world in which different 'tribes' take different stances on this (see Takens & Lietaer, 2004). The debate, in part, rests on therapists' view of diagnosis.

Rogers (1951) was opposed to the use of diagnostic labels applied to psychological dynamics, viewing it as unnecessary, and detrimental to the therapeutic process. Rogers' objection to diagnosis was twofold. First, it places the locus of evaluation in the hands of experts which, he argues, leads to a dependency in clients (1951, p. 224): 'there is a degree of loss of personhood as the individual acquires the belief that only the expert can accurately evaluate him, and that therefore the measure of his personal worth lies in the hands of another'. Second, diagnosis, for Rogers and others, has undesirable social and philosophical implications, such as the diagnostician having control over the client or patient, control which, ultimately, may take the form of assessment, sectioning under mental health (illness) legislation, and confinement.

A further note, which may be an objection for some, and a relief for others, is that diagnosis changes over time. A study of the history of diagnostic categories reveals considerable change over the past 100 years. Perhaps the most infamous example was the removal of homosexuality from the APA's (1968) *DSM II* in the publication of its third edition (*DSM III*) in 1980. In a brief review of the phenomenon of hysterical syndromes, Swildens (2003, p. 8) comments about symptoms and conditions which have disappeared and others which have taken their place: 'Perhaps such fashionable renaming is not so much an expression of a shift in psycho-pathology as a manifestation of the dominance of a different school of therapy.' It seems that our view of what is 'neurotic' is more likely to change according to changing social mores than what we refer to as 'psychotic', which seems more constant across time and cultures. Some of our definitions of what is neurotic depend on what is socially sanctioned or desirable. There is, for instance, current concern about the extent to which the American health insurance industry shapes the categorisation of disorders in the APA's *DSM*. We think this is particularly important for person-centred therapists who, in discussions with practitioners from other theoretical orientations and other professions, as well as with clients, may take a less popular but longer view of the usefulness of particular diagnostic categorisations of symptoms.

Others since have followed and elaborated Rogers' lines of thinking. On the basis that the primary purpose of diagnosis is to determine treatment,

Shlien (1989) argues that, since client-centred therapy has only one 'treatment' for all clients, i.e. working in the context of the necessary and sufficient therapeutic conditions, then diagnosis is irrelevant. This has led to some criticism of person-centred therapy as advancing a kind of therapeutic uniformity. Rogers (1951, pp. 223–4) advances a number of propositional statements regarding diagnosis, concluding that:

> Therapy is basically the experiencing of the inadequacies in old ways of perceiving, the experiencing of new and more accurate perceptions, and the recognition of significant relationships between perceptions.
>
> In a very meaningful and accurate sense, therapy *is* diagnosis, and this diagnosis is a process which goes on in the experience of the client, rather than the intellect of the clinician.

In our view this is both a more moderate and more radical proposition than the complete rejection of diagnosis. It is more moderate in that it retains the concept of diagnosis, a position which, we believe, has led to the recent elaboration of and debate about differential process. It is more radical in that it clearly places the locus of evaluation and control in the hands of the client. There is, for instance, a world and a paradigm of difference between the statements 'The doctor sent me. I'm depressed.' and 'I'm mad and I'm angry.' For Holland (1988) these statements represent a shift from a functionalist to an interpretative paradigm.

In the context of the dominance of the medical/psychiatric model this person-centred attitude to diagnosis is counter-cultural. It can place person-centred therapists outside of, or at least viewed with some suspicion by, institutions such as the National Health Service in the UK. In response, Tudor and Merry (2002) summarise three approaches to diagnosis taken by person-centred practitioners:

1   To eschew diagnosis completely – as represented by Shlien (1989).
2   To seek to understand other systems (medicine, psychology and other psychotherapeutic approaches) and their approaches to psychopathology, diagnosis, assessment and treatment, and to translate them into person-centred language, theory and concepts – for example, Speierer (1990) and Joseph and Worsley (2005).
3   To develop a person-centred/experiential approach:

   i.   To 'illness', 'mental illness' and 'disorder', thus, illness as incongruence (Biermann-Ratjen, 1998; Speierer, 1996); person-centred theory and mental illness (Wilkins, 2005).
   ii. To psychodiagnosis and assessment (Fischer, 1989; Wilkins & Gill, 2003).

iii. To specific 'conditions' such as borderline personality disorder (Bohart, 1990); fragile and dissociated process (Warner, 1991, 1998); neurosis (Lambers, 1994); depression (Catterall, 2005; Rowland, 2002; Schneider & Stiles, 1995); schizophrenic thought disorder (Warner, 2002); narcissistic defence (Swildens, 2004); psychotic functioning (Van Werde, 2005); anti-social personality disorder (McCulloch, 2005); autism and Asperger's syndrome (Knibbs & Moran, 2005); post-traumatic stress (Joseph, 2005).

It is in elaborating these developments that differences have emerged between what is characterised as a more classical person-centred therapy and experiential therapy.

Proponents of process differentiation argue, as the term suggests, that it is useful to differentiate a client's process. As we see (above), Swildens writes about 'the diversification of the client-centred attitude'. This implies that, depending on the client's process (depressive, schizophrenic, border-line, narcissistic, and so on), the therapist offers a diversified and differ-ential response. If such responses are framed in terms of more empathy for this client, more congruence with regard to another, clearer boundaries for one, fewer for another, then this would be clearly at odds with the prin-ciples of person-centred therapy and, specifically, Rogers' therapeutic attitudes or conditions (see Chapter 7), and the process of therapy (see Chapter 8). Acknowledging the advances that person-centred therapy has made with regard to understanding client processes, and citing the work of Prouty (1994) and Warner (2000), Mearns (2004, p. 98) argues: 'It is not that these client processes demand particular therapeutic protocols additional to the principles of person-centred working; rather, it is that these processes create particularly demanding relationships in terms of communication, engagement and trust.'

We think that the answer to what at times appears to be an impasse between two polarised positions is summarised by three propositions:

1   That the therapeutic relationship is a significant curative factor in psychotherapy. As Schmid (2004, p. 41) puts it: 'Since it is the relationship that facilitates the process of personalization, differ-entiated relationships are needed: each person-to-person relationship is different, otherwise it would not be a *personal* relationship.'

2   That the most significant experience of differentiation is the client's. In other words, clients experience and, in various ways, construe their experience: one person is constantly suspicious of her neighbours, another isolates himself, a third experiences acute discomfort in close relationships, a fourth shows disregard for others, and so on. As therapists we may have a number of ways of conceptualising and understanding different differentiations. The ultimate test of these

LIVERPOOL
JOHN MOORES UNIVERSITY
AVRIL ROBARTS LRC
TEL. 0151 231 4022

theories, however, is whether they help us to be empathic, and whether they help the client 'diagnose' herself (see Rogers, 1951). Of course our empathy for different clients is different – because they're different, and because each therapeutic relationship is different. This perspective addresses the 'uniformity myth' that person-centred therapy and therapists are the same. As Schmid (2004, p. 40) puts it, 'the therapeutic answer is: not uniform but unique'.

3   That forms of therapy, such as pre-therapy, or therapeutic techniques (if used at all) are best conceptualised as forms of empathy, whether empathic understanding, empathic attunement, empathic responding, accurate empathy (Truax & Carkhuff, 1967), idiosyncratic empathy (Bozarth, 1984), or different levels (Truax & Carkhuff, 1967) or kinds of empathy (Neville, 1996). This reconceptualisation places such therapy with various forms of differentiated process, i.e. fragile (Warner, 1991), dissociated (Warner, 1998), psychotic, depressed (Rowland, 2002), and disconnected (Mearns & Cooper, 2005), at the heart of the person-centred therapeutic endeavour and process, rather than before it.

Organismic disorganisation

Based on the observation of people with brain injuries, Goldstein (1934/95) formulates certain general rules which determine organismic life. These include two classes of behaviour: ordered and disordered or 'catastrophic' (pp. 48–9):

> In an ordered situation, responses appear to be constant, correct, adequate to the organism to which they belong, and adequate to the species and to the individuality of the organism, as well as to the respective circumstances. The individual himself experiences them with a feeling of smooth functioning, unconstraint, well-being, adjustment to the world, and satisfaction, that is, the source of behavior has a definite order, a total pattern in which all involved organismic factors – the mental and the somatic down to the physiochemical processes – participate in a fashion appropriate to the performance in question.

Goldstein goes on (p. 49):

> The 'catastrophic' reactions, on the other hand, are not only 'inadequate' but also disordered, inconstant, inconsistent, and embedded in physical and mental shock. In these situations, the individual feels himself unfree, buffeted, and vacillating. He experiences a shock affecting not only his own person, but the surrounding world as well. He is in that condition that we usually call anxiety.

If Goldstein's language appears polarised, the intention in his work and a major theme of *The Organism* is the acknowledgement of the value of pathology. This is partly because it illuminates health. Duff (1993, p. 33) suggests that 'illness is to health what dreams are to waking life – the reminder of what is forgotten, the bigger picture working towards resolution'. This echoes another point which Goldstein makes about rehabilitation: that being well means being capable of ordered behaviour despite being ill, 'disordered' or impaired in some way. This represents a two-continua concept of health/order and illness/disorder (see Minister of National Health and Welfare, 1988; Tudor, 1996) and addresses Schmid's point (p. 159) about being both authentic and ill.

According to Rogers (1959b, p. 204), 'anxiety is phenomenologically a state of uneasiness or tension whose cause is unknown . . . Anxiety is the response of the organism to the "subception" that . . . discrepancy may enter awareness, thus forcing a change in the self-concept.' This catches the sense of the non-conscious and the implicit about organismic disorganisation, from the mental and the somatic down to micro-physiochemical processes. In organismic terms anxiety may be expressed in terms of breathlessness, due to oxygen hunger; excitement, marked by increased cardiac activity; and restlessness, represented by increased motoric activity (see Perls, 1947/69). Whilst organismic disorganisation may occur and operate internally on a microbiological level, it is often expressed somatically:

- Internally, in terms of psychosomatic ailments such as back problems or irritable bowel syndrome.
- Externally, through the skin, for example, blushing, psoriasis.
- Externally, in terms of behaviour, such as forms of agitation.

Here, as an example of organismic disorganisation, we discuss the disorder and experience of someone who compulsively overeats. This disorder or disorganisation is widespread, particularly in the so-called advanced economies in which, according to a number of reports, it is reaching epidemic proportions. According to one website (www.aplaceofhope.com) between 10% and 15% of all Americans suffer from some type of serious eating disorder; at least one third of all Americans are now considered to be obese; and 60% are clinically overweight. From an organismic perspective, we cannot understand this outside of the particular environmental context. Thus, it is no coincidence that this disorder is more prevalent in industrialised societies as, in such societies, there is generally an abundance of food available. In the case of anorexia nervosa, this is coupled with expectations about attractiveness which is equated with thinness (see APA, 1994). Compulsive overeating is defined when a person consumes a large amount of food in a short period of time (less than two hours), but does not engage in purging behaviour. It may include a history of dieting, alternating with overeating. The 'compulsive' in 'compulsive eating disorder' refers to the fact that she (and this disorder predominantly affects women) eats without regard to physical cues signalling hunger or satisfaction. 'Eating' refers to a set of eating habits, strategies regarding weight management, and attitudes about weight and body shape. 'Disorder' refers to the degree of impact of such actions, resulting in a loss of self-control; obsession, anxiety, and guilt; alienation from self and others; and physiological imbalances which are potentially life-threatening.

In her discussion of compulsive overeating, Barth (1991) sees four major areas from self psychology which can contribute to a therapist's work (see also Chapter 4). We discuss these with reference to organismic, person-centred psychology.

1   The focus on self-esteem and self-cohesion. Both person-centred psychology and self psychology share a view that human beings strive for regard, from others and from self, and that we have a tendency to seek balance over time, one expression of which is self-cohesion (see Stern, 2000, and Chapter 4). When we lose this, as organisms, we seek to compensate. In the short term, overeating helps to alleviate feelings of fragility, dissociation, confusion and self-hatred. Barth reports one client saying: 'It's better to hate yourself than not to have a self at all.'

2   The view of symptoms as attempts to restore and/or maintain self-esteem and self-cohesion. This is consistent with an organismic view of symptoms (as we discuss in Chapter 2). Hartmann (1958) describes symptoms as not simply evidence of psychopathology, but also often evidence of an adaptive response to an unhealthy or pathological environment. Self-cohesion is, for Stern (1985, 2000), one of the experiences which comprises a sense of core self (see Chapter 4) which, for us, is an aspect of the experiencing organism. Many people with eating disorders have difficulty in articulating their feelings which, from the perspective of both self psychology and person-centred psychology, is viewed as an adaptation to some aspects of their experience and, possibly, a developmental deficit.

3   The use of empathy as a primary therapeutic tool. Given that many people with eating disorders are highly self-critical, a therapist's empathy may be a new, challenging and reparative experience. The use of empathy as a tool, condition or attitude is obviously familiar to the person-centred practitioner. Whilst Barth (op. cit.) acknowledges that Kohut didn't 'invent' empathy, like many other self psychologists, she omits Rogers from her resumé of the concept and its development. One of the contributions of self psychology to our understanding of empathy has been its emphasis on the client's internalisation of the therapist's stance and the development of self-empathy. From a person-centred perspective Snyder (1994, p. 97) discusses self-empathy, which

he defines as 'the attitude of compassion and curiosity regarding one's own experience that enables one to be simultaneously conscious of feelings and detached from them'. Barrett-Lennard (1997) explores this further.

4 The concept of the self-object. For self psychologists, the client's ability to utilise the therapist's empathic attitude is part of the 'self–object transference' (see Chapter 4). Whilst the vocabulary and some of the concepts may differ between self psychology and person-centred psychology, the idea that the therapist may, for a time, fulfil certain needs for the client is, in our view, uncontentious. It is consistent with views about the process of empathy (Greenberg & Elliot, 1997; Stern, 1985, 1990); and with an acknowledgement of the importance of the client's empathy for themselves (Rogers, 1959b); in the context of group therapy, for each other (see Giesekus & Mente, 1986); and of the importance of the client's experience of empathy through contact in the therapeutic relationship (see Erskine, Mousund & Trautmann, 1999). When we are, for instance, working with or thinking about a client with an eating disorder, we may think about this in terms of her self- or organismic regulation of self-esteem, feelings and behaviours.

Organismic reorganisation

From the discussion about the somatic element of organismic disorganisation (p. 167), it follows that 'organismic reorganisation', a term Perls (1947/69) uses, also works – and must work – at a somatic level. In the context of his process conception of psychotherapy, Rogers (1958/67a) suggests that there is a certain physiological loosening at what he identifies as the sixth stage of this process. He reports moistness in the eyes and muscular relaxation, and hypothesises improved circulation and improved conductivity of nervous impulses. He follows this (p. 148) with a transcription of part of a therapy session. The client has expressed the wish that his parents would die or disappear:

Client: They're somehow still so strong. I don't know. There's some umbilical – I can almost feel it inside me – swish (*and he gestures, plucking himself away by grasping at his navel.*)

Therapist: They really do have a hold on your umbilical cord.

Client: It's funny how real it feels . . . It's like a burning sensation, kind of, and when they say something which makes me anxious I can feel it right here (*pointing*). I never thought of it quite that way.

Therapist: As though if there's a disturbance in the relationship between you, then you do just feel it as though it was a strain on your umbilicus.

Client: Yeah, kind of like in my gut here. It's so hard to define the
               feeling that I feel there.

It is this kind of therapeutic work, amongst other examples he cites, that
leads Fernald (2000) to assert that organismic experiencing is the fundamental construct of the person-centred approach, and to claim Rogers as a
body-centred therapist. As Rogers (1953/67a, p. 103) himself puts it:
'psychotherapy (at least client-centered therapy) is a process whereby man
becomes his organism – without self-deception, without distortion . . . [It]
seems to mean a getting back to sensory and visceral experience.'

For instance, when a person experiences her whole body or a part of it as
either 'dead' or as not belonging to her, her thoughts and emotions as not
arising from her, and when her movements are not accompanied by feelings
of spontaneity, she may experience herself as influenced by outside forces.
For Angyal (1941, p. 116) such a 'loss of ego reference'

> refers to a disturbance on the symbolic level. This complex of symp-
> toms indicates, however, that certain factors of the biological subject
> organization are no longer under the government of the total organism,
> but they have fallen out or become segregated from the biological total
> process. They have been segregated possibly because they are
> incompatible with the rest of the personality.

Laing (1965, p. 78) describes this as 'the schizoid condition' in which

> there is a persistent scission between the self and the body. What the
> individual regards as his true self is experienced as more or less
> disembodied, and bodily experience and actions are in turn felt to be
> part of the false-self system.

One example of therapeutic work with this experience state is reported by
Van Werde (2002). He describes his work with 'Henry', a patient who
believes that his internal organs have been relocated, and that the only way
to reorganise them is for him to fall down onto the floor heavily. This was
often accompanied by loud and disturbing screaming. Accepting his frame
of reference, and drawing on the theory and practice of pre-therapy (see
Prouty, 1994; Prouty, Van Werde & Pörtner, 2002), Van Werde helps
Henry to contact his feelings, with the result that his falling and self-
harming behaviour lessens.

Other approaches, especially some forms of gestalt and body psychotherapy, take a more active, interventionist approach to such reorganisation
(see Perls, 1947/69; Staunton, 2002). Perls suggests (p. 73) an addition to
the psychoanalytic rule of free association: that the patient 'is expected

to communicate everything he feels in his *body* . . . A simple method of covering the whole organismic situation is to ask the patient to convey to the analyst whatever he experiences mentally, emotionally and *physically.*' Brown (1990, p. viii), a body psychotherapist who first trained as a Rogerian therapist, for instance, talks about change in terms of dissolving rigidities:

> The positive change and growth process for us hinges upon the degree to which the old rigidities, both energetic and characterological, are dissolved and replaced by new forms of beingness-for-self and beingness-for-others that attest to a more integrated differentiation for the person's embodied soul.

However, Fernald (2000, p. 176) observes that Rogers' ultimate interest is to facilitate organismic experiencing and that he does not push to intensify or to regulate experiences: 'For Rogers the organic movement of contracting or tightening are no less important than those of expanding and loosening.' Although Rogers values fluidity (see Chapters 2 and 8), his empathic tracking of organismic movement in whatever direction shows his commitment to a positive regard which is unconditional of the direction of movement. Fernald's point also echoes our own observations and assertions about the *descriptive* nature of Rogers' process conception of psychotherapy (see Appendix 3).

Self disorder, personality disorder

We discuss these together as we view them as two perspectives on the same phenomenon of 'disorder'. In person-centred psychology, self is a theoretical construct (see Chapter 4) and personality is a functional construct (see Chapter 5). Whilst we may understand 'self' as more reflexive and 'personality' as more social, we cannot understand any form of psychopathology, inauthenticity or alienation without considering both the *intra*personal and the *inter*personal nature of its origins and development, unless it is clearly organic. This view is echoed in recent and current thinking about psychopathology in contributions from psychoanalysis, self psychology and developmental psychology (see, for example, Masterson, 1988, and Ronningstam, 1998). The APA (2000) still uses the term 'personality disorder' and doesn't refer to self disorder. However, most of the literature on personality disorders recasts them in terms of 'disorders of the self' or 'primary disorders of the self'. Also, certain diagnostic categories such as dissociative identity disorder, formerly multiple personality disorder, are being more accurately described as dissociative self disorder. Swildens (2003, p. 9) suggests that 'Self-pathology precedes interpersonally acquired guilt and the ensuing guilt economy. At first, we are primarily preoccupied with ourselves, and consequently of course with the important others who contributed to the formation of our selves.' However, as we argued in earlier chapters, and especially Chapter 4, we cannot understand 'self' outside of the interpersonal field. Self does not precede personality. They are, rather, different ways of thinking about different aspects or manifestations of the human organism.

We discussed Rogers' theory of development and, specifically, self-development in Chapter 4. Here, we take up the story where we left it there, and describe the breakdown of that development, in terms of: the development of incongruence, discrepancies in behaviour, the experience of threat and the process of defence, breakdown and disorganisation. Rogers (1959b, p. 224):

⟶ 'When *self-experiences* of the individual are discriminated by significant others as being more or less worthy of *positive regard*, then *self-regard* becomes similarly selective.'

Rogers uses the word 'when' rather than 'if' as he acknowledges that this process is inevitable. The absence of any conditions of worth is a hypothetical state in which (p. 244) 'the needs for *positive regard* and *self-regard* would never be at variance with *organismic evaluation*'.

⟶ When the individual avoids or seeks an experience solely because it is less or more worthy of regard, by himself or others, then he acquires a condition of worth or value: 'You're only OK, if you . . .'

In moving away from 'that self which one truly is' Rogers (1960/1967) identifies a tendency to move away from pleasing others and, similarly, one away from meeting the expectations of others. Some years later, from a transactional perspective, Kahler and his colleagues, who were interested in the behavioural clues to such expectations and conditionality, identified certain distinctive sets of behaviours, expressed in words, tones, gestures, postures and facial expressions. They listed five of these behaviour sequences: Be Perfect, Please (others), Try Hard, Be Strong, and Hurry Up (Kahler & Capers, 1974; Kahler, 1978).

⟶ Because of the need for self-regard and the regard of others, the individual perceives his experience selectively, in terms of the external conditions of worth he internalises.

⟶ In certain situations experiences which fit with his conditions of worth are perceived and symbolised accurately: 'I did please her, and I am

OK'. Experiences which don't fit with such conditions are perceived selectively and distorted: 'I didn't do that right, so I must be bad or wrong' or 'There's no pleasing them'; are denied to awareness, as if 'I shouldn't want that'; or ignored: 'What desire?' (see Rogers, 1951).

Rogers (ibid., p. 226) comments that 'from the time of the first selective *perception* in terms of *conditions of worth*, the states of *incongruence between self and experience*, of *psychological maladjustment* and of *vulnerability*, exist to some degree'. Bozarth (1998, p. 83) summarises this process: 'Conditionality is the bedrock of Rogers' theory of pathology.'

Although distortion and denial are the two defence mechanisms generally identified within person-centred psychology, a close reading of Rogers' (1951) theory of personality and behaviour shows that he also refers to those experiences which are ignored (p. 503) *'because there is no perceived relationship to the self-structure'*. Despite identifying this third defence mechanism, when he comes to represent the personality in diagrammatic terms, Rogers omits this defence of ignoring or 'ignoration' (see Tudor & Merry, 2002). We consider this to be an example of Rogers emphasising a self-referential view of the individual, and discounting the impact of others in the phenomenal, environmental field.

— Some experiences now occur in the organism which the person does not recognise as self-experiences. He does not accurately symbolise them or organise them into his self-structure.

— This leads to the development of discrepancies in behaviour which are (Rogers, 1959b, p. 227) 'either unrecognized as self-experiences or perceived in distorted or selective *fashion in such a way as to be congruent with the* self'.

For Rogers, this describes the psychological basis for neurotic and psychotic behaviours. Consistent with both his empiricism and his phenomenological perspective (see Chapter 1), Rogers views rationalisation, compensation, fantasy, paranoia, catatonia, and so on as *behaviours*. In doing so, he cuts across the traditional conceptual distinction between neurosis and psychosis, a point we discuss further (below).

Rogers continues (p. 228): 'the incongruence between self and experience is handled by the distorted perception of experience or behaviour, or by the denial of experience . . . or by some combination of distortion and denial'.

— As the organism continues to function, an experience which is incongruent is perceived or subceived as threatening.

LIVERPOOL JOHN MOORES UNIVERSITY
LEARNING SERVICES

This is because if the experience were perceived and symbolised accurately, the self-concept would no longer be a consistent gestalt and the person would feel more anxious. According to Rogers (p. 227), 'The process of *defence* is the reaction which prevents these events from occurring.' In other words: defences are there for protection. However, the consequences of defensiveness are: rigidity of perception, an inaccurate perception of reality, and 'intensionality', which Rogers describes as the characteristic of a person in a defensive state: perceiving his experience in absolute, unconditional and over-generalised terms, and confusing fact with evaluation.

Rogers' theory of defence and, specifically, his use of the word 'threat' was influenced by the work of Hogan (1948). In defining anxiety as a threat Rogers is agreeing with Adler, Goldstein, Horney and May in viewing anxiety as a result of a threat to a value that an organism holds as necessary for existence, as distinct from viewing threat as an instinctual impulse.

⟶ Finally, in this process, if the organism's process of defence is unable to operate successfully, due to a large or significant degree of incongruence, occurring suddenly or obviously, for instance, as a result of a trauma, then a person will experience a state of disorganisation.

Rogers (ibid.) distinguishes between defensive and disorganised behaviours. The distinction is based on a description of a gradual process from discrepancy, threat and defence to a distinct point at which a person's process of defence no longer holds. This experience and concept of disorganisation includes many of the more 'irrational' and 'acute' psychotic behaviours. Rogers argues both that this is a more fundamental classification than the neurotic–psychotic one, and that it avoids the concepts of neurosis and psychosis being viewed as entities in themselves.

Reflecting on this process towards disorganisation, Rogers suggests that, once such acute psychotic behaviours have been exhibited, a further process of defence sets in in order to protect the organism against the painful awareness of such disorganisation. The process of this defence, he tentatively suggests, is characterised by a switch between the denied experiences and an altered self-concept being 'regnant'. This has echoes of Berne's (1961/1975) notion of different ego states having at different times 'executive power'.

Most theories of personality propose a structure to the personality (such as id, ego and superego) and, indeed, in his description and image of the structure of the total personality (Figure 6.1) Rogers (1951) also uses the language of structure. The overlapping area in Figure 6.1 represents that part of the personality which is congruent and integrated, and the distance or gap between experience and self-structure. We refer to the personality as

Self-structure   Experience

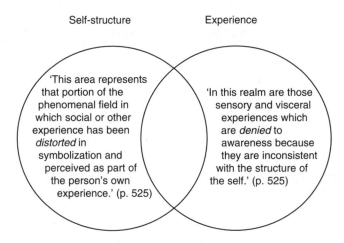

'This area represents
that portion of the
phenomenal field in
which social or other
experience has been
distorted in
symbolization and
perceived as part of
the person's own
experience.' (p. 525)

'In this realm are those
sensory and visceral
experiences which
are *denied* to
awareness because
they are inconsistent
with the structure of
the self.' (p. 525)

Figure 6.1 The total personality – in tension (Rogers, 1951).

being in tension, as that is consistent with Rogers' view of the organism (see Chapter 2).

Although Rogers concludes his outline of a theory of personality and behaviour with this figure, he frames the theory in terms of process. Moreover, his description of self-structure and experience refers to an 'area' and a 'realm' of the phenomenal field. In this sense, his figure of the total personality is a framework within which we may describe the relationship between a person and their environment, including other persons (see Chapter 7). Gendlin (1964) makes a similar point when he argues that personality structure cannot explain personality *change*. Structure arises out of process, a view which is consistent with the principles of constructivism. Given that this figure represents a process, we may use it to symbolise the authentic organism (Figure 6.2) and, drawing on Rogers' distinction, behaving defensively (Figure 6.3) and in a disorganised way (Figure 6.4).

This description of the breakdown of self-development, an increasing alienation from self, together with increasing disordered behaviour, provides the person-centred therapist with a view of self pathology which encompasses 'disorders of the self'. According to Kohut (1977) all addictions to substances (food, alcohol, drugs), as well as to sex, aim to fulfil the structural gap which ensues from having an insecurity about the self and feelings of self-fragmentation. This may be viewed as an example of Rogers' description of a gap between the experience of fragmentation and a concept of self which doesn't allow of such fragmentation.

In Chapter 4 we refer to Clarkson and Lapworth's (1992) interrelated concepts of self (wholeness, interpersonally developed, and moving). Here

Self-structure
Experience

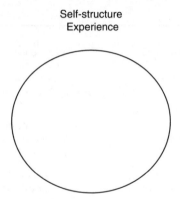

Figure 6.2 The total personality – when experience is symbolised accurately.

Self-structure   Experience

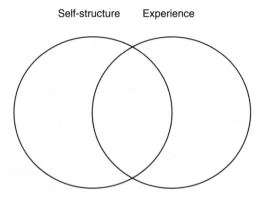

Figure 6.3 The total personality – defensive behaviour.

Self-structure   Experience

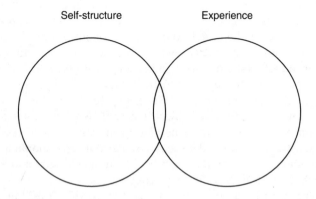

Figure 6.4 The total personality – disorganised behaviour.

we summarise the sense of experiencing a multiplicity of selves and the concept of the true – and false – self.

- 'I wasn't myself', 'He was beside himself with rage' – These describe the sense of someone feeling, or witnessing someone feeling, dislocated. In the second case the subject is, as it were, standing somewhere else, 'beside' himself. In this description the person is dissociated, his rage is discounted and, possibly, his related behaviour is unowned, as in 'I couldn't help myself'. Being 'taken over' in some way (by drink, rage, anxiety or panic) implies that there are parts of the whole person which act independently or 'feel' independent. This may be thought of as false or compliant (see next point); such 'parts' certainly imply a multiple sense of self or a sense of multiple selves which, at an extreme, may be manifested in a multiple personality disorder or dissociative identity disorder. From a client-centred perspective, Warner (1998, 2000) identifies and discusses dissociated process, describing effective therapeutic work based on understanding and empathic connection with clients' multiple presentations.
- 'I'm not feeling myself today' and 'She's back to her old self' – Both these phrases imply a sense of a core or 'true' self, which a person may not be feeling today but which she can get back to. 'I'm so sorry. I don't know what came over me. That wasn't like me at all' – describes a sense of 'not me' or 'false self'. For Winnicott (1960/65) 'me/not me' is an inevitable corollary of the sense of 'I am' and a necessary and important part of human development, one which has parallels in transactional analysis in the concept of impasse (see Mellor, 1980; Clarkson & Lapworth, 1992). The notion of the 'real me' goes back to James (see Chapter 4) and, in the fields of psychiatry and psychotherapy, has been developed notably by Winnicott (1956/58, 1960/65) and later by Masterson (1988). The problem with the interrelated terms of true and false is that they not only posit a split in the self, but also one which implies a judgement of good and bad. It is echoed within person-centred literature by the unhelpful notion of the 'organismic self' (Seeman, 1983). Significantly Winnicott (1956/58) himself views the 'false self' as an aspect of the true self:

> In the cases on which my work is based there has been what I call a true self hidden, protected by a false self. *This false self is no doubt an aspect of the true self.* It hides and protects it, and it reacts to the adaptation failures and develops a pattern corresponding to the pattern of environmental failure. In this way the true self is not involved in the reacting, and so preserves a continuity of being. However, this hidden true self suffers an impoverishment that derives from lack of experience [our emphasis].

Dependency-related 'disorder'

As an example of self disorder we discuss dependency-related disorder. We think this is particularly interesting because, of all mammals, human beings are born the least neurologically mature, with only 25% of adult brain volume; develop the most slowly; and are, in comparison, the most dependent for the longest period of time for nutritional, social and emotional support. We may say that we are 'hard wired' for dependence, and have to learn independence. In the early phases of human infancy, social care is synonymous with physiological regulation (see Chapter 2). From an organismic perspective which acknowledges the importance and impact of the environment, any understanding of dependence must consider the extent to which a person's environment was in particularly active interchange with her as an infant.

The APA (2004, p. 665) defines dependent personality disorder as 'A pervasive and excessive need to be taken care of that leads to submissive or clinging behaviour and fears of separation, beginning by early adulthood and present in a variety of contexts' as indicated by a number of criteria (see Box 6.1). The wording and tone of this description of diagnostic features is passive and blaming. Whose 'need' is it anyway? Given the necessary early dependent relationship between a primary caregiver and child, this could as easily read: 'A pervasive and excessive need to take care of another that leads to submissive or clinging behaviour and fears of separation in the caregiver or child, or both.'

From an organismic perspective we argue that:

- Dependence has its origins in necessary and healthy development. Advice and reassurance (criterion 1), for instance, may be viewed as an expression of the unconditional positive regard of a significant other. Furthermore, as Angyal (1965/73, pp. 106–7) points out, though the word has taken on a pejorative meaning, dependence 'is one aspect of every community formation, an expression of the homonomous trend'. He continues: 'Only the dependence that expresses the neurotic feeling of helplessness, and consequently far exceeds the objective necessity for support, merits negative evaluation.'
- Dependence, therefore, begins in childhood and not in early adulthood. Furthermore, there are many examples of ways in which society, through its institutions, encourages dependency and discourages responsibility (criterion 2). In his critique of the education system, for instance, Gatto (2002) argues that schools themselves can become pathological, and that psychopathic schools encourage dependency and passivity. We see that this is also true of those psychotherapy and counselling trainings which infantilise adult learners or trainees.

Box 6.1 Diagnostic criteria for dependent personality disorder (APA, 2000)

Diagnostic Criteria for 301.6 Dependent Personality Disorder

A pervasive and excessive need to be taken care of that leads to submissive or clinging behaviour and fears of separation, beginning by early adulthood and present in a variety of contexts as indicated by five (or more) of the following:

1) has difficulty making everyday decisions without an excessive amount of advice and reassurance from others
2) needs others to assume responsibility for most major areas of his or her life
3) has difficulty expressing disagreement with others because of fear of loss of support or approval. **Note:** Do not include realistic fears of retribution.
4) has difficulty initiating projects or doing things on his or her own (because of a lack of self-confidence in judgment or abilities rather than a lack of motivation or energy)
5) goes to excessive lengths to obtain nurturance and support from others, to the point of volunteering to do things that are unpleasant
6) feels uncomfortable or helpless when alone because of exaggerated fears of being unable to care for himself or herself
7) urgently seeks another relationship as a source of care and support when a close relationship ends
8) is unrealistically preoccupied with fears of being left to take care of himself or herself

---

- Each of the statements defining the criteria of dependent personality disorder may be turned around. Thus (criterion 3), if a child is not supported or approved of when expressing disagreement, then it is likely that she learns to be acquiescent, and thereby develops a condition of worth: 'I'm only OK if I keep quiet' (see p. 172). In this sense, each of the criteria statements, if turned around, may be viewed as describing a particular form of alienation, of a dependent process, which illustrates the process of defence, breakdown and disorganisation described above (pp. 172–4).
- Most of the statements carry some comparative qualifier (excessive, most, exaggerated, urgently, unrealistically) which implies or relies on a judgement about how the particular person functions and is in any case value-laden and culturally specific. From a person-centred perspective such a judgement can, ultimately, only be made by the 'dependent' person herself, in the context of her environment.

- Dependence is co-created by the primary caregiver/s and significant others in a child's environment, and by how the child responds and is supported to respond. Thus the child may develop authentically or may express her alienation in the form of this 'disorder' or, more accurately, *process.*

In advancing this critique we are not denying the reality of what one client referred to as being 'too dependent on others'. Laing (1965) describes it poignantly, and phenomenologically, with regard to one client who 'could not become a "person"'. He had '"no self", "I am only a response to other people, I have no identity of my own . . . other people supply me with my existence."'

Narcissistic personality 'disorder'

The third example of 'disorder' we use to illustrate our approach to psychopathology as alienation is narcissistic personality disorder, which, following Lasch (1979), we think is still prevalent in Western culture. The disorder or, as we prefer, 'process', takes its name from the Greek myth of Narcissus.

According to myth, Narcissus was the son of a god, extremely handsome, and admired by many. One of the women who loved Narcissus was a nymph called Echo. Echo couldn't speak except to repeat what was said to her, so she couldn't tell Narcissus that she loved him. One day, Narcissus was walking in the woods with some friends. Having become separated from them, he called out 'Is anyone here?' to which Echo replied: 'Here. Here.' She stepped forward with open arms, but Narcissus refused to accept her love. Echo was so upset that she went and hid in a cave, and wasted away until nothing was left of her, except her voice. Nemesis, a goddess, found out about this, and was very angry. She decided to punish Narcissus by making him fall in love with himself. One day, when Narcissus looked at his reflection in a pond, he fell in love with it. He stayed, gazing at his reflection, until he too died, rooted to the spot forever, and taking the form of a flower – narcissus. In other versions it is Aphrodite, the goddess of love, who curses Narcissus for his rejection of romantic love.

As we reflect on this story, we may identify a number of elements:

1 　That Narcissus and others both perceived that he was extremely handsome and admired. There is a view that every Narcissus needs his or her Echo, but in most versions of the myth, the original Narcissus knew that he was handsome and admired before he saw his reflection. This hints at an earlier, developmental process by which he learnt to

love himself rather than to love (an)other, and leads to an egotistical narcissism.

2   That Echo couldn't speak her love to Narcissus acknowledges the fact that narcissism is co-created, in part by the withholding of love or of the communication of love. This process leads to a more dissociative narcissism.

3   That, having become separated from his friends, it is significant that Narcissus calls out 'Is anyone here?' It would be more usual to say 'Is anyone there?' It's as if the movement towards relationship has to be initiated by the other, and even so may well be rejected. Fairbairn (1952) suggests that our greatest motivation is for contact and that, as a consequence of this, our greatest fear is of separation. Similarly, Symington (1993, p. 18) says that, as the self is inherently relational, 'the core of narcissism is a hatred of the relational . . . and one of the ways that narcissism operates is to destroy separateness'.

In this sense narcissism is a form of alienation from self-in-relationship.

According to Kohut (1971, p. 200) the particular affective experiences of narcissistic disorders encompass a spectrum, 'ranging from anxious grandiosity and excitement on the one hand to mild embarrassment and self-consciousness or severe shame, hypochondria, and depression on the other'. It is said that shame loves to hide, and many narcissists hide their shame or fear of shame by being out in the open, often the centre of attention, in the public gaze. A person may deal with a shaming experience by becoming obsessive about himself: 'It's all about me.' The classical 'features' of narcissism include: grandiosity; self-importance, maintained by exaggeration of achievements and talents; being 'special'; requiring excessive admiration; having a sense of entitlement; being exploitative; lacking in empathy; envious; and arrogant. From an holistic perspective, we see this inflation of self as representing a loss of a sense of self as homonomous, and of a sense of others in the relational field.

In the ordinary course of events a child's grandiosity and omnipotence get deflated and challenged by the rough and tumble of life, and by having to deal with others. Masterson (1981) argues that, in the case of people who have a narcissistic disorder, this deflation didn't happen and that this represents an arrest in the child's development. Schore (1994), amongst others, locates the origins of narcissism in the practising phase of child development, especially in transacting reunions following stressful separations. Broucek (1982) identifies two types of narcissism: an 'egotistical' type and a 'dissociative' type, also described by Gabbard (1989) as 'oblivious' and 'hypervigilant', respectively. This is important, as the *DSM-IV* fails to characterise the latter type of narcissism, thereby misrepresenting the range of narcissistic personality process. Schore (1994, p. 430) explains the neurobiology of these emotional developments:

Due to psychobiological regulatory failures the high levels of positive affect that fuel grandiose states are either underregulated or overregulated. An insecure-resistant attachment interaction is a source generator of egotistical narcissistic personalities who possess a sympathetic-dominant limbic system, while an insecure-avoidant one engenders dissociative narcissistic personalities.

Schore's focus on regulation is entirely consistent with the organismic perspective developed in this present work (see especially Chapter 2).

The person with an egotistical narcissistic process will often have been reared by adoring, doting parents who have objectified their child, and failed to provide enough realistic positive and negative evaluation to support, as Broucek (1991, p. 60) puts it, 'some degree of tension between the actual self and the idealized self'. From a person-centred perspective, tension is inherent in the human organism: a fact and necessity of life. However, as we note above (p. 174), it is the degree and extent of tension which distinguishes defensive from disorganised behaviours and personality processes (see Figures 6.3 and 6.4). In narcissistic process, this is fuelled by the degree of idealisation, initially from the mother or primary carer. One mother, informed about her adult son's grandiosity and criminality, became misty-eyed, and could only comment that 'He was such a lovely child, so loving and artistic.' In this case, in the child's development, there was no tension between mother and son, that is, no realistic evaluation of his behaviour or early confrontation of his developing narcissism. In terms of Rogers' (1951) personality theory, we would expect that the further apart a person's experience is from his sense of self-structure, the more extreme the sense of alienation and the more serious the pathological process. However, this is to read Figure 6.3 in only one plane. In the case of narcissistic process, the person's experience is more or less congruent with his sense of self, as he does not let in or allow much, if any, feedback from the environment which doesn't support his grandiosity. One example of this is a person whose behaviour had breached codes of professional and ethical conduct. Confronted by colleagues who were considering taking action against him, he is reported to have said: 'Don't worry. I'm going to complain about myself.' This kind of narcissistic process is represented in Figure 6.5 in which the boundary between the total personality and his environment is shown as thicker or more rigidly defensive and impervious to feedback from the environment of others. The rejection or deflection of such feedback maintains a rigid, though coherent, sense of self-in-isolation.

An egotistical narcissistic process is, in effect, the result of an overdose at a feeling level. Working with the adult narcissist, it is important that the therapist is empathic and that this is experienced by the client as relational. As the client allows himself to experience the therapist's empathy, he also becomes more open to the evaluations of others and thus experiences more

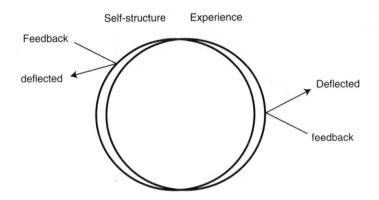

Self-structure   Experience

Feedback

deflected

Deflected

feedback

Figure 6.5 The total personality – egotistical narcissistic process.

dissonance between his experience (of the therapist and others) and his sense of self.

The dissociative type of narcissism, by contrast, is, for the child, the result of being emotionally underwhelmed. Often, a parent who is depressed does not provide sufficient positive vitality affects in mirroring transactions, or help for the child to recover from his shame, with the result that the child often has low self-esteem and diminished energy. As both child and adult he becomes highly sensitive. In contrast to the self-absorption of the egotistical narcissist, the attention of the dissociative narcissist is continually directed towards others. One client continually rejected his therapist's empathy, responding 'Yes, but . . .' to her every empathic response. No matter how hard the therapist tried she '. . . got it wrong' and ended up feeling rejected, blamed and de-skilled (see Figure 6.6).

Both narcissistic processes are based on parental misattunement and lack of regulation. Therapists working with narcissistic process experience what is referred to in the literature as the client's 'narcissistic rage'. The rage of the egotistical narcissistic process is more explosive, and the dissociative process is more implosive. One way of understanding this is that the client experiences the therapist's responses as repetitions of the unempathic approach of his parent or parents. Working with this process is hard for the therapist and, in doing so, we find the following helpful to remember and sometimes hang on to:

1   That the client's rage is a communication of certain needs as perceived by the self.
2   That the client's rage is a form of repair, in that, as a child, he could not be thus rageful or vengeful.
3   That the client's rage is an attempt to create a more responsive other.

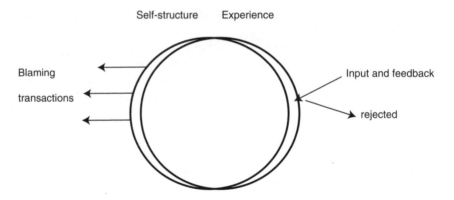

Figure 6.6 The total personality – dissociative narcissistic process.

4   That the very fact of being in therapy is highly evocative for the client as it involves some abandonment of his self-sufficiency, and this quite often leads to premature termination on the part of the client.
5   That, often, and especially early on in therapy, the therapist needs to 'hang on', and maintain her empathic attitude.
6   That empathy has been found to be particularly useful with narcissistic process, a treatment strategy also elaborated by Kohut (1977).
7   That it is important that empathy is viewed and presented in a relational context. In this sense, as we argue throughout the book, we find the concept of homonomy especially useful. Autonomy, both as a value and a goal, can be used to support this pathological process, often in the form of a fierce and rigid self-sufficiency, from a place of mistrust, as if the client feels he'd be poisoned if he were to take in anything from somebody else. The concept of homonomy puts the client in a relational field, with the therapist.

One of the reasons we have focused on narcissistic process, apart from the cultural perspective referred to above, is because therapy itself, and therapists themselves, may be viewed as narcissistic (see Chapter 4). For person-centred therapists there is a danger that we may be, or may be experienced as, 'too empathic'. As Hargaden puts it, in a contribution to an internet discussion group (relationalta@topica.com, 3 October, 2005): 'Therapy based on person-centred or self-psychological perspectives, with their focus on endlessly tolerating the client's needs for mirroring and twinship, can sometimes seem to be quintessentially narcissistic.' Whilst we take issue with Hargaden's use of the word 'endlessly' as, for us, that would simply be bad therapy or misattunement, we think she has a point. She continues: 'The consequence of this is that the therapist becomes idealised, thus making client and therapist the "perfect" narcissistic couple.' Of course, this critique applies equally to therapies which rely on a transferential type of treatment. The notion that a client can only be cured through the analysis of his projections onto the therapist, places the analyst, and her reflective self-analysis, at the centre of the treatment, with the client reduced to an echo. This said, we find it heartening that in psychoanalytical circles there is an increasing interest in empathy; in considering empathy and the client's response as a test of the accuracy and effectiveness of interpretations; and in the relational turn in therapy.

In this chapter we have reviewed three 'disorders' of our times. In doing so we have sought to develop or begin to develop systematic and genuinely person-centred descriptions of alienated and inauthentic processes. With regard to the organismic disorder of compulsive eating we drew on elements of a person-centred self psychology (see Chapter 4). With regard to a dependent 'self' disorder we offered a critique of a particular psychiatric formulation, based on Rogers' (1959) theory of self and personality development. With regard to narcissistic personality processes, we offered an integration of a holistic theory of neurotic process with more recent research in neuroscience, framed in terms of Rogers' (1951) personality theory. The selection of 'disorders' is significant in that, being 'of our times', they may be clearly viewed as organismic and environmental. Finally, our approach to their understanding offers a number of ways in which we may further develop systematic descriptions of pathology, as an aid to theory and practice.

Self reintegration, personality integration

The process of self-reordering or reintegration is described by Rogers (1959b, p. 230) as encompassing and requiring:

1 a decrease in conditions of worth; and an increase in unconditional positive regard, and
2 the unconditional positive regard of a significant other, communicated in a context of empathic understanding, with the consequent increase in the client's own unconditional positive self-regard, whereby threat is reduced, the process of defence reversed and '*experiences* customarily *threatening* are *accurately symbolized* and integrated into the *self concept*'.

A person's ability to integrate, specifically her mastery of her environment and her perception of reality, was one of Jahoda's (1958) criteria for mental health. Within person-centred literature, and specifically with reference to the concept of the fully functioning person, Seeman (1983, 1984) has written about 'personality integration' (see Chapter 5).

If conditionality is, as Bozarth (1998, p. 83) says, 'the bedrock of Rogers' theory of pathology', then unconditionality is fundamental to the process of reintegration. We need only reflect on our own conditionality as therapists, and the conditionality of many environments in the field of mental illness and psychiatry, to appreciate the radical implications of this statement for therapeutic practice and services (see Newnes, Holmes & Dunn, 1999, 2001). The second point about the context of empathy is particularly pertinent in the light of recent research in neuroscience concerning the impact and benefits of empathy (see Chapters 2 and 4).

Paula referred herself to a therapist, describing herself as 'too dependent on others', and wanting some short-term therapy to resolve this. She held a responsible job in a caring profession. She was, however, anxious at work, one expression of which was that she tended to over prepare, in an attempt to seek the approval of her managers, unsuccessfully as it turned out. She lived with her parents, having returned to the family home after college in which she had lived in halls of residence. She had difficulty in making everyday decisions. After a period of individual therapy she joined a therapy group in which, initially, she would often represent the same issue or question, seeking advice and reassurance from other group members. She was generally pleasing, had a somewhat fixed smile, and, initially, rarely disagreed with either her therapist or other group members. She had difficulty in taking the initiative in relationships due to her lack of self-confidence. She had a series of unfulfilling, casual relationships, including one in which she was abused. However, she was reluctant to let the particular man go as she experienced him as caring for her when he was around. This need was partly fuelled by the fact that she felt uncomfortable and helpless when alone. In diagnostic terms she fulfilled the criteria for dependent personality disorder (APA, 2000).

Initially the therapy went well. The therapist liked Paula, and Paula seemed to benefit from feeling acknowledged and supported. She joined a group run by the therapist. Again, she felt supported by the therapist and by the others members of the group, although she found any conflict upsetting. After a while she seemed to be stuck: work was still difficult, she was still living at home, and there were no signs of a supportive partner. At this time the therapist realised that, in subtle ways, he had been avoiding Paula and had been treating her somewhat conditionally, favouring some of her decisions over others. He realised that he needed to pay attention to her and to accept her need to depend upon him. This led to a fruitful period of therapy during which the therapist adopted some of the principles of sharing life therapy (Stamatiadis, 1990), including shorter, more frequent individual sessions, accepting phone calls from her, and so on. Over time and some testing, this led to him experiencing an increase in unconditional positive regard for her and an increase in Paula's own unconditional positive self-regard. Gradually she came to feel less threatened by others and was able to establish independent relationships with friends and, eventually, a partner.

A note on the pathology of organism, and self and person. In our discussions of the 'pathology' of the organism, and self and person, we have aimed to elaborate a person-centred description of inauthentic process. We do not want to create another framework for the categorisation of different forms of mental illness, disorder or disease and specifically do not locate, for example, eating disorders as a form of organismic disorganisation, and – as we outlined earlier – disorders of the self as only self disorders, and personality disorders as only disordering of the person. Rather, from an organismic perspective, we believe that any form of alienation, wherever it originates, is likely to resonate in the whole person, organismically, in relationship with herself, and with others in the context of their environment. We do believe that it is important to acknowledge differentiated processes and we see such processes, such as dependent processes or narcissistic processes, as various and varied expressions of the inauthenticity of organism, as well as the self and person.

Environmental press

Given the views we outline in Chapter 3 concerning the organism's tendency to actualise, it makes no sense to talk in terms of a pathological tendency. However, it does make sense to consider the ways in which external factors influence, support or thwart this inherent organismic tendency. In this consideration we draw on Murray's (1938) concept of 'press'. Although the concept of need had been widely used in psychology before Murray, he was the first psychologist to provide such a complete taxonomy of needs. Murray argues that whilst a person's needs influence their motives, motives are also influenced by external events. Just as the concept of need represents the significant determinants of behaviour *within* the person, the concept of 'press' refers to the significant determinants of behaviour in the *external* environment (1938, p. 121): 'The *press* of an object is what it can *do to the subject* or *for the subject* – the power that it has to affect the well-being of the subject in one way or another.' The connection between press and motive (and implied behaviour) is illustrated by examples in Table 6.1. The examples of press are adapted from Murray's original list.

Murray's concept of environmental press prefigures Lewin's (1952) force field analysis of change, influenced by driving and restraining forces. One example of environmental press might be when you're eating a sandwich. As you finish the sandwich, someone comes in with a take-away. Suddenly

Table 6.1 Examples of press and motive (developed from Murray, 1938)

Press	An example of motive
Parental separation	Desire to bond with partner
Accident	Caution
Loss of possessions	Desire for material objects
Retention of objects	Desire for acquisition
Rejection	Lack of concern
Rivalry	Desire to achieve
Birth of a sibling	Desire to be single
Aggression and maltreatment	Self-effacing
Dominance	Desire for freedom
Indulgence	Desire to be the centre of attention
Tenderness	Desire to be nurturing
Affiliation	Desire to belong
Sex	Desire for sex
Deception or betrayal	Desire for revenge
Inferiority	Desire for conquest

you don't feel satisfied. You lose interest in the sandwich and start to crave for some of the take-away meal. The motive to eat has been restimulated, not by a need but by a stimulus or press from the environment. The slightly old-fashioned phrase 'May I press you to . . . another cake?' echoes the sense of external pressure, polite or otherwise. In elaborating this concept, Murray distinguishes between *beta press*, that is, the significance of environmental objects as a person perceives them, and *alpha press*, that is, the properties of those environmental objects as they exist objectively, such as advertising – and, indeed, the press!

In his book *The Clinical Treatment of the Problem Child*, Rogers (1939) devotes one part to examples of the change of environment as a form of treatment, in terms of the foster home, and institutional placement. He does not, however, extend his acknowledgement of the therapeutic significance of a change of environment to a theoretical level. Murray's concept of press, by contrast, offers a (then) contemporary theoretical elaboration of the significance of the environment in the context, as we note in Chapter 2, of an appreciation of the organism. We think this is significant in a number of ways:

1   It provides the historical ground for other, more recent, considerations of the impact of the environment on the individual within person-centred therapy.
2   It provides a different focus on the person in that the gaze of thera-peutic enquiry is not only on the individual alone. Interestingly, one element of Murray's (op. cit., p. 156) definition of autonomy is 'To be independent and free to act according to impulse. To be unattached, unconditioned, irresponsible. To defy conventions.' The environment,

in the form of the environmental press, and especially the *beta press* the person experiences or perceives, becomes equally the focus of a person (organism or environment)-centred therapy.

3   It provides an environmental context to the organism's tendency to actualise, whatever form, twists and turns that takes. Rather than seeing the person or, for instance, his tendency to self-harm as a problem or the problem, the concept of press promotes an appreciation of the interpersonal, intersubjective and co-created relationship between the person and their environment. Both person and environment, as well as the relationship between them, form the figure and ground of therapy. We now turn to the conditions of that therapy.

Chapter 7

Conditions

It is as though he listened and such listening as his enfolds us in a silence in which we begin to hear what we are meant to be.

Lao Tzu

Love received and love given comprise the best form of therapy.

Gordon Allport

The counselor, then, is one who is skilled in understanding human beings and their perceptions and who provides the conditions under which change in perceptions, and then self-initiated behavior change, can occur.

C.H. Patterson

The conditions serve to keep me on track when I tend to stray. Their richness continues to edify me as I explore their meaning and ramifications. Thus, I begin virtually all of my work by reviewing them.

Ned Gaylin

In this chapter we narrate a history of each therapeutic condition. This is consistent with what we've called our 'back to the future' approach, and allows us to look again at the roots of each condition, identify original understandings, track subsequent deviations and misunderstandings, and consider the implications of any of this for current and future practice. Although we have critiqued and, to some extent, debunked the conditions, at least as far as their logical necessity and sufficiency is concerned, we think it is important, nevertheless, to examine them in some detail. We think this for a number of reasons. Whether they are necessary or sufficient or not:

- They remain implicated in the process of effective therapy.
- They are central to much person-centred literature and thinking.
- They provide a framework for discussion and research within and outside person-centred therapy.

Before we do this we want to remind ourselves that we see the theory of the conditions as a seminal rather than a technological theory. Given this, the process of separating the conditions one from another is necessarily artificial. They are, says Gaylin (2002, p. 340), 'an integral whole, none separable from the others'. We separate them only so as to enrich our understanding of the whole. We close this chapter by looking again at the conditions as a whole, and at some of the ways in which they live with and inform one another in the service of that whole.

Psychological contact

Contact, or psychological contact, specifies for Rogers (1957) a 'minimal relationship', where (p. 96), each person 'makes some perceived difference in the experiential field of the other'. Its sole function in the theory seems to be to anchor his conviction, initially, at least, that meaningful therapeutic change can happen only when two or more people are in relationship. The human need for contact appears in the work of theorists as diverse as Angyal (1941), where it is implicit in the trend to homonomy; Fairbairn (1952), who views contact as the source of our greatest motivation as humans; and Berne (1970/73), who wrote about contact as a human hunger. Psychological contact, therefore, in these terms, is a *sine qua non*, an absolutely necessary condition or pre-condition. Gaylin (2002, p. 340) says that it 'has been virtually overlooked', and that for him it's synonymous with relationship. Sanders and Wyatt (2002, p. 8) describe it as 'a reciprocal interpersonal event, symbolized in awareness'. Although we agree with them that it's both interpersonal and reciprocal, we question whether it needs to be symbolised in awareness. Our grounds for this come from Rogers, who argues (1957, p. 96) that perception is probably not necessary, and that it may be 'sufficient if each makes some "subceived" difference'. Disputing this, Sanders and Wyatt (2002, p. 7) refer to an 'overwhelming body of scientific evidence' which they say militates against the notion of subception, and they wonder why person-centred writers have ignored this.

Rogers (1957, p. 100) defines psychological contact as a binary phenomenon, by which he means that two people are either in psychological contact, or they're not. In his 1959 paper (1959b, p. 215) he says specifically that the other five conditions 'exist on continua', implying that psychological contact, at least as he understands it, does not. Others disagree. Mearns, for instance, asserts (1997, p. 17) that 'the phenomenological reality of psychological contact to both clients and counsellors is that there are *degrees* of contact'. We wonder, in the first instance, how anyone can assert another's phenomenological reality dogmatically, as if it were an uncontested fact. We then need to ask whether clients and counsellors do experience degrees of contact, whether it's necessary or helpful to modify

Rogers' original formulation, and what it might add to our thinking or practice if we do. We see no reason to complicate the idea of contact. We think it's simpler, more elegant and more parsimonious to leave the notion as Rogers defined it, and to agree instead degrees of empathic understanding, unconditional acceptance, communication and perception.

This raises a number of questions, the first and most pressing of which is why we would allow degrees of other conditions, and not psychological contact. One answer to this is historical: because Rogers said so. He notes (1959b, p. 207) that he originally used the word 'relationship' to describe this condition, and found that this led to misunderstanding, 'for it was often understood to represent the depth and quality of a good relationship, or a therapeutic relationship'. He means, rather, to describe 'the *least* or minimum experience which could be called a relationship'. A relationship, then, does not have to begin at depth, nor to have therapeutic qualities from the beginning. Rogers argues simply that therapeutic change starts in and from the existence of relationship *per se*, rather than from any particular qualities of particular relationships. He continues: 'If more than this simple contact between two persons is intended, then the additional characteristics of that contact are specified in the theory.' We think that this is unambiguous, that Rogers saw psychological contact as a binary precondition, and that the burden of argument rests therefore with those who hold that psychological contact comes in degrees. We can sum up our position at this point by saying that psychological contact resembles electrical contact. All parts of a circuit need to be connected before electricity can flow, and the switch that connects is either on or off. Once the switch is on, electricity is flowing, and we can harness its power for all manner of tasks. Likewise, once we are in psychological contact the relationship is, so to speak, current, and all manner of things are possible.

If we define psychological contact as the least that can be called a relationship, then anything more of a relationship is, by definition, something more than psychological contact. We need, therefore, other terms to describe that something more. Rogers (1957, p. 96) says that the remaining five conditions 'define the characteristics of the relationship' which psychological contact allows. They offer ways of describing the degrees of relationship between therapist and client, and we suggest that they are precise enough, flexible enough, and open enough to allow us to describe those relationships in as much detail as they demand and deserve.

Rogers' inclusion of psychological contact as a *necessary* condition raises a question for us: is a relationship between two people really necessary for therapeutic change to occur? Bearing in mind our examination of the notion of necessity in Chapter 1, we are asking whether therapeutic change can ever happen without psychological contact. Rogers seems eventually to have asked himself a similar question. In a chapter published after Rogers' death, Rogers and Sanford (1989, p. 1484) give an example of therapeutic growth precipitated in a man as he is reading, in a prison cell, on his own. Later in the same chapter (p. 1492) they list five conditions as necessary for therapeutic change to take place. Psychological contact is not one of them.

This makes sense to us. Although many people experience moments of change within the immediacy of a relationship, there seems no reason why those moments should necessarily occur *only* in relationship. To return to our electrical analogy: there are some tasks that require electricity, and some that we can achieve more efficiently or effectively with electricity. Electricity, however, is not the only source of power, and some of us, sometimes, cook with gas.

There's another argument for suggesting that psychological contact need not be one of the six conditions. Watson (1984, p. 19) argues that if the other conditions are present, then psychological contact can be assumed and 'does not require its own operational definition'. We agree. If a therapist is experiencing empathic understanding and unconditional positive regard, and if a client is feeling understood and accepted, then the two are necessarily in psychological contact. It's implied in the other conditions and doesn't, therefore, need to be specified as a separate condition.

In the last thirty years, some theorists and practitioners, working within the person-centred approach and associated specifically with experiential therapy, have developed a way of working which they refer to as 'Pre-Therapy' (see Prouty, 1976, 1994; Van Werde, 1994, 1998). They work with people, some of whom are hospitalised, who are 'pre-expressive', 'psychotic' or 'retarded'. Their work is based on the theory of contact functions and behaviour, and the practice of contact reflections, and, as such, is viewed by some as expanding the concept of contact. The term 'pre-therapy' refers to the fact that they work with clients who would normally be considered or thought of as not amenable to therapy by virtue of their inability to make or sustain relationship. Conceptually, we locate this work at stages 1 and 2 of Rogers' (1958/67a) process conception of psychotherapy (see Appendix 3). On these grounds, we understand this as a specialised form of therapy, rather than 'pre'-therapy, and we see contact reflections as particular forms of empathic responses.

Client incongruence

The notion of incongruence refers specifically to an incongruence or inconsistency between experience and self, and captures the idea that aspects of a person's experience and being may be at odds with one another, with psychological, emotional and behavioural consequences. It is, says Rogers (1957, p. 96), 'a basic construct in the theory we have been developing' and 'refers to a discrepancy between the actual experience of the organism and the self picture of the individual insofar as it represents that experience'.

Incongruence is relatively unexamined and undeveloped as a theoretical construct. Once he'd defined it, and despite the significance we think it has for our understanding of psychological distress, Rogers paid less attention to it as a condition in its own right than he did to some of the other conditions. Subsequent writers have followed suit, to the point that a recent series of books on the therapeutic conditions gives congruence, empathic understanding and unconditional positive regard a volume each, contact and perception a shared volume, and incongruence nothing in its own right. There are exceptions. Drawing on the work of Hellmuth Kaiser, and using his terms, Van Kalmthout and Pelgrim (1990, p. 387) suggest that incongruence is a 'universal symptom', one of the 'perennial constants in human problems and their solutions'. Speierer (1990) and Biermann-Ratjen (1996, 1998) also examine incongruence and its relationship to psychopathology.

We think it's important to note that Rogers uses the term to describe a particular kind of incongruence, between particular and named aspects of a person's being: organismic experience and self picture. This definition of incongruence is a precise one, and Brazier (1995, p. 221) reminds us that we can't take all apparent inconsistencies as evidence of incongruence:

> When one is harmonious, one's outward manifestation in behaviour, facial expression, speech and so on is all of a piece with one's inner sentiments, beliefs and thoughts as they arise. However, what is consistent and what is inconsistent is more a function of the depth of perception of the observer than a description of the actual state of the person in question.

Incongruence is one of the organism's ways of protecting itself. It is not, therefore, in and of itself pathological. Biermann-Ratjen (1996, 1998) has described a process by which an organism (a) develops a self-concept in response to its perception of what others think; and (b) becomes incongruent as it defends against organismic experiences which are then inconsistent with that self-concept. Although the development of incongruence, then, has its roots in an organism's tendency to preserve itself in the face of immediate threat, some of the longer-term consequences of incongruence are unsettling or worse. 'There are' says Speierer (1990, p. 339) 'no neuroses nor psychosomatic disorders without incongruence.' This statement suggests that the notion of incongruence helps to describe and explain how people become psychologically distressed. It also paves the way for his later idea (1996, p. 300) that client-centred therapy is, essentially, 'the treatment of incongruence', and that its 'aims include the reduction of experienced incongruence, the improvement of coping with incongruence, the improvement of the ability to self-congruent experiencing, and the enlargement of incongruence tolerance'.

Rogers (1957, p. 96) describes a client's incongruence as if it were a fact: a client 'is in a state of incongruence, being vulnerable or anxious'. In his 1959 paper he identifies three process elements of incongruence: a general and generalised *vulnerability*, a dimly perceived tension or *anxiety*, and an *awareness* of incongruence. We think it's consistent with the otherwise phenomenological nature of person-centred thinking and practice to emphasise especially a client's *awareness* of incongruence. Just as psychological contact marks the beginning of relationship, so a client's awareness of his own incongruence marks the beginning of his search for health and healing. Unless a client is aware that he's unhappy or distressed he's unlikely to think about seeing a therapist. In that sense, we could argue that such awareness precedes psychological contact, since without it a client is unlikely even to find himself sitting with a therapist and available for relationship. In Rogers' words (1958/67a, p. 132), such an individual, unaware of his own incongruence, 'is not likely to come voluntarily for therapy'. Putting a client's awareness of his own incongruence first recognises that without it the therapeutic endeavour doesn't even begin, and that the client is not only at the *centre* of the process, but essential to the *beginning* of it. This is consistent with the view, reported by Tony Merry (personal communication, 18 July 1999), that Rogers also regarded this condition as, in effect, a pre-condition. Another way of saying this is that a client's awareness of incongruence is, in strict terms, a necessary condition, a condition without which therapy will not happen.

Congruence

Of the six conditions, congruence has probably generated the most confusion, a confusion deepened by polemical and polarised arguments about its place in theory and practice. On the one hand, for instance, we have Thorne (1991, p. 189): 'Acceptance, empathy and congruence – these three, as always, but the greatest and the most difficult and the most exciting and the most challenging is congruence.' And on the other we have Bozarth (2001, p. 189): 'When Rogers states that the conditions may be separate and that congruence is the most important, client-centered therapy no longer exists.'

We want first to distinguish between the term congruence and the idea which the term describes, if only to expose the extent to which the idea predates the term. The ideas of personal integrity and personal involvement, and the idea that these qualities are therapeutically helpful, predate the christening of those ideas with the name congruence. Writing in the early 1930s Taft (1933, p. 21), whose work Rogers read, says this:

> In the last analysis, therapy as a qualitative affair must depend upon the personal development of the therapist and his ability to use

consciously for the benefit of his client, the insight and self-discipline which he has achieved in his own struggle to accept self, life and time, as limited, and to be experienced fully only at the cost of fear, pain and loss. I do not mean that knowledge is not necessary, that technical skill is not necessary; they are, but they are of no value therapeutically without the person. To make case work therapeutic, incidentally or deliberately, one must *be* a therapist and only to the extent that this is true are the relationships one sets up therapeutic, regardless of the label, the number of visits or the interpretation recorded in the dictation.

Although she doesn't use the term congruence, Taft is describing some of the elements which we would now understand the term to cover. Implicit in what she says here are the following ideas:

- Therapy depends first upon the therapist's 'personal development' and then upon her willingness to put the fruits of that development – 'insight and self-discipline' – at the service of her client. The person of the therapist is central to the therapeutic endeavour.
- The therapist's self-acceptance is important, and particularly her acceptance of personal limitations – the 'struggle to accept self . . . as limited'. This suggests a need for humility, and both knowledge and acceptance of our own limits.
- The therapist's 'life and time' are also limited, and she must accept this. In some ways this is a recognition of existential givens.
- The therapist needs 'knowledge' and 'skills', but it's not these that are therapeutically valuable. This reminds us of some of what Rogers and Bozarth, among others, have said about the relative non-importance of techniques in person-centred practice.
- The therapist must, above all, '*be* a therapist'. Taft italicises the verb. This echoes her own etymological assertion (1933, p. 3) that therapy is about waiting and serving rather than doing anything to anyone; it prefigures the later Rogerian and person-centred emphasis on therapy as a way of being rather than doing; and foreshadows Bozarth's assertion (2001, p. 197): 'The only goal of the client-centered therapist is to be a certain way.'

Writing in *Client-Centered Therapy* (1951, p. 76), Rogers has this to say about congruence:

> This experience of discovering within oneself present attitudes and emotions which have been viscerally and physiologically experienced, but which have never been recognized in consciousness, constitutes one of the deepest and most significant phenomena of therapy.

We notice two things here:

1 The word congruence doesn't appear in the index to that book, so we can assume that Rogers hadn't named it yet.
2 He describes it as one of the outcomes of effective therapy for a client, and not as one of the conditions that it's necessary for a therapist to hold.

The structure of Rogers' later description of congruence is, though, already in place and will be familiar to readers of his later work. He's describing two worlds: a world of visceral and physiological experience, and a world of recognition 'in consciousness'. He's saying that in therapy those two worlds can become consistent one with the other, and therefore implying that they are often not, that we may often be experiencing feelings or sensations which we have not recognised in consciousness, of which we are not aware.

Ellingham (2001) has articulated some of the problems with this way of thinking about congruence. He points out that it borrows heavily from the Freudian model, and that that in itself carries some implications for person-centred practice. Freudian undertones aren't surprising if we remember that Rogers credits Otto Rank, one of the first generation of psychoanalysts, as an early and significant influence. Although Rank broke with Freud in the mid 1920s, his influence on Rogers puts Rogers only one handshake away from Freud; for more on this, see Kramer (1995).

Later in *Client-Centered Therapy*, Rogers articulates nineteen propositions, the fifteenth of which (p. 513) argues as follows:

> Psychological adjustment exists when the concept of the self is such that all the sensory and visceral experiences of the organism are, or may be, assimilated on a symbolic level into a consistent relationship with the concept of the self.

This resembles the earlier quotation: it posits the same two worlds and sees the still un-named congruence as describing the psychological adjustment of the client rather than a necessary characteristic of the therapist. Both of these quotations suggest that Rogers approached congruence initially from the perspective of what it shows the therapist about the client. This is interesting given that eighteen years earlier Taft had insisted that the therapist needed to be psychologically well-adjusted, not that the client would get to be. We notice also (a) that Rogers says 'are, or may be'; and (b) that he talks about assimilating 'on a symbolic level'. The first point relates to that strand of Rogers' thinking about congruence which argues that it's enough that experience be 'available to awareness'. The second point looks forward to his increasingly common usage of the idea of

LIVERPOOL
JOHN MOORES UNIVERSITY
AVRIL ROBARTS LRC
TEL. 0151 231 4022

symbolising. We'll look at that in more detail shortly. Rogers hasn't yet broached the idea of communicating congruence. He's also still talking about congruence as an outcome for the client, and as an internal process.

Within a year or two, Rogers (1959b, p. 214) is using the word congruence to describe an accurate matching of experience with awareness:

> The 'growing edge' of this portion of the theory has to do with point 3, the congruence or genuineness of the therapist in the relationship. This means that the therapist's symbolization of his own experience in the relationship must be accurate, if therapy is to be most effective. Thus if he is experiencing threat and discomfort in the relationship, and is aware only of an acceptance and understanding, then he is not congruent in the relationship and therapy will suffer. It seems important that he should accurately 'be himself' in the relationship, whatever the self of that moment may be.

Although not published until 1959, this paper was written by the end of 1954 (see Rogers & Hart, 1970), and was certainly available at the same time as the 1957 paper was published (see Chapter 1). This is interesting because some people still talk about the 1957 paper as if it precedes the 1959 paper, and make assumptions therefore that the 1959 paper represents a development in Rogers' thinking over the 1957 paper.

So, by 1954 Rogers is using the word congruence to describe the therapist's wholeness or integrity. He's still describing it in terms of the relationship between two worlds, the world of experience and the world of awareness. And, acknowledging a debt to Angyal, he's using the word symbolisation to describe the process by which congruence is attained. Elsewhere in this paper Rogers (1959b, p. 198) defines accurate symbolisation as the state in which the 'symbols which constitute our awareness . . . match, or correspond to, the "real" experience, or to "reality"'.

A symbol is something which stands for something else. The most obvious symbol is a word, which is a sound that stands for a thing, a something else. The word cup is not the thing cup. The word cup allows us to communicate about the thing cup. The word anger is not the experience anger. The word anger, if we have it, allows us to symbolise the experience anger in awareness, and to communicate the experience. Put words together and you have an elaborate and sophisticated network of symbols called language, with which we can (a) articulate our experience to ourselves and (b) communicate it to others.

So, congruent is what we are when we have symbolised, or given a name to, our experiences, when we can say that this or this or this is what we're feeling or experiencing. It seems reasonable to infer from what Rogers writes that the symbols we make for our experience, the words we use to describe our experience to ourselves, should be both accurate and adequate:

accurate to the nature of whatever we're experiencing; and adequate to its complexity and subtlety.

Rogers stresses five times (!) in the four sentences of this one paragraph that he is talking about the therapist's congruence 'in the relationship'. He argues later in this paper (1959b, p. 215) and again in the 1957 paper that he does not expect any therapist to be 'a completely congruent person at all times'.

In the next paragraph, Rogers addresses the issue of communication, and suggests that there are two sets of circumstances in which a therapist might choose to communicate his or her feelings:

1   'if the therapist finds himself persistently focused on his own feelings rather than those of the client, thus greatly reducing or eliminating any experience of empathic understanding', and
2   if the therapist is 'persistently experiencing some feeling other than unconditional positive regard'.

There are a number of implications to draw out here:

- Rogers' default position at this time seems to be that the demand of congruence covers the relationship between experience and awareness only. It is primarily an internal process that provides the basis or preparation for authentic empathic understanding and unconditional positive regard. The requirement to be congruent does not normally need to extend to communication. This is the position Bozarth arrives at in 1996 and develops (2001, p. 197) five years later:

  > The only goal of the client-centered therapist is to be a certain way. This way of being entails being congruent in the relationship *in order* to experience unconditional positive regard towards, and empathic understanding of, the client's frame of reference.

- In his formal, if-then, description of the conditions, Rogers does not say that communication is necessary (or sufficient). We can infer from this that he at least, at that time, did not see a therapist's communication of his or her experience as ordinarily necessary for the process of therapy. It would have been easy for Rogers to say that communication was necessary. He didn't.
- There are defined circumstances where communication is indicated: where a therapist's feelings 'persistently' (and Rogers uses this word in each of the two exceptions he describes) impede or occlude his or her experience of empathic understanding or unconditional positive regard.
- In those circumstances where a therapist may communicate from his or her own experience, Rogers talks specifically about a therapist communicating feelings, rather than thoughts, ideas or imaginings.

Later in the 1959 paper, Rogers formulates what he calls 'a tentative law of interpersonal relationships'. He describes it as a theory deduced from the theory of therapy, and as 'a theory in the making, rather than a finished product'. He sees therapy relationships as special examples of interpersonal relationships. Speaking explicitly about interpersonal relationships (rather than therapy relationships) he says this (p. 240) about congruent communication:

> the greater the communicated *congruence* of *experience, awareness*, and behavior on the part of one individual, the more the ensuing relationship will involve a tendency toward reciprocal communication with the same qualities, mutually accurate understanding of the communications, improved *psychological adjustment* and functioning in both parties, and mutual satisfaction in the relationship.

Writing again about relationships generally, rather than about therapy relationships specifically, and building on the established notion that congruence covers experience and awareness, Rogers suggests (1961/67a, p. 339) that we might extend it 'to cover a matching of experience, awareness and communication'.

If 'communicated congruence' is so beneficial in interpersonal relationships, why is Rogers so cautious about allowing, endorsing or encouraging it in therapy relationships? We don't have an answer to this, although we note that Rogers identified different kinds of relationships, within which different qualities were relatively more important. In a paper originally published in 1975 he describes (1975/80, p. 160) three kinds of relationship, each of which calls for a particular quality from the helper or therapist:

- What Rogers calls 'the ordinary interactions of life – between marital and sex partners, between teacher and student, employer and employee, or between colleagues or friends' demand congruence, or 'the straightforward expression of personally owned feelings – both negative and positive'. In these relationships 'congruence is a basis for living together in a climate of realness'.
- Other 'nonverbal relationships – between parent and infant, therapist and mute psychotic, physician and very ill patient' call for 'a nurturing climate in which delicate, tentative new thoughts and productive processes can emerge'.
- Other relationships where one person is 'hurting, confused, troubled, anxious, alienated, terrified, or when he or she is doubtful of self-worth, uncertain as to identity' call for a 'deep understanding' which he believes is 'the most precious gift one can give to another'.

There's a lot to draw out here. Rogers talks in the first paragraph about 'the ordinary interactions of life'. What follows suggests that he does not include therapeutic relationships as ordinary: they are extra-ordinary, separate, different. The second paragraph describes what we might call extreme relationships, of the sort that, Prouty, Warner and Van Werde have written about. The third paragraph seems to us to be the one that most clearly describes what most of us would recognise as a therapeutic relationship. And Rogers is saying that in this particular kind of relationship, empathic understanding is most important.

Even where he allows for the explicit communication of awareness, Rogers counsels caution. 'There is' he says (1961/67a, p. 341) 'an important corollary of the construct of congruence which is not at all obvious':

> If an individual is at this moment entirely congruent, his actual physiological experience being accurately represented in his awareness, and his communication being accurately congruent with his awareness, then his communication could never contain an expression of an external fact.

This is an extraordinary statement, simple, obvious and profound. If we are describing our awareness of our *experience*, rather than our perception or our observation, we can speak only of what we feel rather than of facts about the other person, his world or the world in general. This has obvious implications for practice.

Unconditional positive regard

Rogers (1959b, p. 208) describes unconditional positive regard as 'one of the key constructs of the theory'. Bozarth's (2001) history of the idea begins in 1940, and refers briefly to Freud, Rank, Allen and Taft as intellectual forerunners. We think that Taft is especially significant. She describes (1933, p. v) a shift in her own thinking over the course of twenty-five years, a shift that takes her away from seeing therapy as 'a reform of the "other" through superior knowledge of life and psychology' towards 'a therapy which is purely individual, non-moral, non-scientific, non-intellectual, which can take place only when divorced from all hint of control, unless it be the therapist's control of himself in the therapeutic situation'.

This interests us on two counts:

1   It describes a movement away from broadly psychodynamic therapy, which privileges the authority of the therapist, to a broadly humanistic therapy, which privileges the authority of the client.
2   It prefigures some of Rogers' thinking, and especially the notion of non-judgemental acceptance or unconditional positive regard.

Taft's own description of her work with two children includes examples of radical unconditionality which we think is challenging to her clients and challenging even now to us. She describes (1933, p. 60) working in a third-floor room with 7-year-old Helen. Helen 'has her toes resting on the middle frame work of the lower sash and the rest of her is out of the window':

> 'Helen, if you fall out on your head, it's not my fault,' I say in a most indifferent tone of voice.
> 'Whose fault will it be?' she asks.
> 'It's going to be yours. There is nothing I can do about it; just fall if you want to.'
> I am much surprised to find that she responds by being very careful.

Whatever we may think now about such practice, Taft is clearly offering Helen a profoundly challenging level of unconditional acceptance, up to and including an acceptance of her right to hurt herself.

Gaylin (2002, p. 344) suggests that unconditional positive regard really describes two conditions:

1   unconditionality, or 'a non-judgmental stance', and
2   positive regard, or a degree of 'caring, or love'.

This reading makes explicit ideas which are implicit in Rogers' own description. In the first and third of three paragraphs, Rogers (1959b, p. 208) draws attention to the unconditional aspect of the idea, saying that it involves perceiving the other person 'in such a way that no self-experience can be discriminated as more or less worthy of positive regard than any other'. In other words, unconditional positive regard involves responding to any and all of a client's self-experiences even-handedly, valuing all experiences equally, embracing what we might see as resistance as willingly as we would embrace any apparent enthusiasm to grow, and expressions of affection as easily as overt hostility. The message to a client is not that whatever he thinks or feels or does is OK, but that no one thing he thinks or feels or does is more or less valuable or acceptable than any one other. The middle paragraph takes the word 'prizing' from Dewey, adds the word 'acceptance' and suggests that both are 'synonymous with unconditional positive regard'. In other words, unconditional positive regard carries connotations of approval, warmth, and appreciation. If we conflate these two strands, we see that unconditional positive regard involves accepting, appreciating and acknowledging a client equally and without bias across the whole range of her experiences, whatever we might think or feel about them from our own perspective.

This is clearly a counsel of perfection, and Rogers acknowledges as much in a footnote (1957, p. 98n):

> The phrase 'unconditional positive regard' may be an unfortunate one, since it sounds like an absolute, an all or nothing dispositional concept. It is probably evident from the description that completely unconditional positive regard would never exist except in theory.

Nevertheless, as Fernald (2000) points out (see Chapter 2), such radical acceptance elicits deep organismic experiencing.

Rogers (ibid., p. 98) goes on to say that effective therapists probably experience such regard for their clients 'during many moments' of their contact with them, and that they are also likely to experience from time to time 'a conditional positive regard' and perhaps at times 'a negative regard'. 'It is' he concludes 'in this sense that unconditional positive regard exists as a matter of degree in any relationship.' Having heard students and colleagues berate themselves for their failure to offer their clients completely unconditional positive regard at all times, we think this footnote deserves wider exposure.

Bozarth (1996) argues with conviction that a client's experience of her therapist's unconditional positive regard for her is the agent of therapeutic change. A client who experiences herself as unconditionally accepted is challenged to examine whatever conditions she grew up believing she had to meet in order to be accepted. She is then in a position to live her life moment to moment on the basis of what she knows is right for her, rather than on the basis of what she believes she has to do if she wants to stay acceptable. We describe this experience as a challenge for a number of reasons. In the first place, an experience of unconditional positive regard challenges whatever previous experiences a client may have of being conditionally loved and accepted. This may mean she has to review her feelings towards and relationships with those who have loved and accepted her conditionally over the years. It also challenges whatever rules or habits she may have evolved so as to stay acceptable, and leaves her having to decide for herself how to live. Unconditional positive regard sounds like a wonderful and positive experience to offer, and to receive, and in many ways it is. It is also, as Bozarth argues, a potent agent of change, and as such it precipitates processes that question the status quo and demand new responses to life. A client who feels herself to be genuinely and consistently accepted without having to meet any conditions is challenged to review her history, her decisions, her picture of who she is and the way in which she is living. We think it's important to recognise that the offering of an apparently warm and benign acceptance can precipitate such an inherently unsettling process. This view of unconditional positive regard as the basis of change is akin to the paradoxical theory of change in gestalt psychology which states (Beisser, 1970/2004, p. 103) *'that change occurs when one becomes what he is, not when he tries to become what he is not'*.

Speaking to camera before meeting Gloria, Rogers says a little about how he works and about what he thinks makes for effective therapy (Shostrom, 1965). He says that we might fairly call unconditional positive regard a kind of 'non-possessive love'. This makes sense to us. The qualities of unconditional positive regard as Rogers and others have described them do add up to a kind of loving: attentive, permissive, accepting. In this sense, Rogers made room for love within therapeutic relationships, even if his own ambition or reticence, or the strictures of academic psychology in 1950s America, made it difficult for him to use the word. Stickley and Freshwater (2002, p. 252) take a more critical view:

> If Rogers' concept of unconditional positive regard actually equals love, as we are led to believe, it could be argued that Rogers has done much to exorcise the term from the vocabulary of the therapy world. Unconditional positive regard may easily be viewed as a skill, or technique, which diminishes the potency of love in its original form.

We think this is harsh. It fails to recognise the context within and against which Rogers was writing, and pays more attention to terminology than to practice. We agree that unconditional positive regard is an ugly phrase, that it sounds heartless and technical, and that it can invite heartless and technical application. In practice, however, it demands, legitimises and makes room for a kind of loving within the process of therapeutic relationships.

Empathic understanding

Empathic understanding stands in a tradition of psychology that seeks to understand rather than to explain, a tradition which has its roots in the work of Wilhelm Dilthey (1833–1911) who argued in 1894 for a descriptive and analytic psychology. In this sense, empathic understanding is an explicitly phenomenological concept. This reflects the then contemporary use of the term to describe aesthetic experience in and in response to various art forms (see Hunsdahl, 1967). Our emotional responses to a piece of art are, in effect, empathic projections onto an object, a work, an event or a person. Earlier, in 1858, Johann Droysen (1804–1884) was the first to contrast 'understanding' (*Verstehen*) with 'explanation' (*Erklaren*) (see Van Belle, in press, 2005). This distinction underpins the concept of empathic understanding in person-centred therapy, and distinguishes person-centred therapy from therapies which seek to analyse, interpret or explain.

Rogers (1959b, p. 210) says that empathic understanding means 'to perceive the internal frame of reference of another with accuracy, and with the emotional components and meanings which pertain thereto, as if one were the other person, but without ever losing the "as if" condition'. On the basis that this condition describes an act of perceiving, some commentators, such as Hackney (1978), question whether this condition fulfils Rogers' own ambition (1959b, p. 246) to provide 'operationally definable constructs' and (1957, p. 95) 'terms which are clearly defined and measurable'. Such commentators, however, ignore Rogers' (1959b) views on theory and research and, specifically, his elaboration of the problem of measurement and quantification. Whilst arguing for a continuing programme of theory and research which (p. 251) 'would meet the rigorous requirements of the logic of science', Rogers also questions the logical positivist approach in which he was reared in favour of the phenomenon of subjectivity. Nevertheless, some researchers, notably Truax and Carkhuff, together and separately (Truax & Carkhuff, 1965; Truax, 1970; Carkhuff, 1971) have elaborated the second element of Rogers' condition of empathic understanding: that of communication to the client. Hackney (1978) views this as a distinction between the process and outcome of empathy.

Bozarth (1996, p. 48) has argued that empathic understanding is 'the vessel' which carries a therapist's experience of unconditional positive regard, by which he means that it both manifests and communicates a therapist's unconditional acceptance of her client. 'It appears' he continues 'that this is the only pure way that Rogers believed unconditional positive regard could be perceived by the client.' Communicating empathic understanding, then, is what a therapist mainly does, at least in visible behavioural terms.

Although many therapists talk about 'feeling' empathic, we recognise that it is a cognitive process as well as an affective one. This is represented by Wexler (1974) who, with others, chose cognitive learning psychology as a theoretical framework for developing the person-centred approach. He views an empathic response (p. 97) as deliberate and organised:

> when it is optimal, *an empathic response is a structure or group of structures that more fully captures, and better organizes, the meaning of the information in the field that the client is processing than had the structure(s) the client had generated himself.*

A recent research review (Bachelor & Horvath, 1999) reports one study finding that 44% of clients interviewed valued a cognitive-type empathic response.

In a discussion of the difference between affect attunement and empathy, Stern (1985, p. 145) identifies four distinct and probably sequential, cognitive processes to empathy: '(1) the resonance of feeling state; (2) the

LIVERPOOL
JOHN MOORES UNIVERSITY
AVRIL ROBARTS LRC
TEL. 0151 231 4022

abstraction of empathic knowledge from the experience of emotional resonance; (3) the integration of abstracted empathic knowledge into an empathic response; and (4) a transient role identification'. Bohart and Greenberg (1997) cite Tausch's (1988) research comparing the therapy responses of Rogers with those of a cognitive therapist. They observe (p. 21) that 'Rogers' empathic responses were more balanced, with about two thirds focusing predominantly on cognitive aspects of the client's experiences and one third on emotion or on both cognition and emotion.' Greenberg and Elliot (1997) expand the notion of understanding, identifying, in addition to this, four forms of empathic responding: evocation, exploration, conjecture and interpretation. As Tudor and Merry (2002, p. 46) put it:

> The process of therapy can, through appropriate resonance, response and checking out of understanding by the therapist, become a genuine dialogue in which client and therapist engage in a search for deeper levels of understanding of the client's experiencing process and internal frame of reference.

Accurate empathic understanding seems to be potent in two ways. The first is that it helps clients identify, clarify and then symbolise or find words for the nuances of their own experience. This is consistent with what Rogers writes (1951, p. 223) about diagnosis: that 'the purpose of the therapist is to provide the conditions in which the client is able to make, to experience, and to accept the diagnosis of the psychogenic aspects of his maladjustment'. The second way in which empathy is potent follows from this. A client who feels himself accurately understood and still accepted feels less alienated, less alone, and more related to another human being. In 1954 Rogers (1954/67a, p. 358) describes it thus:

> If I say that I 'accept' you, but know nothing of you, this is a shallow acceptance indeed, and you realize that it may change if I actually come to know you. But if I understand you empathically, see you and what you are feeling and doing from your point of view, enter your private world and see it as it appears to you – and still accept you – then this is safety indeed. In this climate you can permit your real self to emerge, and to express itself in varied and novel formings as it relates to the world.

In 1986 he puts it this way (p. 129):

> To my mind, empathy is in itself a healing agent. It is one of the most potent aspects of therapy, because it releases, it confirms, it brings even

the most frightened client into the human race. If a person can be understood, he or she belongs.

We can understand more fully the significance of this aspect of empathy's power if we refer back to Angyal, who explored (1941, p. 182) the concept of homonomy: 'the tendency to conform to, unite with, participate in, and fit into superindividual wholes'. He suggests that this tendency, this urge to belong to a something larger than oneself, is 'a source of profound motivation for human behavior'. Empathic understanding, then, is one way of satisfying this urge, for both therapist and client. When one understands the other, both belong to something larger and more inclusive than either one of them individually.

This way of thinking helps to explain why empathic understanding enriches both client and therapist. Rogers articulates both the risks and the riches of understanding another person. 'If I let myself really understand another person,' he writes (1953/67b, p. 18), 'I might be changed by that understanding. And we all fear change.' In her discussion of empathy, Afuape (2004) echoes this view of its reciprocal nature, and asserts that its basis in the emotional and the intuitive makes it a subjective and fluid response rather than an 'objective' condition.

Of course, Rogers was not alone in promoting the power and efficacy of empathy. He was preceded by Freud (1916/73), and theorists and clinicians from other schools have also used and developed the concept: Moreno in psychodrama; Jaspers, the existential psychoanalyst; Winnicott (1965) in object relations; and, as we discussed in Chapter 4, Kohut in self psychology. Angyal (1965/73, p. 290) references Rogers explicitly:

> With patients whose emotions are not, or no longer, completely submerged or falsified, a sensitive *recognition of all their feelings by the therapist* can do much to increase the patient's awareness of his mental states. Because of this greater differentiation, and also because the therapist naturally resonates to genuine undistorted feelings, this process also furthers their growth. This is one reason why reflection of feelings advocated and practiced by Rogers and his followers often proves so effective.

The contributions of a number of theoretical orientations to reconsidering empathy have been brought together in a volume edited by Bohart and Greenberg (1997). In an otherwise excellent collection, in their own introduction, the editors (Bohart & Greenberg, 1997) somewhat undermine their credibility by perpetuating a common misunderstanding of the conditions by referring to the 'core conditions' only as 'necessary and sufficient'. As we note in Chapters 2 and 4, research in the fields of neuroscience and infant development generally supports the importance of empathy in terms of limbic resonance and in sparking relationship, originally between mother or primary care-giver and child. Schore (1994) discusses the emergence of empathy and its importance in altruistic behaviour, viewing this (p. 351) as 'an essential prerequisite to later social and moral development'. We see this most in therapeutic groups in which group members are able to express empathy for each other (see Giesekus & Mente, 1986). Yalom (1995) sees such altruism as one of the curative factors in group psychotherapy.

Recently, Sayers (2004) argues that:

> Empathy, however, is crucial in therapy not only as a means by which therapists become aware of, and correct their failed empathy. It is also crucial as a means of investigating and researching into the unknown and unconscious factors contributing to the discontents bringing people into therapy.

Citing Rogers, Sayers emphasises the value of empathy as an object of neuropsychological, philosophical and psychotherapy research as well as a mirroring, receptive and projective means of enabling self-knowledge.

Client perception

In his 1959 paper (p. 213), Rogers' sixth condition is formulated thus: 'That the client perceives, at least to a minimal degree, conditions 4 and 5, the unconditional positive regard of the therapist for him, and the empathic understanding of the therapist.' In the 1957 paper, Rogers says (p. 99) that: 'The communication to the client of the therapist's empathic understanding and unconditional positive regard is to a minimal degree achieved.' Van Belle (in press, 2005) outlines the philosophical traditions which support the importance of prizing and understanding others:

> to practice Person-Centered therapy with success one must prize the otherness of others and believe in the importance of empathizing with, or understanding others. One needs to believe in the importance of indwelling a person's personal frame of reference rather than logically dissecting his or her mind for expert treatment. This is the legacy of Romanticism and Anti-Positivism in Person-Centered therapy.

Whether we emphasise the client's perception or the therapist's communication, this is the most significant condition, and the condition by which the process of therapy stands or falls. It is, for Rogers (1958/67a, p. 130), the *assumed* condition:

> I shall assume that the client experiences himself as being fully *received*. By this I mean that whatever his feelings – fear, despair, insecurity,

anger, whatever his mode of expression – silence, gestures, tears or words; whatever he finds himself being in this moment, he senses that he is psychologically *received*, just as he is, by the therapist. There is implied in this term the concept of being understood, empathically, and the concept of acceptance. It is also well to point out that it is the client's experience of this condition which makes it optimal, not merely the fact of its existence in the therapist.

'The organism' says Rogers (1951, p. 484) 'reacts to the field as it is experienced and perceived. This perceptual field is, for the individual, "reality".' This has a number of clear implications for the process and practice of therapy. In the context of the six conditions it provides a rationale for suggesting that this sixth condition, a client's own experience and perception of her own therapy, is the most significant determining factor of its effectiveness. Therapy depends not on the skill of the therapist, nor on particular responses, nor even on the quality of the therapeutic relationship. In so far as it depends on any of these things at all, it depends specifically on the way his client experiences and perceives them, because his client's experiencing and perceiving constitute her reality. It may sometimes seem that we simply 'take in' the world as it exists. However, our perceptual processing is more complex than that. Pally (2000, p. 19) describes how the brain actively constructs perceptions thus:

> Contrary to popular belief, the brain does not operate like a camera taking in a whole scene, but operates more like a feature detector. The brain detects the individual stimulus features of the environment such as edges, contour, line orientation, colour, form, pitch, volume and movement and processes them in separate regions of the cortex. There is no place in the brain 'where it all comes together' as a whole image. To create a perception, the brain takes a pattern of neuronal activity created by the simultaneous processing of all these individual environmental features and compares it with patterns stored in the memory. When a match for the current pattern is found, perception occurs. The vast majority of perception occurs non-consciously.

Whilst this highlights the importance of the therapeutic environment and perhaps calls us as therapists to be mindful of our own consistency in terms of edge, décor, aesthetics, tone, movement and expression, it also offers a relief, in that we can't possibly control or determine the environmental conditions, therapeutic or otherwise. One therapist worked from two different settings and rooms which were, to all intents and purposes, quite different in terms of structure, decoration, and objects. The feedback from clients, however, was consistent: that 'the room', 'this place' was calming. Whilst the clients expressed themselves about the room and the place, what we understand from how we construct perceptions is that they were drawing on much more and, perhaps, much more to do with the therapist, than they were aware of.

This sixth condition puts the client at the centre of the process and outcome of therapy. Clinical research cited by Miller, Hubble and Duncan (1995) indicates that the client is the single most potent factor in therapy, contributing 40% to the outcome of therapy. Because this condition is so important in terms of the process and outcome of therapy, we discuss this further in the next chapter on process. Very little has been written about this condition. One exception to this is a paper by Toukmanian (2002) in which she emphasises perception as the core element in person-centred and experiential psychotherapies. Tudor (2000) refers to this, together with conditions 1 and 2, as 'the lost conditions'.

Other conditions

For as long as people have been helping others professionally and, more specifically, offering psychotherapy, there has been an interest in knowing and researching what works. Rogers' own development of the theory of therapeutic conditions was an attempt to describe, operationalise and, ultimately, evidence the conditions of therapy and of therapeutic change. McLeod (2003, p. 150) assesses Rogers and his colleagues' work as the 'single most important programme of research into therapeutic process'. He identifies two reasons for this: 'Firstly, it pioneered many research methods that have subsequently been widely adopted. Secondly, it used research to test and develop theory in a systematic manner.' Although, to a large extent, the concern and focus of research has moved away from the therapeutic conditions (a discussion we pick up in the next section), practitioners and writers within the approach still addressed 'conditions' of therapy. In this section we consider a number of writers since Rogers who have suggested other conditions that seem to them to be necessary for therapeutic growth to occur.

- Thorne (1991c, p. 74) suggests 'tenderness', not so much as an addition to the established conditions, nor even 'to make them more effective'. He proposes simply that 'if tenderness is present, something qualitatively different may occur'.
- Rebutting critiques of person-centred practice, and reviewing the three therapist conditions of congruence, empathy and unconditional positive regard, Natiello (1987, p. 204) suggests that 'the concept of therapist personal power underlying the approach is so integral to its successful practice that it might be considered a fourth condition'.
- Mearns (1990) suggests 'sufficiency of therapeutic context' as a condition for effective therapy.

- In a paper published in 1986, Rogers (1986/90, p. 137) describes another characteristic of his work:

> when I am at my best, as a group facilitator or a therapist . . . when I am closest to my inner, intuitive self, when I am somehow in touch with the unknown in me, when perhaps I am in a slightly altered state of consciousness in the relationship, then whatever I seem to do seems full of healing. Then simply my *presence* is releasing and helpful. There is nothing I can do to force this experience, but when I can relax and be close to the transcendental core of me . . . at those moments it seems that my inner spirit has reached out and touched the inner spirit of the other.

Thorne (1992) proposes this as a fourth condition, in addition to the three 'core conditions', an argument which we refute as we don't see how presence, as Rogers describes it, however desirable, can be a *condition* of therapy (see Tudor & Worrall, 1994).

- Taking a different slant on the conditions, Land (1996, p. 73) says this:

> I have decided that there is only one necessary and sufficient attitude or predisposition or condition which I can intentionally and rather consistently bring to therapy. Everything else unfolds naturally or is discovered or experienced or invented along the way. (The only efficient cause of therapy, of course, is the client's own ability and choice to change for the better, although clients and therapists clearly need each other.) That one attitude which I can intentionally bring and which I know the client surely needs from me is a sustained and generous interest.

Land acknowledges that whatever a therapist brings to the therapeutic endeavour is limited to the context and occurrence of that endeavour, and that ultimately success in therapy depends more upon the resources of the client than upon anything the therapist does. Bozarth's findings (1998, p. 19) support this idea: 'The data increasingly point to "the active client" and the individuality of the client as the core of successful therapy.' Additionally, Land's idea is broad enough to allow for any number of idiosyncratic and emergent manifestations, and in some ways takes us back to the pragmatism that Rogers describes as characteristic of his own early practice, where the only question worth asking was whether something worked.

- In Chapter 8 we discuss creativity as an important process outcome, and the inner conditions necessary for creativity. Here, briefly, we discuss the external conditions which Rogers identifies as important. His ideas about creativity are not well known. They have been taken up by some, most notably his daughter in her work on creative and expressive therapy (N. Rogers, 1993/2000). Rogers identifies two conditions which foster creativity:

1 Psychological safety. This, in turn, is established by three processes:

   a. Accepting the individual as of unconditional worth.
   b. Providing a climate in which external evaluation is absent.
   c. Understanding empathically.

   It is important to note, from a therapeutic perspective, that this is concerned with providing the conditions under which people may feel 'safe', rather than attempting to guarantee or ensure safety which, in our view, is impossible.

2 Psychological freedom and permissiveness – of *symbolic* expression. It is this emphasis on symbolic expression which Natalie Rogers has taken forward in her use of the expressive arts in healing.

Natalie Rogers (1993/2000) has added a third condition:

3 Offering stimulating and challenging experiences. Whilst the first two conditions may be viewed as the provision of the soil and nutrients for creativity, this third, external condition is offered by the therapist/facilitator in a more active way. The expressive therapist may offer suggestions to the client designed to stimulate and challenge: 'I suggest using chalks with your fingers rather than painting with a brush.' These suggestions are meant to facilitate expression rather than to direct a client's experience. The stimulation of movement, dance, drawing, sculpting and so on are also supported by Gardner's (1983/93) work on multiple intelligences.

The conditions: An holistic view

Having reviewed the conditions separately we consider their interrelationship and them as a whole. First we comment on the ubiquitous use of the term the 'core conditions'.

The 'core conditions'

Before we advance a theory, it is sometimes necessary to state what the theory is not. The term 'core conditions' seems to have been coined by Carkhuff (1969a, 1969b) who used it in the context of identifying 'core, facilitative and action-oriented conditions' from divergent orientations to therapy by which the helper facilitated change in the client (or 'helpee'). In addition to empathic understanding, respect and genuineness, these included: specific emphasis on emotional experiencing, concreteness in problem solving, the ability to confront and the ability to interpret the helping relationship. The term '*the* core conditions' was taken up by people much closer to Rogers than Carkhuff (G. Barrett-Lennard, personal communication, 17 May 1999) and applied to three of the six necessary and sufficient conditions and, although Rogers himself did not use the term, it has nevertheless since become part of the person-centred lexicon. Truax and Carkhuff (1967) refer to the three conditions as 'central therapeutic ingredients', whilst Shlien and Levant (1984) refer to them as 'the facilitative conditions'.

Carkhuff, Truax and, most notably, Egan, all of whom refer to 'core conditions' and are often claimed to be 'person-centred', laid the ground for a human relations *technology* enterprise which, whilst popularising these conditions and attitudes, has in effect also moved a long way from the spirit and substance of Rogers' thought and person-centred practice. Most importantly, the theoretical denial and distortion of this central hypothesis of person-centred therapy and, specifically, the nature of the therapeutic relationship, perpetuates a reduced version of the approach and confirms a partial and insufficient view of person-centred therapy. This has, at worst, led to successive generations of students of person-centred therapy perceiving that it lacks conceptual completeness and theoretical integrity. This misunderstanding has led to a number of problems:

1   The view that the 'core conditions' alone are necessary and sufficient.
2   The view that, by naming them together, they are the same in nature.
3   The view that they are, in some way, 'core' or at the heart of this theory and, more broadly, the person-centred approach.
4   The corollary, that the other three conditions are less 'core' or central.

Reconditioning the conditions

From the preceding discussion we note a number of clarifications to the theory of the therapeutic conditions:

- That there are therapist conditions (1, 3, 4 and 5) and client conditions (1, 2 and 6). This acknowledges the active involvement of the client in the facilitative healing of therapy. It may also explain Rogers' apparent reference to the 'core conditions' as necessary and sufficient attitudes *on the part of the therapist*, whilst reserving discussion of the six conditions as a theoretical statement about relationships (Merry, personal communication, 18 July 1999).

- That client incongruence is more accurately formulated and placed as a precondition. Arguably, the view that the client is herself both necessary and sufficient makes her the only condition of the therapeutic process.
- That there is an important difference between the therapist's condition of congruence on the one hand and those of unconditional positive regard and empathic understanding on the other. The difference is that the client needs to perceive the latter two (Rogers, 1959b) or that the therapist needs to communicate them (Rogers, 1957) for the 'if-then' formulation to be fulfilled. In our view, this makes congruence the quiet condition, whereas both therapist and client need to be more active and explicit about communicating, experiencing and perceiving the other two conditions.

From these two points together we can re-present the conditions thus:

Client	*Therapist*

Client incongruence

⟶ Psychological contact ⟵

Therapist congruence

⟵   Therapist unconditional
Client   positive regard
receives
these   ⟵   Therapist empathic
understanding

- That the central or 'assumed' condition is the client's perception. This radical emphasis on the client's report and reality is, in practice, missing from most accounts of the therapeutic process and relationship. Significantly *Client-Centered Therapy* (Rogers, 1951) contains a long chapter which draws on clients' diaries to describe the relationship 'as experienced by the client'. In it Rogers cites an article by Axline (1950), a close colleague, who invited clients to write descriptions of their experiences. More recently, Duncan and Moynihan's (1994) outcome research utilises the client's frame of reference. For further references to client experiences of therapy see Chapter 8.

From conditions to relationship

Rogers' use of the term 'conditions' supports his 'if-then' formulation of theory which was developed in a particular historical, philosophical and theoretical context designed within and to appeal to the prevailing logical positivist view of science and research methodology. We know that Rogers himself (1959b), although actively engaged in such research, also questioned its limitations, specifically from a subjective, phenomenological perspective. Interestingly, the main ideas in the facilitative-conditions model have informed and been assimilated into research about the therapeutic alliance (Bordin, 1979; Hovarth & Greenberg, 1986) and the therapeutic relationship (Gelso & Carter, 1985). A review of the process-outcome literature in psychotherapy and counselling (Orlinsky, Grawe & Parks, 1994), involving the collation of results of more than 2000 studies concluded:

- That the quality of the client's participation in therapy is the most important determinant of outcome.
- That the therapeutic bond, especially as perceived by the client, is important in mediating the link between process and outcome.
- That the therapist's contribution towards helping the client is made mainly through empathic, affirmative, collaborative and self-congruent engagement with the client.

McLeod (2003) acknowledges the resemblance between these conclusions and Rogers' facilitative conditions and points out (p. 165) what he views as three aspects of process missing from this comparison: 'the type of contract between therapist and client, the active participation of the client, and the active use of interventions by the therapist'. In response to this, we think:

1   That any therapeutic contract needs to follow contact between client and therapist, and to be understood in terms of the principles, theory and conditions of person-centred therapy (see Worrall, 1997). In any case, in his early works, Rogers discusses the practicalities of therapy, including contractual issues such as boundaries and time (Rogers, 1942; Rogers & Wallen, 1946).
2   That the active participation of the client is implied in this current re-reading of the therapeutic conditions; and that we should also be mindful of creating and reifying 'activity' as a condition of therapeutic worth.
3   That the same is true of the relative activity of the therapist; and that the concept of 'interventions', let alone 'active interventions', is itself a construct (see Warner, 2000a).

This said, one of the implications of the language of a therapeutic conditions model is that it implies a somewhat linear 'if-then' process with the therapist 'doing unto' the client, and the client being, at worst, the passive recipient of the therapist's love and understanding. This supports the view of some person-centred practitioners that they 'do' or 'provide' congruence or empathy, as if these conditions were a pill or remedy to be given *per diem* or, more likely, weekly. In order to rectify this, we present the conditions in a relational context, by drawing on person-centred personality theory (see Figure 7.1). This has a number of advantages:

- Both therapist and client are described as total personalities (after Rogers, 1951). The therapist's conditions are seen as they are: located within and emanating from her personality and, ideally, from that part which is congruent and integrated in relationship. Equally, the client 'receives' these conditions (or not) within the context of his personality and the relationship as he experiences it, in the field as he perceives it.
- It illustrates Rogers' (1959b) point that conditions 2 to 6 are each on a continuum. We view this not as an abstract continuum but one which is located in the experience and, therefore, the personality of the participants in the therapeutic encounter.
- Both psychological contact (condition 1) and 'being received' (condition 6) are experienced directly and congruently or, in some way, distorted or denied. In his relationship inventory Barrett-Lennard (1962, 1978) discusses the intensity and intimacy of interpersonal contact. In his presentation the client's experience of being received or, more actively, of experiencing the therapist's love and understanding (condition 6), is more closely linked to this interpersonal contact (condition 1) in a kind of feedback loop. Given that Rogers saw psychological contact as binary, and given what he said about unconditional positive regard and empathic understanding, we argue that a client's *perception* that he is loved and understood results more from his therapist's love and understanding than from the nature or 'depth' of contact.
- Viewing the conditions in the context of person-centred personality theory also illustrates more clearly the dynamic between the therapist offering unconditional positive regard and empathic understanding and the client's experience or perception of these (or not). The client needs to have some self-regard and some regard for the therapist's regard, some empathy for themselves and some empathy for the therapist's empathy in order to experience or perceive these conditions. This is borne out by more recent studies of child development which emphasise the developmental and interpersonal necessity for the child to experience and give love and empathy (see Chapters 2 and 4 and Stern, 1985, 2000).

Finally, there is a further and significant theoretical movement represented by this re-working of the therapeutic conditions model which takes us from

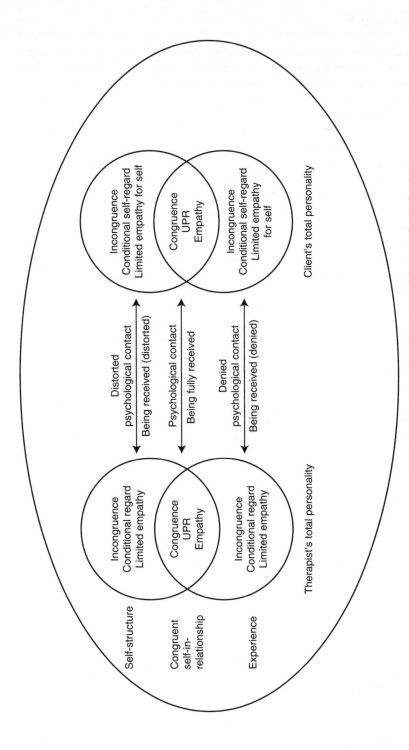

Figure 7.1 The necessary and sufficient conditions – in a relational and cultural context (Tudor, 2000).

the therapeutic relationship as noun to therapeutic relating as an active verb. This keeps the process of therapy active, alive, mutual and co-creative, qualities which we explore in the next chapter.

Chapter 8

Process

We must cultivate the science of human relationships.

Franklin D. Roosevelt

For many years now I have been trying to formulate for myself the process by which change in personality and behavior is achieved in psychotherapy.

Carl Rogers

In his formulation of a theory of therapy, personality and interpersonal relationships, Rogers (1959b) describes what he saw as the conditions, process and outcomes of therapy. In Chapter 7 we discussed the conditions. In this chapter we examine both process and outcomes, which are, for us, inextricably connected. An examination and reformulation of Rogers' process conception of psychotherapy precedes a discussion of process and outcome in terms of fluidity, creativity and personal power. We see the process of effective therapy as, in itself, one of the outcomes of an experience of effective therapy. We see any of the apparent outcomes of effective therapy as more or less sharply differentiated aspects of its process. This way of thinking offers a critique of outcome-based therapy, and of current preoccupations with focus, cure and solution. In the last part of the chapter we draw a distinction between the therapeutic relationship and 'therapeutic relating'. We elaborate this through discussions on the person of the therapist, the person of the client and the process of relating.

Drawing specifically on the work of Jessie Taft, person-centred therapy has always held the relationship between therapist and client as central to whatever potential for healing it offers. Taft (1933, p. 17) called her work 'relationship therapy' and defined it 'as a process in which the individual finally learns to utilize the allotted hour from beginning to end without undue fear, resistance, resentment or greediness'. She went on to say that when he, the client, can take it and also leave it without denying its value, without trying to escape it completely or keep it forever because of this very value, in so far he has learned to live, to accept this fragment of time in and for itself, and strange as it may seem, if he can live this hour he has in his grasp the secret of all hours, he has conquered life and time for the moment and in principle.

By this definition relationship therapy is clearly more about helping people live fulfilling lives than it is about the alleviation of particular local symptoms. We suggest that the same is true of person-centred therapy. Marking it off as a particular kind of therapy, Rogers and Sanford (1989, p. 1483) say this:

> The single element that most sets client-centered psychotherapy apart from the other therapies is its insistence that the medical model – involving diagnosis of pathology, specificity of treatment, and desirability of cure – is a totally inadequate model for dealing with psychologically distressed or deviant persons.

In 1958 Rogers published two articles describing the helping or therapeutic relationship. In one (Rogers, 1958/67b) he describes the characteristics of a helping relationship, as well as certain ways in which the helper or therapist can create that kind of relationship. These, posed in the form of a series of questions, offer a number of meditations and challenges to the helper:

- 'Can I *be* in some way which will be perceived by the other person as trustworthy, as dependable or consistent in some deep sense?' (p. 119)
- 'Am I secure enough within myself to permit him his separateness?' (p. 121)

In the second article, Rogers (1958/67a) attempts to describe a process conception of psychotherapy through seven stages. The task of describing any process is not easy. 'It is' says Tolstoy (1869/1982, p. 974),

> impossible for the human intellect to grasp the idea of absolute continuity of motion. Laws of motion of any kind only become comprehensible to man when he can examine arbitrarily selected units of that motion. But at the same time it is this arbitrary division of continuous motion into discontinuous units which gives rise to a large proportion of human error.

Tolstoy articulates the difficulties and risks of the task which Rogers set himself: to describe in words that are public, linear and discrete a process that is continuous, normally private, often unspoken, always subtle and invariably subjective. The limitations of language make it difficult to catch in words the essence of *any* process in its richness, detail and fluency. Phillips (1994, p. 160) makes the same point: 'All modern theory is written in the shade of Heraclitus. But however inclined we are to the idea of process, our language seems to need punctuation.' It's easier to describe differentiated elements of a process one by one, but that inevitably loses the seamless continuousness which is the essence of process.

The point of examining the process of therapy is to look at what changes happen, and to think then about what causes, allows or invites those changes to happen, in the hope, ultimately, that we will learn what to do to facilitate them more effectively. This is what Rogers was about. He wanted to describe the process of therapy, to see what order he could find in it, and then to develop (1951, p. 132) a theory 'sufficient to contain the evidence thus far available'. He wondered (ibid., p. 131) 'what *really happens* in successful therapy? What are the psychological processes by which change comes about?' These questions preface a chapter in which Rogers presents 'the many hypotheses which are currently held in regard to the process of client-centered therapy, and the research evidence which supports some of them'. The chapter itself includes research findings, theoretical speculations, and case examples, and although Rogers makes a number of interesting points about the process of therapy, the chapter as a whole is less structured and less focused than his later writings on the same theme.

By 1956, when he came to write 'A Process Conception of Psychotherapy', first published in 1958, Rogers had settled on a methodology, and this chapter is much more focused and ordered. He saw that studying the outcomes of therapy would yield little about the process of therapy; that objective research would cast light on individual moments rather than 'ongoing movement'; and (1958/67a, p. 127) that research procedures would probably not 'shed light directly upon the process of personality change'. He resolved instead (ibid., p. 128) 'to take a naturalist's observational, descriptive approach' to the phenomena of therapy, 'and to draw forth those low-level inferences' which seemed to arise most naturally from his observations, and which seemed 'most native to the material itself'. Another way of saying this is that he approached his work phenomenologically, with the intention simply to see and describe what happened there, and to let order, structure and theory emerge gradually out of observation and description.

For the purposes of this venture, Rogers assumed (1958/67a, p. 130) 'a constant and optimal set of conditions' which we discussed in Chapter 7. He summed these up by saying that a client had to experience himself as being 'received'. This notion of being received is a significant one, central to our thinking about the process of therapy. Rogers collapses all that he thought and wrote about the conditions for therapeutic change into this one word. Instead of thinking about six conditions, we can now think more simply and more immediately about how we might receive our clients as fully as possible. A client's experience of being received in therapy furthers a process of change begun before therapy began and continued outside of it. To understand some of how this happens we turn to Proposition XVII (Rogers 1951, p. 517):

> Under certain conditions, involving primarily complete absence of any threat to the self-structure, experiences which are inconsistent with it may be perceived, and examined, and the structure of self revised to assimilate and include such experiences.

Based on an unconditional trust in an organism's tendency to actualise, this proposition suggests that environmental safety is the most a therapist can provide or needs to provide in order for a client to begin or carry on the process of therapeutic change. To offer the 'complete absence of any threat to the self-structure' therapists need both to understand and to accept a client's lived reality, as he experiences it and communicates it, without conditions, evaluation, diagnosis, interpretation or agenda. The proposition asserts that in such safety a client will be increasingly open to experience and will therefore necessarily dissolve overly rigid structures and constructs.

As we note in Chapter 1, the results of a major study into *The Therapeutic Relationship and Its Impact* (Rogers et al., 1967) did not prove the causal relationship between the therapist's attitudes and patient process movement. It did conclude that therapy is more accurately viewed as a mutually interactive process.

The process conception of psychotherapy

Having steeped himself in the phenomena of his work with clients, Rogers then drew from what he noticed seven elements or continua along which he saw clients move, and divided their movement along those continua into seven stages. The seven stages have probably received more attention than the continua, at least on training courses where they provide a relatively friendly, if crude, way of measuring change or progress. They seem to us, though, to be both arbitrary and potentially unhelpful. Rogers (1958/67a, p. 131) admits that the number of stages at least is arbitrary. He says that although he identified seven stages, the process of change in therapy 'is a continuum', and would be a continuum 'whether one discriminated three stages or fifty'. Further to this, we think that they're unhelpful in that they enshrine the notion of progress rather than process, with the seventh stage being the desirable goal, and clients at the fourth stage being more advanced than clients at the second. This invites therapists to think in terms of moving their clients on from one stage to the next, to practise accordingly, and to feel skilled or incompetent themselves according to how well or not their clients are doing. We suggested when we examined the six conditions that Rogers wrote the theory as a description of phenomena, and expected us to read it as such. We think the same here, and we see the same risks as we did there of reading it as a prescription. We also find it unhelpful to think about a process in terms of stages. Process theories and stage theories are qualitatively different. That Rogers uses the language of a stage theory to describe what he says is a process theory seems to us to support our assertion that he straddles a line between quantitative and qualitative, objective and subjective, modern and postmodern.

We are more interested in the continua of change than in the stages. We think that they're helpful in that they describe the lived process of therapy naively and accurately. They articulate a movement from fixed to fluid, from closed to open, from rigid to flowing, and from stasis to process. Thus, for example, during the course of therapy, a client may move from being remote from his feelings, unable or unwilling to acknowledge or experience them in the present, to a process of experiencing them with immediacy as a continually changing flow. Rogers is clear that *he* values fluidity (ibid., p. 135):

> Would everyone agree that this is a desirable process of change, that it moves in valued directions? I believe not. I believe some people do not value fluidity. This is one of the social value judgements which individuals and cultures will have to make.

Notwithstanding this, Rogers views clients in terms of what they are experiencing subjectively, and not according to some 'objective', external diagnosis, including his own. His commitment to regarding a client's organismic experiencing without conditions means that he also values an individual's fixity. His process conception of psychotherapy, thus, is a description rather than a prescription of process. Even more specifically, he acknowledges it (p. 155) as describing a process which is set in motion 'when the individual experiences himself as being fully received'. It is thus a person-centred model rather than a generic one. He is critical of his own descriptive groupings under each stage, which are, in any case, incomplete. In Appendix 3 we include Rogers' own descriptions and examples, completing the gaps in his original work by adding our own.

Rogers describes the continua of change as follows:

- A loosening of feelings.
- A change in the manner of experiencing.
- A shift from incongruence to congruence.
- A change in the manner and extent of communication.
- A loosening of the cognitive maps of experience.

Stage 1	Stage 2	Stage 3	Stage 4	Stage 5	Stage 6	Stage 7
	Only a very modest degree of success with voluntary clients at this stage		Constitutes much of psychotherapy		A distinctive and often dramatic stage	Occurs as much outside as inside the therapeutic relationship
Pre-therapy						Ex therapy Post therapy

Figure 8.1 Rogers' process conception of psychotherapy, showing the location of pre-therapy.

- A change in the individual's relationship to his problems.
- A change in the manner of relating.

Taken together, these continua indicate one of the theoretical outcomes of successful therapy: the 'fully-functioning person' (Rogers 1959b, p. 234) (see next section).

In terms of his conception of this process in *stages*, Rogers makes specific points about some of the stages (see Figure 8.1). He suggests, for instance, that therapists 'have a very modest degree of success in working with' clients at stage 2. Most therapy begins, then, when an individual is 'at' stage 3 (p. 134). Conceptually this means that stages 1 and 2 describe a pre-therapy process of being received. Rogers talks about this happening occasionally in play or group therapy, in which (p. 133) 'the person can be exposed to a receiving climate, without himself having to take any initiative, for a long enough time to experience himself *as received*'. We know both from our own experiences and from those of our clients that often it takes someone a long time to get to therapy. Knowing that a therapist has helped someone else, or has a generally good reputation, can give a potential client enough hope that he will be received to take the first step and to make contact. This conceptualisation also locates 'pre-therapy' (Prouty, 1976, 1994; Van Werde, 1994, 1998) in terms of Rogers' process conception of psychotherapy.

In summary, Rogers' process conception of psychotherapy acknowledges:

- That there is a process pre therapy.
- That stages 4 and 5 (p. 139) constitute 'much of psychotherapy as we know it'.
- That, regarding the sixth stage, (p. 150) 'these moments of immediate, full accepted experiencing are in some sense almost irreversible'.

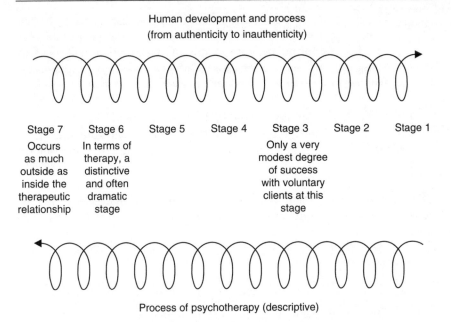

Figure 8.2 Rogers' process conception of therapy and development.

- That there is a stage beyond therapy in which the client is not much in need of the therapist's help – what some other approaches refer to as 'transference cure'.

We complete Rogers' stage conception of the process of psychotherapy (see Appendix 3), with two amendments:

1 We present it principally in terms of the elements or process scales (see Rogers & Rablen, 1958; Rogers, 1959a), as we see a discrepancy between Rogers' emphasis on process and the way in which he presents it (1958/67a) as a stage theory.

2 We present it in reverse, beginning with stage 7, to make and emphasise a point about human development and process (see Figure 8.2). We see that the process of therapy takes place within a process of human development that begins at conception. Rogers (1953/67a, p. 80) notes that 'one of the fundamental directions taken by the process of therapy is the free experiencing of the actual sensory and visceral reactions of the organism without too much of an attempt to relate these experiences to the self'. Rogers (1958/67a, p. 154) describes a person at stage 7 as someone who 'has now incorporated the quality of motion, of flow, of changingness, into every aspect of his psychological life'. Rogers again (1953/67a, p. 80):

LIVERPOOL JOHN MOORES UNIVERSITY
LEARNING SERVICES

The end point of this process is that the client discovers that he can be his experience, with all of its variety and surface contradiction; that he can formulate himself out of his experience, instead of trying to impose a formulation of self upon his experiences, denying to awareness those elements which do not fit.

It is clear from our discussion in Chapter 2 about the nature and development of the organism that this describes an authentic, fully functioning organism or person at any and every age from conception onwards.

It doesn't make sense, then, to talk in terms of an individual as 'reaching' or 'achieving' stage 7. To do so is problematic for a number of reasons:

- It takes us into the realm of stage theory as distinct from process theory.
- It implies a greater valuing of stage 7 over other previous stages and, therefore, a prescriptive model of therapeutic change.
- It contradicts Rogers' (1959a) theory of human development.

Process and outcome

In person-centred therapy, outcomes are process outcomes. In his 1959 paper Rogers lists fifteen different aspects of the outcome of a successful therapeutic experience. All these outcomes follow from a client's increased capacity to experience fully those aspects of herself which she found previously unacceptable in some way. Nearly all of these process outcomes have been measured operationally by various objective measures, including: the thematic apperception test, the Rorschach ink-blot test, Q-sorts, a discomfort-relief quotient, and an emotional maturity scale. Rogers cites thirty-five research studies in support of his hypothesised outcomes.

This view of process outcome is epitomised in the concept of 'the fully functioning person' (see Chapter 5 and Rogers, 1957/67, 1959b). Rogers didn't see such a person as ever existing in the flesh. He describes a fully functioning person (1959b, p. 234) as 'the ultimate in the actualization of the human organism' and the 'ultimate hypothetical person'. It seems clear that he is describing an outcome of therapy that is possible only in theory, and not in actuality.

Given that proviso, is the notion of the fully functioning person helpful? We think it is for a number of reasons:

- It brings together under one heading many of the apparently random or unconnected phenomena we may notice as we work. This helps us therefore make tentative and provisional sense of seeming chaos, and to trust the process even when we're not sure where it's leading.

- It provides us with a description of optimal health which is consistent with the philosophical values of person-centred practice, and which allows us to dialogue with other mental health professionals who may have their own such descriptions.

- It specifies in a general way a possible outcome of effective therapy and allows us therefore to make soft, or impressionistic, assessments of how we and our clients are doing.

One client found this approach to therapy challenging. He saw the changes he needed and wanted to make in his life in functional terms, with the result that he tended to 'fast forward', for instance, from going out with someone to imagining a more intimate relationship. He was then disappointed if a 'date' didn't further his progress towards a permanent relationship. Discussing this with his therapist he came to see that the '"what" is the "how"', a phrase that became a kind of meditation for him. Taking this on, he became more relaxed about 'what' he did and focused more on enjoying the 'how': going out more, meeting more people, enjoying the encounters for their own sake rather than worrying about a particular outcome.

There are three aspects of process which, in our view, are understated and, perhaps underrated in person-centred therapy: fluidity, creativity and personal power. As we acknowledge in Chapter 2, we view these as qualities of the organism. We discuss them here as process outcomes of therapy.

Fluidity

Fluidity is an expression of the organism's tendency to actualise. In a paper on the process of psychotherapy Rogers (1958/67a, p. 158) describes this as 'new experiencing with immediacy' in which 'feeling and cognition inter-penetrate, self is subjectively present in the experience' and 'volition is simply the subjective following of a harmonious balance of organismic direction'. The person 'has changed, but what seems most significant, he has become an integrated process of changingness'. This is an important passage in which there are a number of points worth highlighting:

- 'New experiencing with immediacy' – Rogers is advancing an experi-ential, existential and phenomenological psychology which values new experiencing at least alongside old experiences, and subjectivity over objectivity. The approach is both person-centred and present-centred.

LIVERPOOL
JOHN MOORES UNIVERSITY
AVRIL ROBARTS LRC
TEL. 0151 231 4022

- 'Feeling and cognition interpenetrate' – That we feel and think at the same time is an organismic, integrative perspective, and one which is supported by more recent findings in neuroscience.
- 'Volition is simply the subjective following of a harmonious balance of organismic direction' – This involves free-flowing internal communication with ourselves and similar external communication with others. The key word here is 'balance'. The person-centred approach, along with others, stands accused of promoting the 'selfish gene', or the self-centred person (see Buber in Kirschenbaum & Henderson, 1990; Vitz, 1977). Rogers' emphasis on the pro-social organism addresses this criticism: 'A hurt to one is a hurt to all'; 'In my tendency to actualise I will balance the needs of others', and herein lies the difference between Rogers' view of the actualising tendency or the tendency to actualise on the one hand and Maslow's view of 'self-actualisation' and self-actualised persons on the other (see Chapter 3).
- 'A unity of flow, of motion . . . an integrated process of changingness' – This phrase reflects Rogers' valuing of fluidity. Indeed, his whole theory of the process of psychotherapy is based on a movement from fixity to changingness, from rigid structure to flow, from stasis to process.

Rogers (ibid., p. 155) acknowledges that he values fluidity as a desirable state of being:

> Would everyone agree that this is a desirable process of change, that it moves in valued directions? I believe not. I believe some people do not value fluidity. This will be one of the social value judgements which individuals and cultures will have to make.

He continues: 'Such a process of change can easily be avoided, by reducing or avoiding those relationships in which the individual is fully received as he is.' At the same time, in supporting people in their distress and 'stuckness', it is important to value fixity, an apparent contradiction we addressed in Chapter 7.

There is an interesting link between Rogers' values concerning fixity and fluidity and the notion from neuroscience concerning the 'design' of the brain which strikes a balance between what is referred to as 'circuit permanence' and 'circuit plasticity'. Whilst for cortical functions such as vocabulary and logic there is a lot of plasticity, Pally (2000, p. 15) reports that 'the subcortical limbic "emotional" circuits that develop in infancy have less plasticity . . . [which] therefore may have long-lasting effect on subsequent psychological development'. Thus, we may have less plasticity in our emotional circuits than accounted for in Rogers' theory of process and value concerning fluidity. Such limitation is moderated, however, by two facts: (i) that it is precisely circuit permanence that allows infants to form attachments and, later, adults to seek such relationships; and (ii) that the cortex develops the capacity to modulate the emotional responses of the subcortex. Also, Pally (ibid., p. 15) suggests that: 'Since it is known that consciously attending to and verbalising something can enhance cortical activation . . . treatments such as analysis enhance cortical functioning, and take advantage of cortical plasticity, [so as] to modulate deeply engrained emotional responses.'

Creativity

In her commentary on Whitehead's (1929/78) philosophy of the organism, Emmet (1932/66, p. 73) describes creativity as 'the urge towards differentiation and unification' – and, combining notions of pure potentiality and the principle of individuation, as answering to the idealist Aristotelian concept of 'primary matter'. This places the act and process of creativity at the heart of person-centred theory and practice. Ever the social scientist, Rogers (1954/67a, p. 349) identifies two elements of the creative process and, also characteristically, a relationship between them: '. . . there must be something observable, some product of creation . . . [and] These products must be novel constructions.'

He goes on (p. 150) to define the creative process as: '*the emergence in action of a novel* relational *product, growing out of the uniqueness of the individual on the one hand, and the materials, events, people, or circumstances of his life on the other*' [our emphasis]. Interestingly, in a recently published oral history based on a series of interviews, Rogers reflects on the fact that he wrote this article on creativity, in essence, in one night: 'It was in itself a creative act. It just flowed' (Rogers & Russell, 2002, p. 296). In a brief passage he describes having been tested in terms of right brain/left brain functioning and found to be quite even. He also talks about his one painting (which he prized), and creating mobiles. Rogers hypothesises certain external conditions which foster creativity. We discuss those in Chapter 7.

In a paper first presented in 1954, Rogers (1954/67a) describes also three significant 'inner conditions':

- Openness to experience – or extensionality, the opposite of psychological defensiveness. Rogers describes this explicitly as being aware of *this* existential moment *as it is*.
- An internal locus (or place) of evaluation. 'The value of his product is, for the creative person, established not by the praise or criticism of others, but by himself. Have I created something satisfying to *me*? Does it express part of me?' (p. 354). Rogers refers to this as an organismic reaction to and appraisal of the created product. In our experience this

is often discouraged in family, educational and other social systems where external evaluations abound.

- An ability to toy or play with elements and concepts. Rogers (ibid., p. 355) describes this as:

> the ability to play spontaneously with ideas, colors, shapes, relationships – to juggle elements into impossible juxtapositions, to shape wild hypotheses, to make the given problematic, to express the ridiculous, to translate from one form to another, to transform into improbable equivalents. It is from this spontaneous toying with life that there arises the hunch, the creative seeing of life in a new and significant way.

> A person-centred approach to theory reflects this ability to toy and play. Such toying and playing with ideas is a healthy use of theory, and leads to good practice.

Elsewhere Rogers (1959b) argues that creativity is one of the outcomes of therapy, that there is a social need for creativity (1980a), and that it depends on a nurturing environment. This social need for creativity has been echoed in the UK by Estelle Morris, the then Minister for the Arts, Sports and Culture (and former Minister for Education) in an interview on the Today Programme on BBC Radio 4 (16 October 2003) in which she said:

> creativity itself is more important than ever before. It's the difference between a good business and an excellent business . . . an excellent teacher and a good teacher. I don't think we've got a way of really describing the impact of creativity in our wider life . . . it's undervalued . . . I want to play my part in trying to tell the story of creativity across government and elsewhere. Without creativity the quality of our lives both personally and nationally would be a lot, lot poorer.

Personal power

We can equate the idea of personal power with the notion of autonomy, and with a client's development or reclaiming of an internal locus of evaluation. Rogers argues (1978, p. 239) that an organism's actualisation involves 'a trend toward self-regulation and away from control by external forces'. He thus locates personal power centrally as one of the manifestations of actualisation, and by implication therefore as one of the observable outcomes of effective therapy. This, we think, suggests that he saw personal power as one aspect of the organism in its natural state. A therapist, therefore, does not, and maybe cannot, *empower* her clients. It is simply not in her gift to make them powerful, or more powerful than they already are in potential. She can, however, ensure at least that she does nothing to impede or diminish her clients in their expression of personal power. At best she can help make a space within which they feel free enough to be personally powerful. Paraphrasing Gertrude Stein on Paris, Rogers (1978, p. xii) says: 'It is not that this approach gives power to the person; it never takes it away.'

Natiello (1990) takes up the notion of personal power. She sees it as a way of beginning to nurture what she calls 'collaborative power', a concept which she says (p. 273) 'is implicit in Rogers' work'. She distinguishes collaborative power from authoritarian power, or power over others, which is, she says (1990, p. 268), 'still the primary political orientation in the world'. Recognising that this authoritarian power is, politically, 'inappropriate and ineffective', she makes the point that those of us who favour instead relationships of mutuality and collaboration have tended (p. 270) to 'reject the concept of power in any form'. She sees this as a mistake, points out that non-authoritarian leaders like Mahatma Gandhi and Martin Luther King were particularly powerful, and suggests that therapists too must have a sense of their own personal power if they are to be effective in their work (p. 274): 'Such an empowered presence is inherent in the concept of congruence – the ability and willingness to be as fully one's real self as possible.'

Personal power, as Rogers and Natiello write about it, carries an implicit recognition that the organism is also pro-social. In Angyal's terms, the organism tends towards both autonomy and homonomy. It seeks, that is, both to exert personal power, and to belong to a family, group or community. The dynamic tension between these two tendencies means that personal power is not an excuse for selfish or reckless self-assertion, and that the exercise of personal power will necessarily take both self and other into account. We think that this line of thought answers some of the criticisms of therapy in general, and of some therapies in particular, that they derive from and promote a selfish individualism. We think also that it challenges the practice of some therapists who attend more to an individual client's rights than to his familial or social responsibilities.

Therapeutic relating

In this part we develop (from the previous chapter) our understanding of therapeutic relating through three discussions concerning the person of the therapist, the person of the client and the process of therapeutic relating.

The person of the therapist

We noted earlier Taft's thinking about the significance of the therapeutic relationship. She also had ideas about the person of the therapist. 'In my opinion' she says (1933, p. 19) 'the basis of therapy lies in the therapist himself, in his capacity to permit the use of self which the therapeutic relationship implies as well as his psychological insight and technical skill.' These ideas prefigure some of Rogers' own thinking that the therapist's personal values, beliefs and ways of being are important variables in the therapeutic process. The therapist's 'use of self' has been taken up by different therapeutic traditions, from a psychoanalytic perspective principally with reference to the notion of countertransference, and within humanistic psychology often with reference to Rogers' conditions. These two streams of thinking about the therapist have been brought together in a recent book, co-authored by two practitioners who represent these different traditions (Rowan & Jacobs, 2002).

The therapeutic conditions require the following qualities of the therapist: to be contactful, congruent in the relationship, unconditionally accepting and accurately empathic. Rogers (1958/67b) elaborates these qualities. Although he frames them in terms of the characteristics of a helping relationship (Box 8.1) they are, equally, qualities essential in an effective therapist.

Box 8.1   Characteristics of a helping relationship (Rogers, 1958/67b)

- Can I be trustworthy?
- Can I communicate myself unambiguously?
- Can I let myself experience positive attitudes towards this person?
- Can I be strong enough to be separate (from the other) – and am I secure enough to permit them their separateness?
- Can I let myself enter fully into the world of their feelings and meanings and understand these as they do?
- Can I be acceptant of each facet of this other person?
- Can I act with sufficient sensitivity in the relationship that my behaviour will not be perceived as a threat – and can I free them from the threat of external evaluation?
- Can I meet this person as a person in the process of becoming (or will I be bound by their and my own past)?

These questions invite self-reflection. Both the therapeutic conditions and these qualities, in effect, at least invite us if not require us, as therapists, to take up the challenge of the ancient injunction, variously attributed to Greek or Egyptian origins, to 'Know thyself'. Whether we engage in this self-knowing informally by means of personal self-reflection or, more formally, through supervision, is a matter of debate, for more on which see Wilkins (1997) and Tudor and Worrall (2004). Boy and Pine (1982) identify a number of professional values, including a 'commitment' to ongoing self-assessment as well as periodic evaluation.

Of course, the qualities of the person that is the therapist are not abstract. They are specific, relational, and effective in so far as his clients perceive them. Rogers (1959b, p. 213) embodies this in the sixth condition: 'That the client perceives, at least to a minimal degree . . . the unconditional positive regard of the therapist for him, and the empathic understanding of the therapist.' Lake (1966, p. 36) puts it well:

> Patients are in general more sensitive to the fact that it is the quality of spirit and personality that differentiates the psychiatrists who help them from those who do not . . . It is the power of being, the power of acceptance, and the spiritual strength of the therapist which is his main curative resource.

Patients or clients are also sensitive to perceived inconsistencies in the therapist, for instance, between thought or speech and action. In this respect the person-centred approach, perhaps more than other approaches to therapy, challenges the therapist to be themselves not only as a therapist but as a person, and to embody the qualities required not only in the consulting room but in their lives. Robbins (1977, p. 253) puts this robustly: 'Any psychiatrist or psychologist whose own life isn't happy and whole enough to be exemplary isn't worth the hide it takes to upholster his couch. He ought to be horsewhipped and sued for malpractice.' Whilst we might not advocate such a punitive response, we endorse the demand for consistency and integrity.

Working in a way which relies on her personal qualities, and indeed on the person of the therapist herself, demands more of the therapist. Being congruent or integrated in the relationship, for example, requires us to acknowledge and accept our own fears, failings and vulnerabilities, and to risk feeling or being incongruent and disintegrated. This brings us to a second ancient injunction, a proverb, cited in the gospel of Saint Luke (4: 23): 'And he said unto them, Ye will surely say unto me this proverb, "Physician, heal thyself".' Again, quite how psychotherapists do this is the subject of much debate in professional circles. The debate centres, for the most part, around whether or not therapists should be required to have personal therapy. For registration with the United Kingdom Council for Psychotherapy (UKCP), for instance, it is a requirement that all psychotherapists undertake their own personal therapy throughout their training: 'The Trainee must engage in a continuous process of analysis and self-examination, before, during and after training' (UKCP Special General Meeting Resolution, May 1990). Further to this, a document produced by the UKCP's Training Standards Committee in 1993 states that 'any training shall include arrangements to ensure that the trainees can identify and manage appropriately their personal involvement in and contribution to the processes of the psychotherapies that they practice'. Further, the

Training Standards Committee within the Humanistic and Integrative Psychotherapy Section of the UKCP, states (1992) that:

> For membership of this Section, it is a requirement of a training course that trainees have personal psychotherapy with an experienced psycho-therapist as part of their training. This should be at least as intensive in terms of frequency and duration as the form of psychotherapy to be practiced.

From a person-centred perspective which values autonomy and non-directiveness, it is clearly antithetical to *require* or *direct* someone to be in therapy (see Mearns, 1994). It is nevertheless consistent, in our view, that students who wish to be accredited or registered respond to the require-ments of organisations and bodies of which they wish to be members.

We discussed fluidity, creativity and personal power earlier in relation to the person in process (pp. 227ff.). In relation to the person of the therapist these qualities manifest in a number of ways: curiosity; non-defensiveness; a willingness both to follow the client's process, and to engage robustly in the process of relationship; non-attachment to particular outcomes or per-spectives; an ability to be stimulating and challenging (see N. Rogers, 1993/2000); continence, or a capacity to contain thoughts, feelings, hunches, intuitions and experiences. This is not an exhaustive list.

Finally, in a paper on the philosophical roots of person-centred therapy in the history of Western thought, Van Belle (in press, 2005) summarises some of the necessary beliefs of the person-centred therapist:

1   A belief in people's capacity to heal through self-reflection.
2   A prizing of 'the otherness of others'.
3   A trust in others and in their exercise of free will.
4   A belief in people's ability and right to choose, as well as their capacity to reason.
5   A love of 'the ambiguity of therapy': 'One must prefer the disorder of emotion to the order of logic, for the Person-Centered therapeutic process is anything but linear and predictable.'

The person of the client

The general psychotherapeutic literature contains little about the person of the client. Most studies, reports and vignettes focus on the client's problems and pathology and are, by definition, particular and partial descriptions of the person. The logic of this present approach and its emphasis on organ-ismic psychology within a broader tradition of health psychology offers a more holistic view of the person of the client. Bergner and Holmes (2000) see Rogers as someone who assigned to all of his clients the status of an unconditionally acceptable human being, not on the basis of observation, but *a priori*. Person-centred therapy provides a relationship in which clients, independently of the facts about their lives and persons, are genuinely regarded and treated as acceptable persons. Bergner and Holmes elaborate this and advocate that therapists assign a large number of statuses to the client. Where Rogers assigned one status, they suggest a 'status dynamic therapy', in which the client is regarded and treated, *a priori*, as a person: (1) who is acceptable; (2) who makes sense; (3) whose best interests come first in the therapeutic relationship; (4) who is important and significant to the therapist; (5) who already possesses enabling strengths, knowledge, and other resources for solving problems; (6) who, given a choice between equally realistic but differentially degrading appraisals of him or her, is to be given the benefit of the doubt; and (7) who is an agent, i.e. an individual capable of entertaining behavioural options and selecting from among them, as opposed to a helpless victim of genetic, historical, environmental, or other forces (Bergner & Staggs, 1987). We think this is an interesting elaboration which is consistent with Rogers' assumptions about the person. It is also consistent with the developmental perspective outlined earlier (see pp. 110ff.).

The process of relating

As far as the therapeutic relationship or therapeutic relating is concerned, the logic of client- or person-centred therapy is to centre or focus on the client. However, there is comparatively little in the psychotherapeutic literature from the client's perspective. As we note in Chapter 7, Rogers devotes a long chapter in *Client-Centered Therapy* (1951) to the relationship as experienced by the client, and he was one of the first therapists and theoreticians to do so. At the end of the chapter Rogers refers to other accounts and studies of clients' experiences of therapy, including Snyder (1947), Lipkin (1948) and Axline (1950). In this tradition there is a small number of books written by clients about their experiences of therapy, including the failure of therapy and therapists, from a technical article about libido development written by an analysand (Brunswick, 1940), and a personal story of a psychoanalysis (Knight, 1950), to more recent accounts by Tilmann (1977), von Drigalski (1986), France (1988), Heyward (1993), Alexander (1995), Gordon (2000), and Sands (2000, 2001). Yalom (1974) offers his own account of a therapeutic relationship alongside his client's account. Some research into therapeutic process has elicited open-ended accounts from clients, including: a relationship inventory, based on Rogers' process conception of psychotherapy (Barrett-Lennard, 1986); a content analysis of 'received' empathy (Bachelor, 1988); client accounts of what they found helpful and hindering in client-centred/experiential psychotherapy

(Lietaer, 1992); and a study of how clients make therapy work (Bohart & Tallman, 1999).

In this final part, we bring together these two persons, the therapist and the client, and consider some ideas which inform the way they relate to each other in the service of the client's healing. We discuss this with reference to non-directivity, intersubjectivity and co-creative therapeutic relating; the question of transference in person-centred therapeutic relating; dialogue; and mutuality. Although we think that person-centred therapy has, from its beginnings, made a particular contribution to our understanding of 'relationship therapy', we recognise that we are not alone in this interest. Over a number of years, other therapeutic approaches have become increasingly interested in the relational perspective.

Non-directivity

We indicated in the Introduction (p. 1) that person-centred therapy was originally called 'non-directive' therapy. In part, Rogers described his work as such so as to distinguish it from prevailing models of therapy, whose practitioners accrued to themselves a level of expertise and authority that allowed them, legitimately in their own eyes, to hold and express views about what clients should or shouldn't do in their lives. The term also describes practice that both devolves from and manifests an unconditional trust in an individual client's tendency and capacity to actualise as fully as environmental conditions allow. As Levitt (2005, p. i) puts it in his preface to a recently edited volume on the subject: 'Non-directivity is the distinguishing feature of the revolutionary, anti-authoritarian approach to psychotherapy and human relations developed by Carl Rogers.' Raskin (1948) points out that Rogers' predecessors, including Freud, Rank, Taft and Allen were also non-directive in various aspects of their work, and to varying degrees.

Taft is perhaps the most immediate forerunner. She describes (1933, p. v) her move over twenty-five years away from 'the notion of a reform of the "other" through superior knowledge of life and psychology, a concept closely allied to that of scientific control in the field of emotions and behavior' and towards 'a therapy which is purely individual, non-moral, non-scientific, non-intellectual, which can take place only when divorced from all hint of control, unless it be the therapist's control of himself in the therapeutic situation'. The case studies which constitute the bulk of her book show her working with a degree of permissiveness which we think is still radical today (see Chapter 7). Rogers (1942, p. 127) puts it this way:

> The non-directive viewpoint places a high value on the right of every individual to be psychologically independent and to maintain his psychological integrity. The directive viewpoint places a high value

upon social conformity and the right of the more able to direct the less able. These viewpoints have a significant relationship to social and political philosophy as well as to techniques of therapy.

The term, though, is problematical in a number of ways. It defines the process of therapy (a) in terms of therapist rather than client, since it is the therapist who is non-directive; and (b) in terms of what the therapist doesn't do, rather than in terms of what he does. This exposes person-centred therapists to the accusation that they are merely reflective, passive, uncommitted and not engaged. It is perhaps for these reasons that Rogers begins to call his work 'client-centred' rather than 'non-directive'. Cain (1989, p. 125) goes further, and points out that Rogers 'barely addresses the issue' after about 1942.

Setting aside the question of what we call the approach, the principle that person-centred practitioners are essentially non-directive in their work with their clients has been more or less central to the practice of person-centred therapy since its beginning. To be completely non-directive, though, even if desirable, is clearly unattainable. Lietaer (1998, p. 63) says that 'it makes little sense to wonder whether a therapist is directive or not. It only makes sense to see *in what way* he or she is directive or task-oriented.' Brodley (1997, 1999/2005) on the other hand asserts the view that non-directivity refers to an attitude and not to specific behaviour, for example, asking questions of clients. 'Further' Brodley (1999/2005, p. 1) argues: 'attitudes are not defined in terms of behavior, although they affect behavior. They are defined in terms of intentions, sensibilities, feelings and values. Attitudes are manifested in intentions that adapt to particular circumstances – thus they cannot be rigid.' The view that the person-centred therapist should never ask a client a question is a rigid rule of behaviour. We are more interested in the therapist's underlying attitude and value, which may result in her asking a question of a client. If the intention of any question is to understand the client, and not to be inquisitive or clever, then the behaviour of asking a question is congruent with the non-directive attitude. Merry (1999, p. 75) also promotes the value of non-directiveness as an underlying attitude: 'a general non-authoritarian attitude maintained by a counselor whose intention is empathically to understand a client's subjective experience'. He continues (pp. 75–6) and makes the connection between this non-directive attitude and the belief in the person's tendency to actualise:

It refers also to the theory that the actualising tendency can be fostered in a relationship of particular qualities, and that whilst the general direction of that tendency is regarded as constructive and creative, its particular characteristics in any one person cannot be predicted, and should not be controlled or directed.

Writing about what he refers to as the paradox of non-directiveness Cain (1989) suggests that to be non-directive on principle and with all clients fails to recognise or attend to the different needs of individual clients, some of whom might benefit from a therapist who is more rather than less directive.

Responding to Cain, Grant (1990) argues for a distinction between 'principled' and 'instrumental' non-directiveness. He suggests that principled non-directiveness arises out of a therapist's commitment to be non-directive *on principle*, and without any attachment as to particular outcome. It is, he says (ibid., p. 81), 'an attitude that provides a "space" for growth, not one that intends to cause it'. Instrumental non-directiveness (ibid., p. 78) is more an expression of a pragmatic strategy 'to bring about growth or empower clients'. 'Respect for the client' he says (ibid., p. 79) 'is not absent, but is allied to or tempered with a pragmatic concern with promoting growth.' The debate about whether person-centred therapy is non-directive or not is, he says (ibid., p. 79), 'better understood as a dispute about what is the morally best way of doing therapy'. This echoes Rogers' conviction above that the choice to be non-directive or not carries more than merely clinical implications. Grant continues (ibid., p. 79):

> We must be able to argue why it is good to engage in the practices we advocate. We should be able to do this because psychotherapy is a moral enterprise. It is an activity which can and does affect the well-being of others, and which is based on ideas about right and wrong.

Patterson (2000b, p. 181) calls Grant's distinction 'ridiculous, patent nonsense'! 'Therapy' he says (ibid., p. 182) 'is an influencing process. The intent of the therapist is to influence the client. If this were not so, the therapist would not be practicing.' These comments indicate that the debate is not simply about whether we're directive or non-directive, but more subtly about how directive we are, and in what areas, and to what ends. As therapists we have, may negotiate, and maintain structure, for example, with regard to time and fees. We may offer structure in terms of providing materials for creative, expressive therapy. This does not mean that we direct the client to have a particular experience. In the context of research into group facilitation, Coghlan and McIlduff (1990) draw a useful distinction between intervention and structure on the one hand and direction on the other.

Brazier (1995, p. 102) provides one way out of the impasse:

> Some would say that in therapy one should never go beyond what the client has given us. On the other hand, the whole purpose of therapy is to help the client go beyond what they have come with. In order to tune into the client's world, the rule of staying within what the client has expressed is vitally important. Once one has tuned in, however,

therapist and client are together occupying a privileged space in which new possibilities may spontaneously occur to either of them. What is crucial then is whether they ring true to the client rather than whether the client actually spoke them first.

We find this argument compelling. Brazier sees the significance of sustained empathic attention, and sees also that when therapist and client achieve a level of mutuality, the debate about what's directive and what's not becomes less important. This is also echoed by Brodley (1999/2005, p. 1) who views the non-directive attitude as intrinsic to Rogers' formulation of the therapeutic conditions: 'The concept of non-directivity comes into existence *within the meaning* of these therapeutic attitudes – they are the source of the non-directive principle.'

Intersubjectivity

Therapist and client meet as two subjective persons. To this encounter a therapist may bring an understanding of intersubjectivity (see Chapter 4), or the meeting of two subjective worlds or frames of reference. As Laing (1967, p. 53) puts it: 'Human beings relate to each other not simply externally, like two billiard balls, but by the relations of the two worlds of experience that come into play when two people meet.' Rogers (1959b) offers a theoretical framework which includes a theory of self and ideas about how a therapist may use his experience in the service of the client. As we acknowledge in Chapter 4, this 'use of self' has subsequently been elaborated by self psychologists, who offer a particular understanding of how therapeutic relationships are disrupted and restored. If we focus on the intersubjective world, we will ask 'What is happening here between us?', rather than 'What's happening to you?' or 'What's happening to me?'. Stolorow and Atwood (1992) frame this question in terms of the interface between the therapist's subjective world and the client's subjective world, and the meanings of the dynamics that this interface creates.

Parlett (1991, p. 75) suggests that one implication of this approach is that 'when two people converse or engage with one another in some way, something comes into existence which is a product of neither of them exclusively . . . there is a shared field, a common communicative home, which is mutually constructed'. Intersubjectivity thus supports a 'two-person' mode of therapeutic action (see Stark, 2000).

Co-creative relating

This brings us to the concept of co-creativity. We discussed constructivism in Chapter 1. This philosophical perspective argues that 'reality' is constructed. Two people talking together co-construct their shared reality.

This, of course, includes disputing and negotiating, constructing and deconstructing. As Sapriel (1998, p. 42) puts it:

> this better reflects the reality that meaning is being co-created by both subjectivities . . . with neither person holding a more objectively 'true' version of reality than the other. It reflects an appreciation of the inevitable, moment-by-moment participation of the therapist's subjective organisation of experience in a system of mutual influence.

For us, this describes an active, engaged and participative approach to therapeutic relating which is entirely compatible with person-centred principles and therapeutic process.

Writing about transactional analysis, Summers and Tudor (2000) identify three principles which underpin co-creative therapy:

1   The principle of 'we'-ness. That the therapeutic relationship or therapeutic relating is a more potent phenomenon than either therapist or client alone. Therapists seem to avoid the 'we' word as if it connotes some form of collusion with the client. We think that using 'we' can be more inclusive and sharing, and can acknowledge and support a sense of homonomy.
2   The principle of shared responsibility. That co-creative therapy (p. 24) 'supports the practical manifestation of interdependence, co-operation and mutuality within the therapeutic relationship by emphasizing shared client–therapist responsibility for the therapeutic process'. *One partially deaf client kept apologising for not hearing what his therapist had said. The therapist responded by owning her own responsibility to talk more clearly and more loudly and, at the same time, asked the client to tell her when he couldn't hear her so well.*
3   The principle of present-centred development. Co-creative therapy emphasises the importance of a present-centred perspective on human development as distinct from a past-centred model of child development (see Chapters 2 and 4). What follows from this principle (p. 25) is that 'the therapeutic focus is on supporting the here-and-now developmental direction of the client'. This principle, in particular, runs counter to conventional wisdom about transference, to which we turn.

Transferential relating

Rogers acknowledges that the notion of transference is useful in so far as it describes a process by which patterns of past relationships inform and influence the way we make relationships in the present. In keeping with his phenomenological, experiential and existential leanings, however, he is more interested in exploring what's present and immediate than he is in unearthing what's past. This means that person-centred practice is inherently present-centred rather than past-centred, and attends to relationships for what they signify in the present rather than for anything they may tell us about the past.

This does not deny the existence, or even the significance, of transference or 'transference attitudes' (Rogers, 1951). It does, however, recognise that even if we're talking about the past, and even if we're relating to our therapist as if she were our mother or father, we're doing so inevitably in the immediate present. An analyst might foster a transference as a way of helping a patient expose and examine the past, in order to make eventual sense of the present. A person-centred practitioner is more likely to stay with what's present in the belief that that will expose whatever a client most needs to attend to next.

Shlien (1984) takes a more extreme view than Rogers. He argues that transference is a myth, and that we don't need to look at all to the past to explain or make sense of present behaviour. There are, he says, enough reasons in the present to account for present behaviour. Even if we behave now as we did then, we do so not *because* we did so then, but *for the same reasons* as we did so then.

These thoughts about past, present and future remind us that Taft, whose influence Rogers acknowledges, sees time as one of the inevitable limitations of therapeutic relationships. She argues (1933, p. 12) that a client's relationship with and use of the therapeutic hour indicates, or even mirrors, his relationship with and use of his life:

> Time represents more vividly than any other category the necessity of accepting limitations as well as the inability to do so, and symbolizes therefore the whole problem of living. The reaction of each individual to limited or unlimited time betrays his deepest and most fundamental life pattern, his relation to the growth process itself, to beginnings and endings, to being born and to dying.

If he resolves his relationship with the limitations of the therapeutic hour he will, therefore, also resolve his relationship with the existential limitations of his life.

Finally in this section, Bohart *et al.* (1993) suggest that human beings tend naturally to look towards the future rather than at the past, and suggest that therapists can, in the present, choose to attend to and empathise with whatever their clients express of hope or future aspiration.

Dialogue and mutuality

The ideas above to do with intersubjectivity and co-creative relating mean that person-centred relating is characterised by dialogue and mutuality. If we see constructivism as the philosophy of process, and intersubjectivity and co-creativity as constituting the theory, then dialogue is the practice and mutuality the outcome.

Dialogue implies a conversation or exchange between two (or more) people. Frankl (1963), De Maré, Piper and Thompson (1991), and Friedman (1992) all talk about dialogue as a form of therapy. Friedman's thinking about the place of dialogue in therapy is influenced by the psychological views of Martin Buber, whose influence Rogers also acknowledges. Through dialogue, client and therapist acknowledge each other's voices and co-create the meaning of what they hear. It is the visible outworking of the philosophy and theory.

The concept of mutuality in person-centred therapy refers to the idea that the therapeutic relationship is, in some ways, reciprocal. The client learns from their work with the therapist; the therapist learns about herself from her work with the client. Mearns (1994, p. 6) describes mutuality as 'where the counsellor and client understand each other across different levels of perspective'. Merry (1999, p. 67) regards some degree of mutuality as characteristic of effective therapy relationships: 'there is a sense that the two people are mutually engaged in exploring meanings and working towards understanding. In successful therapeutic relationships, mutuality can develop into an intimate and close sharing of thoughts, emotions and experiences.' We think this epitomises effective therapy in which the two parties co-regulate (see Chapter 2). We may say, to paraphrase Schore (1994), that person-centred therapy facilitates the patterns of affect regulation that integrate organismic growth, and allows for a continuity of inner experience. Whilst we see this process as co-created and co-regulated, we do not see mutuality as symmetrical. Aron (1996) makes the point that mutuality is not symmetrical, and that the focus of attention remains with the client's process.

In this chapter we conclude our discussion of the theory and practice of person-centred therapy. In the next and final chapter we consider the environmental context of this therapy.

Chapter 9

Environment

An old text says, 'If you do not know a man, look at his friends; if you do not know a ruler look at his attendants.' Environment is the important thing! Environment is the important thing!

Hsun-tzu

Always think of the universe as one living organism, with a single substance and a single soul; and observe how all things are submitted to the single perceptivity of this one whole, all are moved by its single impulse, and all play their part in the causation of every event that happens. Remark the intricacy of the skein, the complexity of the web.

Marcus Aurelius

We must recognize that the human organism is not an isolated entity, sufficient unto itself. Every individual is born, lives, and dies inseparably from the larger contexts of physical, social, political, and spiritual influences. The laws governing the physical universe are not separate from those governing the functions of living organisms . . . we must begin by comprehending clearly the setting in which the human being is found, how it influences him, and in turn how he affects it.

George Vithoulkas

Person-centred therapy is an environmental model of therapy. First, the notion of therapeutic conditions, necessary, sufficient or otherwise, makes the therapeutic environment integral to the process and outcome of therapy. Client and therapist are heteronomous to each other, each a part of the other's environment. Together they co-create the therapeutic environment. Second, and perhaps more centrally, as others including Angyal (1941) and Barrett-Lennard (1996) and we argue, the organism cannot be understood outside of its environment. As we emphasise throughout this book, the organism – and, more broadly, the person – is in a dynamic, transactional relationship with its environment (see Rogers, 1959b). We think it is relevant, therefore, to discuss the environment or context of the client, whether individual, couple, family or group. Taking this one step further we also think it is important to reflect on person-centred therapy in its environmental context. Our focus in this last chapter, therefore, is on the environment external to person-centred therapy: the field, as it were, in which person-centred therapy and its practitioners stand, act, interact and impact. In the first part of the chapter we consider three environments: the intellectual, the ethical and the professional. In the second part we discuss the extent to which person-centred therapy is or may be seen as an integrative therapy. In the third part, which also concludes this book, we reflect on person-centred therapy in its own terms.

Person-centred therapy: Environmental understandings

We think that the broader, environmental context of theory and practice is important, especially from an organismic perspective. Just as the environment is the context for the organism, so the social, political and cultural environment is the context for person-centred therapy itself. Two books have addressed this especially. Van Belle's (1980) study of Rogers in relation to his view of therapy, personality and interpersonal relations is a major, if relatively unknown, contribution to the literature. Barrett-Lennard (1998) discusses the sociopolitical and cultural context of the beginnings of client-centred therapy, including Franklin Roosevelt's 'New Deal' programme, and juxtaposes his presidency with Rogers' directions, steps and style.

The intellectual environment

In this book we acknowledge the intellectual environment of person-centred therapy, with regard to the ideas and historical antecedents which have informed and shaped it. We comment on the autobiographical nature of theory (see Rogers, 1967, and the Introduction). We emphasise the organismic origins and the relational nature of person-centred theory. We note that person-centred therapy is often located within the school or third 'force' of humanistic psychology. We share Mearns and Thorne's (2000) critique of this broad categorisation (see the Introduction) which, in any case, does not do justice to Maslow's (1962) vision of humanistic psychology as 'epi-Freudian' and 'epi-behaviouristic', that is, building upon previous analytic and behavioural forces. For us, Pine's (1990) quadripartite analysis of conceptual domains of psychoanalysis offers a more coherent, meta-theoretical framework for an understanding of the more general field of psychotherapy. In his eponymous book, he summarises the substantive phenomena of *Drive, Ego, Object and Self* (see Box 9.1).

Box 9.1 Pine's taxonomy of drive, ego, object relations and self psychology

Drive psychology   Urges, motivation
Ego psychology   Modes of defence and adaptation
Object relations psychology   Relationships, their internalisation, distortion
                              and repetition
Self psychology   Phenomena of differentiation and boundary
                              formation, of personal agency and
                              authenticity, and of self-esteem

---

Pine omits organismic psychology from his conceptual analysis, probably because he was more concerned with the history of psychoanalysis, and with an integrative view of the phenomena under discussion, than with providing a comprehensive, conceptual history of psychology. In this book, we reclaim the conceptual domain of organismic psychology as the underpinning of person-centred therapy. In doing so, we consider the phenomena Pine identifies from an organismic perspective and framework (see Box 9.2).

Box 9.2 The location of discussions in this present work, in terms of Pine's
         taxonomy

Drive, urges, motivation   Discussed in the context of the
                                            organism's tendency to actualise
                                            (Chapter 3)

Ego, defence and adaptation   Discussed in terms of self and person
                                            (Chapters 4 and 5)

Object relations, relationships, their   Discussed as 'subject relations'
internalisation, distortion and   (Chapters 4, 6 and 8)
repetition

Self, differentiation and boundary   Discussed in relation to the organism
formation, personal agency and   (Chapter 2) and self (Chapter 4)
authenticity, and self-esteem

Organismic theory takes a holistic approach to the study of the person (see Chapter 2). Research investigations based on organismic theory focus on the *total* person, within the context of her environment, and not on isolated psychological functions and functioning. Within person-centred therapy such research has taken different forms: from early research based on the methodology of the Q-sort, which informs a number of contributions in Rogers and Dymond (1954); co-operative experiential enquiry (see Reason & Heron, 2002/1986); heuristics, a method of enquiry which proceeds towards an unknown goal by incremental exploration (see, for example, Barrineau & Bozarth, 2002/1989; Moustakas, 1990; Merry, 2004); through to hermeneutic inquiry, which is based on the view that the study of person can only be carried out through a distinctive human science (see, for instance, Guba & Lincoln, 1990).

Organismic theory is also all-encompassing. Hall and Lindzey (1978) argue that it offers a broad base for understanding the total organism. They distinguish this from a narrow preoccupation with such things as learning and perception, for example, which they say is true of gestalt psychology. This reminds us of the importance of and necessity for a holistic, multi-dimensional and multi-disciplinary approach to the study of the organism. Viewing and locating person-centred psychology as an organismic psychology forges its intellectual links historically with psychobiology (see Rennie, 1943), psychosomatics (see Dunbar, 1954), neurology (see Taylor, 1931), neuropsychiatry (see Goldstein, 1934/95) and, currently, with developments in neuroscience and evolutionary psychology (see Chapters 2 and 4).

Person-centred therapy is widely acknowledged (McLeod, 2003) as one of the first approaches to psychotherapy to conduct substantial research into its own processes and outcomes, research which has informed and still influences psychotherapy research in general. Van Belle (in press, 2005) also acknowledges that Rogers was probably the first therapist to advocate and to practice empirical research, and that, in some sense, this makes him a positivist. However, Van Belle goes on to argue that, in terms of his basic intent and the tools that he and his colleagues used, Rogers was anti-positivist.

Research in psychotherapy is as important now as ever, and perhaps even more important, given the gap between research and practice for most practitioners, for discussion of which see McLeod (2003). We see a number of reasons for promoting this aspect of the intellectual environment which person-centred and other therapies inhabit:

- Holism – and diversity. We live in a diverse world, culturally, spiritually, politically, intellectually, and therapeutically. As we espouse holism, we take a holistic approach to the study of the person and a particular approach to therapy. This means adopting research methods which are consistent with the approach *and*, as we stated in the Introduction, being open to research which refutes theory or practice.
- Duty of care. Some people view research as part of a duty of care that practitioners have towards their clients. This involves being able to read and understand the implications of research across theoretical orientations, and to be cognisant of research methods and findings. With the increase in psychotherapy training courses validated at Masters' level, and especially those offering MSc degrees, this perceived duty is

becoming increasingly framed as a necessary skill to fulfil both academic and professional requirements.

- The therapeutic relationship and therapeutic relating. Psychotherapy outcome research shows consistently that the therapeutic relationship is a significant factor in determining the effectiveness of therapy. Some studies put the significance of this factor as high as 40%. Given the history of person-centred therapy as 'relationship therapy', person-centred therapists are – or should be – particularly interested in this. The number of approaches to therapy suggests that no one approach has a monopoly on the truth. This makes it more important that we have an overview of such factors as the significance of the therapeutic relationship.

- Reflexivity. Reflective and critical consciousness is a feature of the human condition and our tendency to actualise, our aspiration, or *physis* (see Chapter 3). In this we draw on Rogers' (1969, 1983) own views about education and learning, as well as Schon's (1983) seminal work *The Reflective Practitioner*. Merry (2004) takes this logic further and sees supervision as a form of heuristic inquiry.

- Advancing the approach. As we have said, person-centred therapy has, historically, been well researched (see Rogers, 1942; Rogers *et al.*, 1967; Seeman, 1990). In 1956 the American Psychological Association honoured Rogers, along with Wolfang Köhler and Kenneth W. Spence, with its first Distinguished Scientific Contribution Award. His citation acknowledged him: 'for formulating a testable theory of psychotherapy, and for extensive systematic research to exhibit the value of the method and explore and test the implications of the theory' (cited in Kirschenbaum & Henderson, 1990b, p. 201). More recently, person-centred therapy has stood the test of comparative trials (see Friedli *et al.*, 1997; King *et al.*, 2000).

  In addition to the more generic reasons outlined above, research into person-centred therapy may also counter some of the misrepresentations of the theory. For instance, most researchers acknowledge the person-centred contribution to process research and the identification of process variables which make a difference to outcome (see Chapter 8).

The professional environment

Since the birth of psychotherapy, there have been fierce debates, at times leading to splits, about the nature of this activity, its status as a profession allied to medicine, and the requirements for training and qualification. Whether we like it or not we inhabit a professional environment, full of stimulation and support, co-operation and competition, envy and gossip. The professional environment in the UK and many other countries is highly organised and structured. Professional associations and bodies accredit or validate training courses and register individual therapists. There is also in the UK currently a move towards the statutory registration of psycho-therapists, a move which government and key professional bodies support. The professional environment is also increasingly competitive. Students and trainees are increasingly expected to gain multiple qualifications, vocational and academic, and to seek accreditation or registration.

Person-centred therapy holds a particular position in this environment on several counts:

1   Psychotherapy & counselling. Person-centred therapy, historically, holds that there is no difference between psychotherapy and coun-selling. Perceived differences are, in our view, based on spurious claims about 'depth' (see Chapter 1), focus, or self-defining assertions: that one is 'long-term', for example, and the other 'short-term'. Differences between psychotherapy and counselling are often based on history, context, organisation, interest, politics, and theoretical orientation (see Tudor, 1997). Generally, psychotherapy and psychotherapists have more status than counselling and counsellors and, for various historical reasons, the person-centred approach is seen as more aligned to counselling than psychotherapy. This prejudice has resulted in some person-centred therapists experiencing a glass ceiling in terms of qualification, registration and access to employment.

2   Anti-institutional. The second count lies in the autobiography of person-centred therapy, and, in effect, of Carl Rogers himself. In a series of papers written towards the end of his life, when he was more interested in wider social issues and applications of his theory, he (1978) talks about 'a new political figure' gaining influence and fostering an emerging culture. In 1980(a) he describes twelve qualities of the 'person of tomorrow', including: having a desire for authenticity, and wholeness; having an authority within; being a process person; and being anti-institutional. What this means is that, in her practice and in her professional life, the person-centred therapist is often free-thinking, questioning, assertive and anti-institutional. The principal argument used in favour of statutory registration, for instance, is that it protects the public. Despite Mowbray's (1995) excellent work which debunks this argument, it is still widely used to support the move towards statutory registration. Person-centred therapists are – or should be – sceptical of and opposed to any mandatory or coercive system, including any regulation based exclusively on external standards.

3   Deconstruction. We have argued that the principles of constructivism are consistent with person-centred philosophy, and that an appreciation of its principles enhances both our understanding of theory, and our practice of therapy (see Introduction). Constructivism involves

deconstruction, the analysis and dissolution of fixed concepts or discourses. Parker (1999) and House (2003) have both made significant contributions to the process of deconstructing some of the givens of psychotherapy. House deconstructs a number of specific psychotherapeutic ideas, such as boundaries, confidentiality, resistance, safety, and what he refers to as 'profession-centred therapy'. From its beginnings, person-centred theory has enshrined a similar willingness to question both 'received' wisdom and its own evolving customs and practice.

As individual therapists we help individual clients to examine their own fixed ideas and to find the words which describe their experiences most comprehensively and accurately. This demands of both client and therapist a willingness to deconstruct and reconstruct meaning and understanding continuously in the light of new experiencing. Consistent with our point in Chapter 8 about co-creative relating, we see this as a co-constructive process. Similarly, we believe that it is consistent with person-centred philosophy and principles to deconstruct and reconstruct our professional environment in the light of organismic experiencing.

The ethical environment

'The greatest trust between man and man' says Bacon (1625/1906, p. 62),

> is the trust of giving counsel. For in other confidences men commit the parts of life; their lands, their goods, their children, their credit, some particular affairs; but to such as they make their counsellors, they commit the whole: by how much the more they are obliged to all faith and integrity.

Bacon's argument is the basis for our assertion, which we hope is uncontentious, that the practice of psychotherapy and counselling makes ethical demands of its practitioners. If, as Angyal argues, the organism tends as much towards homonomy as autonomy; and if, as Rogers argues, the organism of both therapist and client is essentially trustworthy, truth-seeking and pro-social; then we might reasonably imagine that codes of ethics and professional practice, and procedures for complaints, would be rarely necessary.

One person in crisis or distress, however, seeks help from another who offers it. The potential for abuse or exploitation is obvious. Masson (1988/89) goes so far as to suggest that this potential is so great and so intrinsic to the process of therapy that the whole endeavour is necessarily compromised from the start, whether potential becomes actual or not. Concern about exploitation and fear of litigation show in the many recent books and articles about boundaries, ethics, complaints and grievances, and in the energy and attention with which professional bodies revise, maintain and implement their various ethical codes and frameworks.

The central question for us is whether these responses to the risk of abuse or exploitation are necessary, adequate or helpful. They seem to us to start from a position of mistrust, and to work on a model of punishment. While we acknowledge the problem they set out to address, our view is that they encourage therapists to adopt a protected or defensive stance that may, indeed, limit the risk to their clients but which, at the same time, almost certainly also limit the likelihood of deeply creative or radical therapeutic practice. With Murdoch (1985, p. 78) we take the view that concern about ethics offers more than this: 'Ethics should not be merely an analysis of ordinary mediocre conduct, it should be a hypothesis about good conduct and about how this can be achieved.'

Person-centred therapy as an integrative therapy

Integration is the *zeitgeist* in psychotherapy. It's the new eclectic. Despite the argument that integration requires a meta-theoretical framework into which to integrate the separate parts or elements of therapy, there are many 'integrative' practitioners who have completed a first-level training which introduces them to a breadth of psychotherapeutic approaches but not a depth of any one approach, discipline or organising principle. As a public description of a modality of or approach to therapy, 'integrative' does not *per se* define or describe the integrating principle or model used. So, people who use the term and want to communicate what they do, have to explain their organising principle, whether it's therapeutic conditions (Rogers, 1957, 1959b), 'phenomenological considerations' (Thorne, 1967), the therapeutic relationship (Gelso & Carter, 1985, 1994; Clarkson, 1990), or a conceptual, paradigm analysis (Tudor, 1996).

Frameworks for integration

There are a number of ideas within person-centred psychology and therapy which provide organising frameworks for integrating theory and therapeutic practice. Here we are concerned to identify meta-theoretical frameworks. We differ in this from Worsley (2004) who explicitly eschews this task, preferring to describe his own 'idiosyncratic' practice of being integrative. We discuss two of these frameworks: the organism and its tendency to actualise; and the integrative nature of the therapeutic conditions. These frameworks are relevant to person-centred therapists and to therapists who work within and draw on other theoretical approaches and methods.

The first point to make here is that organismic theory is integrative. According to Hall and Lindzey (1978, p. 298): 'Organismic theory emphasizes the unity, integration, consistency, and coherence of the normal personality. Organization is the natural state of the organism; disorganization is pathological and is usually brought about by the impact of an oppressive or threatening environment.' Personality integration is viewed as criterial to mental health, a perspective which has been elaborated by researchers and practitioners in the generic field of mental health, such as Jahoda (1958), as well as by writers within the person-centred tradition, such as Seeman (1984). In the field of psychology, psychotherapy and counselling there has, particularly over the past twenty years, been a growing interest in integrative theory. We view the person-centred theory of therapy, rooted in organismic theory, as *ipso facto*, an integrative theory and practice. Thus when, as therapists, we help a client to acknowledge health, alongside their illness, we are helping them to have a more integrated view of themselves, which we may see in terms of their personality (see Chapter 5). We note in Chapter 7 that Rogers often uses 'integrated' as a synonym for 'congruent'.

Rogers (1957) describes the six conditions which his own clinical experience and 'pertinent research' suggested were both necessary and sufficient for effecting therapeutic personality change. He makes the point that these describe the conditions and qualities relevant for therapists or helpers in *any* situation in which constructive personality change occurs. In this paper Rogers (p. 230) says explicitly that 'it is not stated that these six conditions are the essential conditions for client-centered therapy, and that other conditions are essential for other types of psychotherapy'. In other words these conditions pertain for all types of therapy. Thus, this paper may be viewed, as Bozarth (1996) puts it, as an 'integrative statement'. The integrative nature of Rogers' 1957 statement of the conditions is, arguably, made more clear by the fact that he refers (a) to relationships which occur in everyday life, and (b) to programmes other than therapy that are aimed at constructive personality growth, such as leadership and educational programmes, and the work of community agencies.

From integration to integrating

In the same way as we prefer the term 'relating' to 'relationship' (see Chapter 8), we advocate a shift in thinking from 'integration' (noun) and even 'integrative' (adjective) to 'integrating' (verb). This acknowledges the *process* of integrating and carries a sense of movement and fluidity rather than fixity or rigidity. Again, we look for a meta-theoretical perspective, and find this within the person-centred and experiential tradition. Warner (2000) has developed a framework by which she characterises different therapist responses and styles or 'levels of interventiveness':

- Level 1 describes the therapist's pure intuitive contact (and is largely a hypothetical level).

- Level 2 is when the therapist conveys their understanding of the client's internal frame of reference.
- Level 3 describes the situation in which the therapist brings material into the therapeutic relationship in ways which foster client choice.
- Level 4 is when the therapist brings material into the therapeutic relationship from their own frame of reference, from a position of authority or expertise.
- Level 5 describes when the therapist brings material into the therapeutic relationship that is outside the client's frame of reference, and in such a way that the client is unaware of both the intervention/s and the therapist's purpose or motivation.

Warner suggests that there is a fundamental dividing line between levels 3 and 4: between the more client-directed therapies which focus on the nature of the client's process (levels 1 to 3), and more authoritative therapies (levels 4 and 5). Warner also suggests (p. 34) that 'there are very real dangers in trying to mix interventions and theories at different levels of intervention, since these therapies are grounded in quite different types of therapeutic relationship'. We view this framework as person-centred in that it has the concept of the client's internal frame of reference as the criterion for its distinctions. Whilst Warner uses this framework to generalise about 'therapies', we take this as more descriptive of how a therapist intervenes from moment to moment. We also view this as an integrating framework in that we may use it to understand different therapies as well as different therapeutic 'interventions', transactions and responses.

Reflecting on the logic of integration in the context of training, Clarkson (1995, p. 280) suggests that 'a systemic integrative approach to psychotherapy integration does not necessarily seek to provide one true model of integration'. Respecting the vitality of individual difference of both trainees and clients, she argues that training needs to be *integrating* rather than integrative. In this sense, with its emphasis on personal development, a person's training in person-centred therapy is – or should be – based on a thorough, personal process of integrating ideas into a whole, which is consistent with the student's personal philosophy, theory, and practice.

Final reflection

We end with a brief reflection on what Sanders (2000) identifies as three 'primary principles' of the person-centred approach:

- The primacy of the actualising tendency.
- The necessity and sufficiency of six therapeutic conditions.
- The primacy of the non-directive attitude, at least in terms of the content of the helping situation.

Sanders distinguishes these principles from secondary principles such as autonomy, equality and holism. We and others have found Sanders' clarification and presentation of these principles helpful (see Tudor, 2003; Embleton Tudor *et al.*, 2004). We have a number of reservations about Sanders' formulation:

1   We have already discussed our preference for referring to 'the tendency to actualise' rather than 'the actualising tendency'.
2   Sanders conflates philosophical principles, such as primacy, necessity and sufficiency, with clinical principles, such as the non-directive attitude. Primacy and necessity are evaluations of principles, based on philosophical logic (see Chapter 6) rather than the principles themselves. We prefer to keep them separate.
3   By ordering them in the way he does, Sanders appears to separate the non-directive attitude from the tendency to actualise, from which it arises and which it follows.
4   Finally, distinguishing secondary from primary principles creates a false hierarchy, especially as some of the 'secondary' principles are, as we discuss above, qualities or properties of the organism (Chapter 2) and its tendency to actualise (Chapter 3).

Placing the organism at the heart of the theory of the person-centred approach clarifies a number of problems about this formulation, and allows us to revise it as follows:

- Principle 1: That the human organism, as other organisms, has a tendency to actualise.
- Principle 2: That, therefore, in order to be facilitative of another, a therapist adopts a non-directive attitude to her client's experience.
- Principle 3: That, therapist and client create, and continually co-create, certain facilitative conditions.

Appendix 1
References for Epigrams

Introduction

Eliot, G. (1995) *Daniel Deronda*. Harmondsworth: Penguin. (Original work published 1876)

Tawney, R.H. (1961) *The Acquisitive Society*. London: Fontana.

Rogers, C.R. & Wood, J.K. (1974) Client–centered theory: Carl Rogers. In A. Burton (ed.) *Operational Theories of Personality* (pp. 211–58). New York: Brunner/Mazel.

Chapter 1

Whitehead, A.N. (1978) *Process and Reality* (D.R. Griffin & D.W. Sherburne, eds.) (corrected edn.). New York: The Free Press. (Original work published 1929)

Goldstein, K. (1995) *The Organism*. New York: Zone Books. (Original work published 1934)

Rogers, C.R. (1957) The necessary and sufficient conditions of therapeutic personality change. *Journal of Consulting Psychology*, *21*, 95–103.

Murdoch, I. (1985) The idea of perfection. In *The Sovereignty of Good* (pp. 1–45). London: Routledge. (Originally published in 1970)

Chapter 2

Goldstein op. cit.

Perls, F. (1969) *Ego, Hunger and Aggression*. New York: Vintage. (Original work published 1947)

Vithoulkhas, G. (1986) *The Science of Homeopathy*. New York: Grove Press.

Rogers, C.R. (1967) Some of the directions evident in therapy. In *On Becoming a Person* (pp. 73–106). London: Constable. (Original work published 1953)

Chapter 3

Aurelius, M. (1964) *Meditations* (M. Staniforth, trans.). Harmondsworth: Penguin.

Vogel, A. (undated). Cited online at www.alexander-essentials.com/vogel-nature-doctor.php3

Rogers, C.R. (1963) The actualizing tendency in relation to 'motives' and to consciousness. In M.R. Jones (ed.) *Nebraska Symposium on Motivation. Volume XI in the series Current Theory and Research in Motivation* (pp. 1–24). Lincoln, NR: University of Nebraska Press.

Chapter 4

Rogers, C.R. (1951) *Client-Centered Therapy*. London: Constable.
Tillich, P. (1952) *The Courage to Be*. London: Fontana.
Mathews, F. (1991) *The Ecological Self*. London: Routledge.

Chapter 5

Shakespeare, W. (1600) *Henry IV Part 2*.
Macmurray, J. (1991) *Persons in Relation. Volume II of The Form of the Personal*. London: Faber & Faber. (Original work published 1961)

Chapter 6

Marx, K. (1964) *Pre-Capitalist Economic Formations*. London: Lawrence & Wishart. (Original work published 1858)
Scott Peck, M. (1985) *The Road Less Travelled*. London: Rider. (Original work published 1978)
Bozarth, J. (1998) Unconditional positive regard. In J.D. Bozarth (1998) *Person-Centered Therapy: A Revolutionary Paradigm* (pp. 83–8). Llangarron: PCCS Books.
Schmid, P. (2004) Back to the client: A phenomenological approach to the process of understanding and diagnosis. *Person-Centered & Experiential Psychotherapies*, *3*(1), 36–51.

Chapter 7

Lao Tzu (1962) *The Way of Life According to Lao Tzu* (W. Bynner, trans.). New York: Capricorn Books.
Allport, G.W. (1983) *Becoming: Basic Considerations for a Psychology of Personality*. New Haven, CT: Yale University Press. (Original work published 1955)
Patterson, C.H. (2000a) A unitary theory of motivation and its counseling implications. In C.H. Patterson *Understanding Psychotherapy: Fifty Years of Client-Centred Theory and Practice* (pp. 10–21). Llangarron: PCCS Books. (Original work published 1964)
Gaylin, N. (2002) The relationship: The heart of the matter. In J.C. Watson, R.N. Goldman & M.S. Warner (eds.) *Client-Centered and Experiential Psychotherapy in the 21st Century: Advances in Theory, Research and Practice* (pp. 339–47). Llangarron: PCCS Books.

LIVERPOOL
JOHN MOORES UNIVERSITY
AVRIL ROBARTS LRC
TEL. 0151 231 4022

Chapter 8

Roosevelt, F.D. (1972) Undelivered speech. In J.P. Lasch (ed.) *Eleanor: The Years Alone* (p. 210). New York: W.W. Norton. (Original work unpublished 1945)

Rogers, C.R. (1970) The process equation of psychotherapy. In J.T. Hart & T.M. Tomlinson (eds.) *New Directions in Client-Centered Therapy* (pp. 190–205). Boston: Houghton Mifflin. (Original work published 1961)

Chapter 9

Hsun-tzu (2000) Human nature is evil. In L. Stevenson (ed.) *The Study of Human Nature: A Reader* (2nd edn.) (pp. 27–33). Oxford: Oxford University Press.

Aurelius op. cit.

Vithoulkhas op. cit.

Appendix 2
Philosophical contributions to the understanding of self

Concept	Definition/Summary	Origins/Authors	Developments
Ātman	Eternal self/individual soul/'soul of the All'/ultimate or essential self.	Hinduism	Jung (1921), Wilber (1980).
Selflessness The illusion of the self	. . . based on transcendentalism.	Buddhism Siddhartha Gautama (The Buddha) (c.560–c.480BCE)	Three dimensions of the self: • The 'boundless self' (the highest) • The 'inner self' (*kokoro*), a fixed core for self-identity and subjectivity • The social or interactional, 'face-sensitive' self (the lowest) (Lebra, 1992).
Communitas			An idealised state of being, involving collapsing the boundaries between self and other (Turner, 1967).
			See also Zukav (1979), Capra (1983), Parfit (1984).
Cogito ergo sum (I think therefore I am)	The self is an innate idea, discernable through intellectual intuition.	René Descartes (1596–1650)	Rationalist philosophy (Spinoza, Leibnitz).
Conatus	The impulse for self-preservation.	Baruch de Spinoza (1632–1677)	Self – 'this special kind of individual, whose autonomy and integrity are a function of its interconnectedness with its environment' (Mathews, 1994, p. 108).
Personal identity	Self as personal identity, united through consciousness.	John Locke (1632–1704)	Empiricist philosophy (Berkeley, Hume).

Concept	Definition/Summary	Origins/Authors	Developments
Perception	Self as a perceiving, active being.	George Berkeley (1685–1753)	Phenomenalism $\longrightarrow$ Kant $\longrightarrow$ phenomenology.
	Self as 'but a bundle or collection of different perceptions' (Hume, 1738/1968, p. 239), unsupported by senses, to which we mistakenly ascribe an identity.	David Hume (1711–1776)	
Experiencing self Self-consciousness		Immanuel Kant (1724–1804)	Kant's philosophy, also referred to as the 'Copernican revolution', synthesised rationalism and empiricism $\longrightarrow$ provides the philosophical basis for Ryce-Menuhin's (1988) analytic psychology of the self.
Self-awareness Self-alienation		Georg Hegel (1770–1831)	
'Authenticity'[1]	1) Authenticity as spontaneous choice. 2) Authenticity as actualising potential.	Friedrich Nietzsche (1844–1990)	$\longrightarrow$ existentialism (Husserl, Heidegger, Sartre, Merleau-Ponty). 'To be that self which one truly is' (Kierkegaard), a phrase Rogers (1960/67b) uses in a paper on personal goals.
Sense-experience	'a self . . . is, in fact, a logical construction out of sense-experiences . . . [which] constitute the sense-history of a self' (Ayer, 1936/71, p. 165).	Alfred J. Ayer (1910–1989)	
Quantum self	Self as elementary particle system, carrying the properties of waves and particles.	Danah Zohar (b.1945)	

1 Whilst Nietzsche did not use the term 'authenticity' explicitly, the notion of *Wahrhaftigkeit* (truthfulness) is virtually a synonym for what is referred to in the later existentialist literature as authentic.

Appendix 3
A process conception of development and psychotherapy

Here we present a process version of Rogers' (1958/67a) stage conception of the process of psychotherapy (see Chapter 6). We complete the gaps in his original work by adding our own (in italic type). We also change some of the language Rogers uses so that, as much as possible, the elements/scales may be read either way.

Stage 7	Stage 6	Stage 5	Stage 4	Stage 3	Stage 2	Stage 1
					Only a modest degree of success with voluntary clients at this stage	Feelings neither recognised nor owned
Occurs as much outside as inside the therapeutic relationship	A distinctive and often dramatic stage					

A loosening of **feelings**

From a process of experiencing a continually changing flow of feelings . . . to remote, unowned feelings, not present . . .

Stage 7	Stage 6	Stage 5	Stage 4	Stage 3	Stage 2	Stage 1
Feelings are experienced with immediacy and richness of detail	Feelings are experienced with immediacy	Feelings are expressed freely as in the present	Feelings are described as objects in the present	Fewer/more expression of feelings, as past	Feelings described as unowned or as past objects	
'In therapy here, what has counted is sitting down and saying, "This is what's bothering me" and play[ing] around with it for a while.'	'. . . and there's that same feeling, being scared that I've so much of this. (*Tears*)'	'That kinda came out and I just don't understand it. (*Long pause*) I'm trying to get hold of what that terror is.'	'It discourages me to feel dependent because it means I'm kind of hopeless about myself.'	'There were so many things I couldn't tell people – nasty things I did. I felt so sneaky and bad.'	'The symptom was – it was – just being very depressed.'	'*I don't know why she said anything to you. I'm fine. It's the anger that she gets upset about.*'

A change in the manner of experiencing

From living freely and acceptantly in a fluidity of experiencing ... to a fixity and remoteness of experiencing ...

Stage 7	Stage 6	Stage 5	Stage 4	Stage 3	Stage 2	Stage 1
Process experiencing: situations are experienced and interpreted in their newness	The immediacy of experiencing is accepted	Experience is loose, not remote, and frequently occurs with little delay	Experiencing more/less bound by structure of past, more/less remote, and may occur with delay	Expression about self-related experiences as objects	Experiencing is bound by the structure of the past	Fixity and remoteness of experiencing ...
'When I'm working on an idea, the whole idea develops like [a] latent image ... It comes in *all over*.'	'The butterflies are the thoughts closest to the surface. Underneath there's a deeper flow. I feel very removed from it.'	'I'm still having a little trouble trying to figure out what this sadness – and this weepiness – means.'	'I feel bound – by something or other. It must be me! There's nothing else that seems to be doing it.'	'And yet there is the matter of, well, how much do you leave yourself open to marriage ... it does place a limitation on your contacts.'	'I suppose the compensation I always make is ... well, shall we say, being on an intellectual level.'	'I don't think it's useful that one should get too caught up in emotions.'

Congruence

From congruence ... to incongruence ...

Stage 7	Stage 6	Stage 5	Stage 4	Stage 3	Stage 2	Stage 1
Awareness, living that awareness, open communication in the present	Incongruence between experience and awareness vividly experienced through expressed congruence	A desire to live feelings and to be the 'real me' ... a tendency towards exactness in differentiation	Realisation of concern about contradictions and incongruencies between experience and self	Some recognition of vulnerability and of contradictions in experience	Incongruence: anxiety and tension	Incongruence, i.e. discrepancy between the self as perceived and organismic experiencing
'You know, I feel great, and that's partly because I don't feel like I have to say "I'm feeling great" when I'm not.'	'Who, Me? Beg? ... That's an emotion I've never felt clearly at all ... I've got such a confusing feeling ... to have these new things come out of me.'	'... some tension that grows in me, or some hopelessness, or some kind of incompleteness ... Seems to be, the closest thing it gets to, is *hopelessness*.'	'I'm not living up to what I am. I really should be doing more than I am.'	'I have great expectations. I really want to achieve something in my life, but I'm not sure if I'm up to the work involved. I know I'm lazy.'	'I don't know. There's no reason to be unhappy. I'm not really sure why I'm here.'	'My boss said I'd lose my job if I didn't come.'

Communication

From a willingness to communicate a changing awareness of internal experiencing . . . to an unwillingness to communicate . . .

Open communication of ever-changing self	Self as object tends to disappear, communication of self	Feelings expressed freely as in the present	Some communication of self	Less/freer flow of expression about the self as object	Reluctance to communicate self	Unwillingness to communicate self
'I realised "I'm acting childishly" and somehow I chose to do that.'	'I am sad. I am, right now, my sadness. There's nothing else.'	'I expected kinda to get a severe rejection – this I expect all the time . . . somehow I guess I even feel it with you.'	'You know, I think I'm beginning to feel more and to feel OK about telling you what I'm feeling.'	'I try hard to be perfect with her – cheerful, friendly, intelligent, talkative – because I want her to love me.'	'I'm OK, really, and even if I were not I'm not sure what good it would do to talk about it.'	'Well, I'll tell you, it always seems a little nonsensical to talk about one's self except in times of dire necessity.'

Constructs

From developing constructions which are modifiable by each new experience . . . to construing experience in rigid ways . . .

Personal constructs tentatively reformulated, validated against further experience, held fluidly	The relevant personal construct is dissolved in experiencing	Less/further discovery of personal constructs as such, critical examination and questioning of them	Some discovery and recognition of personal constructs and questioning of their validity	Personal constructs becoming/still rigid, but may be recognised as constructs	Constructs becoming more/still rigid, unrecognised as such, thought of as facts	Personal constructs are extremely rigid
'I can see . . . what it would be like – that it doesn't matter if I don't please people.'	'I was living so much of my life, and seeing so much of my life in terms of being scared of something.'	'This idea of needing to please – of having to do it – that's really been kind of a basic assumption of my life.'	'It amuses me . . . it's a little stupid of me and I feel a little tense about it . . . Humour has been my bulwark all my life.'	'I felt so guilty for so much of my life that I felt I deserved to be punished . . . whenever affection is involved it means submission.'	'I can't do anything right – I can't ever finish it.'	'That was a silly thing to do. I am stupid.'

The individual's relationship to their problems

From living problems subjectively, and being responsible for their part in the development of problems . . . to problems being unrecognised (and, therefore, the individual having no desire to change) . . .

	Stage 1	Stage 2	Stage 3	Stage 4	Stage 5	Stage 6	Stage 7
	No problems are recognised or perceived	Problems are perceived as external to self	Some recognition of problems	Vacillating feelings of self-responsibility for problems	Decreasing/increasing quality of acceptance of self-responsibility for problems	Problems owned and lived	Problems are not external or internal, only phases of problems lived subjectively
	'I don't have any problems. In any case, you can't change what you've been given.'	'Disorganisation keeps cropping up in my life.'	'Well, it seems as if I must have a problem. People keep telling me I should get some help . . .'	'Yes, I do recognise that not saying things to people is my problem. At the same time, some people don't make it easy.'	'Something in me is saying, "What more do I have to give up? . . . This is me talking to me . . . It's complaining now."'	'Of course I have problems; the difference is that I recognise them as my problems and, most of the time, I am more interested in how I can resolve them.'	'At best, I think 'problems" are challenges from which I haven't yet learned what I need to learn!'

The individual's manner of relating

From living openly and freely in relation to others . . . to avoiding close relationships . . .

	Stage 1	Stage 2	Stage 3	Stage 4	Stage 5	Stage 6	Stage 7
	Close and communicative relationships are construed as dangerous	Little relating to others	Some relating to others	Risks relating on the basis of feeling	Decreasingly/increasingly freer dialogues with others on the basis of dialogues within the self	Internal and external communication decreasingly/increasingly clear	Experiencing of effective choice in new ways of being
	'People either let you down or stab you in the back.'	'I'm a "lone ranger" . . . I've had my fingers burned too many times to get too involved with someone.'	'I can feel myself smiling sweetly the way my mother does.'	'I'm not quite sure how to put this but I was feeling a little upset with how you treated me last week.'	'The real truth of the matter is that I'm not the sweet, forbearing guy that I try to make out I am . . . I don't know why I should pretend I'm not that way.'	'I feel like I know myself better. I know what's going on "inside" and can talk more to others about this.'	'I realise how much I've changed, like I've got back to where I was: I'm more effective; more confident; more assertive when I need to be – and less so when I don't need to be.'

© Keith Tudor 1994, 1996, 2004

References

Adorno, T.W., Frenkel-Brunswik, E., Levinson, D.J. & Sanford, R.N. (1969) *The Authoritarian Personality*. New York: Norton.

Afuape, T. (2004) Challenge to obscuring difference: Being a Black woman psychologist using SELF in therapy. *Journal of Critical Psychology, Counselling and Psychotherapy*, 4(3), 165–75.

Alexander, R. (1995) *Folie à Deux*. London: Free Association Books.

Allen, J.R. & Allen, B.A. (1997) A new type of transactional analysis and one version of script work with a constructivist sensibility. *Transactional Analysis Journal*, 27(2), 89–98.

Allport, G.W. (1961) Comment on earlier chapters. In R. May (ed.) *Existential Psychology* (pp. 94–9). New York: Random House.

Allport, G.W. (1983) *Becoming: Basic Considerations for a Psychology of Personality*. New Haven, NJ: Yale University Press. (Original work published 1955)

American Psychiatric Association. (1968) *Diagnostic and Statistical Manual of Mental Disorders* (2nd edn.). Washington, DC: APA.

American Psychiatric Association. (1980) *Diagnostic and Statistical Manual of Mental Disorders* (3rd edn.). Washington, DC: APA.

American Psychiatric Association (1994) *Diagnostic and Statistical Manual of Mental Disorders* (4th edn.). Washington, DC: APA.

Anderson, R. & Cissna, K. (1997) *The Martin Buber – Carl Rogers Dialogue: A New Transcript with Commentary*. Albany, NY: Suny Press.

Anderson, W.T. (1990) *Reality Isn't What It Used to Be: Theatrical Politics, Ready-to-Wear Religion, Global Myths, Primitive Chic, and Other Wonders of the Postmodern World*. San Francisco: Harper & Row.

Angyal, A. (1941) *Foundations for a Science of Personality*. New York: Commonwealth Fund.

Angyal, A. (1973) *Neurosis & Treatment: A Holistic Theory*. New York: John Wiley & Sons. (Original work published 1965)

Antonovsky, A. (1979) *Health, Stress and Coping: New Perspectives on Mental and Physical Well-Being*. San Francisco, CA: Jossey-Bass.

Aristotle (1955) *Ethics* (J.A.K. Thomson, trans). Harmondsworth, UK: Penguin.

Aron, L. (1996) *A Meeting of Minds: Mutuality in Psychoanalysis*. Hillsdale, NJ: The Analytic Press.

Atwood, G. & Stolorow, R. (1996) *A Meeting of Minds: Mutuality in Psycho-analysis*. Hillsdale, NJ: The Analytic Press.

Aurelius, M. (1964) *Meditations* (M. Staniforth, trans). Harmondsworth, UK: Penguin.

Axline, V. (1950) Play therapy experiences as described by child participants. *Journal of Consulting Psychology, 14*, 53–63.

Ayer, A.J. (1971) *Language, Truth and Logic*. Harmondsworth, UK: Penguin. (Original work published 1936)

Bachelor, A. (1988) How clients perceive therapist empathy: A content analysis of 'received' empathy. *Psychotherapy, 25*, 227–40.

Bachelor, A. & Horvath, A. (1999) The therapeutic relationship. In M.A. Hubble, B.L. Duncan & S.D. Miller (eds.) *The Heart and Soul of Change: What Works in Therapy* (pp.133–78). Washington, DC: American Psychological Association.

Bacon, F. (1625/1906) *Essays*. London: Dent.

Barker, P. (1996) *Psychotherapeutic Metaphors: A Guide to Theory and Practice*. New York: Brunner/Mazel.

Barker, R., Dembo, T. & Lewin, K. (1941) *Frustration and Regression: An Experiment with Young Children*. Iowa City, IA: University of Iowa Press.

Barrett-Lennard, G.T. (1962) Dimensions of therapist response as causal factors in therapeutic change. *Psychological Monographs, 76*(43).

Barrett-Lennard, G.T. (1978) The relationship inventory: Later developments and applications. JSAS *Catalog of Selected Documents in Psychology, 8*(68). (MS No. 1732)

Barrett-Lennard, G.T. (1979) A new model of communicational-relational systems in intensive groups. *Human Relations, 32*, 841–9.

Barrett-Lennard, G.T. (1986) The relationship inventory now: Issues and advances in theory, method and use. In L.S. Greenberg & W.M. Pinsof (eds.) *The Psychotherapeutic Process: A Research Handbook* (pp. 439–76). New York: Guilford Press.

Barrett-Lennard, G.T. (1996) Therapy and groups in context: A study of developmental episodes in adulthood. In R. Hutterer, G. Pawlowsky, P.F. Schmid & R. Stipsits (eds.) *Client-Centered and Experiential Psychotherapy: A Paradigm in Motion* (pp. 185–96). Frankfurt am Main: Peter Lang.

Barrett-Lennard, G.T. (1997) The recovery of empathy – toward others and self. In A.C. Bohart & L.S. Greenberg (eds.) *Empathy Reconsidered: New Directions in Psychotherapy* (pp. 103–21). Washington, DC: American Psychological Association.

Barrett-Lennard, G.T. (1998) *Carl Rogers' Helping System*. London: Sage.

Barrett-Lennard, G.T. (2002) The helping conditions in their context: Expanding change theory and practice. *Person-Centered & Experiential Psychotherapies, 1*(1&2), 144–55.

Barrett-Lennard, G.T. (2005) *Relationship at the Centre: Healing in a Troubled World*. London: Whurr.

Barrineau, P. & Bozarth, J.D. (2002) A person-centered research model. In D. Cain (ed.) *Classics in the Person-Centered Approach* (pp. 317–22). Ross-on-Wye: PCCS Books. (Original work published 1989)

Barth, D. (1991) When the patient abuses food. In H. Jackson (ed.) *Using Self Psychology in Psychotherapy* (pp. 223–42). Northvale, NJ: Jason Aronson.

Beaumont, H. (1993) Martin Buber's 'I-Thou' and fragile self-organization: Gestalt couples therapy. *British Gestalt Journal*, *2*(2), 85.

Beck, C.E. (1963) *Philosophical Foundations of Guidance*. Englewood Cliffs, NJ: Prentice-Hall.

Becker, H.S. (1967) Whose side are we on? In W.J. Filstead (ed.) *Qualitative Methodology: Firsthand Involvement with the Social World* (pp. 239–247). Chicago, IL: Markham.

Beech, C. & Brazier, D. (1996) Empathy for a real world. In R. Hutterer, G. Pawlowsky, P.F. Schmid & R. Stipsits (eds.) *Client-Centered and Experiential Psychotherapy: A Paradigm in Motion* (pp. 331–46). Frankfurt am Main: Peter Lang.

Beisser, A. (2004) The paradoxical theory of change. *International Gestalt Journal*, *27*(2), 103–7. (Original work published 1970)

Benjamin, J.B., Li, L., Greenberg, B.D., Murphy, D.L. & Hamer, D.H. (1996) Population and familial association between the dopamine regulator gene and measures of novelty seeking. *Nature Genetics*, *12*, 81–4.

Bergner, R. & Staggs, J. (1987) The positive therapeutic relationship as accreditation. *Psychotherapy*, *24*, 315–20.

Bergner, R.M. & Holmes, J.R. (2000) Self-concepts and self-concept change: A status dynamic approach. *Psychotherapy*, *37* 36–44.

Berne, E. (1968) *Games People Play*. Harmondsworth, UK: Penguin. (Original work published 1964)

Berne, E. (1971) *The Mind in Action*. New York: Simon & Schuster. (Original work published 1947)

Berne, E. (1973) *Sex in Human Loving*. Harmondsworth: Penguin. (Original work published 1970)

Berne, E. (1975) *Transactional Analysis in Psychotherapy*. London: Souvenir Press. (Original work published 1961)

Biermann-Ratjen, E.-M. (1996) On the way to a client-centered psychopathology. In R. Hutterer, G. Pawlowsky, P.F. Schmid & R. Stipsits (eds.) *Client-Centered and Experiential Psychotherapy: A Paradigm in Motion* (pp. 11–24). Frankfurt am Main: Peter Lang.

Biermann-Ratjen, E.-M. (1998) Incongruence and psychopathology. In B. Thorne & E. Lambers (eds.) *Person-Centred Therapy: A European Perspective* (pp. 119–30). London: Sage.

Bion, W. (1961) *Experience in Groups and Other Papers*. London: Tavistock.

Bohart, A.C. (1990) A cognitive client-centered perspective on borderline personality development. In G. Lietaer, J. Rombauts & R. Van Balen (eds.) *Client-Centered and Experiential Psychotherapy in the Nineties* (pp. 599–621). Leuven: Leuven University Press.

Bohart, A.C. (1991) Empathy in client-centered therapy: A contrast with psychoanalysis and self psychology. *Journal of Humanistic Psychology*, *31*(1), 34–48.

Bohart, A.C. (2004) How do clients make empathy work? *Person-Centered & Experiential Psychotherapies*, *3*(2), 102–16.

Bohart, A.C. & Greenberg, L.S. (eds.) (1997) *Empathy Reconsidered: New Directions in Psychotherapy*. Washington, DC: American Psychological Association.

Bohart, A.C., Humphrey, A., Magallanes, M., Guzman, R., Smiljanich, K. &

Aguallo, S. (1993) Emphasizing the future in empathy responses. *Journal of Humanistic Psychology*, *33*(2), 12–29.

Bohart, A.C. & Tallman, K. (1999) *How Clients Make Therapy Work*. Washington, DC: American Psychological Association.

Bohm, D. (1983) *Wholeness and the Implicate Order*. London: Ark. (Original work published 1980)

Bordin, E. (1979) The generalizability of the psychoanalytic concept of the working alliance. *Psychotherapy: Theory, Research and Practice*, *16*, 252–60.

Boring, E.G. & Lindzey, G. (eds.) (1967) *A History of Psychology in Autobiography, Vol. V*. New York: Appleton-Century-Crofts.

Bowen, M., Miller, M., Rogers, C.R. & Wood, J.K. (1980) Learnings in large groups: Their implications for the future. In C.R. Rogers *A Way of Being* (pp. 316–35). Boston: Houghton Mifflin.

Boy, A.V. & Pine, G. (1982) *Client-Centered Counseling: A Renewal*. Boston, MA: Allyn & Bacon.

Boyeson, G. & Boyeson, M.L. (1981) *Collected Papers from Biodynamic Psychology Vol.1*. London: Biodynamic Psychology Publications.

Boyeson, G. & Boyeson, M.L. (1982) *Collected Papers from Biodynamic Psychology Vol.2*. London: Biodynamic Psychology Publications.

Bozarth, J.D. (1984) Beyond reflection: Emergent modes of empathy. In R. Levant & J. Shlien (eds.) *Client-Centered Therapy and the Person-Centered Approach: New Directions in Theory, Research and Practice* (pp. 59–75). New York: Praeger.

Bozarth, J.D. (1993) Not necessarily necessary, but always sufficient. In D. Brazier (ed.) *Beyond Carl Rogers* (pp. 92–105). London: Constable.

Bozarth, J.D. (1996) A theoretical reconceptualization of the necessary and sufficient conditions for therapeutic personality change. *The Person-Centered Journal*, *3*(1), 44–51.

Bozarth, J.D. (1998) Playing the probabilities in psychotherapy. *Person-Centred Practice*, *6*(1), 9–21.

Bozarth, J.D. (2001) Congruence: A special way of being. In G. Wyatt (ed.) *Congruence* (pp. 174–83). Llangarron: PCCS Books.

Brazier, D. (ed.) (1993a) *Beyond Carl Rogers*. London: Constable.

Brazier, D. (1993b) Introduction. In D. Brazier (ed.) *Beyond Carl Rogers* (pp. 7–13). London: Constable.

Brazier, D. (1993c) *Congruence*. Occasional Paper No.28. Available from Eigenwelt Interskill, 53 Grosvenor Place, Newcastle upon Tyne NE2 2RD.

Brazier, D. (1993d) The necessary condition is love: Going beyond self in the person-centred approach. In D. Brazier (ed.) *Beyond Carl Rogers* (pp. 72–91). London: Constable.

Brazier, D. (1995) *Zen Therapy*. London: Constable.

Brodley, B.T. (1997) The non-directive attitude in client-centered therapy. *The Person-Centered Journal*, *4*(1), 18–30.

Brodley, B.T. (1999) The actualizing tendency concept in client-centered theory. *The Person-Centered Journal*, *6*(2), 108–20.

Brodley, B.T. (2005) Introduction: About the non-directive attitude. In B. Levitt (ed.) *Embracing Non-Directivity: Reassessing Person-Centered Theory and Practice in the 21st Century* (pp. 1–4). Ross-on-Wye, UK: PCCS Books. (Original work published 1999)

Bronson, M.B. (2000) *Self-Regulation in Early Childhood*. New York: Guilford Press.

Broucek, F.J. (1982) Shame and its relationship to early narcissistic developments. *International Journal of Psycho-Analysis*, *63*, 369–78.

Brown, M. (1990) *The Healing Touch: An Introduction to Organismic Psychotherapy*. Mendocino, CA: Liferhythm.

Browning, D. (1966) *Atonement and Psychotherapy*. Philadelphia, PA: The Westminster Press.

Brunswick, R.M. (1940) The pre-Oedipal phase of libido development. *The Psychoanalytic Quarterly*, *11*, 293–319.

Bulhan, H.A. (1980) Fritz Fanon: The revolutionary psychiatrist. *Race & Class*, *21*, 251–70.

Butler, J.M. & Haigh, G.V. (1954) Changes in the relation between self-concepts and ideal concepts consequent upon client-centered counseling. In C.R. Rogers & R.F. Dymond (eds.) *Psychotherapy and Personality Change* (pp. 55–75). Chicago, IL: University of Chicago Press.

Butler, J.M. & Rice, L.N. (1963) Adience, self-actualization and drive theory. In J.M. Wepman & R.W. Heine (eds.) *Concepts of Personality* (pp. 79–110). Chicago, IL: Aldine.

Cain, D.J. (1989) The paradox of nondirectiveness in the person-centered approach. *Person-Centered Review*, *4*(2), 123–31.

Cain, D.J. (1990) Celebration, reflection, and renewal: 50 years of client-centered therapy and beyond. *Person-Centered Review*, *5*(4), 357–63.

Cambray, J. & Carter, L. (2004) Analytic methods revisited. In J. Cambray & L. Carter (eds.) *Analytic Psychology: Contemporary Perspectives in Jungian Analysis*. London: Brunner-Routledge.

Campos, L. (1980) 'Cure' as finding the right metaphor. *Transactional Analysis Journal*, *10*(2), 172–4.

Capra, F. (1983) *The Turning Point*. London: Fontana.

Carkhuff, R.R. (1969a) *Helping and Human Relations Vol. I: Selection and Training*. New York: Holt, Rinehart & Winston.

Carkhuff, R.R. (1969b) *Helping and Human Relations Vol. II: Practice and Research*. New York: Holt, Rinehart & Winston.

Carkhuff, R.R. (1971) *The Development of Human Resources*. New York: Holt, Rinehart & Winston.

Carroll, R. (2002) Biodynamic massage in psychotherapy: Re-integrating, re-owning and re-associating through the body. In T. Staunton (ed.) *Body Psychotherapy* (pp. 78–100). London: Brunner-Routledge.

Cartwright, D. (1957) Annotated bibliography of research and theory construction in client-centred therapy. *Journal of Consulting Psychology*, *4*, 82.

Cartwright, D.S. & Graham, M.J. (1984) Self-concept and identity: Overlapping portions of a cognitive structure of self. In R.S. Levant & J.M. Shlien (eds.) *Client-Centered Therapy and the Person-Centered Approach* (pp. 108–30). New York: Praeger.

Caspary, W. (1991) Carl Rogers – Values, persons and politics. The dialectic of individual and community. *Journal of Humanistic Psychology*, *31*(4), 8–31.

Catterall, E. (2005) Working with maternal depression: Person-centred therapy as part of a multidisciplinary approach. In S. Joseph & R. Worsley (eds.) *Person-*

Centred Psychopathology: A Positive Psychology of Mental Health (pp. 202–25). Ross-on-Wye, UK: PCCS Books.

Chesterton, G.K. (1994) *What's Wrong with the World?* San Francisco, CA: Ignatius Press. (Original work published 1910)

Clarkson, P. (1990) A multiplicity of psychotherapeutic relationships. *British Journal of Psychotherapy*, 7, 148–63.

Clarkson, P. (1992) *Transactional Analysis Psychotherapy: An Integrated Approach.* London: Routledge.

Clarkson, P. (1995) *The Therapeutic Relationship.* London: Whurr.

Clarkson, P. & Lapworth, P. (1992) The psychology of the self in TA. In P. Clarkson *Transactional Analysis Psychotherapy: An Integrated Approach* (pp. 175–203). London: Routledge.

Cloninger, C.R., Svrakic, D.M. & Pryzbeck, T.R. (1993) A psychobiological model of temperament and character. *Archives of General Psychiatry*, 30, 975–90.

Coghlan, D. & McIlduff, E. (1990) Structuring and non directiveness in group facilitation. *Person-Centered Review*, 5, 13–29.

Combs, A.W. (1948) Phenomenological concepts in non-directive therapy. *Journal of Consulting Psychology*, 12(4), 197–208.

Cooper, M. (2003) *Existential Therapies.* London: Sage.

Cooper, M. (2004) Existential approaches to therapy. In P. Sanders (ed.) *The Tribes of the Person-Centred Nation* (pp. 95–124). Llangarron: PCCS Books.

Corker, M. (2003) Developing anti-disabling counseling practice. In C. Lago & B. Smith (eds.) *Anti-Discriminatory Counselling Practice* (pp. 33–49). London: Sage.

Cornelius-White, J.H.D. & Godfrey, P.C. (2004) Pedagogical crossroads: Integrating feminist critical pedagogies and the person-centred approach to education. In R. Moodley, C. Lago & A. Talahite (eds.) *Carl Rogers Counsels a Black Client: Race and Culture in Person-Centred Counselling* (pp. 166–78). Llangarron: PCCS Books.

Cortina, M. (2003) Defensive processes, emotions and internal working models. A perspective from attachment theory and contemporary models of the mind. In M. Cortina & M. Marrone (eds.) *Attachment Theory and the Psychoanalytic Process* (pp. 307–33). London: Whurr.

Corwall, R. & Reeves, P. (2003, 14 November) Iraq: The crumbling coalition. *The Independent*, p.1.

Dalla Costa, M. (1972) *Women and the Subversion of the Community.* Bristol, UK: Falling Wall Press.

Damasio, A. (1996) *Descartes' Error: Emotion, Reason and the Human Brain.* London: Penguin. (Original work published 1994)

Damasio, A. (1999) *The Feeling of What Happens: Body, Emotion and the Making of Consciousness.* London: Heinemann.

Davies, D. & Neal, C. (eds.) (1996) *Pink Therapy: A Guide for Counsellors and Therapists Working with Lesbian, Gay and Bisexual Clients.* Buckingham, UK: Open University Press.

Davies, D. & Neal, C. (eds.) (2000) *Therapeutic Perspectives on Working with Lesbian, Gay, Bisexual and Transgender Clients.* Buckingham, UK: Open University Press.

Davies, P. (1995) *About Time: Einstein's Unfinished Revolution.* Harmondsworth, UK: Penguin.

De Maré, P., Piper, R. & Thompson, S. (1991) *Koinonia: From Hate, Through Dialogue, to Culture in the Large Group.* New York: Brunner/Mazel.

Dewey, J. (1928) Philosophies of freedom. In H. Kallen (ed.) *Freedom in the Modern World.* New York: Coward-McCann.

Dewey, J. (1960) Philosophies of freedom. In R.J. Berstein (ed.) *Experience, Nature and Freedom.* New York: Bobs-Merrill. (Original work published 1928)

Diefenbeck, J.A. (1995) *A Subjective Theory of Organism.* Lanham, MD: University Press of America.

Donner, S. (1991) The treatment process. In H. Jackson (ed.) *Using Self Psychology in Psychotherapy* (pp. 51–70). Northvale, NJ: Jason Aronson.

Duff, K. (1993) *The Alchemy of Illness.* London: Virago.

Dunbar, H.F. (1954) *Emotions and Bodily Changes* (4th edn.). New York: Columbia University Press.

Duncan, B.L. & Moynihan, D.W. (1994) Applying outcome research: Intentional utilization of the client's frame of reference. *Psychotherapy, 31,* 294–301.

Dymond, R.F. (1954) Adjustment changes over therapy from self-sorts. In C.R. Rogers & R.F. Dymond (eds.) *Psychotherapy and Personality Change* (pp. 76–84). Chicago: University of Chicago Press.

Edelman, G.M. (1992) *Bright Air Brilliant Fire: On the Matter of the Mind.* New York: Basic Books.

Edelman, G.M. & Tononi, G. (2000) *Consciousness: How Matter Becomes Imagination.* London: Penguin.

Edwards, P. (ed.) (1967) *Encyclopedia of Philosophy.* New York: Macmillan.

Eiden, B. (2002) Application of post-Reichian psychotherapy: A Chiron perspective. In T. Staunton (ed.) *Body Psychotherapy* (pp. 27–55). London: Brunner-Routledge.

Ellingham, I. (1995) Quest for a paradigm: Person-centred counselling/ psychotherapy versus psychodynamic counselling and psychotherapy. *Counselling, 6*(4), 288–90.

Ellingham, I. (1997) On the quest for a person-centred paradigm. *Counselling, 8*(1), 52–55.

Ellingham, I. (1998) Person-centred porridge. *Person-Centred Practice, 6*(2), 110–12.

Ellingham, I. (1999a) Carl Rogers' 'congruence' as an organismic, not a Freudian concept. *The Person-Centered Journal, 6*(2), 121–40.

Ellingham, I. (1999b) On transcending person-centred postmodernist porridge. *Person-Centred Practice, 7*(2), 62–78.

Ellingham, I. (2001) Carl Rogers' congruence as an organismic, not a Freudian concept. In G. Wyatt (ed.) *Congruence* (pp. 96–115). Llangarron: PCCS Books. (Original work published 1999)

Ellingham, I. (2002) Foundation for a person-centred, humanistic psychology and beyond: The nature and logic of Carl Rogers' 'formative tendency'. In J.C. Watson, R.N. Goldman & M.S. Warner (eds.) *Client-Centered and Experiential Psychotherapy in the 21st Century: Advances in Theory, Research and Practice* (pp. 16–35). Llangarron: PCCS Books.

Embleton Tudor, L., Keemar, K., Tudor, K., Valentine, J. & Worrall, M. (2004) *The Person-Centred Approach: A Contemporary Introduction.* Basingstoke, UK: Palgrave.

Embleton Tudor, L. & Tudor, K. (ed.) (2002) Psyche and soma [Theme issue]. *Person-Centred Practice*, 10(2).

Emmet, D. (1966) *Whitehead's Philosophy of the Organism* (2nd edn.). New York: Macmillan. (Original work published 1932)

Erskine, R.G. (1998) Attunement and involvement: Therapeutic responses to relational needs. *International Journal of Psychotherapy*, 3(3), 235–43.

Erskine, E., Moursund, J. & Trautmann, R. (1999) *Beyond Empathy – A Therapy of Contact-in Relationship.* New York: Brunner/Mazel.

Evans, D. & Zarate, O. (1999) *Introducing Evolutionary Psychology.* Cambridge: Icon Books.

Evans, R.I. (1981) *Dialogue with Carl Rogers.* New York: Praeger. (Original work published 1975)

Fairbairn, W.R.D. (1952) *An Object Relations Theory of the Personality.* New York: Basic Books.

Fairhurst, I. (1999) *Women Writing in the Person-Centred Approach.* Llangarron: PCCS Books.

Federn, P. (1952) *Ego Psychology and the Psychoses.* New York: Basic Books.

Feldenkreis, M. (1981) *The Elusive Obvious.* Cupertino, CA: Meta Publications.

Ferenczi, S. (1995) *The Clinical Diary of Sándor Ferenczi* (J. Dupont, ed. & M. Balint & N.Z. Jackson, trans). Cambridge, MA: Harvard University Press. (Original work published 1932)

Fernald, P.S. (2000) Carl Rogers: Body-centered counselor. *Journal of Counselling & Development*, 78, 172–9.

Finke, J. (1990) Dream work in client-centered psychotherapy. In G. Lietaer, J. Rombauts & R. Van Balen (eds.) *Client-Centered and Experiential Psychotherapy in the Nineties* (pp. 507–10). Leuven: Leuven University Press.

Finke, J. (2002) Aspects of the actualizing tendency from a humanistic psychology perspective. *Person-Centered and Experiential Psychotherapies*, 1(1&2), 28–40.

Fischer, C.T. (1989) The life-centered approach to psychodiagnostics: Attending to lifeworld, ambiguity and possibility. *Person-Centered Review*, 4(2), 163–170.

Fordham, M. (1957) *New Developments in Analytical Psychology.* London: Routledge & Kegan Paul.

Fowles, J. (1981) *The Aristos* (rev. edn.). London: Triad/Granada. (Original work published 1964)

France, A. (1988) *Consuming Psychotherapy.* London: Free Association Books.

Frankl, V. (1963) *Man's Search for Meaning.* New York: Simon & Schuster.

Freud, S. (1958) Recommendations to physicians practicing psychoanalysis. In *The Standard Edition of the Complete Psychological Works of Sigmund Freud. Vol 12* (J. Strachey, ed. & trans., pp. 111–20). London: Hogarth Press. (Original work published 1912)

Freud, S. (1962) The question of lay-analysis. In *Two Short Accounts of Psycho-Analysis* (J. Strachey, ed. & trans., pp. 89–170). Harmondsworth, UK: Pelican. (Original work published 1926)

Freud, S. (1973) Introductory lectures on psychoanalysis. In *The Pelican Freud Library, Vol. 1: Introductory Lectures on Psychoanalysis* (J. Strachey & A. Richards, eds., J. Strachey, trans.). Harmondsworth, UK: Pelican.

Frie, R. (ed.) (2003) *Understanding Experience: Psychotherapy and Postmodernism.* London: Routledge.

Friedli, K., King, M., Lloyd, M. & Horder, J. (1997) Randomised controlled assessment of non-directive psychotherapy versus routine general practitioner care. *Lancet*, *350*, 1662–5.

Friedman, M. (1992) *Dialogue and the Human Image: Beyond Humanistic Psychology*. Newbury Park, CA: Sage.

Fromkin, V. & Rodman, R. (1983) *Introduction to Language*. London: Holt-Saunders.

Fromm, E. (1971) *The Crisis of Psychoanalysis*. London: Jonathon Cape.

Fuller, R.C. (1984) Rogers's impact on pastoral counselling and contemporary religious reflection. In R. Levant & J. Shlien (eds.) *Client-Centered Therapy and the Person-Centered Approach: New Directions in Theory, Research and Practice* (pp. 352–69). New York: Praeger.

Gabbard, G.O. (1989) Two subtypes of narcissistic personality disorder. *Bulletin of the Menninger Clinic*, *53*, 527–32.

Gallagher, S. (1998) *Personalism: A Brief Account*. Paper available online at http://www2.canisius.edu/~gallaghr/pers.html

Gardner, H. (1993) *Frames of Mind: The Theory of Multiple Intelligences* (2nd edn.). London: Fontana Press. (Original work published 1983)

Gatto, J.T. (2002) *Dumbing Us Down: The Hidden Curriculum of Compulsory Schooling*. Gabriola Island, BC: New Society Publishers.

Gaylin, N. (2002) The relationship: The heart of the matter. In J.C. Watson, R.N. Goldman & M.S. Warner (eds.) *Client-Centered and Experiential Psychotherapy in the 21st Century: Advances in Theory, Research and Practice* (pp. 339–47). Llangarron: PCCS Books.

Geggus, P. (2002) Zero balancing: Person-centred bodywork – or body-centred personwork. *Person-Centred Practice*, *10*(2), 88–95.

Gelb, A. & Goldstein, K. (1920) *Psychologische Analysen Hirnpathologischer Fälle* [*Psychological Analysis in Brain Pathological Cases*]. Leipzig: Barth.

Gelso, C.J. & Carter, J.A. (1985) The relationship in counseling and psychotherapy: Components, consequences and theoretical antecedents. *The Counseling Psychologist*, *13*(2), 115–243.

Gelso, C. & Carter, J. (1994) Components of the psychotherapy relationship: Their interaction and unfolding during treatment. *Journal of Counseling Psychology*, *41*, 296–306.

Gendlin, E.T. (1961) Experiencing: A variable in the process of therapeutic change. *American Journal of Psychotherapy*, *15*, 233–45.

Gendlin, E. T. (1964) A theory of personality change. In P. Worchal & D. Byrne (eds.) *Personality Change* (pp. 102–48). New York: Wiley.

Gendlin, E.T. (1981) *Focusing* (rev. edn.). New York: Bantam.

Gendlin, E. (1986) *Let Your Body Interpret Your Dreams*. Wilmette, IL: Chiron.

Gergen, K.J. (1991) *The Saturated Self*. New York: Basic Books.

Giesekus, U. & Mente, A. (1986) Client empathic understanding in client-centered therapy. *Person-Centered Review*, *1*, 163–171.

Gilligan, C. (1982) *In a Different Voice: Psychological Theory and Women's Development*. Cambridge, MA: Harvard University Press.

Goldstein, K. (1940) *Human Nature in the Light of Psychopathology*. Cambridge, MA: Harvard University Press.

Goldstein, K. (1995) *The Organism*. New York: Zone Books. (Original work published 1934)

Golomb, J. (1995) *In Search of Authenticity*. London: Routledge.

Gomez, L. (1997) *Introduction to Object Relations*. London: Tavistock.

Gordon, D. (1978) *Therapeutic Metaphors*. Cupertino, CA: Meta Publications.

Gordon, E.F. (2000) *Mockingbird Years*. New York: Basic Books.

Graf, C.L. (1984) A comparison of Carl Rogers' and Heinz Kohut's humanistic theories of the fully functioning person. In A.S. Segrera (ed.) *Proceedings of the First International Forum on the Person-Centered Approach*. Oaxrepec, Moreles, Mexico: Universidad Iberamericana.

Grant, B. (1990) Principled and instrumental nondirectiveness in person-centered and client-centered therapy. *The Person-Centered Review*, 5(1), 77–88.

Gray, J. (2003) *Straw Dogs: Thoughts on Humans and Other Animals*. London: Granta. (Original work published 2002)

Greenberg, L.S. & Elliot, R. (1997) Varities of empathic responding. In A.C. Bohart & L.S. Greenberg (eds.) *Empathy Reconsidered: New Directions in Psychotherapy* (pp. 167–86). Washington, DC: American Psychological Association.

Griffin, D.R. (1976) *God, Power and Evil: A Process Theodicy*. Philadelphia, PA: Westminster.

Guba, E.G. & Lincoln, Y.S. (1990) Can there be a human science?: Constructivism as an alternative. *Person Centred Review*, 5(2), 130–54.

Hackney, H. (1978) The evolution of empathy. *Personnel and Guidance Journal*, 35–38.

Hall, C. & Lindzey, G. (1957) *Theories of Personality*. New York: Wiley.

Hall, C. & Lindzey, G. (1970) *Theories of Personality* (2nd edn.). New York: Wiley.

Hall, C. & Lindzey, G. (1978) *Theories of Personality* (3rd edn.). New York: Wiley.

Harré, R. (1998) *The Singular Self*. London: Sage.

Hartmann, H. (1958) *Ego Psychology and the Problem of Adaptation*. New York: International Universities Press.

Hartshorne, C. (1962) *The Logic of Perfection and Other Essays in Neoclassical Metaphysics*. La Salle, IL: Open Court.

Haule, J.R. (1996) *The Love Cure: Therapy Erotic and Sexual*. Woodstock, CT: Spring Publications.

Hayashi, S. & Kara, A. (2002) Understanding self through Taoist emptiness. In J.C. Watson, R.N. Goldman & M.S. Warner (eds.) *Client-Centered and Experiential Psychotherapy in the 21st Century: Advances in Theory, Research and Practice* (pp. 73–8). Llangarron: PCCS Books.

Hayashi, S., Kuno, T., Morotomi, Y., Osawa, M., Shimizu, M. & Suetake, Y. (1994) *A Reevaluation of the Client-Centered Therapy Through the Work of F. Tomoda and Its Cultural Implications in Japan*. Paper presented at the Third International Conference on Client-Centered and Experiential Psychotherapy, Gmunden, Austria.

Heyward, C. (1993) *When Boundaries Betray Us*. New York: HarperCollins.

Hillman, J. & Ventura, M. (1992) *We've Had a Hundred Years of Psychotherapy and the World's Getting Worse*. San Francisco, CA: Harper.

Hoffman, L. (1993) A reflective stance for family therapy. In S. McNamee & K.J. Gergen (eds.) *Therapy as Social Construction* (pp. 7–24). London: Sage.

Hogan, R. (1948) *The Development of a Measure of Client Defensiveness in the*

Counselling Relationship. Unpublished doctoral dissertation, University of Chicago.

Holdstock, L. (1990) Can client-centered therapy transcend its monocultural roots? In G. Lietaer, J. Rombauts & R. Van Balen (eds.) *Client-Centered and Experiential Psychotherapy in the Nineties* (pp. 109–21). Leuven: Leuven University Press.

Holdstock, L. (1993) Can we afford not to revision the person-centred concept of self? In D. Brazier (ed.) *Beyond Carl Rogers* (pp. 229–52). London: Constable.

Holdstock, L. (1996a) Discrepancy between the person-centered theories of self and of therapy. In R. Hutterer, G. Pawlowsky, P.F. Schmid & R. Stipsits (eds.) *Client-Centered and Experiential Psychotherapy: A Paradigm in Motion* (pp. 163–81). Frankfurt am Main: Peter Lang.

Holdstock, L. (1996b) Implications of developments regarding the concept of self for client-centered theory and practice. In U. Esser, H. Pabst & G.-W. Speierer (eds.) *The Power of the Person-Centred Approach: New Challenges – Perspectives – Answers* (pp. 83–90). Köln: Gesellschaft für wissenschaftliche Gesprächspsychotherapie.

Holland, R. (1977) *Self in Social Context.* London: Macmillan.

Holland, S. (1988) Defining and experimenting with prevention. In S. Ramon & M.G. Giannichedda (eds.) *Psychiatry in Transition* (pp. 125–37). London: Pluto Press.

Horkheimer, M. & Adorno, T.M. (1972) *Dialectic of Enlightenment.* New York: Herder & Herder.

Horney, K. (1939) *New Ways in Psychoanalysis.* New York: W.W. Norton.

Horvarth, A.O. & Greenberg, L.S. (1986) Development of the working alliance inventory. In L.S. Greenberg & W.M. Pinsof (eds.) *The Psychotherapeutic Process: A Research Handbook.* New York: Guilford Press.

Hospers, J. (1967) *An Introduction to Philosophical Analysis* (2nd edn.). London: Routledge & Kegan Paul.

House, R. (2003) *Therapy Beyond Modernity: Deconstructing and Transcending Profession-Centred Therapy.* London: Karnac.

Howard, A. (2000) *Philosophy for Counselling and Psychotherapy: Pythagoras to Postmodernism.* Basingstoke, UK: Macmillan.

Hume, D. (1968) *A Treatise of Human Nature. Volumes 1 and 2.* London: Dent. (Original work published 1738)

Hunsdahl, J.B. (1967) Concerning Einfühlung (empathy): A concept analysis of its origin and early development. *Journal of the History of the Behavioral Sciences, 3,* 180–91.

Hutterer, R., Pawlowsky, G., Schmid, P.F. & Stipsits, R. (eds.) (1996) *Client-Centered and Experiential Psychotherapy: A Paradigm in Motion.* Frankfurt am Main: Peter Lang.

Ivey, A.E., Ivey, M.B. & Simek-Morgan, L. (1993) *Counseling and Psychotherapy* (3rd edn.). London: Allyn & Bacon.

Jackson, H. (ed.) (1991) *Using Self Psychology in Psychotherapy.* Northvale, NJ: Jason Aronson.

Jacobs, M. (1998) *The Presenting Past.* Buckingham, UK: Open University Press.

Jacobson, E. (1964) *The Self and the Object World.* New York: International Universities Press.

Jahoda, M. (1958) *Current Concepts of Positive Mental Health*. New York: Basic Books.

James, S. (1975) *Sex, Race and Class*. Bristol: Falling Wall Press.

James, W. (1890) *Principles of Psychology. Vol.1*. New York: Henry Holt.

James, W. (1999) The self. In R.F. Baumeister (ed.) *The Self in Social Psychology* (pp. 68–77). Philadephia, PA: Psychology Press. (Original work published 1892)

Jennings, J.L. (1986) The dream is the dream is the dream. *The Person-Centered Review, 1*(3), 310–33.

Jones, M. (1996) Person-centred theory and the post-modern turn. *Person-Centred Practice, 4*(2), 19–26.

Joseph, S. (2005) Understanding post-traumatic stress from the person-centred perspective. In S. Joseph & R. Worsley (eds.) *Person-Centred Psychopathology: A Positive Psychology of Mental Health* (pp. 190–201). Ross-on-Wye, UK: PCCS Books.

Joseph, S. & Worsley, R. (2005) Psychopathology and the person-centred approach: Building bridges between disciples. In S. Joseph & R. Worsley (eds.) *Person-Centred Psychopathology: A Positive Psychology of Mental Health* (pp. 1–8). Ross-on-Wye, UK: PCCS Books.

Josselson, R. (1987) *Finding Herself: Pathways to Identity Development in Women*. London: Jossey-Bass.

Jung, C.G. (1964) Psychological types. In *The Collected Works of C.J. Jung. Vol. 6: Psychological Types* (H. Read, M. Fordham & G. Adler, eds., R.F.C. Hull, trans.). London: Routledge & Kegan Paul. (Original work published 1921)

Jung, C.G. (1967) *The Collected Works of C.J. Jung. Vol. 12: Psychology and Alchemy* (H. Read, M., Fordham & G. Adler, eds., R.F.C. Hull, trans.). London: Routledge & Kegan Paul. (Original work published 1944)

Kahler, T. (1978) *Transactional Analysis Revisited*. Little Rock, AR: Human Development Publications.

Kahler, T. with Capers, H. (1974) The miniscript. *Transactional Analysis Journal, 4*(1), 26–42.

Kahn, E. (1985) Heinz Kohut and Carl Rogers: A timely comparison. *American Psychologist, 40*, 893–904.

Kahn, E. (1989a) Carl Rogers and Heinz Kohut. On the importance of valuing the 'self'. In D.W. Dettick & S.P. Dettick (eds.) *Self Psychology: Comparisons and Contrasts* (pp. 213–28). Hillsdale, NJ: The Analytic Press.

Kahn, E. (1989b) Carl Rogers and Heinz Kohut: Toward a constructive collaboration. *Psychotherapy, 26*(4), 555–63.

Kahn, E. (1996) The intersubjective perspective and the client-centered approach: Are they one at their core? *Psychotherapy, 33*(1), 30–42.

Kahn, E. & Rachman, A.W. (2000) Carl Rogers and Heinz Kohut: A historical perspective. *Psychoanalytic Psychotherapy, 17*(2), 294–312.

Kant, I. (2005) *Critique of Pure Reason* (M. Weigelt, ed.). London: Penguin. (Original work published 1781)

Kantor, J.R. (1924a) *Principles of Psychology. Vol.1*. New York: Knopf.

Kantor, J.R. (1924b) *Principles of Psychology. Vol.2*. New York: Knopf.

Kearney, A. (1997) Class, politics and the training of counsellors. *Person-Centred Practice, 5*(2), 11–15.

Keen, S. (1983) *The Passionate Life: Stages of Loving*. London: Gateway Books.

Kegan, R. (1982) *The Evolving Self: Problem and Process in Human Development*. Cambridge, MA: Harvard University Press.

Keil, S. (1996) The self as a systemic process of interaction of 'inner persons'. In R. Hutterer, G. Pawlowsky, P.F. Schmid & R. Stipsits (eds.) *Client-Centered and Experiential Psychotherapy* (pp. 53–66). Frankfurt am Main: Peter Lang.

Kelly, G.A. (1955) *The Psychology of Personal Constructs. Vol.1.* New York: W.W. Norton.

Kelly, G.A. (1962) Europe's matrix of decision. In M.R. Jones (ed.) *Nebraska Symposium on Motivation, 1962* (pp. 83–123). Lincoln, NE: University of Nebraska Press.

Keys, S. (1999) The person-centred counsellor as an agent of human rights. *Person-Centred Practice*, 7(1), 41–7.

Kiesler, D.J., Mathieu, P.L. & Klein, M.H. (1967) A summary of the issues and conclusions. In C.R. Rogers, E.T. Gendlin, D.J. Kiesler & C.B. Truax (eds.) *The Therapeutic Relationship and Its Impact: A Study of Psychotherapy with Schizophrenics* (pp. 295–311). Madison, WI: University of Wisconsin Press.

King, M., Lloyd, M., Sibbald, B., Gabbay, M., Ward, E. & Byford, S. (2000) Randomised controlled trial of non-directive counselling, cognitive behaviour therapy and usual general practitioner care in the management of depression as well as mixed anxiety and depression in primary care. *Health Technology Assessment*, 4(19).

Kirkpatrick, F.G. (1991) Introduction. In J. Macmurray (ed.) *Persons in Relation* (pp. ix–xxv). London: Faber & Faber. (Original work published 1961)

Kirschenbaum, H. (1979) *On Becoming Carl Rogers*. New York: Delacorte Press.

Kirschenbaum, H. & Henderson, V.L. (eds.) (1990a) *Carl Rogers: Dialogues*. London: Constable.

Kirschenbaum, H. & Henderson, V.L. (eds.) (1990b) *The Carl Rogers Reader*. London: Constable.

Knibbs, J. & Moran, H. (2005) Autism and Asperger syndrome: Person-centred approaches. In S. Joseph & R. Worsley (eds.) *Person-Centred Psychopathology: A Positive Psychology of Mental Health* (pp. 260–75). Ross-on-Wye, UK: PCCS Books.

Knight, J. (1950) *The Story of My Psychoanalysis*. New York: McGraw-Hill.

Knox, J. (2004) Developmental aspects of analytical psychology: New perspectives from cognitive neuroscience and attachment theory. In J. Cambray & L. Carter (eds.) *Analytic Psychology: Contemporary Perspectives in Jungian Analysis*. London: Brunner-Routledge.

Koch, S. (ed.) (1959) *Psychology: A Study of a Science, Vol. 3: Formulation of the Person and the Social Context*. New York: McGraw-Hill.

Kohak, E. (1997) Personalism: Towards a philosophical delineation. *Personalist Forum*, 13(1), 3–11.

Kohlberg, L. (1976) Moral stages and moralization: The cognitive-developmental approach. In T. Lickona (ed.) *Moral Development and Behavior: Theory, Research and Social Issues* (pp. 31–53). New York: Holt Rinehart & Winston.

Köhler, W. (1940) *Dynamics in Psychology*. New York: Liveright Publishing Corporation.

Kohut, H. (1959) Introspection, empathy and psychoanalysis: An examination of the relationship between mode of observation and theory. In P.H. Ornstein (ed.)

The Search for Self Vol. 1 (pp. 205–32). New York: International Universities Press.

Kohut, H. (1971) *The Analysis of the Self*. New York: International Universities Press.

Kohut, H. (1977) *The Restoration of the Self*. New York: International Universities Press.

Kohut, H. (1981) On empathy. In P.H. Ornstein (ed.) *The Search for Self Vol. 4* (pp. 525–35). New York: International Universities Press.

Kohut, H. (1982) Introspection, empathy and the semicircle of mental health. *International Journal of Psychoanalysis*, *63*, 395–408.

Kohut, H. (1984) *How Does Analysis Cure?* Chicago, IL: University of Chicago Press.

Kramer, R. (1995) The birth of client-centered therapy: Carl Rogers, Otto Rank, and 'The beyond'. *Journal of Humanistic Psychology*, *35*(4), 54–110.

Lago, C. & Clark, J. (2004) Growing race awareness in the therapist (Reflections on Carl Rogers' videotaped session with Dadisi). In R. Moodley, C. Lago & A. Talahite (eds.) *Carl Rogers Counsels a Black Client: Race and Culture in Person-Centred Counselling* (pp. 148–59). Llangarron: PCCS Books.

Lago, C. & MacMillan, M. (eds.) (1999) *Experiences in Relatedness: Groupwork and the Person-Centred Approach*. Llangarron: PCCS Books.

Laing, R.D. (1965) *The Divided Self*. Harmondsworth, UK: Penguin.

Laing, R.D. (1967) *The Politics of Experience* and *The Bird of Paradise*. Harmondsworth, UK: Penguin.

Lake, F. (1966) *Clinical Theology: A Theological and Psychiatric Basis to Clinical Pastoral Care*. London: Darton Longman & Todd.

Lambers, E. (1994) The person-centred perspective on psychopathology: The neurotic client. In D. Mearns (ed.) *Developing Person-Centred Counselling* (pp. 105–9). London: Sage.

Land, D. (1996) Partial views. In R. Hutterer, G. Pawlowsky, P.F. Schmid & R. Stipsits (eds.) *Client-Centered and Experiential Psychotherapy: A Paradigm in Motion* (pp. 67–74). Frankfurt am Main: Peter Lang.

Lapworth, P. (2003, April) *Introjective Transference in Working with Lesbian, Gay and Bisexual Clients Who are Addressing Their Sexual Identity*. Workshop, Institute of Transactional Analysis Conference, Swansea.

Lasch, C. (1979) *The Culture of Narcissism*. New York: Warner Books.

Laungani, P. (1999) Client centred or culture centred counselling. In S. Palmer & P. Laungani (eds.) *Counselling in a Multicultural Society* (pp. 133–52). London: Sage.

Leary, D.E. (ed.) (1990) *Metaphors in the History of Psychology*. Cambridge: Cambridge University Press.

Lebra, T.S. (1992) Self in Japanese culture. In N. Rosenberger (ed.) *Japanese Sense of Self* (pp. 105–20). Cambridge: Cambridge University Press.

Lecky, P. (1945) *Self-Consistency: A Theory of Personality*. New York: Island Press.

Le Doux, J. (1995) Emotion: Clues from the brain. *Annual Review of Psychology*, *46*, 209–35.

Le Doux, J. (1998) *The Emotional Brain*. London: Weidenfeld & Nicholson.

Levitt, B.E. (2005) Preface. In B. Levitt (ed.) *Embracing Non-Directivity: Reassess-*

ing Person-Centered Theory and Practice in the 21st Century (pp. i–iii). Ross-on-Wye, UK: PCCS Books.

Lewin, K. (1952) *Field Theory in Social Science.* New York: Harper & Row.

Lewontin, R.C. (2000) *The Triple Helix: Gene, Organism and Environment.* Cambridge, MA: Harvard University Press.

Lietaer, G. (1992) Helping and hindering processes in client-centered/experiential psychotherapy: A content analysis of client and therapist postsession perceptions. In S.G. Toukmanian & D.L. Rennie (eds.) *Psychotherapy Process Research: Theory-Guided and Phenomenological Research Strategies* (pp. 134–62). Newbury Park, CA: Sage.

Lietaer, G. (1998) From non-directive to experiential: A paradigm unfolding. In B. Thorne & E. Lambers (eds.) *Person-Centred Therapy: A European Perspective* (pp. 62–73). London: Sage.

Lietaer, G., Rombauts, J. & Van Balen, R. (1990) *Client-Centered and Experiential Psychotherapy in the Nineties.* Leuven: Leuven University Press.

Lipkin, S. (1948) The client evaluates nondirective psychotherapy. *Journal of Consulting Psychology, 12,* 137–46.

Littman, R.A. (1958) Motives, history and causes. In M.R. Jones (ed.) *Nebraska Symposium on Motivation 1958* (pp. 114–68). Lincoln, NR: University of Nebraska Press.

Lucretius (1951) *On the Nature of the Universe* (R.E. Latham, trans.). Harmondsworth, UK: Penguin.

Lynch, G. (1997) Words and silence: Counselling and psychotherapy after Wittgenstein. *Counselling, 8*(2), 126–8.

Lynch, V.J. (1991) Basic concepts. In H. Jackson (ed.) *Using Self Psychology in Psychotherapy* (pp. 15–25). Northvale, NJ: Jason Aronson.

MacIsaac, D.S. (1997) Empathy: Heinz Kohut's contribution. In A.C. Bohart & L.S. Greenberg (eds.) *Empathy Reconsidered: New Directions in Psychotherapy* (pp. 245–64). Washington, DC: American Psychological Association.

Macmurray, J. (1991) *The Self as Agent. Volume I of The Form of the Personal.* London: Faber & Faber. (Original work published 1957)

Macmurray, J. (1991) *Persons in Relation. Volume II of The Form of the Personal.* London: Faber & Faber. (Original work published 1961)

Marques-Teixeira, J. & Antones, S. (2000) *Client-Centered and Experiential Psychotherapy.* Linda a Velha, Portugal: Vale & Vale.

Martel, Y. (1996) *Self.* London: Faber & Faber.

Marx, K. (1964) *Pre-Capitalist Economic Formations.* London: Lawrence & Wishart. (Original work published 1858)

Maslow, A.H. (1954) *Motivation and Personality.* New York: Harper & Row.

Maslow, A.H. (1962) *Towards a Psychology of Being.* New York: Van Nostrand.

Masson, J. (1989) *Against Therapy.* London: Collins. (Original work published 1988)

Masterson, J.F. (1981) *The Narcissistic and Borderline Disorders.* New York: Brunner/Mazel.

Masterson, J.F. (1985) *The Real Self: A Developmental, Self, and Object Relations Approach.* New York: Brunner/Mazel.

Masterson, J.F. (1988) *The Search for the Real Self: Unmasking the Personality Disorders of Our Age.* New York: The Free Press.

Mathews, F. (1991) *The Ecological Self*. London: Routledge.

May, R. (ed.) (1961a) *Existential Psychology*. New York: Random House.

May, R. (1961b) The emergence of existential psychology. In R. May (ed.) *Existential Psychology* (pp. 11–51). New York: Random House.

Maylon, A. (1982) Psychotherapeutic implications of internalized homophobia in gay men. In J. Gonsiorek (ed.) *Homosexuality and Psychotherapy*. New York: Haworth Press.

McCleary, R.A. & Lazarus, R.S. (1949) Autonomic discrimination without awareness. *Journal of Personality, 18*, 171–79.

McCulloch, L.A. (2005) Anti-social personality disorder and the person-centred approach. In S. Joseph & R. Worsley (eds.) *Person-Centred Psychopathology: A Positive Psychology of Mental Health* (pp. 169–189). Ross-on-Wye, UK: PCCS Books.

McDougall, W. (1908) *Introduction to Social Psychology*. London: Methuen.

McDougall, W. (1932) *The Energies of Men: A Study of the Fundamentals of Dynamic Psychology*. London: Methuen.

McLeod, J. (2003) *Doing Counselling Research* (2nd edn.). London: Sage.

Mead, G.H. (1934) *Mind, Self and Society* (ed. C.W. Morris). Chicago, IL: University of Chicago Press.

Mearns, D. (1990) The counsellor's experience of success. In D. Mearns & W. Dryden (eds.) *Experiences of Counselling in Action* (pp. 97–112). London: Sage.

Mearns, D. (1994) *Developing Person-Centred Counselling*. London: Sage.

Mearns, D. (1996) Working at relational depth with clients in person-centred therapy. *Counselling, 7*(4), 306–11.

Mearns, D. (1997) *Person-Centred Counselling Training*. London: Sage.

Mearns, D. (1999) Person-centred therapy with configurations of the self. *Counselling, 10*(2), 125–130.

Mearns, D. (2002) Further theoretical propositions in regard to self theory within the person-centered therapy. *Person-Centered and Experiential Psychotherapies, 1*(1&2), 14–27.

Mearns, D. (2004) Foreword. In M. McMillan (ed.) *The Person-Centred Approach to Therapeutic Change*. London: Sage.

Mearns, D. & Cooper, M. (2005) *Working at Relational Depth*. London: Sage

Mearns, D. & Thorne, B. (2000) *Person-Centred Therapy Today: New Frontiers in Theory and Practice*. London: Sage.

Mellor, K. (1980) Impasses: A developmental and structural understanding. *Transactional Analysis Journal, 10*(3), 213–20.

Merry, T. (1999) *Learning and Being in Person-Centred Counselling*. Llangarron: PCCS Books.

Merry, T. (2003) The actualisation conundrum. *Person-Centred Practice, 11*(2), 83–91.

Merry, T. (2004) Supervision as heuristic research enquiry. In K. Tudor & M. Worrall (eds.) *Freedom to Practise: Person-Pentred Approaches to Supervision* (pp. 189–99). Ross-on-Wye: PCCS Books.

Miller, J.G. (1988) Bridging the content-structure dichotomy: Culture and the self. In M.H. Bond (ed.) *The Cross-Cultural Challenge to Social Psychology* (pp. 266–81). London: Sage.

Miller, S., Hubble, M. & Duncan, B. (1995, March/April) No more bells and whistles. *The Family Therapy Networker*, 53–63.

Minister of National Health and Welfare. (1988) *Mental Health for Canadians*. Ottawa: MNHW.

Mitchell, J. (1975) *Psychoanalysis and Feminism*. Harmondsworth, UK: Penguin.

Molina, V. (1977) *Notes on Marx and the Problem of Individuality*. Working Paper in Cultural Studies 10. University of Birmingham: Centre for Contemporary Cultural Studies.

Moodley, R. (2003) Double, triple, multiple jeopardy. In C. Lago & B. Smith (eds.) *Anti-Discriminatory Practice* (pp. 120–34). London: Sage.

Moodley, R., Lago, C. & Talahite, A. (eds.) (2004) *Carl Rogers Counsels a Black Client: Race and Culture in Person-Centred Counselling*. Llangarron: PCCS Books.

Moore, J. (1997) Who is the person in the person-centred approach? *Person-Centred Practice*, *5*(2), 21–5.

Moustakas, C. (1990) Heuristic research: Design and methodology. *Person-Centered Review*, *5*(2), 170–90.

Mowbray, R. (1995) *The Case Against Psychotherapy Registration: A Conservation Issue for the Human Potential Movement*. London: Transmarginal Press.

Murdoch, I. (1985) The idea of perfection. In *The Sovereignty of Good* (pp. 1–45). London: Routledge. (Originally published in 1970)

Murphy, G. (1947) *Personality: A Biosocial Approach to Origins and Structure*. New York: Harper.

Murray, H.A. (1938) *Explorations in Personality*. Oxford: Oxford University Press.

Natiello, P. (1987) The person-centered approach: From theory to practice. *Person-Centered Review*, *2*, 203–16.

Natiello, P. (1990) The person-centered approach, collaborative power, and cultural transformation. *Person-Centered Review*, *5*(3), 268–86.

Naysmith, S. (2003) Scotland at forefront of radical plan to improve behaviour. *The Scotsman*.

Neville, B. (1996) Five kinds of empathy. In R. Hutterer, G. Pawlowsky, P.F. Schmid & R. Stipsits (eds.) *Client-Centered and Experiential Psychotherapy: A Paradigm in Motion* (pp. 439–53). Frankfurt am Main: Peter Lang.

Newnes, C. (2004) Psychology and psychotherapy's potential for countering the medicalization of everything. *Journal of Humanistic Psychology*, *44*, 358–76.

Newnes, C., Holmes, G. & Dunn, C. (eds.) (1999) *This is Madness: A Critical Look at Psychiatry and the Future Mental Health Services*. Llangarron: PCCS Books.

Newnes, C., Holmes, G. & Dunn, C. (eds.) (2001) *This is Madness Too: Critical Perspectives on Mental Health Services* (pp. 147–60). Llangarron: PCCS Books.

Nobles, W.W. (1973) Psychological research and the black self-concept: A critical review. *Journal of Social Issues*, *29*, 11–31.

Norris, C. (1995) Post-modernism. In T. Honderich (ed.) *The Oxford Companion to Philosophy* (p. 708). Oxford: Oxford University Press.

Northrup, C. (1998) *Women's Bodies, Women's Wisdom: The Complete Guide to Women's Health and Wellbeing*. London: Piatkus Books.

O'Connor, N. & Ryan, J. (1993) *Wild Desires and Mistaken Identities: Lesbianism and Psychoanalysis*. New York: Columbia University Press.

O'Hara, M. (1984) Person-centered gestalt: Toward a holistic synthesis. In R.S.

Levant & J.M. Shlien (eds.) *Client-Centered Therapy and the Person-Centered Approach* (pp. 203–21). New York: Praeger.

O'Hara, M. (1989) Person-centered approach as conscientizaçao: The works of Carl Rogers and Paulo Freire. *Journal of Humanistic Psychology, 29*(1), 11–36.

O'Hara, M. (1995) Streams: On becoming a postmodern person. In M.M. Suhd (ed.) *Positive Regard: Carl Rogers and Other Notables He Influenced* (pp. 105–55). Palo Alto, CA: Science & Behavior Books.

O'Hara, M. (1999) Moments of eternity: Carl Rogers and the contemporary demand for brief therapy. In I. Fairhurst (ed.) *Women Writing in the Person-Centred Approach* (pp. 63–77). Llangarron: PCCS Books.

Orange, D.M., Atwood, G.E. & Stolorow, R.D. (2001) *Working Intersubjectively: Contextualism in Psychoanalytic Practice*. New York: The Analytic Press.

Orlinsky, D.E., Grawe, K. & Parks, B.K. (1994) Process and outcome in psychotherapy: Noch einmal. In A.E. Bergin & S.L. Garfield (eds.) *Handbook of Psychotherapy and Behavior Change* (4th edn., pp. 270–376). New York: John Wiley & Sons.

Ornstein, A. (1986) Supportive psychotherapy: A contemporary view. *Clinical Social Work, 14*, 14–30.

Paglia, C. (1994) No law in the arena. In C. Paglia (ed.) *Vamps and Tramps* (pp. 19–94). New York: Vintage,

Paglia, C. (1995, 19 September) *AOL Transcript Camille Paglia*. Document available online at http://archive.aclu.org/about/transcripts/paglia.htlm

Pally, R. (2000) *The Mind–Brain Relationship*. London: Karnac Books.

Panksepp, J. (1998) *Affective Neuroscience: The Foundations of Human and Animal Emotions*. Oxford: Oxford University Press.

Parfit, D. (1984) *Reasons and Persons*. Oxford: Oxford University Press.

Parker, I. (1999) *Deconstructing Psychotherapy*. London: Sage.

Parlett, M. (1991) Reflections on field theory. *The British Gestalt Journal, 1*, 69–81.

Parsons, T. (1959) An approach to psychological theory in terms of the theory of action. In S. Koch (ed.) *Psychology: A Study of Science. Vol. 3: Formulation of the Person and the Social Context* (pp. 612–711). New York: McGraw-Hill.

Patterson, C.H. (1965) *Theories of Counseling and Psychotherapy*. New York: Harper & Row.

Patterson, C.H. (2000a) A unitary theory of motivation and its counseling implications. In C.H. Patterson, *Understanding Psychotherapy: Fifty Years of Client-Centred Theory and Practice* (pp. 10–21). (Original work published 1964)

Patterson, C.H. (2000b) On being non-directive. In C. H. Patterson, *Understanding Psychotherapy: Fifty Years of Client-Centred Theory and Practice* (pp. 181–4). Llangarron: PCCS Books.

Peake, M. (1950) *The Glass Blowers*. London: Eyre & Spottiswoode.

Perls, F. (1969) *Ego, Hunger and Aggression*. New York: Vintage. (Original work published 1947)

Perls, F., Hefferline, R.F. & Goodman, P. (1973) *Gestalt Therapy: Excitement and Growth in the Human Personality*. (Original work published 1951)

Philippson. P. (2004) *Gestalt Therapy and the Culture of Narcissism*. Article available online from Manchester Gestalt Centre website: www.123webpages.co.uk

Phillips, A. (1994) *On Flirtation*. London: Faber & Faber.

Piaget, J. (1954) *The Construction of Reality in the Child*. New York: Basic Books. (Original work published 1937)

Pine, F. (1988) The four psychologies of psychoanalysis and their place in clinical work. *Journal of the American Psychoanalytic Association*, *36*, 571–96.

Pine, F. (1990) *Drive, Ego, Object and Self: A Synthesis for Clinical Work*. New York: Basic Books.

Piontelli, A. (1992) *From Fetus to Child: An Observational and Psychoanalytic Study*. London: Tavistock/Routledge.

Poitier, S. (2000) *The Measure of a Man: A Memoir*. London: Simon & Schuster.

Politzer, G. (1976) *Elementary Principles of Philosophy*. London: Lawrence & Wishart.

Proctor, G. & Napier, M.B. (eds.) (2004a) *Encountering Feminism: Intersections between Feminism and the Person-Centred Approach*. Llangarron: PCCS Books.

Proctor, G. & Napier, M.B. (2004b) Introduction. In G. Proctor & M.B. Napier (eds.) *Encountering Feminism: Intersections between Feminism and the Person-Centred Approach* (pp. 1–11). Llangarron: PCCS Books.

Prouty, G.F. (1976) Pre-therapy, a method of treating pre-expressive, psychotic and retarded patients. *Psychotherapy: Theory, Research and Practice*, *13*(3), 290–5.

Prouty, G.F. (1994) *Theoretical Evolutions in Person-Centered/Experiential Therapy: Applications to Schizophrenic and Retarded Psychoses*. Westport, CT: Praeger.

Prouty, G.F., Van Werde, D. & Pörtner, M. (2002) *Pre-Therapy*. Llangarron: PCCS Books.

Purton, C. (2004) *Person-Centred Therapy: The Focusing-Oriented Approach*. Basingstoke, UK: Palgrave.

Putnam, S.P., Spritz, B.L. & Stifter, C.A. (2002) Mother–child coregulation during delay of gratification at 30 months. *Infancy*, *3*(2), 209–25.

Quinton, A. (1995) Philosophy. In T. Honderich (ed.) *The Oxford Companion to Philosophy* (pp. 666–70). Oxford: Oxford University Press.

Raimy, V. (1943) *The Self-Concept as a Factor in Counseling and Personality Organization*. Unpublished PhD thesis, Ohio State University.

Raimy, V. (1948) Self reference in counseling interviews. *Journal of Consulting Psychology*, *12*, 153–63.

Raimy, V. (1975) *Misconceptions of the Self*. San Francisco, CA: Jossey-Bass.

Ramachandran, V.S. (2003) Hearing colors, tasting shapes. *Scientific American*, *288*(5), 52–9.

Rank, O. (1989) *The Double: A Psychoanalytic Study* (H. Tucker, trans. & ed.). London: Karnac. (Original work published 1914)

Rank, O. (1941) *Beyond Psychology*. New York: Dover Publications.

Rapaport, D. (1959) The structure of psychoanalytic theory: A systematizing attempt. In S. Koch (ed.) *Psychology: A Study of Science. Vol. 3: Formulation of the Person and the Social Context* (pp. 55–183). New York: McGraw-Hill.

Raskin, N.J. (1948) The development of non-directive psychotherapy. *Journal of Consulting Psychology*, *13*, 154–6.

Reason, P. & Heron, J. (2002) Research with people: The paradigm of cooperative experiential enquiry. In D. Cain (ed.) *Classics in the Person-Centered Approach* (pp. 293–304). Ross-on-Wye: PCCS Books. (Original work published 1986)

Reich, W.R. (1983) *The Function of the Orgasm*. London: Souvenir Press. (Original work published 1924)

Rennie, T.A.C. (1943) Adolf Meyer and his psychobiology; the man, his methodology and its relation to therapy. *Papers of the American Congress of General Semantics*, *2*, 156–65.

Robbins, T. (1977) *Even Cowgirls Get the Blues*. London: Corgi. (Original work published 1976)

Robinson, D.N. (1995) *An Intellectual History of Psychology* (3rd edn.) London: Arnold. (Original work published 1976)

Rodgers, B.J. (2003) An exploration into the client at the heart of therapy: A qualitative perspective. *Person-Centered & Experiential Psychotherapies*, *2*(1), 19–30.

Rogers, A. (2001) Do we need 'a' theory of personality. *Person-Centred Practice*, *9*(1), 37–42.

Rogers, C.R. (1931) *Measuring Personality Adjustment in Children Nine to Thirteen*. New York: Teachers College, Columbia University, Bureau of Publications.

Rogers, C.R. (1939) *The Clinical Treatment of the Problem Child*. Boston: Houghton Mifflin.

Rogers, C.R. (1941) Psychology in clinical practice. In J.S. Gray (ed.) *Psychology in Use. A Textbook in Applied Psychology* (pp. 114–67). New York: American Book Company.

Rogers, C.R. (1942) *Counseling and Psychotherapy: Newer Concepts in Practice*. Boston: Houghton Mifflin.

Rogers, C.R. (1947) Some observations on the organization of personality. *American Psychologist*, *2*, 358–68.

Rogers, C.R. (1951) *Client-Centered Therapy*. London: Constable.

Rogers, C.R. (1956) Intellectualized psychotherapy. [Review of *The Psychology of Personal Constructs*]. *Contemporary Psychology*, *1*(12), 357.

Rogers, C.R. (1957) The necessary and sufficient conditions of therapeutic personality change. *Journal of Consulting Psychology*, *21*, 95–103.

Rogers, C.R. (1959a) A tentative scale for the measurement of process in psychotherapy. In E.A. Ruenstein & M.B. Parloff (eds.) *Research in Psychotherapy. Vol. I* (pp. 96–107). Washington, DC: American Psychological Association.

Rogers, C.R. (1959b) A theory of therapy, personality and interpersonal relationships, as developed in the client-centred framework. In S. Koch (ed.) *Psychology: A Study of Science. Vol. 3: Formulation of the Person and the Social Context* (pp. 184–256). New York: McGraw-Hill.

Rogers, C.R. (1963) The actualizing tendency in relation to 'motive' and to consciousness. In M. Jones (ed.) *Nebraska Symposium on Motivation 1963* (pp. 1–24). Lincoln, NE: University of Nebraska Press.

Rogers, C.R. (1967a) Some of the directions evident in therapy. In *On Becoming a Person* (pp. 73–106). London: Constable. (Original work published 1953)[1]

---

1 A number of Rogers' books comprise previously published material. For historical interest and accuracy, we refer to separate chapters in these books, citing them in the text, for example, as 'Rogers (1957/67)'. Where two papers were previously published in the same year we adopt the convention 'Rogers (1953/67a)' and so on.

Rogers, C.R. (1967b) 'This is me'. In *On Becoming a Person* (pp. 3–27). London: Constable. (Original work published 1953)

Rogers, C.R. (1967a) Toward a theory of creativity. In *On Becoming a Person* (pp. 347–59). London: Constable. (Original work published 1954)

Rogers, C.R. (1967b) What it means to become a person. In *On Becoming a Person* (pp. 107–24). London: Constable. (Original work published 1954)

Rogers, C.R. (1967a) Personality change in psychotherapy. In *On Becoming a Person* (pp. 225–42) London: Constable. (Original work published 1955)

Rogers, C.R. (1967b) Persons or science? A philosophical question. In *On Becoming a Person* (pp. 199–224) London: Constable. (Original work published 1955)

Rogers, C.R. (1967) A therapist's view of the good life: The fully functioning person. In *On Becoming a Person* (pp. 183–96). London: Constable. (Original work published 1957)

Rogers, C.R. (1967a) A process conception of psychotherapy. In *On Becoming a Person* (pp. 125–59). London: Constable. (Original work published 1958)

Rogers, C.R. (1967b) The characteristics of a helping relationship. In *On Becoming a Person* (pp. 39–57). London: Constable. (Original work published 1958)

Rogers, C.R. (1967a) Client-centered therapy in its context of research. In *On Becoming a Person* (pp. 243–70). London: Constable. (Original work published 1960)

Rogers, C.R. (1967b) 'To be that self which one truly is': A therapist's view of personal goals. In *On Becoming a Person* (pp. 163–82). London: Constable. (Original work published 1960)

Rogers, C.R. (1967a) A tentative formulation of a general law of interpersonal relationships. In *On Becoming a Person* (pp. 338–46). London: Constable. (Original work published 1961)

Rogers, C.R. (1967b) *On Becoming a Person: A Therapist's View of Psychotherapy*. London: Constable. (Original work published 1961)

Rogers, C.R. (1967c) Personal thoughts on teaching and learning. In *On Becoming a Person: A Therapist's View of Psychotherapy* (pp. 273–8) London: Constable. (Original work published 1961)

Rogers, C.R. (1967d) The place of the individual in the new world of the behavioral sciences. In *On Becoming a Person* (pp. 384–402). London: Constable. (Original work published 1961)

Rogers, C.R. (1967e) What we know about psychotherapy – Objectively and subjectively. In *On Becoming a Person* (pp. 59–69). London: Constable. (Original work published 1961)

Rogers, C.R. (1967) Carl R. Rogers. In E.G. Boring & G. Lindzey (eds.) *A History of Psychology in Autobiography, Vol. V* (pp. 343–84). New York: Appleton-Century-Crofts.

Rogers, C.R. (1968) Some thoughts regarding the current presuppositions of the behavioral sciences. In C.R. Rogers & W.R. Coulson (eds.) *Man and the Science of Man* (pp. 55–72). Columbus, OH: Charles E. Merrill.

Rogers, C.R. (1969) *Freedom to Learn*. Columbus, OH: Charles E. Merrill.

Rogers, C.R. (1970) The process equation of psychotherapy. In J.T. Hart & T.M. Tomlinson (eds.) *New Directions in Client-Centered Therapy* (pp. 190–205). Boston: Houghton Mifflin. (Original work published 1961)

Rogers, C.R. (1973) *Carl Rogers on Encounter Groups*. New York: Harper & Row. (Original work published 1970)

Rogers, C.R. (1973) *Becoming Partners: Marriage and Its Alternatives*. London: Constable.

Rogers, C.R. (1978) *Carl Rogers on Personal Power*. London: Constable.

Rogers, C.R. (1979) The foundations of the person-centred approach. *Education*, *100*(2), 98–107.

Rogers, C.R. (1980) Ellen West – and loneliness. In C.R. Rogers *A Way of Being* (pp. 164–80). Boston: Houghton Mifflin. (Original work published 1961)

Rogers, C.R. (1980) The foundations of a person-centred approach. In C.R. Rogers *A Way of Being* (pp. 113–36). Boston: Houghton Mifflin. (Original work published 1963)

Rogers, C.R. (1980) Some new challenges to the helping professions. In C.R. Rogers *A Way of Being* (pp. 235–59). Boston: Houghton Mifflin. (Original work published 1973)

Rogers, C.R. (1980) Can learning encompass both ideas and feelings? In C.R. Rogers *A Way of Being* (pp. 263–91). Boston: Houghton Mifflin. (Original work published 1974)

Rogers, C.R. (1980) Empathic: An unappreciated way of being. In C.R. Rogers *A Way of Being* (pp. 137–63). Boston: Houghton Mifflin. (Original work published 1975)

Rogers, C.R. (1980) Beyond the watershed: And where now? In C.R. Rogers *A Way of Being* (pp. 292–315). Boston: Houghton Mifflin. (Original work published 1977)

Rogers C.R. (1980) Do we need 'a' reality? In C.R. Rogers *A Way of Being* (pp. 96–108). Boston: Houghton Mifflin. (Original work published 1978)

Rogers, C.R. (1980a) *A Way of Being*. Boston: Houghton Mifflin.

Rogers, C.R. (1980b) Introduction. In C.R. Rogers *A Way of Being* (pp. vii–x). Boston: Houghton Mifflin.

Rogers, C.R. (1981) The emerging person: A new revolution. In R.I. Evans *Dialogue with Carl Rogers* (pp. 147–75). New York: Praeger. (Original work published 1975)

Rogers, C.R. (1983) *Freedom to Learn for the 80s*. Columbus, OH: Charles E. Merrill.

Rogers, C.R. (1986) Rogers, Kohut, and Erickson: A personal perspective on some similarities and differences. *Person-Centred Review*, *1*(2), 125–40.

Rogers, C.R. (1990) A client centered/person-centered approach to therapy. In H. Kirschenbaum & V.L. Henderson (eds.) *The Carl Rogers Reader* (pp. 135–52). London: Constable. (Original work published 1986)

Rogers, C.R. & Dymond, R.F. (eds.) (1954) *Psychotherapy and Personality Change*. Chicago, IL: University of Chicago Press.

Rogers, C.R. & Freiberg, H.J (1994) *Freedom to Learn* (3rd edn.). Columbus, OH: Charles E. Merrill.

Rogers, C.R., Gendlin, E.T., Kiesler, D.J. & Truax, C.B. (eds.) (1967) *The Therapeutic Relationship and Its Impact: A Study of Psychotherapy with Schizophrenics*. Madison, WI: University of Wisconsin Press.

Rogers, C.R. & Hart, J. (1970) Looking back and looking ahead: A conversation with Carl Rogers. In J.T. Hart & T.M. Tomlinson (eds.) *New Directions in Client-Centered Therapy* (pp. 502–34). Boston: Houghton Mifflin.

Rogers, C.R. & Rablen, R.A. (1958) *A Scale of Process in Psychotherapy.* Mimeographed manual. University of Wisconsin.

Rogers, C.R. & Russell, D.E. (2002) *Carl Rogers the Quiet Revolutionary: An Oral History.* Roseville, CA: Penmarin Books.

Rogers, C.R. & Sanford, R. (1989) Client-centered psychotherapy. In H.I. Kaplan & B.J. Sadock (eds.) *Comprehensive Textbook of Psychiatry, Vol. 2.* (pp. 1482–1501). Baltimore: Williams & Wilkins.

Rogers, C.R. & Wallen, J.L. (1946) *Counseling with Returned Servicemen.* New York: McGraw-Hill.

Rogers, C.R. & Wood, J.K. (1974) Client-centered theory: Carl Rogers. In A. Burton (ed.) *Operational Theories of Personality* (pp. 211–58). New York: Brunner/Mazel.

Rogers, N. (2000) *The Creative Connection.* Llangarron: PCCS Books. (Original work published 1993)

Ronningstam, E. (1998) *Disorders of Narcissism.* Washington DC: American Psychiatric Press.

Rowan, J. (1990) *Subpersonalities.* London: Routledge.

Rowan, J. & Jacobs, M. (2002) *The Therapist's Use of Self.* Maidenhead, UK: Open University Press.

Rowland, B. (2002) Depressed process: A person-centred view of depression. *Person-Centred Practice, 10*(1), 27–34.

Roy, B. (1988) Loss of power – Alienation. In B. Roy & C. Steiner (eds.) *Radical Psychiatry: The Second Decade* (pp. 3–13). Unpublished manuscript. See www.emotional-literacy.com/rp0.htm

Ryce-Menuhin, J. (1988) *The Self in Early Childhood.* London: Free Association Books.

Sacks, O. (1995) Foreword. In K. Goldstein *The Organism* (pp. 7–14). New York: Zone Books. (Original work published 1934)

Sander, L.W. (1982) Polarities, paradox, and the organizing process. In J. Call, E. Galenson & R. Tyson (eds.) *Proceedings of the First World Congress on Infant Psychiatry* (pp. 871–908). New York: Basic Books.

Sander, L.W. (2002) Thinking differently: Principles of process in living systems and the specificity of being known. *Psychoanalytic Dialogues, 5,* 11–42.

Sanders, P. (2000) Mapping person-centred approaches to counselling and psychotherapy. *Person-Centred Practice, 8*(2), 62–74.

Sanders, P. (ed.) (2004) *The Tribes of the Person-Centred Nation.* Llangarron: PCCS Books.

Sanders, P. & Tudor, K. (2001) This is therapy: A person-centred critique of the contemporary psychiatric system. In C. Newnes, G. Holmes & C. Dunn (eds.) *This Is Madness Too: Critical Perspectives on Mental Health Services* (pp. 147–60). Llangarron: PCCS Books.

Sanders, P. & Wyatt, G. (2002) The history of conditions one and six. In G. Wyatt & Sanders, P. (eds.) *Contact and Perception* (pp. 1–24). Llangarron: PCCS Books.

Sands, A. (2000) *Falling for Therapy.* London: Macmillan.

Sands, A. (2001, 22 September) *Psychotherapy from a Client's Point of View. Talk to the British Psychological Society.* Paper available online at www.therapy-abuse.net/information/articles.anna_sands_bps_talk.htm.

Sapriel, L. (1998) Can gestalt therapy, self-psychology and intersubjectivity theory be integrated? *The British Gestalt Journal,* 7(1), 33–44.

Sayers, J. (2004) Therapy as research: Focusing on empathy. *Journal of Critical Psychology, Counselling and Psychotherapy,* 4(2), 86–93.

Scheerer, M. (1954) Cognitive theory. In G. Lindzey (ed.) *Handbook of Social Psychology Vol. I* (pp. 91–142). New York: Random House.

Schiff, J.L., Schiff, A.W., Mellor, K., Schiff, E., Schiff, S., Richman, D. *et al.* (1975) *Cathexis Reader: Transactional Analysis Treatment of Psychosis.* New York: Harper & Row.

Schlebusch, P. (2004) Review [Problem drinking: A person-centred dialogue]. *Person-Centered & Experiential Psychotherapies,* 3(1), 70–2.

Schmid, P. (1998) 'On becoming a person-centred approach': A person-centred understanding of the person. In B. Thorne & E. Lambers (eds.) *Person-Centred Therapy: A European Perspective* (pp. 38–52). London: Sage.

Schmid, P. (2004) Back to the client: A phenomenological approach to the process of understanding and diagnosis. *Person-Centered & Experiential Psychotherapies,* 3(1), 36–51.

Schneider, C.K. & Stiles, W.B. (1995) A person-centered view of depression: Women's experiences. *The Person-Centered Journal,* 2, 67–77.

Schon, D.A. (1983) *The Reflective Practitioner.* New York: Basic Books.

Schore, A.N. (1994) *Affect Regulation and the Origin of the Self: The Neurobiology of Emotional Development.* Hillsdale, NJ: Lawrence Erlbaum Associates Inc.

Schore, A.N. (2003) *Affect Regulation and the Repair of the Self.* New York: W.W. Norton.

Schwartz, B. (1986) *The Battle for Human Nature: Science, Morality, and Modern Life.* New York: W.W. Norton.

Seeman, J. (1983) *Personality Integration: Studies and Reflections.* New York: Human Sciences Press.

Seeman, J. (1984) The fully functioning person: Theory and research. In R.F. Levant & J. Shlien (eds.) *Client-Centered Therapy and the Person-Centered Approach: New Directions in Theory, Research and Practice* (pp. 131–52). New York: Praeger.

Seeman, J. (ed.) (1990) Human inquiry and the person-centered approach [Special Issue]. *Person-Centered Review,* 5(2).

Shlien, J. (1984) A countertheory of transference. In R. Levant & J. Shlien (eds.) *Client-Centered Therapy and the Person-Centered Approach: New Directions in Theory, Research and Practice* (pp. 153–81). New York: Praeger.

Shlien, J. (1989) Boy's person-centered perspective on psychodiagnosis. A response. *Person-Centered Review,* 4(2), 157–62.

Shlien, J.M. & Levant, R.F (1984) Introduction. In R.F. Levant & J.M. Shlien (eds.) *Client-Centered Therapy and the Person-Centered Approach: New Directions in Theory, Research and Practice* (pp. 1–16). New York: Praeger.

Shostrom, E. (Producer) (1965) *Three Approaches to Psychotherapy.* Santa Ana: Psychological Films.

Siegel, D.J. (1999) *The Developing Mind.* New York: Guilford Press.

Smith, P. (1978) Domestic labour and Marx's theory of value. In A. Kuhn & A

Wolpe (eds.) *Feminism and Materialism* (pp. 198–219). London: Routledge & Kegan Paul.

Smuts, J. (1987) *Holism and Evolution*. New York: Macmillan. (Original work published 1926)

Snyder, W.U. (1947) The present status of psychotherapeutic counseling. *Psychological Bulletin*, *44*, 297–386.

Snyder, W.U. (1994) *The Psychotherapy Relationship*. New York: Macmillan. (Original work published 1961)

Solms, M. & Turnbull, O. (2002) *The Brain and the Inner World*. London: Karnac.

Sontag, S. (1989) *AIDS and Its Metaphors*. Harmondsworth, UK: Penguin.

Speierer, G.-W. (1990) Toward a specific illness concept of client-centered therapy. In G. Lietaer, J. Rombauts & R. Van Balen (eds.) *Client-Centered and Experiential Psychotherapy in the Nineties* (pp. 337–59). Leuven: Leuven University Press.

Speierer, G.-W. (1996) Client-centered psychotherapy according to the differential incongruence model (DIM). In R. Hutterer, G. Pawlowsky, P.F. Schmid & R. Stipsits (eds.) *Client-Centered and Experiential Psychotherapy: A Paradigm in Motion* (pp. 299–311). Frankfurt am Main: Peter Lang,

Spielhofer, H. (2003) Organism and subjectivity — 1: The concept of 'organism' and 'actualizing tendency'. *Person-Centered & Experiential Psychotherapies*, *2*(2), 75–88.

Spinelli, E. (1989) *The Interpreted World: An Introduction to Phenomenological Psychology*. London: Sage.

Spinelli, E. (1997) *Tales of Un-Knowing: Therapeutic Encounters from an Existential Perspective*. London: Duckworth.

Spinoza, B. de (1993) *Ethics*. (G.H.R. Parkinson, ed. & rev., A. Boyle, trans.). London: Everyman. (Original work published 1677)

Stamatiadis, R. (1990) Sharing life therapy. *Person-Centered Review*, *5*(3), 287–307.

Standal, S. (1954) *The Need for Positive Regard: A Contribution to Client-Centered Theory*. Unpublished PhD dissertation, University of Chicago.

Stanton, M. (1990) *Sándor Ferenczi: Reconsidering Active Intervention*. London: Free Association Books.

Stark, M. (2000) *Modes of Therapeutic Action: Enhancement of Knowledge, Provision of Experience, Engagement in Relationship*. Northvale, NJ: Jason Aronson.

Staunton, T. (ed.) (2002) *Body Psychotherapy*. London: Brunner-Routledge.

Steiner, C. (1971) *Games Alcoholics Play*. New York: Grove Press.

Steiner, C. (1981) *The Other Side of Power*. New York: Grove Press.

Steiner, C. (2000) Radical psychiatry. In R.J. Corsini (ed.) *Handbook of Innovative Therapy* (pp. 578–86). Chichester, UK: Wiley.

Steiner, C., Wyckoff, H., Golstine, D., Lariviere, P., Schwebel, R., Marcus, J. & Members of the Radical Psychiatry Center. (1975) *Readings in Radical Psychiatry*. New York: Grove Press.

Stern, D.N. (1985) *The Interpersonal World of the Infant*. New York: Basic Books.

Stern, D.N. (1991) *Diary of a Baby*. London: Fontana.

Stern, D.N. (2000) *The Interpersonal World of the Infant* (rev. edn.). New York: Basic Books.

Stern, D.N. (2004) *The Present Moment in Psychotherapy and Everyday Life*. New York: W.W. Norton & Co.

Stickley, T. & Freshwater, D. (2002) The art of loving and the therapeutic relationship. *Nursing Inquiry*, *9*(4), 250–6.

Stige, B. (1998) Perspectives on meaning in music therapy. *British Journal of Music Therapy*, *12*(1), 20–7.

Stinckens, N., Lietaer, G. & Leijssen, M. (2002) The valuing process and the inner critic in the classical and current client-centered/experiential literature. *Person-Centered and Experiential Psychotherapies*, *1*(1&2), 41–55.

Stolorow, R. & Atwood, G. (1992) *Contexts of Being: The Intersubjective Foundations of Psychological Life.* Hillsdale, NJ: The Analytic Press.

Stolorow, R.D. (1976) Psychoanalytic reflections on client-centered therapy in the light of modern conceptions of narcissism. *Psychotherapy: Theory, Research & Practice*, *13*, 26–9.

Stolorow, R.D., Brandchaft, B. & Atwood, G. (1987) *Psychoanalytic Treatment: An Intersubjective Approach.* Hillsdale, NJ: The Analytic Press.

Strawson, P.F. (1959) *Individuals.* London: Methuen.

Stumm, G. (2002) The person-centered approach and self psychology. In J.C. Watson, R.N. Goldman & M.S. Warner (eds.) *Client-Centered and Experiential Psychotherapy in the 21st Century: Advances in Theory, Research and Practice* (pp. 108–26). Llangarron: PCCS Books.

Summers, G. & Tudor, K. (2000) Cocreative transactional analysis. *Transactional Analysis Journal*, *30*(1), 23–40.

Swildens, H. (2004) Self-pathology and postmodern humanity: Challenges for person-centered psychotherapy. *Person-Centered & Experiential Psychotherapies*, *3*(1), 4–18.

Symington, N. (1993) *Narcissism – A New Theory.* London: Karnac Books.

Taft, J. (1933) *The Dynamics of Therapy in a Controlled Relationship.* New York: Macmillan.

Takens, R.J. & Lietaer, G. (2004) Process differentiation and person-centredness: A contradiction? *Person-Centered & Experiential Psychotherapies*, *3*(2), 77–87.

Tausch, R. (1988) The relationship between emotions and cognition: Implications for therapist empathy. *Person-Centred Review*, *3*, 277–91.

Taylor, J. (1931) *Selected Writings of John Hughlings Jackson Vols. I & II.* London: Hodder & Stoughton.

Thorne, B. (1991a) Carl Rogers and the doctrine of original sin. In B. Thorne *Person-Centred Counselling: Therapeutic and Spiritual Dimensions* (pp. 126–34). London: Whurr.

Thorne, B. (1991b) *Person-Centred Counselling: Therapeutic and Spiritual Dimensions.* London: Whurr.

Thorne, B. (1991c) The quality of tenderness. In B. Thorne *Person-Centred Counselling: Therapeutic and Spiritual Dimensions* (pp. 73–81). London: Whurr. (Original work published 1982)

Thorne, B. (1992) *Carl Rogers.* London: Sage.

Thorne, B. (2003) *Carl Rogers* (2nd edn.). London: Sage.

Thorne, B. & Lambers, E. (ed.) (1998) *Person-Centred Therapy: A European Perspective.* London: Sage.

Thorne, F.C. (1967) *Integrative Psychology.* Brandon, VT: Clinical Publishing Co.

Tillich, P. (1952) *The Courage to Be.* London: Fontana.

Tilmann, M. (1977) *Years of Apprenticeship on the Couch.* New York: Urizen.

Tobin, S.A. (1991) A comparison of psychoanalytic self psychology and Carl Rogers' person-centered therapy. *Journal of Humanistic Psychology, 30,* 9–33.

Tolan, J. (2002) The fallacy of the 'real' self: In praise of self-structure. In J.C. Watson, R.N. Goldman & M.S. Warner (eds.) *Client-Centered and Experiential Psychotherapy in the 21st Century: Advances in Theory, Research and Practice* (pp. 144–9). Llangarron: PCCS Books.

Tolman, E.C. & Brunswik, E. (1935) The organism and the causal texture of the environment. *Psychological Review, 42,* 43–77.

Tolstoy, L. (1982) *War and Peace* (R. Edmonds, trans.). Harmondsworth, UK: Penguin. (Original work published 1869)

Tophoff, M. (1984) *The Dynamics of Person-Centered Body Work in a Group Setting.* Paper presented at the VIIIth International Congress of Group Psychotherapy, Mexico City.

Toukmanian, S. (2002) Perception: The core element in person-centered and experiential psychotherapies. In G. Wyatt & P. Sanders (eds.) *Contact and Perception* (pp. 115–32). PCCS Books: Llangarron.

Trevarthen, C. (1993) The foundations of intersubjectivity: Development of interpersonal and cooperative understandings in infants. In D. Olsen (ed.) *Essays in Honor of Jerome S. Bruner* (pp. 316–42). New York: W.W. Norton. (Original work published 1980)

Truax, C.B. (1970) *A Tentative Scale of the Measurement of Accurate Empathy.* Unpublished paper, University of Calgary, Canada.

Truax, C.B. & Carkhuff, R. (1965) Client and therapist transparency in the psychotherapeutic encounter. *Journal of Counseling Psychology, 12,* 3–9.

Truax, C.B. & Carkhuff, R.R. (1967) *Toward Effective Counseling and Psychotherapy. Training and Practice.* Chicago, IL: Aldine.

Truax, C.B. & Mitchell, K.K. (1971) Research on certain interpersonal skills in relation to process and outcome. In A.E. Bergin & S.L. Garfield (eds.) *Handbook of Psychotherapy and Behaviour Change: An Empirical Analysis* (pp. 299–344). New York: Wiley & Sons.

Tudor, K. (1996) *Mental Health Promotion: Paradigms and Practice.* London: Routledge.

Tudor, K. (1997) Being at dis-ease with ourselves: Alienation and psychotherapy. *Changes, 15*(2), 143–50.

Tudor, K. (1999) 'I'm OK, You're OK – and They're OK': Therapeutic relationships in transactional analysis. In C. Feltham (ed.) *Understanding the Counselling Relationship* (pp. 109–119). London: Sage.

Tudor, K. (2000) The case of the lost conditions. *Counselling, 11*(1), 33–7.

Tudor, K. (2003) The neopsyche: The integrating adult ego state. In C. Sills & H. Hargaden (eds.) *Ego states* (pp. 201–31). London: Worth Reading.

Tudor, K. (2004) Mental health promotion. In I.J. Norman & I. Ryrie (eds.) *The Art and Science of Mental Health Nursing: A Textbook of Principles and Practice* (pp. 35–65). Buckingham, UK: McGraw Hill/Open University Press.

Tudor, K. & Merry, T. (2002) *Dictionary of Person-Centred Psychology.* London: Whurr.

Tudor, K. & Worrall, M. (1994) Congruence reconsidered. *British Journal of Guidance and Counselling, 22*(2), 197–206.

Tudor, K. & Worrall, M. (2002) The unspoken relationship: Financial dynamics in freelance therapy. In. J. Clark (ed.) *Freelance Counselling and Psychotherapy* (pp. 80–90). London: Sage.

Tudor, K. & Worrall, M. (eds.) (2004a) *Freedom to Practise: Person-Centred Approaches to Supervision*. Llangarron: PCCS Books.

Tudor, K. & Worrall, M. (2004b) Issues, questions, dilemmas and domains in supervision. In K. Tudor & M. Worrall (eds.) *Freedom to Practise: Person-Centred Approaches to Supervision* (pp. 79–96). Llangarron: PCCS Books.

Turner, V. (1967) *Forest of Symbols*. Ithaca, NY: Cornell University Press.

UKCP (United Kingdom Council for Psychotherapy Humanistic and Integrative Section Training Standards Committee) (1992) *Entry Requirements and Curriculum Contents*. London: UKCP.

United Nations. (1948) *Declaration of Human Rights*. New York: UN.

Van Belle, H.A. (1980) *Basic Intent and Therapeutic Approach of Carl R. Rogers*. Toronto: Wedge Publishing Foundation.

Van Belle, H.A. (1990) Rogers' later move towards mysticism: Implications for client-centered therapy. In G. Lietaer, J. Rombauts & R. Van Balen (eds.) *Client-Centered and Experiential Psychotherapy in the Nineties* (pp. 47–57). Leuven: Leuven University Press.

Van Belle, H.A. (in press, 2005) Philosophical roots of person-centered therapy in the history of western thought. *The Person-Centered Journal*.

Van Kalmthout, M. (1998a) Personality change and the concept of self. In B. Thorne & E. Lambers (eds.) *Person-Centred Therapy: A European Perspective* (pp. 53–61). London: Sage.

Van Kalmthout, M. (1998b) Person-centred theory as a system of meaning. In B. Thorne & E. Lambers (eds.) *Person-Centred Therapy: A European Perspective* (pp. 11–22). London: Sage.

Van Kalmthout, M. (2002) The farther reaches of person-centered psychotherapy. In J.C. Watson, R.N. Goldman & M. Warner (eds.) *Client-Centered and Experiential Psychotherapy in the 21st Century: Advances in Theory, Practice and Research* (pp. 127–43). Llangarron: PCCS Books.

Van Kalmthout, M.A. & Pelgrim, F.A. (1990) In search of universal concepts in psychopathology and psychotherapy. In G. Lietaer, J. Rombauts & R. Van Balen (eds.) *Client-Centered and Experiential Psychotherapy in the Nineties* (pp. 381–96). Leuven: Leuven University Press,

Van Werde, D. (1994) An introduction to client-centred pre-therapy. In D. Mearns *Developing Person-Centred Counselling* (pp. 121–5) London: Sage.

Van Werde, D. (1998) 'Anchorage' as a core concept in working with psychotic people. In B. Thorne & E. Lambers (eds.) *Person-Centred Therapy* (pp. 195–205) London: Sage.

Van Werde, D. (2002) The falling man: Pre-therapy applied to somatic hallucinating. *Person-Centred Practice*, *10*(2), 101–7.

Van Werde, D. (2005) Facing psychotic functioning: Person-centred contact work in residential psychiatric care. In S. Joseph & R. Worsley (eds.) *Person-Centred Psychopathology: A Positive Psychology of Mental Health* (pp. 158–68). Ross-on-Wye, UK: PCCS Books.

Vargas, M.J. (1954) Changes in self-awareness during client-centered therapy. In C.R. Rogers & R.F. Dymond (eds.) *Psychotherapy and Personality Change* (pp. 145–66). Chicago, IL: University of Chicago Press.

Vitz, P. (1977) *Psychology as Religion: The Cult of Self-Worship*. Grand Rapids, MI: William B. Eerdmans.

von Broembsen, F. (1999) *The Sovereign Self: Toward a Phenomenology of Self Experience*. Northvale, NJ: Jason Aronson.

von Drigalski, D. (1986) *Flowers on Granite*. Berkeley, CA: Creative Arts Book Company.

Vossen, T.J. (1990) Client-centered dream therapy. In G. Lietaer, J. Rombauts & R. Van Balen (eds.) *Client-Centered and Experiential Psychotherapy in the Nineties* (pp. 511–48). Leuven: Leuven University Press.

Wann, T.W. (ed.) (1965) *Behaviorism and Phenomenology: Contrasting Bases for Modern Psychology*. Chicago & London: Phoenix Books. (Original work published 1964)

Warner, M.S. (1991) Fragile process. In L. Fusek (ed.) *New Directions in Client-Centered Therapy: Practice with Difficult Client Populations (Monograph Series 1)* (pp. 41–58). Chicago, IL: Chicago Counseling and Psychotherapy Center.

Warner, M.S. (1997) Does empathy cure? A theoretical consideration of empathy, processing and personal narrative. In A.C. Bohart & L.S. Greenberg (eds.) *Empathy Reconsidered: New Directions in Psychotherapy* (pp. 125–40). Washington, DC: American Psychological Association.

Warner, M.S. (1998) A client-centered approach to therapeutic work with dissociated and fragile process. In L. Greenberg, J. Watson & G. Lietaer (eds.) *Handbook of Experiential Psychotherapy* (pp. 368–87). New York: Guilford Press.

Warner, M.S. (1999) The language of psychology as it affects women and other traditionally disempowered groups. In I. Fairhurst (ed.) *Women Writing in the Person-Centred Approach* (pp. 193–8). Llangarron: PCCS Books.

Warner, M.S. (2000a) Person-centered psychotherapy: One nation, many tribes. *The Person-Centered Journal*, 7(1), 28–39.

Warner, M.S. (2000b) Person-centred therapy at the difficult edge: A developmentally based model of fragile and dissociated process. In D. Mearns & B. Thorne *Person-Centred Therapy Today: New Frontiers in Theory and Practice* (pp. 144–71). London: Sage.

Warner, M.S. (2002) Luke's dilemmas: A client-centered/experiential model of processing with a schizophrenic thought disorder. In J.C. Watson, R.N. Goldman & M.S. Warner (eds.) *Client-Centered and Experiential Psychotherapy in the 21st Century: Advances in Theory, Research and Practice*. Llangarron: PCCS Books.

Waterhouse, R.L. (1993) Wild women don't have the blues: A feminist critique of person-centered counseling and therapy. *Feminism and Psychology*, 3(1), 55–71.

Watson, J.C., Goldman, R.N. & Warner, M.S. (ed.) (2002) *Client-Centered and Experiential Psychotherapy in the 21st Century: Advances in Theory, Research and Practice*. Llangarron: PCCS Books.

Watson, N. (1984) The empirical status of Rogers's hypotheses of the necessary and sufficient conditions for effective psychotherapy. In R.F. Levant & J.M. Shlien (eds.) *Client-Centered Therapy and the Person-Centered Approach: New Directions in Theory, Research and Practice* (pp. 17–40). New York: Praeger.

Watzlawick, P., Beavin, J.H. & Jackson, D.D. (1967) *Pragmatics of Human Communication: A Study of Interactional Patterns, Pathologies, and Paradoxes*. New York: W.W. Norton & Company.

Werner, H. (1948) *Comparative Psychology of Mental Development* (rev. edn.). Chicago, IL: Follett.

Wexler, D.A. (1974) A cognitive theory of experiencing, self-actualization and therapeutic process. In D.A. Wexler & L.N. Rice (eds.) *Innovations in Client-Centered Therapy* (pp. 49–116). New York: Wiley.

Wheeler, R.H. (1940) *The Science of Psychology* (2nd edn.). New York: Crowell.

White, M. & Epstein, D. (1990) *Narrative Means to Therapeutic Ends*. New York: Norton.

Whitehead, A.N. (1920) *The Concept of Nature*. Cambridge: Cambridge University Press.

Whitehead, A.N. (1933) *Adventures of Ideas*. London: Pelican.

Whitehead, A.N. (1954) *Dialogues of Alfred North Whitehead* (L. Price, ed.) Westorrt, CT: Greenwood Press.

Whitehead, A.N. (1967) *Science and the Modern World*. New York: The Free Press. (Original work published 1925)

Whitehead, A.N. (1971) *Function of Reason*. Boston, MA: Beacon Press. (Original work published 1958)

Whitehead, A.N. (1978) *Process and Reality* (D.R. Griffin & D.W. Sherburne, eds., corrected edn.). New York: The Free Press. (Original work published 1929)

Wilber, K. (1980) *The Atman Project: A Transpersonal View of Human Development*. Wheaton, IL: The Theosophical Publishing House.

Wilber, K. (1990) *Eye to Eye: The Quest for the New Paradigm*. Boston: Shambhala.

Wilkins, P. (1997) *Personal and Professional Development for Counsellors*. London: Sage.

Wilkins, P. (2003) *Person-Centred Therapy in Focus*. London: Sage.

Wilkins, P. (2005) Person-centred theory and 'mental illness'. In S. Joseph & R. Worsley (eds.) *Person-Centred Psychopathology: A Positive Psychology of Mental Health* (pp. 43–59). Ross-on-Wye, UK: PCCS Books.

Wilkins, P. & Gill, M. (2003) Assessment in person-centered therapy. *Person-Centered & Experiential Psychotherapies*, *2*(3), 172–87.

Winnicott, D.W. (1958) Clinical varieties of transference. In D.W. Winnicott *Through Paediatrics to Psycho-Analysis*. London: Hogarth Press/Institute of Psycho-Analysis. (Original work published 1956)

Winnicott, D.W. (1965) Ego distortion in terms of true and false self. In D.W. Winnicott *The Maturational Processes and the Facilitating Environment: Studies in the Theory of Emotional Development* (pp. 140–52). London: Hogarth Press/ Institute of Psycho-Analysis. (Original work published 1960)

Winnicott, D.W. (1965) *The Maturational Processes and the Facilitating Environment: Studies in the Theory of Emotional Development*. London: Hogarth Press.

Wittgenstein, L. (1974) *Philosophical Investigations*. Oxford: Blackwell. (Original work published 1922)

Wittgenstein, L. (2001) *Tractatus Logico-Philosophicus* (D.F. Pears & B.F. McGuinness trans. & eds.). London: Routledge. (Original work published 1921)

Wolter-Gustafson, C. (1999) The power of the premise: Reconstructing gender and human development with Rogers' theory. In I. Fairhurst (ed.) *Women Writing in the Person-Centred Approach* (pp. 199–214). Llangarron: PCCS Books.

Wolter-Gustafson, C. (2004) Toward convergence: Client-centered and feminist assumptions about epistemology and power. In G. Proctor & M.B. Napier (eds.)

Encountering Feminism: Intersections between Feminism and the Person-Centred Approach (pp. 97–115). Llangarron: PCCS Books.

Wood, J.K. (1984) Communities for learning: A person-centered approach. In R.S. Levant & J.M. Shlien (eds.) *Client-Centered Therapy and the Person-Centered Approach* (pp. 297–316). New York: Praeger.

Wood, J.K. (1996) The person-centered approach: Towards an understanding of its implications. In R. Hutterer, G. Pawlowsky, P.F. Schmid & R. Stipsits (eds.) *Client-Centered and Experiential Psychotherapy: A Paradigm in Motion* (pp. 163–81). Frankfurt am Main: Peter Lang.

Wood, J.K. (1999) Toward an understanding of large group dialogue and its implications. In C. Lago & M. MacMillan (eds.) *Experiences in Relatedness: Groupwork and the Person-Centred Approach* (pp. 137–65). Llangarron: PCCS Books.

Woodfin, R. & Groves, J. (2001) *Introducing Aristotle*. Cambridge: Icon Books.

Woodworth, R.S. with Sheehan, M. (1965) *Contemporary Schools of Psychology* (3rd edn.). New York: The Ronald Press Co. (Original work published 1931)

Wordsworth, W. (1850) The Prelude. In T. Hutchinson (ed.) *Poetical Works* (pp. 494–588, 1904). Oxford: Oxford University Press. (Revised by E. de Selincourt, 1936)

Worrall, M. (1997) Contracting within the person-centred approach. In C. Sills (ed.) *Contracts in Counselling* (pp. 65–75). London: Sage.

Wyatt, G. (2001) The multifaceted nature of congruence within the therapeutic relationship. In G. Wyatt (ed.) *Congruence* (pp. 79–95). Llangarron: PCCS Books.

Yalom, I. (1974) *Everyday Gets a Little Closer*. New York: Basic Books.

Yalom, I. (1995) *The Theory and Practice of Group Psychotherapy* (4th edn.). New York: Basic Books.

Zimring, F.M. (1988) Attaining mastery. The shift from the 'me' to the 'I'. *Person-Centered Review*, *3*(2), 165–75.

Zimring, F.M. (1995) A new explanation for the beneficial results of client-centered therapy: The possibility of a new paradigm. *The Person-Centered Journal*, *2*(2), 36–48.

Zohar, D. (1991) *The Quantum Self*. London: Flamingo.

Zuckerkandl, V. (1973) *Man the Musician*. Princeton: Princeton University Press.

Zukav, G. (1979) *The Dancing Wu Li Masters*. London: Rider.

Zúñiga, G.L. (2001) What is economic personalism? A phenomenological analysis. *Journal of Markets & Morality*, *4*(2), 151–75.

Author index

Taft, J. 86, 195–6, 202, 219, 231–2, 236, 241
Takens, R.J. 163
Talahite, A. 33
Tallman, K. 236
Tausch, R. 206
Tawney, R.H. 1
Taylor, J. 246
Thompson, S. 242
Thorne, B. 3, 25, 46, 108, 129, 130, 195, 210, 211, 244
Thorne, F.C. 250
Tillich, P. 29, 101, 128
Tilmann, M. 235
Tobin, S.A. 116, 118, 121, 122
Tolan, J. 90, 108
Tolman, E.C. 46
Tolstoy, L. 220
Tononi, G. 96, 97
Tophoff, M. 68
Toukmanian, S. 210
Trautmann, R. 169
Trevarthen, C. 79
Truax, C.B. 3, 166, 205, 213
Tudor, K. 3, 4, 9, 10, 12, 34, 40, 69, 102, 123, 124, 129, 144, 152, 153, 157, 160, 164, 167, 173, 206, 210, 211, 217, 232, 240, 248, 250, 253
Turnbull, O. 55–6, 84, 95, 97
Turner, V. 257

United Nations 35

Van Belle, H.A. 23, 25, 27, 42, 204, 208, 234, 244, 246
Van Kalmthout, M.A. 85, 99, 102, 153, 194
Van Werde, D. 165, 170, 193, 224
Vargas, M.J. 107
Ventura, M. 31
Vithoulkas, G. 45, 243
Vitz, P. 152, 228

Vogel, A. 85
von Broembsen, F. 115
von Drigalski, D. 235
Vossen, T.J. 96

Wallen, J.L. 215
Wann, T.W. 23
Warner, M.S. 4, 35, 62, 116, 120, 122, 165, 166, 177, 215, 251–2
Waterhouse, R.L. 31
Watson, J.C. 2
Watson, N. 3, 193
Watzlawick, P. 129
Werner, H. 46
Wexler, D.A. 129, 205
Wheeler, R.H. 46
White, M. 40
Whitehead, A.N. 13, 40, 49, 50, 51, 56, 60, 80, 83, 84, 95, 132, 145, 146, 160, 161, 229
Wilber, K. 64, 65, 257
Wilkins, P. 33, 34, 46, 164, 232
Winnicott, D.W. 102, 116, 177, 207
Wittgenstein, L. 14, 15, 124
Wolter-Gustafson, C. 34, 128
Wood, J.K. 1, 11, 22–3
Woodfin, R. 145
Woodworth, R.S. 92, 137
Wordsworth, W. 98
Worrall, M. 9, 10, 12, 152, 211, 215, 232
Worsley, R. 164, 250
Wyatt, G. 43, 191

Yalom, I. 208, 235

Zarate, O. 72
Zimring, F.M. 16, 112, 125, 126, 127, 130
Zohar, D. 59, 96
Zuckerkandl, V. 124
Zukav, G. 257
Zúñiga, G.L. 139

Subject index